Readings on Adolescence and Emerging Adulthood

Jeffrey Jensen Arnett
University of Maryland

Prentice Hall

Upper Saddle River, New Jersey 07458

Library of Congress Cataloging-in-Publication Data

Arnett, Jeffrey Jensen.
    Readings on adolescence and emerging adulthood / Jeffrey Jensen Arnett.
      p. cm.
    Companion book to the author's: Adolescence and emerging adulthood.
    Includes bibliographical references.
    ISBN 0-13-089455-9
    1. Adolescence. 2. Teenagers. 3. Young adults. I. Arnett, Jeffrey Jensen. Adolescence
and emerging adulthood. II. Title.

HQ796.A7265 2002
305.235—dc21

                                    2001046152

VP/Editorial Director: Laura Pearson
Senior Acquisitions Editor: Jennifer Gilliland
Editorial Assistant: Nicole Girrbach
Senior Managing Editor: Mary Rottino
Production Liaison: Fran Russello
Project Manager: Linda B. Pawelchak
Prepress and Manufacturing Buyer: Tricia Kenny
Cover Director: Jayne Conte
Cover Design: Bruce Kenselaar
Executive Marketing Manager: Sheryl Adams
Copy Editing: Roaring Mountain Editorial Services

This book was set in 9/11 New Baskerville by Pine Tree Composition
and was printed and bound by R.R. Donnelly & Sons Company.
The cover was printed by Phoenix Color Corp.

 ©2002 by Pearson Education, Inc.
Upper Saddle River, New Jersey 07458

Printed in the United States of America
10 9 8 7 6 5 4 3

ISBN 0-13-089455-9

Pearson Education LTD., *London*
Pearson Education Australia PTY. Limited, *Sydney*
Pearson Education Singapore, Pte. Ltd.
Pearson Education North Asia Ltd., *Hong Kong*
Pearson Education Canada, Ltd., *Toronto*
Pearson Educación de Mexico, S.A. de C.V.
Pearson Education—Japan, *Tokyo*
Pearson Education Malaysia, Pte. Ltd.

Contents

Preface

This book of readings can be used to supplement a textbook in an undergraduate course on adolescent development or as a foundation of readings for a graduate course. I assembled and edited this book as a companion to my textbook *Adolescence and Emerging Adulthood: A Cultural Approach* (2001, Prentice Hall), but it should also work well as a companion to other textbooks. The readings cover a broad range of topics found in most textbooks, from biological and cognitive development to relationships with family and friends to young people's experiences with school, work, and media, among other topics.

A good textbook provides students with a credible, well-informed, and comprehensive overview of a field, but even the best textbook must translate and paraphrase research rather than present it directly. To understand how scholarship in a field is conducted, it is important for students to read original theoretical and research papers. This book contains 27 papers to inform students of the range of scholarship currently taking place on development from age 10 to 25.

The principles that determined the selection of the papers here were similar to those that guided my writing of the textbook: take a cultural approach, include emerging adulthood (roughly age 18 to 25) as well as adolescence, and draw from a variety of disciplines. Taking a cultural approach allows students to see what adolescents are like in different parts of the world. This approach is intended to inspire readers to examine their assumptions about the "natural" course of development in adolescence and also analyze the assumptions sometimes made by scholars on adolescence. In my experience, students are fascinated by learning about how different adolescence can be from what they have experienced themselves, and their understanding is expanded by this knowledge.

Emerging adulthood is also included because doing so reflects the profound changes that took place in the nature of "adolescence" in the twentieth century. In that time span, puberty moved about 2 years earlier in the life course of people in industrialized societies so that most young people now show the first physical changes of puberty at age 10 to 12. Meanwhile, since 1950 the typical age of entering marriage and parenthood has risen steeply; it is now in the late twenties in every industrialized country.

In my view, the age range of 10 to 25 is too broad, and the changes that take place during that period too vast, to be considered one developmental period of adolescence. I have proposed emerging adulthood as a separate period, different from adolescence but not fully adult. I included material on emerging adulthood in my textbook, and this book of readings contains several selections that pertain to this age period, including a theoretical framework for understanding it (Reading 1.3). Students enjoy readings on this age period, in part because for many of them it is a period they are in themselves or have passed through recently.

The readings are taken from a variety of disciplines, including psychology, sociology, anthropology, and education. I believe it is important to draw from all these disciplines, because each has information and insights to offer that contribute to a whole portrait of adolescence and emerging adulthood. Drawing from a variety of disciplines also means representing a variety of methods, including questionnaires, text analysis, interviews, and ethnographies. My goal was to present a broad view so that students learn about many different ways that scholarship in the field is conducted.

In selecting the readings, then, I sought to represent a variety of different cultures, to represent scholarship on emerging adulthood as well as adolescence, and to draw from numerous disciplines. In addition, I sought readings that were written clearly and with a minimum of arcane terminology so that they could be digested by students. I avoided articles that simply reviewed an area of the field, because students get enough of that in their textbooks. I did, however, include theoretical articles, which go beyond reviewing an area to add new ideas, and articles that combine theory and research.

One theme that was part of my textbook but is not part of this book of readings is a historical approach. I was not able to include readings from different eras of research on adolescence and still have room for a variety of cultures,

emerging adulthood as well as adolescence, and a variety of disciplines. Thus, with the exception of one reading by G. Stanley Hall and the two readings on cognitive development, all the readings are from works that have been published since 1990, most have been published since 1995, and nearly one-fourth were published in 1999 or 2000. Together, the readings should provide students with an understanding of how scholarship on adolescence and emerging adulthood is conducted now, in our time.

I edited each reading, some more extensively than others. Some had to be trimmed considerably because the original length was much too great to fit comfortably into a book of readings. Some contained extensive statistical analyses that few students would be able to follow. In general, I avoided editing that would change the style or the wording of the readings. Instead, I tried to choose readings that were already written in a lively and accessible way.

Each reading contains a brief introduction in which I provide background information and describe the key points of the reading. Following each reading is a series of Thinking Critically questions. The purpose of these questions is to encourage students to analyze the validity of the material in the readings, to consider hypothetical questions, and to apply the material to their own lives and their own society. Instructors may wish to use these questions to initiate class discussions or as questions for student essays.

I wish to thank the many colleagues who sent papers to me in response to my request for material to consider for this book. Although I was not able to use them all, I read and benefited from each, gaining knowledge of the current scholarship taking place in each area. I hope any scholar who has a paper that may be suitable for this book will send it to me to consider for future editions. I would also like to acknowledge the following reviewers: Karen G. Howe, The College of New Jersey; Mary Ann Manos, Bradley University; Virginia Navarro, University of Missouri–Saint Louis; and Merryl Patterson, Austin Community College.

Jeffrey Jensen Arnett
University Park, Maryland

I Introduction, History, and General Issues

The History of Adolescence

G. Stanley Hall is the founder of the scientific study of adolescence. In a landmark two-volume work published in 1904, he sought to include everything that was known at the time about adolescence, from biological development to sexuality to family relationships to religious development, among many other topics. In the chapter from which the following reading is taken, Hall sought to present adolescence as it had been portrayed through the centuries in literature, biography, and history. The reading should give you a sense of Hall's approach to writing and scholarship on adolescence and also provide you with some examples of how adolescence has been viewed in the past. As you read, keep in mind that in Hall's view, adolescence extended from age 14 to 24.

Reading 1.1

Adolescence in Literature, Biography, and History

G. S. Hall

Romance, poetry, and biography furnish many admirable descriptions of the psychic states and changes characteristic of every stage of the adolescent transformation, and now it may be well to pause and consider a few examples.

The Platonic dialogues (5th century B.C.) are among the best of all literary sources for the study of the pedagogy of adolescence. Some of the best of them owe their charm to the noble love of adolescent boys. Of the twenty-seven dialogues, with about one hundred and ten characters, twelve or fourteen are obviously adolescents.

Charmides is perhaps the most glorious of all Plato's boys. He is portrayed as being drawn to a conversation of Socrates concerning temperance. His friend and lover, Chaerephon, a crazy-brained, impetuous young man, had pronounced him the reigning beauty of the day, whom all his companions loved, and he was always followed by a train of admirers. There was a flutter when he entered, and all made place to have him sit beside them. His soul was found to be as beauteous as his body, so that he best illustrates the Greek ideal of a fair soul in a fair body. As Socrates converses with him on temperance, he appears an almost ideal illustration of this also.

Lysis seems, with his shyness, impulsiveness, and artless candor, his insatiable eagerness to hear more, perhaps the youngest of Plato's boys. Socrates, with characteristic sympathy, easily engages him in conversation. Your parents love you and want you to be happy, but do they gratify all your wishes? When he replies No, that even his father's servants can drive horses which he cannot, Socrates expresses surprise, but leads on to the truth that men are trusted in things they know.

The most radiant boy beauty of all the juvenile interrogators of Socrates is Alcibiades. He appears when he is very young and about to enter public life, and would persuade the people, but to what end? Socrates leads him to say that he would seek justice rather than wealth or power. Only the virtuous deserve freedom. "Are you free?" asks Socrates, and he replies, "I feel that I am not, but I hope, Socrates, that by your aid I may become free, and from this day forward I will never leave you." We have another glimpse of this favorite in the Protagoras, where we are told his beard is just appearing. He seems in his early twenties, and intrudes intoxicated with his followers into the assemblage, lawless, a lion's whelp, but already known as one of the ablest and gifted of all Greeks. He tells of his vain effort to ensnare Socrates by his homosexual charms, and then proceeds to the most brilliant eulogy of his character.

Aristotle (4th century B.C.) has given the best ancient characterization of youth. He says:

The young are in character prone to desire and ready to carry any desire they may have formed into action. Of bodily desires it is the sexual to which they are most disposed to give way, and in regard to sexual desire they exercise no self-restraint. They are changeful, too, and fickle in their desires, which are as transitory as they are vehement; for their wishes are keen without being permanent, like a sick man's fits of hunger and thirst. They are passionate, irascible, and apt to be carried away by their impulses. They are the slaves, too, of their passion, as their ambition prevents their ever brooking a slight and renders them indignant at the mere idea of enduring an injury. They are charitable rather than the reverse, as they have never yet been witnesses of many villianies; and they are trustful, as they have not yet been often deceived. They are sanguine, too, for the young are heated by Nature as drunken men by wine, not to say that they have not yet experienced frequent failures. Their lives are lived principally in hope. They have high aspirations; for they have never yet been humiliated by the experience of life, but are unacquainted with the limiting force of circumstances. Youth is the age when people are most devoted to their friends, as they are then extremely fond of social intercourse. If the young commit a fault, it is always on the side of excess and exaggeration, for they carry everything too far, whether it be their love or hatred or anything else. Finally, they are fond of laugher and consequently facetious, facetiousness being disciplined insolence.

Keim, who has written one of the most comprehensive and scholarly of all the lives of Jesus, thinks that many, if not most, of his disciples, when he chose them, were adolescents. He says:

> Though some of the disciples may have been married, yet an age of not much more than twenty years is plainly indicated in the case of most of them, for they are represented as coming directly from the houses of their parents, and Jesus cautions them against preferring their parents to their Teacher, and administers to them truly paternal censures.

A radically different type and ideal of adolescence arose in the early Christian Church and persisted for centuries. The mental life was in many ways narrowed and impoverished by the intense struggles for purity of body and soul which the new religion had inspired. Instead of the harmony between them that pervaded Greek thought, soul and body were now violently sundered, and asceticism assumed that the transient life of the body must be subordinated to the eternal life of the spirit, and mortification of the flesh, visions, and ecstatic communion with the divine were the ideals. The most precious and abundant data for illustrating this new attitude are fortunately at hand.

Although the historical character of the records may be questioned, they show how strong were the motives that impelled young men and women of all stations to take religious vows and enter upon lives of sanctity. Here are a few examples:

St. Ephraem the Syrian (born 378 A.D.) was a wild boy and indulged in various escapades, but at eighteen felt remorse, was baptized, and began to discipline his body and soul with great severity, fasting and lying on the bare ground all night in prayer.

St. Benedict (born 543 A.D.), of illustrious birth, was scarcely fourteen when he renounced fortune, family, and worldly joy, plunged into the wild gorges over the savage hills, put on monastic habit of skin, and took up his abode in a dark and inaccessible cave, drawing up each day with a cord, when warned by a bell, the loaf of bread which a friend provided. Here he lived three years, and when shepherds found him was thought to be a wild beast till he instilled grace into their rustic souls. When he was strongly tempted to sexual fantasies, stripping himself naked he rolled in a clump of thorns and briars until his body was all one wound, but also until he had extinguished forever the eternal fire which inflamed him even in the desert.

St. Bernard (born 1153) at the age of twelve had a vision in which his just dead mother urged him to become a monk, but his mind was expanding; the schools of Paris were stimulating; philosophy began to weave its wondrous spell; and it was only after a long struggle that he was able to quell the fervent straining of his mind for intellectual activity and condemn it to bondage to the soul, whose welfare alone he resolved to cultivate. So, persuading a brother to desert his young wife, they fled to the desert and cloister.

St. Ven (born 1158) early dedicated her soul and body to God and resisted her parents' efforts to make her marry. At the wedding, when asked if she would take this man, cried out before the whole church that she would not. When force was used and preparation again made, it was found that she had cut off her nose. Thus she had her way.

In a very interesting paper, entitled "Shakespeare and Adolescence," Dr. M. F. Libby very roughly reckons seventy-four interesting adolescents among the comedies, forty-six among the tragedies, and nineteen among the histories. He selects thirty characters who, either on account of direct references to their age, or because of their love stories, or because they show the emotional and intellectual plasticity of youth, may be regarded as typical adolescents, including Romeo, Juliet, Hamlet, Ophelia, and Prince Hal, among others. Libby holds that besides these, the sonnets and poems of Shakespeare perhaps show a yet greater, more profound and concentrated knowledge of adolescence. The series of sonnets culminates in Sonnet 116, which makes love the sole beacon of humanity. It might be said that it is connected by a straight line with the best teachings of Plato, and that here humanity picked up the clue lost in the great interval.

In looking over biographies of well-known modern men who deal with their boyhood, one finds deplorable carelessness of their biographers concerning the facts and influences of their youth. In exploring such sources we soon see how few writers have given true pictures of the chief traits of this developmental period, which can rarely be ascertained with accuracy. The adult finds it hard to recall the emotional and instinctive life of the teens which is banished without a trace, save as scattered hints may be gathered from diaries, chance experiences, or the recollections of others. But the best observers see but little of what goes on in the youthful soul, the development of which is very largely subterranean. Only when the feelings erupt in some surprising way is the process manifest. The best of these sources are the autobiographies, and of these only few are full of the details of this stage.

John Stuart Mill's *Autobiography* is one of the most remarkable. No boy ever had more diligent and earnest training than his father gave him or responded better. He cannot remember when he began to learn Greek, but was told that it was at the age of three. The list of classical authors alone that he read in the original, to say nothing of history, political, scientific, logical, and other works before he was twelve, is perhaps unprecedented in all history.

From the age of fifteen he had an object in life: to reform the world. This gave him happiness, and the idea of struggling to promote the reform of the world seemed an inspiring program for life. But in the autumn of 1826, when he was twenty years of age, he fell into "a dull state of nerves," where he could no longer enjoy, and what had produced pleasures appeared insipid. In his Autobiography he recalls that

In this state of mind it occurred to me to put the question directly to myself: "Suppose that all your objects in life were realized; that all the changes in institutions and opinions which you are looking forward to could be completely effected at this very instant; would this be a great joy and happiness to you?" And an irrepressible self-consciousness distinctly answered, "No." At this my heart sank within me: the whole foundation on which my life was constructed fell down. All my happiness was to have been found in the continual pursuit of this end. The end had ceased to charm, and how could there ever again be any interest in the means? I seemed to have nothing left to live for. At first I hoped that the cloud would pass away of itself, but it did not. I carried it with me into all companies, all occupations. Hardly anything had power to cause me even a few minutes oblivion of it. For some months the cloud seemed to grow thicker and thicker.

In vain I sought relief from my favorite books, those memorials of past nobleness and greatness from which I had always hitherto drawn strength and animation. I read them now without feeling, and I became persuaded that my love of mankind, and of excellence for its own sake, had worn itself out. I sought no comfort by speaking to others of what I felt. Of friends, I had at that time none to whom I had any hope of making my condition intelligible. It was, however, abundantly intelligible to myself, and the more I dwelt upon it the more hopeless it appeared.

I asked myself if I could or if I was bound to go on living, when life must be passed in this manner. I generally answered to myself that I did not think I could possibly bear it beyond a year.

But within about half that time, in reading a moving passage about how a mere boy felt that he could save his family and take the place of all they had lost, a vivid conception of the scene came over him, and he was moved to tears. From that moment his burden grew lighter. He saw that his heart was not dead and that he still had some stuff left of which character and happiness were made; and although there were several later lapses, some of which lasted many months, he was never again as miserable as he had been.

It is, I believe, high time that adolescent literature should be recognized as a class by itself. Much of it should be individually prescribed for the reading of the young, for whom it has a singular zest and is a true stimulus and corrective. Here the young appeal and listen to each other as they do not to adults, and in a way the latter have failed to appreciate. Again, no biography, and especially no autobiography, should henceforth be complete if it does not describe this period of transformation so all-determining for future life to which it alone can often give the key. Lastly, many if not most young people should be encouraged to enough of the confessional private journalism to teach them self-knowledge, for the art of self-expression usually begins now if ever, when it has a wealth of subjective material and needs forms of expression peculiar to itself.

REFERENCES

Keim, T. (1877). *The history of Jesus of Nazara*. London: [no publisher indicated].

Libby, M. F. (1901). Shakespeare and adolescence. *Pediatric Seminar*, June.

THINKING CRITICALLY

1. Consider Aristotle's description of youth. How many of Aristotle's claims about young people are still familiar today? Is it or is it not justifiable to describe young people in such general terms, as if they all share common characteristics?

2. Do you agree with Hall's assertion, "The adult finds it hard to recall the emotional and instinctive life of the teens which is banished without a trace"? Think of yourself at age 13 or 14. How vividly do you think you can recall the thoughts and feelings you experienced at that time?

3. Hall relies almost entirely on individual case examples in this chapter. To what extent are such examples generalizable to all adolescents? In your answer, include a consideration of historical and cultural issues.

The Storm and Stress Debate

The question of whether or not adolescence is necessarily a difficult time, a time of "storm and stress," was originally raised by G. Stanley Hall in his 1904 book, from which the previous reading was taken. Hall's view was that adolescent storm and stress is both universal and biologically based. Since he stated this view, some scholars have agreed with him, but others have strongly disagreed. This reading provides a history of the debate over adolescent storm and stress and attempts to reconcile the opposing views.

Reading 1.2

Adolescent Storm and Stress, Reconsidered

J. J. Arnett

Nearly one hundred years after G. Stanley Hall (1904) proposed that adolescence is inherently a time of storm and stress, his view continues to be addressed by psychologists. For the most part, contemporary psychologists reject the view that adolescent storm and stress is universal and inevitable (e.g., Eccles et al., 1993; Offer & Schonert-Reichl, 1992; Petersen et al., 1993; Steinberg & Levine, 1997). However, the storm and stress view is usually invoked by psychologists only in passing, in the course of addressing some other topic. Rarely has the storm and stress view been considered directly, and its merits and limitations evaluated in depth.

Hall initiated the scientific study of adolescence, and since his time (especially in the past 20 years), research on adolescence has produced a great deal of information that bears upon the question of adolescent storm and stress. As we approach the centennial of Hall's (1904) ground-breaking work on adolescence, this may be an appropriate time to evaluate the merits of the view for which he is best known today. I will argue here that a case can be made

for the validity of a modified storm and stress view. The claim that adolescent storm and stress is characteristic of all adolescents, and that the source of it is purely biological, is clearly false. However, evidence supports the existence of some degree of storm and stress—at least for adolescents in the middle-class American majority culture—with respect to conflict with parents, mood disruptions, and risk behavior. Not all adolescents experience storm and stress in these areas, but adolescence is the period when storm and stress is *more likely* to occur than at other ages. It is emphasized that there are individual differences among adolescents in the extent to which they exhibit storm and stress, and that there are cultural variations in the pervasiveness of adolescent storm and stress.

Storm and Stress: A Brief History

Hall (1904) was the first to consider the storm and stress issue explicitly and formally in relation to adolescent development, but he was not the first in the history of Western thought to re-mark on the emotional and behavioral distinc-tiveness of adolescence. Aristotle stated that youth "are heated by Nature as drunken men by wine." Socrates characterized youth as in-clined to "contradict their parents" and "tyran-nize their teachers." Rousseau relied on a stormy metaphor in describing adolescence: "As the roaring of the waves precedes the tem-pest, so the murmur of rising passions an-nounces the tumultuous change. . . . Keep your hand upon the helm," he advised parents, "or all is lost" (Rousseau, 1762/1962, pp. 172–173).

Around the time Rousseau was writing, an influential genre of German literature was developing, known as "sturm und drang" litera-ture—roughly translated as "storm and stress." The quintessential work of the genre was Goethe's "The Sorrows of Young Werther" (1774/1989), a story about a young man who commits suicide in despair over his doomed love for a married woman. There were numer-ous other stories at the time that depicted youthful anguish and angst. The genre gave rise to popular use of the term "storm and stress," which Hall adopted a century later when writing his magnum opus on adolescent development.

Hall (1904) favored the Lamarckian evo-lutionary ideas that were considered by many prominent thinkers in the early 20th century (Freud and Jung included) to be a better expla-nation of evolution than Darwin's theory of nat-ural selection. In Lamarck's now-discredited theory, evolution takes place as a result of accu-mulated experience. Organisms pass on their characteristics from one generation to the next not in the form of genes (which were unknown at the time Lamarck and Darwin devised their theories) but in the form of *memories and ac-quired characteristics*. Thus Hall, considering de-velopment during adolescence, judged it to be "suggestive of some ancient period of storm and stress" (1904, vol. 1, p. xiii). In his view, there must have been a period of human evolu-tion that was extremely difficult and tumul-tuous; the memory of that period had been passed ever since from one generation to the next, and was *recapitulated* in the development

of each individual as the storm and stress of adolescent development. To Hall, this legacy of storm and stress was particularly evident in ado-lescents' tendency to question and contradict their parents, in their mood disruptions, and in their propensity for reckless and antisocial behavior.

Although Hall is often portrayed as de-picting adolescent storm and stress as universal and biological, in fact his view was more nu-anced. He acknowledged individual differ-ences, noting for example that conflict with parents was more likely for adolescents with "ruder natures" (vol. 2, p. 79). Also, he believed that a *tendency* toward storm and stress in ado-lescence was universal and biologically based, but that culture influenced adolescents' expres-sion and experience of it. He saw storm and stress as more likely to occur in the United States of his day than in "older lands with more conservative traditions" (vol. 1, p. xvi). In his view the storm and stress of American adoles-cence was aggravated by growing urbanization, with all its temptations to vice, and by the clash between the sedentary quality of urban life and what he saw as adolescents' inherent need for activity and exploration. Hall also believed that adolescent storm and stress in his time was ag-gravated by the failure of home, school, and re-ligious organizations to recognize the true nature and potential perils of adolescence and adapt their institutions accordingly, a view not unlike that of many more recent scholars (e.g., Eccles et al., 1993; Simmons & Blythe, 1987).

In the century since Hall's work estab-lished adolescence as an area of scientific study, the debate over adolescent storm and stress has simmered steadily and boiled to the surface pe-riodically. Anthropologists, led by Margaret Mead (1928), countered the claim that a ten-dency toward storm and stress in adolescence is universal and biological by describing non-Western cultures in which adolescence was neither stormy nor stressful. In contrast, psy-choanalytic theorists, particularly Anna Freud (1946, 1958, 1968, 1969), have been the most outspoken proponents of the storm and stress view. Like Hall, psychoanalytic theorists viewed adolescent storm and stress as rooted in the *recapitulation* of earlier experiences, but as a recapitulation of ontogenetic oedipal conflicts from early childhood rather than phylogenetic epochs (Blos, 1962). This recapitulation of oedipal conflicts provoked emotional volatility (as the adolescent ego attempted to gain ascendancy over resurgent instinctual drives), depressed mood (as the adolescent mourned the renunciation of the oedipal parent) and conflict with parents (in the course of making this renunciation) (Blos, 1962). Furthermore, the resurgence of instinctual drives was regarded as likely to be acted out in "dissocial, even criminal" behavior (Freud, 1968, p. 18).

Anna Freud (1958, 1968, 1969) viewed adolescents who did *not* experience storm and stress with great suspicion, claiming that their outward calm concealed the inward reality that they must have "built up excessive defenses against their drive activities and are now crippled by the results" (1968, p. 15). She, much more than Hall, viewed storm and stress as universal and immutable, to the extent that its absence signified psychopathology: "To be normal during the adolescent period is by itself abnormal" (1958, p. 267).

In recent decades, two types of studies concerning adolescent storm and stress have appeared. A handful of studies, mostly by Buchanan and Holmbeck (Buchanan et al., 1990; Buchanan, 1998; Buchanan & Holmbeck, 1998; Holmbeck & Hill, 1988; Offer, Ostrov, & Howard, 1981), have focused on public perceptions of adolescence as a time of storm and stress. These studies (using American middle-class samples) have consistently found that most people in the American majority culture perceive adolescence as a time of relative storm and stress. For example, Buchanan et al. (1990, 372) found that the majority of both parents and teachers agreed with statements such as "Early adolescence is a difficult time of life for children and their parents/teachers." Buchanan and Holmbeck (1998) reported that college students and parents of early adolescents viewed adolescents as more likely than elementary school children to have problems such as symptoms of internalizing disorders (e.g., anxious, insecure, depressed) and risk

taking/rebelliousness (e.g., reckless, impulsive, rude). Similarly, the majority of college students surveyed by Holmbeck and Hill (1988) agreed with statements such as "adolescents frequently fight with their parents."

A second type of contemporary study has addressed the actual occurrence of adolescent storm and stress, in the specific areas of conflict with parents (Gecas & Seff, 1990; Steinberg, 1987), emotional volatility (Larson & Richards, 1994), negative affect (Brooks-Gunn & Warren, 1989, Buchanan, Eccles, & Becker, 1992; Petersen et al., 1993), and risk behavior (Arnett, 1992; Moffitt, 1993). Storm and stress tends to be mentioned in these studies not as the primary focus but in the course of addressing another topic. Consistently, these studies reject the claim—usually attributed to Hall—that adolescent storm and stress is universal and find only weak support for the claim that it is biologically based. However, the studies also consistently support a modified storm and stress thesis, that adolescence is a time when various types of problems are *more likely* to arise than at other ages. The primary goal of this paper is to draw together the evidence from these areas and present an argument for the validity of the modified storm and stress thesis.

Defining "Storm and Stress"

It is important at this point to address directly the question of what is included under the concept of "adolescent storm and stress." Taking historical and theoretical views in combination with contemporary research, the core of the storm and stress view seems to be the idea that adolescence is a period of life that is *difficult* (Buchanan et al., 1990)—more difficult in some ways than other periods of life, and difficult for adolescents as well as for the people around them. This idea, that adolescence is difficult, includes *three key elements:*

1. *Conflict with parents.* Adolescents have a tendency to be rebellious and resist adult authority. In particular, adolescence is a time when conflict with parents is especially high.

2. *Mood disruptions.* Adolescents tend to be more volatile emotionally than either children or adults. They experience more extremes of mood, and more swings of mood from one extreme to the other. They also experience more frequent episodes of depressed mood.

3. *Risk behavior.* Adolescents have higher rates of reckless, norm-breaking, and antisocial behavior than either children or adults. Adolescents are more likely to cause disruptions of social order, and to engage in behavior that carries the potential for harm to themselves and/or the people around them.

This is not an all-inclusive list of the possible elements of adolescent storm and stress. Occasionally, storm and stress has been discussed in terms of other elements such as school difficulties (Eccles et al., 1993) and self-image (Offer & Offer, 1975). However, the three elements discussed here appear consistently in the writings of Hall (1904), the anthropologists (Mead, 1928), the psychoanalysts (Blos, 1962; Freud, 1968, 1969), and contemporary scholars (e.g., Buchanan, 1998; Eccles et al., 1993; Offer & Schonert-Reichl, 1992; Petersen et al., 1993; Steinberg & Levine, 1997). Thus these three elements are the focus of this discussion.

Before proceeding, one more comment is in order, about the length of adolescence. Hall (1904) viewed adolescence and its accompanying storm and stress as lasting through the early twenties (vol. 1, p. xix). Other observers of adolescent storm and stress, from Aristotle to the present, have applied their comments not just to early adolescence but to a middle and late adolescence/emerging adulthood extending through the late teens and early twenties (see Kett, 1977). Here, too, the evidence related to the storm and stress view will be considered for an extended adolescent age range. Different elements of storm and stress have different peaks—conflict with parents in early adolescence (Paikoff & Brooks-Gunn, 1991), mood disruptions in mid-adolescence (Petersen et al., 1993), risk behavior in late adolescence/emerging adulthood (Arnett, 1992;

2000). Each of these elements represents a different kind of difficulty to be experienced, for adolescents as well as for those around them. It is in combination that they create a perception of adolescence as a difficult period of life.

We now consider each of the three elements of the storm and stress view, in order of their developmental peak during adolescence: conflict with parents, mood disruptions, and risk behavior.

Conflict With Parents

Hall (1904) viewed adolescence as a time when "the wisdom and advice of parents and teachers is overtopped, and in ruder natures may be met by blank contradiction" (vol. 2, p. 79). He viewed this as due not only to human evolutionary history but also to the incompatibility between adolescents' need for independence and the fact that "parents still think of their offspring as mere children, and tighten the rein where they should loosen it" (vol. 2, p. 384). Contemporary studies have established that conflict with parents increases in early adolescence, compared to preadolescence, and typically remains high for a couple of years before declining in late adolescence (Laursen, Coy, & Collins, 1998; Paikoff & Brooks-Gunn, 1991; Smetana, 1989). One naturalistic study of early adolescents' conflicts with parents and siblings reported a rate of two conflicts every three days, or 20 per month (Montemayor & Hanson, 1985). During the same time that the number of daily conflicts between parents and their early adolescent children increases (compared to preadolescence), declines occur in the amount of time they spend together and in their reports of emotional closeness (Larson & Richards, 1994). Conflict is especially frequent and intense between mothers and early adolescent daughters (Collins, 1990).

This conflict makes adolescence difficult not just for adolescents but for their parents. Parents tend to perceive adolescence as the most difficult stage of their children's development (Buchanan et al., 1990; Pasley & Gecas, 1984; Small, Cornelius, & Eastman, 1983). However, it should be added that there are substantial individual differences, and there are many parents and adolescents between whom there is little conflict, even if overall rates of conflict between parents and children rise in adolescence. Conflict between parents and adolescents is more likely when the adolescent is experiencing depressed mood (Cole & McPherson, 1993), when the adolescent is experiencing other problems such as substance abuse (Petersen, 1988), and when the adolescent is an early-maturing girl (Buchanan, Eccles, & Becker, 1992).

Almost without exception, contemporary scholars emphasize that higher rates of conflict with parents in adolescence do not indicate a serious or enduring breach in parent-adolescent relationships (e.g., Hill & Holmbeck, 1987; Montemayor, 1986; Offer & Offer, 1975; Rutter, Graham, Chadwick, & Yule, 1976; Steinberg & Levine, 1997). Even amidst relatively high conflict, parents and adolescents tend to report that overall their relationships are good, that they share a wide range of core values, and that they retain a considerable amount of mutual affection and attachment. The conflicts tend to be over apparently mundane issues such as personal appearance, dating, curfews, and the like (Smetana, 1988). Even if they disagree on these issues, they tend to agree on more serious issues such as the value of honesty and the importance of education. This point seems well established, but it does not mean that adolescence is not a difficult time for both adolescents and their parents as a result of their minor but frequent conflicts.

Furthermore, the principal issues of conflict between adolescents and their parents may not be as trivial as they seem on the surface. Conflicts between adolescents and their parents often concern issues such as when adolescents should begin dating and whom they should date, where they should be allowed go, and how late they should stay out. All of these issues can serve as proxies for arguments over more serious issues such as substance use, automobile driving safety, and sex. By restricting when adolescents can date and with whom, parents indirectly restrict adolescents' sexual opportunities. By attempting to restrict where adolescents can go and how late they should stay out, parents may be attempting to limit adolescents' access to alcohol and drugs, to shield adolescents from the potentially dangerous combination of substance use and automobile driving, and to restrict adolescents' opportunities for sexual exploration.

Some scholars (e.g., Steinberg, 1990) have suggested that conflict between adolescents and their parents is actually beneficial to adolescents' development, because it promotes the development of individuation and autonomy within the context of a warm relationship. This may be true, but high conflict may make adolescence a difficult time for adolescents and their parents even if the conflict ultimately has benefits.

Mood Disruptions

The claim of a link between adolescence and extremes of emotion (especially negative) is perhaps the most ancient and enduring part of the storm and stress view. Hall (1904) viewed adolescence as "the age of . . . rapid fluctuation of moods" (vol. 1, p. xv), with extremes of both elation and depressed mood. What does contemporary research tell us about whether adolescence is distinguished by high emotional volatility and a tendency toward negative moods? In general, studies that have assessed mood at frequent intervals have found that adolescents do indeed report greater extremes of mood and more frequent changes of mood, compared to preadolescents or adults. Also, a number of large longitudinal studies concur that negative affect increases in the transition from preadolescence to adolescence (see Buchanan et al., 1992, for a review).

One of the most interesting and enlightening lines of research on this topic in recent years has involved studies using the Experience Sampling Method (ESM; e.g., Csikszentmihalyi & Larson, 1984; Larson & Ham, 1993; Larson & Richards, 1994). Also known as the "beeper" method, this research entails having adolescents (and others) carry beepers throughout the day and record their thoughts, behavior, and emotions when they are beeped at random times. This method has provided an unprecedented look into the daily lives of adolescents, including how their emotions vary in the course of a day and how these variations compare to the emotions recorded by preadolescents and adults using the same method.

The results of this research indicate that there is truth to the storm and stress claim that adolescence is a time of greater mood disruptions. Adolescents report experiencing extremes of emotion (positive as well as negative, but especially negative) more often than their parents do (Larson & Richards, 1994; also see Larson, Csikszentmihalyi, & Graef, 1980). They report feeling "self-conscious" and "embarrassed" two to three times more often than their parents and are also more likely to feel awkward, lonely, nervous, and ignored. Adolescents also report greater mood disruptions when compared to preadolescents. Comparing preadolescent 5th graders to adolescent 9th graders, Larson and Richards (1994) describe the emotional "fall from grace" that occurs in that interval, as the proportion of time experienced as "very happy" declines by 50%, and similar declines take place in reports of feeling "great," "proud," and "in control." The result is an overall "deflation of childhood happiness" (p. 85) as childhood ends and adolescence begins.

In addition to the ESM studies, other studies have found negative moods to be prevalent in adolescence, especially for girls. In their review of adolescent depression, Petersen et al. (1993) described a "midadolescence peak" that has been reported in studies of age differences in depressed mood, indicating that adolescents have higher rates of depressed mood than either children or adults. Petersen et al. (1993) analyzed 14 studies of nonclinical samples of adolescents and concluded that depressed mood ("above which a score is thought to be predictive of clinical depression" ([p. 157]) applied to over one-third of adolescents at any given time.

Adolescents vary in the degree to which they experience mood disruptions. A variety of factors have been found to make mood disruptions in adolescence more likely, including low popularity with peers, poor school performance, and family problems such as marital discord and parental divorce (Petersen et al., 1993). The more negative life events adolescents experience, the more likely they are to experience mood disruptions (Brooks-Gunn & Warren, 1989). Although these individual differences should be kept in mind, overall the results of research indicate support for the storm and stress view that adolescence is more likely than other age periods to be a time of emotional difficulty.

Risk Behavior

At the beginning of a scene in "The Winter's Tale," Shakespeare has an older man deliver a soliloquy about the youth of his day. "I would that there were no age between ten and three-and-twenty, or that youth would sleep out the rest," he grumbles, "for there is nothing in between but getting wenches with child, wronging the ancientry, stealing, fighting." This lament should ring familiar to anyone living in Western societies in recent centuries, and to people in many other societies as well. Adolescence has long been associated with heightened rates of antisocial, norm-breaking, and criminal behavior, particularly for males. Hall (1904) included this as part of his view of adolescent storm and stress, agreeing that "a period of semicriminality is normal for all healthy [adolescent] boys" (vol. 1, p. 404).

Contemporary research confirms that in the United States and other Western countries, the teens and early twenties are years of highest prevalence of a variety of types of risk behavior (i.e., behavior that carries the potential for harm to self and/or others). This pattern exists for crime as well as for behavior such as substance use, risky automobile driving, and risky sexual behavior (Arnett, 1992; Moffitt, 1993). Unlike conflict with parents or mood disruptions, rates of risk behavior peak in late adolescence/ emerging adulthood rather than early or middle adolescence (Arnett, 2000). Rates of crime rise in the teens until peaking at age 18, then drop steeply (Gottfredson & Hirschi, 1990). Rates of most types of substance use peak at about age 20 (Johnston, O'Malley, & Bachman, 1994). Rates of automobile accidents and fatalities are highest in the late teens (U.S. Deptartment of Transportation, 1995). Rates of sexually transmitted diseases (STDs) peak in the early twenties (Stein, Newcomb, & Bentler, 1994), and two-thirds of all STDs are contracted by people who are under twenty-five years old (Hatcher, Trussell, Stewart, & Stewart, 1994).

The variety of respects in which adolescents engage in risk behavior at greater rates than children or adults lends further validity to the perception of adolescence as a difficult time, a time of storm and stress. Although adolescents generally experience their participation in risk behavior as pleasurable (Arnett, 1992; Lyng, 1991), suffering the consequences of such behavior—contact with the legal system, treatment for an STD, involvement in an automobile accident, and so on—is likely to be experienced as difficult. Furthermore, it is understandable that parents may find it difficult to watch their children pass through the ages when such behavior is most likely to occur.

In this area, as with conflict with parents and mood disruptions, it is important to recognize individual differences. Adolescents vary a great deal in the extent to which they participate in risk behavior. To some extent, these differences are forecast by behavior prior to adolescence. Persons who exhibit behavior problems in childhood are especially likely to engage in risk behavior as adolescents (Moffitt, 1993). Individual differences in characteristics such as sensation seeking and impulsivity also contribute to individual differences in risk behavior during adolescence (Arnett, 1992; Zuckerman, 1983). Nevertheless, although not all adolescents engage in risk behavior, the majority of adolescents take part occasionally in risk behavior of one kind or another (Arnett, 1992; Moffitt, 1993). This lends substantial credence to the view that adolescence is a period of storm and stress.

Why Storm and Stress?

Even if we accept the argument that adolescence is a time of heightened tendency toward storm and stress, the question remains as to why this should be so. To what extent do the roots of storm and stress lie in the biological changes that take place in the course of puberty? To what extent are the roots cultural, with adolescent storm and stress being especially pronounced in cultures that value individualism?

Current evidence indicates that biological changes make some contribution. With respect to mood disruptions, reviews of the effects of hormones on adolescents' moods have concluded that the dramatic hormonal changes that accompany puberty contribute to emotional volatility (Buchanan et al., 1992) and negative moods (Brooks-Gunn, Graber, & Paikoff, 1994), particularly in early adolescence when the rate of hormonal change is steepest. However, scholars in this area emphasize that the hormonal contribution to adolescent mood disruptions appears to be small and tends to exist only in interaction with other factors (Brooks-Gunn et al., 1994; Brooks-Gunn & Warren, 1989; Susman, 1997).

It is clear that the biological changes of puberty do not make adolescent storm and stress universal and inevitable. This is easily and unmistakably demonstrated by the fact that not all cultures experience the same levels of adolescent storm and stress, and some evidently do not experience it at all. Margaret Mead's (1928) original assertion to this effect has more recently been confirmed by Schlegel and Barry (1991), in their analysis of adolescence in 186 "traditional" (preindustrial) cultures worldwide. They reported that most traditional cultures experience less storm and stress among their adolescents, compared to the West.

A key difference between traditional cultures and the West, Schlegel and Barry (1991) observed, is the degree of *independence* allowed by adults and expected by adolescents. In the majority cultures of the West, because of cultural values of individualism, it is taken for granted by adolescents and their parents (as well as by most Western social scientists) that children should become independent from their parents during the course of adolescence, and attain full independence by the end of adolescence. A substantial amount of adolescent storm and stress arises from regulating the pace of adolescents' growing independence (Steinberg, 1987). Differences of opinion over the proper pace of this process are a source of conflict between adolescents and their parents, and part of parents' perception of adolescence as difficult results from their concern that the adolescent's growing independence may lead to participation in risk behavior (Pasley & Gecas, 1984). In contrast, independence for adolescents is less likely to be expected by adolescents and their parents in traditional cultures, so it is less likely to be a source of adolescent storm and stress (Dasen, 1998).

Even in traditional cultures, adolescent storm and stress is not unknown. Biological changes in combination with changing family obligations and changing economic responsibilities are common to adolescence virtually everywhere, and inherently involve new challenges and—for some adolescents, at least—difficulty. Some ethnographies on adolescence describe conceptions in traditional cultures of adolescence as a time of mood disruptions (e.g., Davis & Davis, 1989; Kirkpatrick, 1987). It should also be noted that differences exist among traditional cultures, with cultures that exclude adolescent boys from the activities of men being more likely to have problems with their adolescent boys than cultures in which boys take part daily in men's activities (Schlegel & Barry, 1991). Nevertheless, adolescent storm and stress is generally more common in the industrialized societies of the West than in traditional cultures.

However, all over the world, traditional cultures are becoming integrated into the global economy and are being influenced by Western (especially American) cultures through growing economic ties and through exposure to Western movies, music, and television (Barber, 1995). Within traditional cultures, it is often the adolescents who are the most enthusiastic consumers of Western media (Barber, 1995; Schlegel, 1998), and there is evidence that they may embrace the individualism of the West more readily than their parents do (Feldman, Mont-Reynaud, & Rosenthal, 1992). A potentially rich topic for research in the com-

ing years would be to monitor changes in the degree of adolescent storm and stress in traditional cultures as globalization proceeds.

This does not mean that storm and stress is likely to increase in all respects for all adolescents in traditional cultures. Individual differences will undoubtedly exist, as they do in the West. Indeed, increased individualism means broadening the boundaries of socialization, so that a greater range of individual differences is allowed expression (Arnett, 1995). Furthermore, the increased individualism fostered by globalization is likely to result in benefits for adolescents along with increased storm and stress. Cultural changes toward globalization and individualism are likely to mean that adolescents in traditional cultures will have a greater range of educational and occupational opportunities than previously, less constrained by gender and other factors (Dasen, 1998; Noble et al., 1996). However, the cost may be greater adolescent storm and stress. It is even possible that storm and stress will become more characteristic of adolescence in traditional cultures than in the West, because adolescents in rapidly changing societies will be confronted with multiple changes not only in their immediate lives but in their societies as well (Dasen, 1998).

Similar issues exist within American society. Currently, there is evidence that adolescent storm and stress may be more likely in the majority culture—the largely White middle class—than in other cultures that are part of American society. For example, parent-adolescent conflict has been found to be more frequent in White middle-class families than in Mexican American families (Suarez-Orozco & Suarez-Orozco, 1996). In the same way that values of individualism make adolescent storm and stress more likely in the American majority culture compared to non-Western traditional cultures, a similar difference in values may make storm and stress more likely in the American majority culture than in certain minority cultures that are part of American society. And in the same way that adolescence in traditional cultures may become more stormy and stressful as the influence of the West increases, adolescents in American minority cultures may exhibit storm and stress to the extent they adopt the individualistic values of the American majority culture.

Thus it might be expected that adolescent storm and stress will increase with the number of generations an adolescents' family has been in the United States. Among Asian American adolescents, for example, it has been found that the greater the number of generations their families have been in the United States, the more likely the adolescents are to exhibit aspects of storm and stress (Fletcher & Steinberg, 1994; Steinberg, 1996; also see Rosenthal, 1984). However, as with the issues involving traditional cultures, the direct exploration of storm and stress issues involving adolescents in American minority cultures has been minimal thus far and represents a promising area for further investigation.

Conclusion

Adolescent storm and stress is not simply a myth that has captured the popular imagination but a real part of life for many adolescents and their parents in contemporary American society. Although the extreme portrayal of adolescent storm and stress by certain psychoanalytic theorists (Freud, 1958, 1968, 1969) is a caricature of normal adolescent development, there is support for Hall's (1904) view that a tendency toward some aspects of storm and

stress exists in adolescence. In their conflicts with parents, in their mood disruptions, and in their higher rates of a variety of types of risk behavior, many adolescents exhibit a heightened degree of storm and stress compared to other periods of life. Their parents, too, often experience difficulty—from increased conflict when their children are in early adolescence, from mood disruptions during mid-adolescence, and from anxiety over the increased possibility of risk behavior when their children are in late adolescence. However, storm and stress in adolescence is not something written indelibly into the human life course. On the contrary, there are cultural differences in storm and stress, and within cultures there are individual differences in the extent to which adolescents exhibit the different aspects of it.

Finally, to view adolescence as a time of storm and stress is not to say that adolescence is characterized *only* by storm and stress. Even amidst the storm and stress of adolescence, most adolescents take pleasure in many aspects of their lives, are happy with most of their relationships most of the time, and are hopeful about the future (Offer & Schonert-Reichl, 1992). G. S. Hall (1904) saw adolescence as stormy and stressful, but also as "the birthday of the imagination" (vol. 1, p. 313), "the best decade of life" (vol. 1, p. xviii), when "the life of feeling has its prime" (vol. 1, p. 59). The paradox of adolescence is that it can be at once a time of storm and stress and a time of exuberant growth.

REFERENCES

Arnett, J. J. (1992). Reckless behavior in adolescence: A developmental perspective. *Developmental Review, 12,* 339–373.

Arnett, J. J. (1995). Broad and narrow socialization: The family in the context of a cultural theory. *Journal of Marriage and the Family, 57,* 617–628.

Arnett, J. J. (2000). Emerging adulthood: A conception of development from the late teens through the twenties. *American Psychologist, 55,* 469–480.

Barber, B. R. (1995). *Jihad vs. McWorld: How globalism and tribalism are reshaping the world.* New York: Ballantine.

Blos, P. (1962). *On adolescence: A psychoanalytic interpretation.* New York: Free Press.

Brooks-Gunn, J., Graber, J. A., & Paikoff, R. L. (1994). Studying links between hormones and negative affect: Models and measures. *Journal of Research on Adolescence, 4,* 469–486.

Brooks-Gunn, J., & Warren, M. P. (1989). Biological and social contributions to negative affect in young adolescent girls. *Child Development, 60,* 40–55.

Buchanan, C. M. (1998). *Parents' category-based beliefs about adolescence: Links to expectations for one's own child.* Manuscript submitted for publication.

Buchanan, C. M., Eccles, J., & Becker, J. (1992). Are adolescents the victims of raging hormones? Evidence for activational effects of hormones on moods and behavior at adolescence. *Psychological Bulletin, 111,* 62–107.

Buchanan, C. M., Eccles, J. S., Flanagan, C., Midgley, C., Feldlaufer, H., & Harold, R. D. (1990). Parents' and teachers' beliefs about adolescents: Effects of sex and experience. *Journal of Youth and Adolescence, 19,* 363–394.

Buchanan, C. M., & Holmbeck, G. N. (1998). Measuring beliefs about adolescent personality and behavior. *Journal of Youth and Adolescence, 27,* 609–629.

Cole, D. A., & McPherson, A. E. (1993). Relation of family subsystems to adolescent depression: Implementing a new family assessment strategy. *Journal of Family Psychology, 7,* 119–133.

Collins, W. A. (1990). Parent-child relationships in the transition to adolescence: Continuity and change in interaction, affect, and cognition. In R. Montemayor, G. R. Adams, & T. P. Gullotta (Eds.), *From childhood to adolescence: A transitional period?* (pp. 85–106). Newbury Park, CA: Sage.

Csikszentmihalyi, M., & Larson, R. W. (1984). *Being adolescent: Conflict and growth in the teenage years.* New York: Basic Books.

Dasen, P. (1998). Rapid social change and the turmoil of adolescence: A cross-cultural perspective. *International Journal of Group Tensions, 29,* 17–49.

Davis, S. S., & Davis, D. A. (1989). *Adolescence in a Moroccan town.* New Brunswick, NJ: Rutgers.

Eccles, J. S., Midgely, C., Wigfield, A., Buchanan, C. M., Reuman, D., Flanagan, C., & MacIver, D. (1993). Development during adolescence: The impact of stage-environment fit on young adolescents' experiences in schools and in families. *American Psychologist, 48,* 90–101.

Feldman, S. S., Mont-Reynaud, R., & Rosenthal, D. A. (1992). When East moves West: The acculturation of values of Chinese adolescents in the U.S. and Australia. *Journal of Research on Adolescence, 2,* 147–175.

Fletcher, A., & Steinberg, L. (1994, February). *Generational status and country of origin as influences on psychological adjustment of Asian-American adolescents.* Paper presented at the biennial meeting of the Society for Research on Adolescence, San Diego, CA.

Freud, A. (1946). *The ego and the mechanisms of defense.* New York: International Universities Press.

Freud, A. (1958). Adolescence. *Psychoanalytic Study of the Child, 15,* 255–278. New York: International Universities Press.

Freud, A. (1968). Adolescence. In A. E Winder & D. Angus (Eds.), *Adolescence: Contemporary studies* (pp. 13–24). New York: American Book.

Freud, A. (1969). Adolescence as a developmental disturbance. In G. Caplan & S. Lebovici (Eds.), *Adolescence: Psychosocial perspectives* (pp. 5–10). New York: Basic Books.

Gecas, V., & Seff, M. A. (1990). Families and adolescents: A review of the 1980s. *Journal of Marriage and the Family, 52,* 941–958.

Goethe, J. W. von (1774/1989). *The sorrows of young Werther, by Johann Wolfgang von Goethe,* translated by M. Hulse, with an Introduction and Notes. London, England: Penguin.

Gottfredson, M. R., & Hirschi, T. (1990). *A general theory of crime.* Stanford, CA: Stanford University Press.

Hall, G. S. (1904). *Adolescence: Its psychology and its relation to physiology, anthropology, sociology, sex, crime, religion, and*

education, Vols. 1 & 2. Englewood Cliffs, NJ: Prentice Hall.

Hatcher, R. A., Trussell, J., Stewart, F., & Stewart, G. (1994). *Contraceptive technology.* New York: Irvington.

Hill, J., & Holmbeck, G. (1987). Disagreements about rules in families with seventh-grade girls and boys. *Journal of Youth and Adolescence, 16,* 221–246.

Holmbeck, G. N., & Hill, J. (1988). Storm and stress beliefs about adolescence: Prevalence, self-reported antecedents, and effects of an undergraduate course. *Journal of Youth and Adolescence, 17,* 285–306.

Johnston, L. D., O'Malley, P. M., & Bachman, J. G. (1994). *National survey results on drug use from the monitoring the future study, 1975–1993* (NIH Publication No. 94-3810). Washington, DC: U.S. Government Printing Office.

Kett, J. F. (1977). *Rites of passage: Adolescence in America, 1790 to the present.* New York: Basic Books.

Kirkpatrick, J. (1987). Taure'are'a: A liminal category and passage to Marquesan adulthood. *Ethos, 15,* 382–405.

Larson, R., Csikszentmihalyi, M., & Graef, R. (1980). Mood variability and the psycho-social adjustment of adolescents. *Journal of Youth and Adolescence, 9,* 469–490.

Larson, R., & Ham, M. (1993). Stress and "storm and stress" in early adolescence: The relationship of negative life events with dysphoric affect. *Developmental Psychology, 29,* 130–140.

Larson, R., & Richards, M. H. (1994). *Divergent realities: The emotional lives of mothers, fathers, and adolescents.* New York: Basic Books.

Laursen, B., Coy, K. C., & Collins, W. A. (1998). Reconsidering changes in parent-child conflict across adolescence: A meta-analysis. *Child Development, 69,* 817–832.

Mead, M. (1928). *Coming of age in Samoa.* New York: Morrow.

Michael, R. T., Gagnon, J. H., Laumann, E. O., & Kolata, G. (1994). *Sex in America.* Boston: Little, Brown.

Moffitt, T. (1993). Adolescence-limited and life-course persistent antisocial behavior: A developmental taxonomy. *Psychological Review, 100,* 674–701.

Montemayor, R. (1986). Family variation in adolescent storm and stress. *Journal of Adolescent Research, 1,* 15–31.

Montemayor, R., & Hanson, E. (1985). A naturalistic view of conflict between adolescents and their parents and siblings. *Journal of Early Adolescents, 5,* 23–30.

Noble, J., Cover, J., & Yanagishita, M. (1996). *The world's youth.* Washington, DC: Population Reference Bureau.

Offer, D., & Offer, J. B. (1975). *From teenage to young manhood.* New York: Basic Books.

Offer, D., Ostrov, E., & Howard, K. I. (1981). The mental health professional's concept of the normal adolescent. *Archives of General Psychiatry, 38,* 149–153.

Offer, D., & Schonert-Reichl, K. A. (1992). Debunking the myths of adolescence: Findings from recent research. *Journal of the American Academy of Child and Adolescent Psychiatry, 31,* 1003–1014.

Paikoff, R., & Brooks-Gunn, J. (1991). Do parent-child relationships change during puberty? *Psychological Bulletin, 110,* 47–66.

Pasley, K., & Gecas, V. (1984). Stresses and satisfactions of the parental role. *Personnel and Guidance Journal, 2,* 400–404.

Petersen, A. C. (1988). Adolescent development. *Annual Review of Psychology, 39,* 583–607.

Petersen, A. C., Compas, B. E., Brooks-Gunn, J., Stemmler, M., Ey, S., & Grant, K. E. (1993). Depression in adolescence. *American Psychologist, 48,* 155–168.

Rosenthal, D. A. (1984). Intergenerational conflict and culture: A study of immigrant and nonimmigrant adolescents and their parents. *Genetic Psychology Monographs, 109,* 53–75.

Rousseau, J. J. (1762/1962). *The Emile of Jean Jacques Rousseau* (W. Boyd, Ed. and Trans.). New York: Teachers College Press, Columbia University.

Rutter, M., Graham, P. Chadwick, F., & Yule, W. (1976). Adolescent turmoil: Fact or fiction? *Journal of Child Psychiatry and Psychology, 17,* 35–56.

Schlegel, A. (1998). The global spread of adolescent culture. In L. Crockett & R. K. Silbereisen (Eds.), *Negotiating adolescence in a time of social change.* Cambridge: Cambridge University Press.

Schlegel, A., & Barry, H., III. (1991). *Adolescence: An anthropological inquiry.* New York: Free Press.

Simmons, R., & Blythe, D. (1987). *Moving into adolescence: The impact of pubertal change and school context.* Hawthorn, NY: Aldine de Gruyter.

Small, S. A., Cornelius, S., & Eastman, G. (1983). *Parenting adolescent children: A period of adult storm and stress?* Paper presented at the annual meeting of the American Psychological Association, Anaheim, CA.

Smetana, J. G. (1988). Concepts of self and social convention: Adolescents' and parents' reasoning about hypothetical and actual family conflicts. In M. Gunnar & W. A. Collins (Eds.), *Minnesota Symposium on Child Psychology, Vol. 21* (pp. 79–122). Hillsdale, NJ: Erlbaum.

Smetana, J. G. (1989). Adolescents' and parents' reasoning about actual family conflict. *Child Development, 60,* 1052–1067.

Stein, J. A., Newcomb, M. D., & Bentler, P. M. (1994). Psychosocial correlates and predictors of AIDS risk behaviors, abortion, and drug use among a community sample of young adult women. *Health Psychology, 13,* 308–318.

Steinberg, L. (1987). Family processes in adolescence: A developmental perspective. *Family Therapy, 14,* 77–86.

Steinberg, L. (1990). Autonomy, conflict, and harmony in the family relationship. In S. Feldman & G. Elliott (Eds.), *At the threshold: The developing adolescent,* (pp. 255–276). Cambridge, MA: Harvard University Press.

Steinberg, L. (1996). *Beyond the classroom: Why school reform has failed and what parents need to do.* New York: Simon and Schuster.

Steinberg, L., & Levine, A. (1997). *You and your adolescent: A parents' guide for ages 10 to 20.* New York: Harper Perennial.

Suarez-Orozco, C., & Suarez-Orozco, M. (1996). *Transformations: Migration, family life, and achievement motivation among Latino adolescents.* Palo Alto, CA: Stanford University Press.

Susman, E. J. (1997). Modeling developmental complexity in adolescence: Hormones and behavior in context. *Journal of Research on Adolescence, 7,* 283–306.

U.S. Department of Transportation (1995). *Understanding youthful risk taking and driving.* (DOT Publication No. HS 808-318). Springfield, VA: National Technical Information Service.

Zuckerman, M. (Ed.). (1983). *Biological bases of sensation seeking, impulsivity, and anxiety.* Hillsdale, NJ: Lawrence Erlbaum Associates.

THINKING CRITICALLY

1. Analyze Anna Freud's assertion, "To be normal during the adolescent period is by itself abnormal." What does she mean by this statement? How might her belief that this statement is true be based in her experience of treating disturbed adolescents as a clinical psychotherapist?

2. Arnett defines storm and stress as including conflict with parents, mood disruptions, and risk behavior. Do you agree or disagree with this definition? What other elements might you include in your own definition?

3. What do you think explains why conflict with parents is higher in early adolescence than in later adolescence? How are early and late adolescence different in ways that might explain it?

4. Arnett argues that the main reason industrialized cultures have higher rates of adolescent storm and stress than traditional, preindustrial cultures is the higher value placed on independence for adolescents in industrialized cultures. Considering the three main aspects of storm and stress—conflict with parents, mood disruptions, and risk behavior—what other differences between industrialized cultures and traditional cultures may help explain differences in their rates of adolescent storm and stress?

The Concept of Emerging Adulthood

Reading 1.1 noted that G. S. Hall defined the age range of adolescence as extending from 14 to 24. Today, most scholars view adolescence as beginning at about age 10 and ending at age 18 or 19. It has been argued recently that there is a new period of life in industrialized societies extending from about age 18 to about age 25 that can be clearly distinguished from the adolescence that proceeds it and the young adulthood that follows it. This reading presents an outline for the new theory of that age period, termed emerging adulthood.

Reading 1.3

Emerging Adulthood: A Theory of Development from the Late Teens Through the Twenties

J. J. Arnett

When our mothers were our age, they were engaged. . . . They at least had some idea what they were going to do with their lives. . . . I, on the other hand, will have a dual degree in majors that are ambiguous at best and impractical at worst (English and political science), no ring on my finger and no idea who I am, much less what I want to do. . . . Under duress, I will admit that this is a pretty exciting time. Sometimes, when I look out across the wide expanse that is my future, I can see beyond the void. I realize that having nothing ahead to count on means I now have to count on myself; that having no direction means forging one of my own.

—Kristen, age 22 (Page, 1999, pp. 18, 20).

For most young people in industrialized countries, the years from the late teens through the twenties are years of profound change and importance. During this time many young people obtain the level of education and training that will provide the foundation for their incomes and occupational achievements for the remainder of their adult work lives (Chisholm & Hurrelmann, 1995; William T. Grant Commission on Work, Family, and Citizenship, 1988). It is for many people a time of frequent change as various possibilities in love, work, and worldviews are explored (Erikson, 1968; Rindfuss, 1991). By the end of this period, the late twenties, most people have made more definite life choices that have enduring ramifications. When adults later consider the most important events in their lives, they most often name events that took place during this period (Martin & Smyer, 1990).

Sweeping demographic shifts have taken place over the past half century that have made the late teens and early twenties not simply a brief period of transition into adult roles but a distinct period of the life course, characterized by change and exploration of possible life directions. As recently as 1970, the median age of marriage in the United States was about 21 for females and 23 for males; by 1996, it had risen to 25 for females and 27 for males (U.S. Bureau of the Census, 1997). Age of first childbirth followed a similar pattern. Also, since mid-century the proportion of young Americans obtaining higher education after high school has risen steeply, from 14% in 1940 to over 60% by the mid-1990s (Arnett & Taber, 1994; Bianchi & Spain, 1996). Similar changes have taken place in other industrialized countries (Chisholm & Hurrelmann, 1995; Noble, Cover, & Yanagishita, 1996).

These changes over the past half century have altered the nature of development in the late teens and early twenties for young people in industrialized societies. Because marriage and parenthood are delayed until the mid-to-late twenties for most people, it is no longer normative for the late teens and early twenties to be a time of entering and settling into long-term adult roles. On the contrary, these years are more typically a period of frequent change and exploration (Arnett, 1998; Rindfuss, 1991).

In this discussion, I will propose a new theory of development from the late teens through the twenties, with a focus on ages 18–25. I will argue that this period, *emerging adulthood*, is neither adolescence nor young adulthood, but theoretically and empirically distinct from them both. Emerging adulthood is distinguished by relative independence from social roles and from normative expectations. Having left the dependency of childhood and adolescence, and not yet having entered the enduring responsibilities that are normative in adulthood, emerging adults often explore a variety of possible life directions in love, work,

and worldviews. Emerging adulthood is a time of life when many different directions remain possible, when little about the future has been decided for certain, when the scope of independent exploration of life's possibilities is greater for most people than it will be at any other period of the lifespan. For most people, the late teens through the mid-twenties are the most *volitional* years of life. However, cultural influences structure and sometimes limit the extent to which emerging adults are able to use their late teens and twenties in this way, and not all young people in this age period are able to use these years for independent exploration.

The theoretical background will be discussed first. Then evidence will be presented to illustrate how emerging adulthood is a distinct period demographically, subjectively, and in terms of identity explorations. Next I will explain how emerging adulthood can be distinguished from adolescence and young adulthood. Finally, I will discuss the economic and cultural conditions under which emerging adulthood is most likely to exist as a distinct period of the life course.

The Theoretical Background

There have been a number of important theoretical contributions to the understanding of development from the late teens through the twenties. One early contribution was made by Erik Erikson (1950, 1968). Erikson rarely discussed specific ages in his writings, and in his theory of human development across the lifespan he did not include a separate stage that could be considered analogous to emerging adulthood as proposed here. Rather, he wrote of development in adolescence and of development in young adulthood. However, he also commented on the "prolonged adolescence" typical of industrialized societies, and the *psychosocial moratorium* granted to young people in such societies, "during which the young adult through free role experimentation may find a niche in some section of his society" (1968, p. 156). Thus Erikson seems to be distinguishing—without naming—a period that is in some ways adolescence and in some ways young adulthood yet not strictly either one, a period in which adult commitments and responsibilities are delayed while the role experimentation that began in adolescence continues and in fact intensifies.

Another theoretical contribution can be found in the work of Daniel Levinson (1978). Levinson interviewed men at midlife, but he had them describe their earlier years as well, and on the basis of their accounts he developed a theory that included development in the late teens and the twenties. He called ages 17–33 "the novice phase" of development and argued that the overriding task of this phase is to move into the adult world and build a stable life structure. During this process, according to Levinson, there is a considerable amount of change and instability as the young person sorts through various possibilities in love and work in the course of establishing a life structure. Levinson acknowledged that his conception of the novice phase was similar to Erikson's ideas about the role experimentation that takes place during the psychosocial moratorium (Levinson, 1978, pp. 322–323).

Perhaps the best-known theory of development in the late teens through the twenties is Kenneth Keniston's theory of "youth." Like Erikson and Levinson, Keniston (1971) conceptualized youth as a period of continued role experimentation between adolescence and young adulthood. However, Keniston wrote at a time when American society and some Western European societies were convulsed by highly visible "youth movements" protesting U.S. involvement in the Vietnam War (among other things). His description of youth as a time of "tension between self and society" (p. 8) and "refusal of socialization" (p. 9) reflect that historical moment rather than any enduring characteristics of the period.

More important, his application of the term "youth" to this period is problematic. "Youth" has a long history in the English language as a term for childhood generally and for what later became called adolescence (e.g., Ben-Amos, 1994), and it continues to be used popularly and by many social scientists for these purposes (as reflected in terms such as "youth organizations"). Keniston's choice of

the ambiguous and confusing term "youth" may explain in part why the idea of the late teens and twenties as a separate period of life never became widely accepted by developmental scientists after his articulation of it. However, as I will argue in the following sections, there is good empirical support for conceiving this period—proposed here as emerging adulthood—as a distinct period of life.

Emerging Adulthood Is Distinct Demographically

Although Erikson (1968), Levinson (1978), and Keniston (1971) all contributed to the theoretical groundwork for emerging adulthood, the nature of the period has changed considerably since the time of their writings more than twenty years ago. As noted at the outset of this discussion, demographic changes in the timing of marriage and parenthood in recent decades have made a period of emerging adulthood typical for young people in industrialized societies. Postponing these transitions until at least the late twenties leaves the late teens and early twenties available for exploring various possible life directions.

An important demographic characteristic of emerging adulthood is that there is a great deal of demographic variability, reflecting the wide scope of individual volition during these years. Emerging adulthood is the only period of life in which *nothing is normative*, demographically (Rindfuss, 1991; Wallace, 1995). During adolescence, up to age 18, there is little variation in a variety of key demographic areas. Over 95% of American adolescents aged 12–17 live at home with one or more parents, over 98% are unmarried, fewer than 10% have had a child, and over 95% are enrolled in school (U.S. Bureau of the Census, 1997). By age 30, new demographic norms have been established: about 75% of thirty year-olds have married, about 75% have become parents, and fewer than 10% are enrolled in school (U.S. Bureau of the Census, 1997).

In between these two periods, however, and especially from age 18 to 25, a person's demographic status in these areas is very difficult to predict on the basis of age alone. The demographic diversity and unpredictability of emerging adulthood is a reflection of the experimental and exploratory quality of the period. Talcott Parsons (1942) called adolescence the "roleless role," but this is a term that applies much better to emerging adulthood. Emerging adults tend to have a wider scope of possible activities than persons in other age periods because they are less likely to be constrained by role requirements, and this makes their demographic status unpredictable.

One demographic area that especially reflects the exploratory quality of emerging adulthood is residential status. Most young Americans leave home by age 18 or 19 (Goldscheider & Goldscheider, 1994). In the years that follow, during emerging adulthood, there is a great deal of diversity in living situations. About one-third of emerging adults "go off to college" after high school and spend the next several years in some combination of independent living and continued reliance on adults, for example in a college dormitory or a fraternity or sorority house (Goldscheider & Goldscheider, 1994). For them this is a period of

"semiautonomy" (Goldscheider & Davanzo, 1986), as they take on some of the responsibilities of independent living but leave others to their parents, college authorities, or other adults. About 40% move out of their parental home not for college but for independent living and full-time work (Goldscheider & Goldscheider, 1994). About two-thirds experience a period of cohabitation with a romantic partner (Michael, Gagnon, Laumann, & Kolata, 1995). Some remain at home while attending college or working or some combination of the two. Only about 10% of males and 30% of females remain at home until marriage (Goldscheider & Goldscheider, 1994).

Amidst this diversity, perhaps the unifying feature of the residential status of emerging adults is the instability of it. Emerging adults have the highest rates of residential change of any age group, as shown in Figure 1.3.1. For about 40% of the current generation of emerging adults, residential changes include moving back into their parents' home and then out again at least once in the course of their late teens and twenties (Goldscheider & Goldscheider, 1994). Frequent residential changes

FIGURE 1.3.1 Residential change by age, 1998 (Source: U.S. Bureau of the Census, 2000, *Geographic mobility: March 1997 to March 1998. Current Population Reports,* Series P-20, No. 520. Washington, DC: U.S. Government Printing Office).

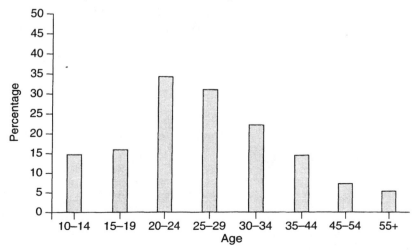

during emerging adulthood reflect the exploratory quality of it, because these changes often take place at the end of one period of exploration or the beginning of another—the end of a period of cohabitation, for example, or entering or leaving college, or the beginning of a new job in a new place.

School attendance is another area in which there is substantial change and diversity among emerging adults. The proportion of American emerging adults who enter higher education in the year following high school is at its highest level ever, over 60% (Bianchi & Spain, 1996). However, this figure masks the expanding diversity in the years that follow. Only 32% of young people aged 25–29 have completed four years or more of college (U.S. Bureau of the Census, 1997). For emerging adults, college education is often pursued in a non-linear way, frequently combined with work and punctuated by periods of non-attendance. For those who do eventually graduate with a four-year degree, college is increasingly likely to be followed by graduate school. About one-third of those who graduate with a bachelor's degree are enrolled in postgraduate education the following year (Mogelonsky, 1996). In European countries, too, the length of education has become extended in recent decades (Chisholm & Hurrelmann, 1995).

Overall, then, the years of emerging adulthood are characterized by a high degree of demographic diversity and instability, reflecting the emphasis on change and exploration. It is only in the transition from emerging adulthood to young adulthood, in the late twenties, that the diversity narrows and the instability eases, as young people make more enduring choices in love and work.

Emerging Adulthood Is Distinct Subjectively

Emerging adults do not see themselves as adolescents, but many of them also do not see themselves as entirely adults. Figure 1.3.2 shows that when they are asked whether or not they feel they have reached adulthood, the majority of Americans in their late teens and early twenties answer neither no nor yes but the ambiguous "in some respects yes, in some respects no" (Arnett, 2000a). This reflects a subjective sense on the part of most emerging adults that they have left adolescence but have not yet completely entered young adulthood (Arnett, 1994a, 1997, 1998). They have no name for the period they are in—as the society they live in has no name for it—so they regard themselves as being neither adolescents nor adults, in between the two but not really one or the other. As Figure 1.3.2 shows, it is only in their late twenties and early thirties that a clear majority of people indicate that they feel they have reached adulthood. However, age is only the roughest marker of the subjective transition from emerging adulthood to young adulthood. Even in their late twenties and early thirties, nearly one-third of the persons in the study illustrated in Figure 1.3.2 did not feel their transition to adulthood was complete.

One might expect that emerging adults' subjective sense of ambiguity in attaining full adulthood arises from the demographic diversity and instability described above. Perhaps it is difficult for young people to feel they have reached adulthood before they have established a stable residence, finished school, settled into a career, and married (or at least committed themselves to a long-term love relationship). However, perhaps surprisingly, the research evidence indicates strongly that these demographic transitions have little to do with emerging adults' conceptions of what it means to reach adulthood. Consistently, in a variety of studies with young people in their teens and twenties, demographic transitions such as finishing education, settling into a career, marriage, and parenthood rank at the *bottom* in importance among possible criteria considered necessary for the attainment of adulthood (Arnett, 1997, 1998, 2001; Greene, Wheatley, & Aldava, 1992; Scheer, Unger, & Brown, 1994).

The characteristics that matter most to emerging adults in their subjective sense of attaining adulthood are not demographic transitions but individualistic *qualities of character* (Arnett, 1998). Specifically, the two top criteria for the transition to adulthood in a variety

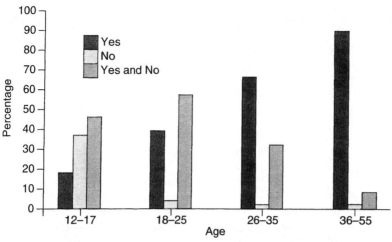

FIGURE 1.3.2 Subjective conceptions of adult status, in response to the question, "Do you feel that you have reached adulthood?" *N* = 519. (Adapted from Arnett, 2001.)

of studies have been found to be *accepting responsibility for one's self* and *making independent decisions* (Arnett, 1997, 1998; Greene et al., 1992; Scheer et al., 1994). A third criterion, also individualistic but more tangible, *becoming financially independent,* also ranks consistently near the top.

The prominence of these criteria for the transition to adulthood reflects an emphasis in emerging adulthood on becoming a self-sufficient person (Arnett, 1998). During these years, the character qualities most important to becoming successfully self-sufficient—accepting responsibility for one's self and making independent decisions—are being developed. Financial independence is also crucial to self-sufficiency, so it is also important in emerging adults' conceptions of what is necessary to become an adult. It is only after these character qualities have reached fruition, and financial independence has been attained, that emerging adults experience a subjective change in their developmental status, as they move out of emerging adulthood and into young adulthood. For most young people in American society, this occurs some time during the twenties and is usually accomplished by the late twenties (Arnett, 2001a).

Although emerging adults do not view demographic transitions as *necessary* for attaining adulthood, it should be noted that parenthood in particular is often *sufficient* for marking a subjective sense of adult status. Parenthood ranks low in young people's views of the essential criteria for adulthood for *people in general,* but those who have had a child tend to view becoming a parent as the most important marker of the transition to adulthood *for themselves* (Arnett, 1998). The explorations that occur in emerging adulthood become sharply restricted with parenthood, because it requires taking on the responsibilities of protecting and providing for a young child. With parenthood, the focus of concern shifts inexorably from responsibility for one's self to responsibility for others.

Emerging Adulthood Is Distinct for Identity Explorations

A key feature of emerging adulthood is that it is the period of life that offers the most opportunity for identity explorations in the areas of love and work. Of course, it is adolescence rather than emerging adulthood that has typically been associated with identity formation. Erikson (1950) designated identity vs. role confusion as the central crisis of the adolescent stage of life, and in the decades since he articulated this idea the focus of research on identity has been on adolescence (Adams, 1999). However, as noted, Erikson (1950; 1968) clearly believed that industrialized societies allow a "prolonged adolescence" for extended identity explorations. If adolescence is the period from age 10–18 and emerging adulthood is the period from (roughly) age 18–25, most identity exploration takes place in emerging adulthood rather than adolescence. Although research on identity formation has focused mainly on adolescence, this research has shown that identity achievement has rarely been reached by the end of high school (Montemayor, Brown, & Adams, 1985; Waterman, 1982) and that identity development continues through the late teens and the twenties (Valde, 1996; Whitbourne & Tesch, 1985).

The focus on identity issues in emerging adulthood can be seen from an examination of the two main areas of identity exploration: love and work. Identity formation involves trying out various life possibilities and gradually moving toward making enduring decisions. In all three of these areas, this process begins in adolescence but takes place mainly in emerging adulthood. With regard to love, American adolescents typically begin dating around age 12–14 (Padgham & Blyth, 1991). However, because any serious consideration of marriage is a decade or more away for most 14–15 year olds, young people view the early years of dating as primarily recreational (Roscoe, Dian, & Brooks, 1987). For adolescents, dating provides companionship, the first experiences of romantic love, and sexual experimentation; but their dating relationships typically last only a few weeks or months (Feiring, 1996), and few adolescents expect to remain with their "high school sweetheart" much beyond high school.

In emerging adulthood, explorations in love become more intimate and serious. Dating in adolescence often takes place in groups, as adolescents pursue shared recreation such as parties, dances, and "hanging out" (Padgham & Blyth, 1991). By emerging adulthood, dating is more likely to take place in couples, and the focus is less on recreation and more on exploring the potential for emotional and physical intimacy. Romantic relationships in emerging adulthood last longer than in adolescence, are more likely to include sexual intercourse, and may include cohabitation (Michael et al., 1995). Thus in adolescence, explorations in love tend to be tentative and transient; the implicit question is, "who would I enjoy being with, here and now?" In contrast, explorations in love in emerging adulthood tend to involve a deeper level of intimacy, and the implicit question is more identity focused: "Given the kind of person I am, what kind of person do I wish to have as a partner through life?"

With regard to work there is a similar contrast between the transient and tentative explorations of adolescence and the more serious and focused explorations of emerging adulthood. In the United States, the majority of high school students are employed part-time (Barling & Kelloway, 1999). Although adolescents often report that their work experiences enhance their abilities in areas such as managing their time and money (Mortimer, Harley, & Aronson, 1999), for the most part their jobs do not provide them with knowledge and experience that will be related to their future occupations (Greenberger & Steinberg, 1986; Steinberg & Cauffman, 1995). Most adolescents are employed in service jobs—restaurants, retail stores, and so on—in which the cognitive challenges are minimal and the skills learned are few. Adolescents tend to view their jobs not as occupational preparation but as a way to obtain the money that will support an active leisure life—CDs, concerts, restaurant meals, clothes, cars, travel, and so on (Bachman & Schulenberg, 1993; Shanahan, Elder, Burchinal, & Conger, 1996; Steinberg & Cauffman, 1995).

In emerging adulthood, work experiences become more focused on preparation for adult work roles. Emerging adults begin to consider how their work experiences will lay the groundwork for the jobs they may have through adulthood. In exploring various work possibilities, they explore identity issues as well: "What kind of work am I good at? What kind of work would I find satisfying for the long term? What are my chances of getting a job in the field that seems to suit me best?"

Emerging adults' educational choices and experiences explore similar questions. In their educational paths they try out various possibilities that would prepare them for different kinds of future work. College students often change majors more than once, especially in their first two years, as they try on possible occupational futures, discard them, and pursue others. With graduate school becoming an increasingly common choice after an undergraduate degree is obtained, emerging adults' educational explorations often continue through their early-to-mid twenties. Graduate school allows emerging adults to switch directions again from the path of occupational preparation they had chosen as undergraduates.

For both love and work, the goals of identity explorations in emerging adulthood are not limited to direct preparation for adult roles. On the contrary, in part the explorations of emerging adulthood are explorations for their own sake, as part of obtaining a broad range of life experiences before taking on enduring—and limiting—adult responsibilities. The absence of enduring role commitments in emerging adulthood makes possible a degree of experimentation and exploration that is not likely to be possible during the thirties and beyond. For people who wish to have a variety of romantic and sexual experiences, emerging adulthood is the time for it, when parental surveillance has diminished and there is as yet little normative pressure to enter marriage. Similarly, emerging adulthood is the time for trying out unusual work and educational possibilities. For this reason, short-term volunteer jobs in programs such as Americorps and the Peace Corps are more popular with emerging adults than with persons in any other age period. Emerging adults may also travel to a different part of the country or the world on their own for a limited period, often in the context of a limited-term work or educational experience. This, too, can be part of their identity explorations, part of expanding their range of

personal experiences prior to making the more enduring choices of adulthood.

Although the identity explorations of emerging adulthood make it an especially full and intense time of life for many people, these explorations are not always experienced as enjoyable. Explorations in love sometimes result in disappointment, disillusionment, or rejection. Explorations in work sometimes result in a failure to achieve the occupation most desired, or in an inability to find work that is satisfying and fulfilling. Also, to a large extent emerging adults pursue their identity explorations on their own, without the daily companionship of either their family of origin or their family-to-be (Jonsson, 1994; Morch, 1995). Young Americans aged 19–29 spend more of their leisure time alone than any persons except the elderly, and more of their time in productive activities (school and work) alone than any other age group under 40 (Larson, 1990). Nevertheless, emerging adults tend to view their lives more positively than persons in any other age group (Rossi & Rossi, 1990), and for the most part emerging adults are highly optimistic about ultimately achieving their goals (Arnett, 2000a). In one national poll of 18–24 year-olds in the United States (Hornblower, 1997), nearly all—96%—agreed that "I am very sure that someday I will get to where I want to be in life."

Other Notable Findings on Emerging Adulthood

The three areas outlined earlier—demographics, subjective perceptions, and identity explorations—are the three areas where information on the distinctiveness of emerging adulthood is most abundant. However, there is evidence available from other areas that suggests possible lines of inquiry for future research on emerging adulthood. One of these areas is risk behavior. Although there is a voluminous literature on adolescent risk behavior and relatively little research on risk behavior in emerging adulthood (Jessor, Donovan, & Costa, 1991), prevalence of several types of risk behavior peak not during adolescence but during emerging adulthood (ages 18–25), including unprotected sex, most types of substance use, and risky driving behaviors such as driving at high speeds or while intoxicated (Arnett, 1992; Bachman, Johnston, O'Malley, & Schulenberg, 1996).

What is it about emerging adulthood that lends itself to such high rates of risk behavior? To some degree, emerging adults' risk behavior can be understood as part of their identity explorations, that is, as one reflection of the desire to obtain a wide range of experiences before settling down into the roles and responsibilities of adult life. One of the motivations consistently found to be related to participation in a variety of types of risk behavior is sensation seeking, which is the desire for novel and intense experiences (Arnett, 1994b). Emerging adults can pursue novel and intense experiences more freely than adolescents because they are less likely to be monitored by parents, and more freely than adults because they are less constrained by roles. Upon marriage, adults are constrained from taking part in risk behavior by the responsibilities of the marriage role, and once they have a child, by the parenting role. In one example of this, Bachman et al. (1996) used longitudinal data to show how substance use rises to a peak in the early twenties during the role hiatus of emerging adulthood, then declines steeply and sharply following marriage, and declines further following the entry to parenthood. The responsibilities of these roles leads to lower rates of risk behavior as emerging adulthood is succeeded by young adulthood.

These findings provide a foundation for research into development during emerging adulthood. There is, of course, much more work to be done on virtually every aspect of development during this period. To what extent do emerging adults rely on friends for support and companionship, given that this is a period when most young people have left their family of origin but have not yet entered marriage? To what extent are the explorations of emerging adulthood different for males and females? Do emerging adults have especially high rates of media use, given that they spend so much time

alone? These and many other questions about the period await investigation. Establishing emerging adulthood as a distinct developmental period may help to promote this research.

Why Emerging Adulthood Is Not Adolescence

It is widely known that the scientific study of adolescence began with the publication of G. Stanley Hall's two-volume magnum opus nearly a century ago (Hall, 1904). What is less widely known, however, is that in Hall's view adolescence extended from age 14 to age 24 (Hall, 1904, vol. 1, p. xix). In contrast, contemporary scholars generally consider adolescence to begin at age 10 or 11 and end by age 18 or 19. The cover of every issue of the *Journal of Research on Adolescence*, the flagship journal of the Society for Research on Adolescence, proclaims that adolescence is defined as "the second decade of life." What happened between Hall's time and our own to move scholars' conceptions of adolescence forward in the life course?

Two changes stand out as possible explanations. One is the decline that has taken place during the 20th century in the typical age of the initiation of puberty. At the beginning of the 20th century, the median age of menarche in Western countries was about 15 (Eveleth & Tanner, 1976). Because menarche takes place relatively late in the typical sequence of pubertal changes, this means that the initial changes of puberty would have begun at about age 13–15 for most people, which is just where Hall designated the beginning of adolescence. However, the median age of menarche (and, by implication, other pubertal changes) declined steadily between 1900 and 1970 before leveling out, so that by now the typical age of menarche in the United States is 12.5 (Brooks-Gunn & Paikoff, 1997). The initial changes of puberty usually begin about two years earlier, thus the designation of adolescence as beginning with the entry into "the second decade of life."

As for the age when adolescence ends, the change in this age may have been inspired not by a biological change but by a social change: the growth of high school attendance to a normative experience for adolescents in the United States. In 1900, only 10% of persons aged 14–17 were enrolled in high school. However, this proportion rose steeply and steadily over the course of the twentieth century, to 95% by 1985 (Arnett & Taber, 1994). This makes it easy to understand why Hall would not have chosen 18 as the end of adolescence, because for most adolescents of his time no significant transition took place at that age. Education ended earlier, work began earlier, leaving home took place later. Marriage and parenthood did not take place for most people until their early-to-mid-twenties (Arnett & Taber, 1994), which may have been why Hall designated age 24 as the end of adolescence. (Hall himself did not explain why he chose this age.)

In our time, it makes sense to define adolescence as ages 10–18. Young people in this age group have in common that they live with their parents, they are experiencing the physical changes of puberty, they attend secondary school, and they are part of a school-based peer culture. None of this remains normative after age 18, which is why it is not adequate simply to call the late teens and early twenties "late adolescence." Age 18 also marks a variety of legal transitions, such as being allowed to vote and sign legal documents.

Although some scholars have suggested that the late teens and early twenties should be considered late adolescence (e.g., Elliott & Feldman, 1990), for the most part scholars on adolescence focus on ages 10–18 as the years of adolescent development. Studies published in the major journals on adolescence rarely include samples with ages higher than 18. For example, in 1997, 90% of the studies published in *Journal of Research on Adolescence* and *Journal of Youth and Adolescence* were on samples of high school age or younger. College students have been the focus of many research studies, but most often as "adults" in social psychology studies. Sociologists have studied the late teens and twenties for patterns of demographic events viewed as part of the transition to adulthood (e.g., Hogan & Astone, 1986; Rindfuss, 1991).

However, few studies have recognized the late teens through the twenties as a distinct developmental period.

Why Emerging Adulthood Is Not Young Adulthood

But (it might be objected) do we not already have a paradigm for the years of the late teens and the twenties? Is that not what young adulthood is? The answer is no. There are a number of reasons why "young adulthood" is unsatisfactory as a designation for this developmental period.

One reason is that the use of "young adulthood" implies that adulthood has been reached at this point. As we have seen, most young people in this age period would disagree that they have reached adulthood. They see themselves as gradually making their way into adulthood, so *emerging* adulthood seems a better term for their subjective experience. More generally, the term *emerging* captures the dynamic, changeable, fluid quality of the period.

Also, if ages 18–25 are "young adulthood," what would that make the thirties? Young adulthood is a term better applied to the thirties, which are still young but are definitely adult in a way that the years 18–25 are not. It makes little sense to lump the late teens, twenties, thirties together and call the entire period "young adulthood." The period from age 18–25 could hardly be more distinct from the thirties. The majority of young people aged 18–25 do not believe they have reached full adulthood, whereas the majority of people in their thirties believe that they have (Arnett, 2001). The majority of people aged 18–25 are still in the process of obtaining education and training for a long-term adult occupation, whereas the majority of people in their thirties have settled into a more stable occupational path. The majority of people aged 18–25 are unmarried, whereas the majority of people in their thirties are married. The majority of people aged 18–25 are childless, whereas the majority of people in their thirties have had at least one child. The list could go on. The point should be clear. Emerging adulthood and young adulthood should be distinguished as separate developmental periods.

It should be emphasized, however, that age is only a rough indicator of the transition from emerging adulthood to young adulthood. Eighteen is a good age marker of the end of adolescence and the beginning of emerging adulthood, because it is the age at which most young people finish secondary school, leave their parents' home, and reach the legal age of adult status in a variety of respects. However, the transition from emerging adulthood to young adulthood is much less definite with respect to age. There are 19 year olds who have reached adulthood—demographically, subjectively, and in terms of identity formation—and 29 year olds who have not. Nevertheless, for most people the transition from emerging adulthood to young adulthood intensifies in the late twenties and is reached by age 30 in all of these respects.

Emerging Adulthood Across Cultures

Thus far the focus of this discussion has been on emerging adulthood among young people in the West, especially in the United States. Is emerging adulthood a period of life that is restricted to certain cultures and certain times?

The answer to this question appears to be yes. For example, in Schlegel and Barry's (1991) comprehensive integration of information on adolescence in 186 traditional non-Western cultures, they concluded that adolescence as a life stage is virtually universal, but a further period between adolescence and adulthood ("youth," in the terminology they used) existed in only 20% of the cultures they studied. In the cultures in their sample, adulthood was typically signified by entry into marriage, and marriage usually took place at about age 16–18 for girls and about age 18–20 for boys. This early timing of marriage allowed for a period of adolescence but not for a period of emerging adulthood.

Emerging adulthood, then, is not a universal period but a period that exists only in cultures that postpone the entry into adult roles and responsibilities until well past the late teens. Thus emerging adulthood would be most likely to be found in countries that are highly industrialized or "postindustrial." Such countries require a high level of education and training for entry into the information-based professions that are the most prestigious and lucrative, so many of their young people remain in school into their early to mid-twenties. Marriage and parenthood are typically postponed until well after schooling has ended, which allows for a period of exploration of various relationships before marriage and exploration of various jobs before taking on the responsibility of supporting a child financially. Table 1.3.1 shows the median ages of marriage in a range of highly industrialized countries, contrasted with the median ages of marriage in selected developing countries.

Although median marriage ages are typically calculated on a country-wide basis, it should be noted that emerging adulthood is best understood as a characteristic of cultures rather than countries. Within some highly industrialized countries, members of minority cultures may have cultural practices that lead to a shortened period of emerging adulthood or no emerging adulthood at all. Limitations in educational and occupational opportunities also influence the extent to which young people can experience their late teens and twenties as a volitional period. The young woman who has a child outside of marriage at age 16 and spends her late teens and early twenties alternating between welfare and low-paying jobs has little chance for exploration of possible life directions; nor does the young man who drops out of school and spends most of his late teens and early twenties unemployed and looking unsuccessfully for a job (Cote & Allahar, 1996). Because opportunities tend to be less widely available in minority cultures than in the majority culture in most industrialized countries, members of minority groups may be less likely to experience ages 18–25 as a period of independent exploration of possible life directions (Morch, 1995). However, social class may be more important than ethnicity, with young people in the middle class or above having more opportunities for the explorations of emerging

TABLE 1.3.1 Median Marriage Age (Females) in Selected Countries

INDUSTRIALIZED COUNTRIES	AGE	DEVELOPING COUNTRIES	AGE
United States	25.2	Egypt	21.9
Canada	26.0	Morocco	22.3
Germany	26.2	Ghana	21.1
France	26.1	Nigeria	18.7
Italy	25.8	India	20.0
Japan	26.9	Indonesia	21.1
Australia	26.0	Brazil	22.6

Note. All data are from Noble, Cover, and Yanagishita (1996).

adulthood than young people who are working class or below. Alternatively, it may be that explorations are not fewer in the working class but different, with more emphasis on work explorations and fewer in education. These are possibilities to be investigated.

Currently in economically developing countries, there tends to be a distinct cultural split between urban and rural areas. Young people in urban areas of countries such as China and India are more likely to experience emerging adulthood, because they marry later, have children later, obtain more education, and have a greater range of occupational and recreational opportunities than young people in rural areas. In contrast, young people in rural areas of developing countries often receive minimal schooling, marry early, and have little choice of occupations except agricultural work. Thus in developing countries emerging adulthood is often experienced in urban areas but rarely in rural areas.

However, it should also be noted that emerging adulthood is likely to become more pervasive worldwide in the decades to come, with the increasing globalization of the world economy. Between 1980 and 1995, the proportion of young people in developing countries who attended secondary school rose sharply, and the median ages of marriage and first childbirth rose in these countries as well (Noble et al., 1996). As developing countries are becoming more integrated into a global economy, there is an increasing number of higher-paying jobs in these countries that require young people to obtain higher educa-

tion. At the same time, as technology becomes increasingly available in these countries, particularly in agriculture, the labor of young people is becoming less and less necessary for family survival, making it possible for many of them to attend school instead.

These changes open up the possibility for the spread of emerging adulthood in developing countries. Economic development makes possible a period of the independent role exploration that is at the heart of emerging adulthood. As societies become more affluent, they are more likely to grant young people the opportunity for the extended moratorium of emerging adulthood, because they have no urgent need for young people's labor. Similarly, economic development is usually accompanied by increased life expectancy, and devoting years to the explorations of emerging adulthood becomes more feasible and attractive when people can expect to live to be at least 70 or 80 rather than 40 or 50. Thus it seems possible that by the end of the 21st century emerging adulthood will be a normative period for young people worldwide, although it is likely to vary in length and content both within and between countries (Arnett, 2000c). The growth and variability of emerging adulthood in countries and cultures around the world would make an important and fascinating topic for a nascent scholarly field of emerging adulthood.

Summary and Conclusion

Emerging adulthood has become a distinct period of the life course for young people in industrialized societies. It is a period characterized for most people by change and exploration, as they examine the life possibilities open to them and gradually arrive at more enduring choices in love, work, and worldviews. Not all young people experience their late teens and twenties as years of change and exploration, even in industrialized societies. Some lack the opportunities to use those years as a volitional period, others may be inclined by personality or circumstances to limit their explorations or to seek a relatively early resolution to them. Nevertheless, we can characterize emerging adulthood as a period when change and exploration are common, even as we recognize the heterogeneity of the period and in-

vestigate this heterogeneity as one of emerging adulthood's distinguishing characteristics.

Emerging adulthood merits scholarly attention as a distinct period of the life course in industrialized societies. It is in many respects the age of possibilities, a period in which many different potential futures remain possible, and personal freedom and exploration of the possibilities of life are higher for most people than at any other time. It is also a period of life that is likely to grow in importance in the coming century, as countries around the world reach a point in their economic development where they may allow the prolonged period of exploration and freedom from roles that constitutes emerging adulthood.

REFERENCES

Adams, G. R. (1999). *The objective measure of ego identity status: A manual on theory and test construction.* Guelph, Ontario: Author.

Arnett, J. (1992). Reckless behavior in adolescence: A developmental perspective. *Developmental Review, 12,* 339–373.

Arnett, J. J. (1994a). Are college students adults? Their conceptions of the transition to adulthood. *Journal of Adult Development, 1,* 154–168.

Arnett, J. (1994b). Sensation seeking: A new conceptualization and a new scale. *Personality and Individual Differences, 16,* 289–296.

Arnett, J. J. (1997). Young people's conceptions of the transition to adulthood. *Youth and Society, 29,* 1–23.

Arnett, J. J. (1998). Learning to stand alone: The contemporary American transition to adulthood in cultural and historical context. *Human Development,* 295–315.

Arnett, J. J. (2000a). High hopes in a grim world: Emerging adults' views of their futures and of "Generation X." *Youth and Society, 31,* 267–286.

Arnett, J. J. (2000b). *Emerging adulthood: Prospects for the 21st century.* Manuscript submitted for publication.

Arnett, J. J. (2001). *Conceptions of the transition to adulthood from adolescence through midlife.* Manuscript submitted for publication.

Arnett, J. & Taber, S. (1994). Adolescence terminable and interminable: When does adolescence end? *Journal of Youth and Adolescence, 23,* 517–537.

Bachman, J. G., Johnston, L. D., O'Malley, P., & Schulenberg, J. (1996). Transitions in drug use during late adolescence and young adulthood. In J. A. Graber, J. Brooks-Gunn, & A. C. Petersen (Eds.), *Transitions through adolescence: Interpersonal domains and context* (pp. 111–140). Mahwah, NJ: Erlbaum.

Bachman, J. G., & Schulenberg, J. (1993). How part-time work intensity relates to drug use, problem behavior, time use, and satisfaction among high school seniors: Are these consequences or just correlates? *Developmental Psychology, 29,* 220–235.

Ben-Amos, I. K. (1994). *Adolescence and youth in early modern England.* New Haven, CT: Yale University Press.

Bianchi, S. M., & Spain, D. (1996). Women, work, and family in America *Population Bulletin, 51*(3), 1–48.

Brooks-Gunn, J., & Paikoff, R. (1997). Sexuality and developmental transitions during adolescence. In J. Schulenberg, J. L. Maggs, & K. Hurrelmann (Eds.), *Health risks and developmental transitions during adolescence* (pp. 190–219). New York: Cambridge University Press.

Chisholm, L., & Hurrelmann, K. (1995). Adolescence in modern Europe: Pluralized transition patterns and their implications for personal and social risks. *Journal of Adolescence, 18,* 129–158.

Cote, J. E., & Allahar, A. L. (1996). *Generation on hold: Coming of age in the late twentieth century.* New York: New York University Press.

Elliott, G. R., & Feldman, S. S. (1990). Capturing the adolescent experience. In S. S. Feldman & G. R. Elliott (Eds.), *At the Threshold: The Developing Adolescent* (pp. 1–14). Cambridge, MA: Harvard University Press.

Erikson, E. H. (1950). *Childhood and society.* New York: Norton.

Erikson, E. H. (1968). *Identity: Youth and crisis.* New York: Norton.

Evelyth, P., & Tanner, J. (1976). *Worldwide variation in human growth.* New York: Cambridge University Press.

Feiring, C. (1996). Concepts of romance in 15-year-olds. *Journal of Research on Adolescence, 6,* 181–200.

Goldscheider, F., & Davanzo, J. (1986). Semiautonomy and leaving home during early adulthood. *Social Forces, 65,* 187–201.

Goldscheider, F., & Goldscheider, C. (1994). Leaving and returning home in 20th century America. *Population Bulletin, 48*(4), 1–35. Washington, DC: Population Reference Bureau, Inc.

Greenberger, E., & Steinberg, L. (1986). *When teenagers work: The psychological and social costs of adolescent employment.* New York: Basic Books.

Greene, A. L., Wheatley, S. M., & Aldava J. F., IV. (1992). Stages on life's way: Adolescents' implicit theories of the life course. *Journal of Adolescent Research, 7,* 364–381.

Hall, G. S. (1904). *Adolescence: Its psychology and its relation to physiology, anthropology, sociology, sex, crime, religion, and education,* Vol. 1. Englewood Cliffs, NJ: Prentice Hall.

Hogan, D. P., & Astone, N. M. (1986). The transition to adulthood. *Annual Review of Sociology, 12,* 109–130.

Hoge, D. R., Johnson, B., & Luidens, D. A. (1993). Determinants of church involvement of young adults who grew up in Presbyterian churches. *Journal of the Scientific Study of Religion, 32,* 242–255.

Hornblower, M. (1997, June 9). Great Xpectations. *Time,* pp. 58–68.

Jonsson, B. (1994, March). *Youth life projects and modernization in Sweden: A cross-sectional study.* Paper presented at the biennial meeting of the Society for Research on Adolescence, San Diego, CA.

Keniston, K. (1971). *Youth and dissent: The rise of a new opposition.* New York: Harcourt Brace Jovanovich.

Larson, R. W. (1990). The solitary side of life: An examination of the time people spend alone from childhood to old age. *Developmental Review, 10,* 155–183.

Levinson, D. J. (1978). *The seasons of a man's life.* New York: Ballantine.

Martin, P., & Smyer, M. A. (1990). The experience of micro- and macroevents: A life span analysis. *Research on Aging, 12,* 294–310.

Michael, R.T., Gagnon, J.H., Laumann, E.O., & Kolata, G. (1995). *Sex in America: A definitive survey.* New York: Warner Books.

Mogelonsky, M. (1996, May). The rocky road to adulthood. *American Demographics,* 26–36, 56.

Montemayor, R., Brown, B., & Adams, G. (1985). *Changes in identity status and psychological adjustment after leaving home and entering college.* Paper presented at the biennial meeting of the Society for Research on Child Development, Toronto.

Morch, S. (1995). Culture and the challenge of adaptation: Foreign youth in Denmark. *International Journal of Comparative Race and Ethnic Studies, 2,* 102–115.

Mortimer, J. T., Harley, C., & Aronson, P. J. (1999). How do prior experiences in the workplace set the stage for transitions to adulthood? In A. Booth, A. C. Crouter, & M. J. Shanahan (Eds.), *Transitions to adulthood in a changing economy: No work, no family, no future?* (pp. 131–159). Westport, CT: Praeger.

Noble, J., Cover, J., & Yanagishita, M. (1996). *The world's youth.* Washington, DC: Population Reference Bureau.

Padgham, J. J., & Blyth, D. A. (1991). Dating during adolescence. In R.M. Lerner, A.C. Petersen, & J. Brooks-Gunn (Eds.), *Encyclopedia of adolescence* (pp. 196–198). New York: Garland.

Page, K. (1999, May 16). The graduate. *Washington Post Magazine,* pp. 18, 20.

Parsons, T. (1942). Age and sex in the social structure of the United States. *American Sociological Review, 7,* 604–616.

Rindfuss, R. R. (1991). The young adult years: Diversity, structural change, and fertility. *Demography, 28,* 493–512.

Roscoe, B., Dian, M. S., & Brooks, R. H. (1987). Early, middle, and late adolescents' views on dating and the factors influencing partner selection. *Adolescence, 22,* 59–68.

Rossi, A. S., & Rossi, P. H. (1990). *Of human bonding: Parent-child relations across the life course.* New York: Aldine de Gruyter.

Scheer, S. D., Unger, D. G., & Brown, M. (1994, February). *Adolescents becoming adults: Attributes for adulthood.* Poster presented at the biennial meeting of the Society for Research on Adolescence, San Diego, CA.

Schlegel, A., & Barry, H., III. (1991). *Adolescence: An anthropological inquiry.* New York: Free Press.

Shanahan, M., Elder, G.H., Jr., Burchinal, M., & Conger, R. D. (1996). Adolescent earnings and relationships with parents: The work-family nexus in urban and rural ecologies. In J. T. Mortimer & M. D. Finch (Eds.), *Adolescents, work, and family: An intergenerational developmental analysis* (pp. 97–128). Thousand Oaks, CA: Sage.

Steinberg, L., & Cauffman, E. (1995). The impact of employment on adolescent development. In R. Vasta (Ed.), *Annals of child development, Vol. 11.* London: Jessica Kingsley Publishers.

U.S. Bureau of the Census (1997). *Statistical abstracts of the United States: 1997.* Washington, DC: U.S. Bureau of the Census.

Valde, G. A. (1996). Identity closure: A fifth identity status. *Journal of Genetic Psychology, 157,* 245–254.

Wallace, C. (1995). *How old is young and young is old? The restructuring of age and the life course in Europe.* Paper presented at Youth 2000: An International Conference, Middlesborough, UK.

Waterman, A. L. (1982). Identity development from adolescence to adulthood: An extension of theory and a review of research. *Developmental Psychology, 18,* 341–358.

Whitbourne, S. K., & Tesch, S. A. (1985). A comparison of identity and intimacy statuses in college students and alumni. *Developmental Psychology, 21,* 1039–1044.

William T. Grant Foundation Commission on Work, Family, and Citizenship (1988, February). *The forgotten half: Non-college-bound youth in America.* Washington, DC: William T. Grant Foundation.

THINKING CRITICALLY

1. At the beginning of the reading, the author describes three previous theoretical concepts of the late teens–early twenties age period. Explain how, in your view, the author does or does not make a convincing case in the course of the reading that emerging adulthood fits better as a conception of this age period.

2. What criteria are most important to you in marking your own transition to adulthood? Are your criteria consistent with the individualistic qualities of character valued as criteria for adulthood by most young Americans?

3. Do you agree with the author's explanation for why risk behavior tends to be highest in emerging adulthood? What might you add to the explanation here?

4. Do you agree with the author's prediction that emerging adulthood will become more common worldwide as developing countries are influenced by globalization? What other possible consequences of globalization are possible for young people in their late teens and early twenties in developing countries?

Puberty Rituals in Melanesia

Menarche, a girl's first menstrual period, is marked in many nonindustrialized cultures by a ritual that recognizes it as the initiation of puberty and the girl's entry into adolescence. The ritual described here takes place in the Rauto culture of Melanesia, a region of islands northeast of Australia. The ritual demonstrates that cultures often have complex beliefs about the significance of menarche. Although the biological significance of menarche is that it indicates a girl is reaching the potential for sexual reproduction, the Rauto ritual illustrates that human cultures often add other meanings to indicators of biological development. The Rauto ritual has several parts; the first part, involving the presentation of menstrual skirts, is described in this reading.

Reading 2.1

Mythic Images and Objects of Myth in Rauto Female Puberty Rituals

T. Maschio

From *To Remember the Faces of the Dead: The Plentitude of Memory in Southwestern New Britain.* Copyright © 1995. Published by The University of Wisconsin Press. Reprinted by permission from the author.

During one of the last days of my first field stay with the Rauto, I saw a performance of the ritual that marks a woman's menarche. The ceremony took one full day, from dawn to dusk, and its poetry and beauty both moved me and helped me understand the type of power a Rauto woman can draw on to express and construct her identity. The rite also appeared to be a formal celebration of the part Rauto women play in helping to form the social identities of female adolescents, and it demonstrated that Rauto women are considered the producers and possessors of important aspects of their culture's religious imagination.

This ritual has an extremely simple structure. During its performance two senior women—usually the initiates' paternal aunts—who are known for their skill in song magic and respected as women of economic influence, present the initiates with a number of objects associated mainly, though not exclusively, with subsistence production and the exchange activities of women. Other objects specifically convey ideas about the power, influence, and privileges of prominent, or "big," women *(ilim alang)*. As they are presented, special magical songs *(aurang)* are sung by the senior women conducting the ritual and by a rather large number of the adolescents' female kin on her mother's side. These songs are said to promote the adolescents' growth and enhance their beauty and health. Their poetry alludes to the uses to which women put the objects presented and represents a celebration of the aesthetic aspect of women's activities. The songs and mimetic acts of the rite also refer to some of the different phases or ages of a woman's life from preadolescence to mature adulthood.

During the rite, the adolescents are instructed in the names and proper uses of the objects presented, instructions that outline the "picture" Rauto have of women's reality. By manipulating ideas and objects that define the nature of an adult woman—especially of a socially prominent "big woman"—aspects of Rauto ethos and worldview are drawn into relationship; the aesthetic feel Rauto women have for their way of life is synthesized with their "pic-ture" of this life. For the Rauto, then, the ritual construction of gender is a way of expressing ideas about human nature, social and moral life, and power and status.

To say that Rauto women are "disseminators" of aspects of the moral tone and aesthetic style and mood of their culture is to say that they control an aspect of cultural or mythic memory. The significance of the acts and images of the puberty rite is that they place initiates in contact with cultural and personal memories that are contained by customary objects and events or scenarios that the rite mimes. The mimesis of the rite demonstrates that song, heirloom, necklace, diadem, and menstrual skirt are a woman's "gesture manifesting some myth from which" she "draws her life" (Leenhardt 1948, p. 138). These myths are the stories of custom, the stories of collective and personal memory that explain the origins and original uses of the objects used during the rite. In the puberty ritual some of these stories add meaning to the enacted song images, images that portray concretely experienced events in the life of a woman.

Ethnographic Background

The Rauto number about 2,500 people and live along the coast and in the interior rain forest of the southwest portion of New Britain. Their lowland forest environment is crisscrossed by many streams and rivers, and the general topography is quite rugged. They are intensive horticulturalists, obtaining most of their subsistence from the slash-and-burn cultivation of taro, yam, and sweet potato, supplemented by banana and amaranth. Their diet is rounded out by coconut, breadfruit, and occasionally pork and wild game, such as cassowary or wallaby, with fish a frequent addition to the diet of coastal villagers.

Both coastal and interior groups usually live in hamlet settlements of twelve to thirty residents, occupying anywhere from five to ten family houses, with one or two large ceremonial houses. The number of residents fluctuates, however, since people frequently leave the hamlet to attend ceremonials or visit and take up temporary residence with trading partners or distant kin.

Ceremonial life essentially consists of a series of song ceremonies performed for persons at major intervals of their life cycles. Most performances are religiously meaningful because they provide contexts for the expression of magical speech and of songs.

Some Obvious Social Meanings and Functions of the Rite

One of the obvious social functions of the Rauto puberty rite is "to raise the name," or enhance the social reputation, of the adolescents for whom it is performed. The rite is most often performed for the eldest or most intelligent and socially promising daughters of prominent men and women, and marks the girls for assumption of a special social status, that of "big woman." It also demonstrates the economic wherewithal of the sponsoring family, thereby becoming also a social marker for the girl's immediate family and extended kin group. Finally, it provides an opportunity for the senior women who perform it to demonstrate their knowledge of ritual and song scripts and, through their performance of various songs, the power of their voices to promote the girls' growth and health. This expression of self is integrally related to the affirmation of the social and cultural identity of senior women. It is a demonstration that their voices have social, moral, and magical power. This is significant because of the particular importance voice and song have in this society (Maschio, 1994); song is a social marker.

One of the most interesting aspects of Rauto female puberty ritual is that, by celebrating the role big women especially play in production and exchange, song serves as an expression of ideals of female social identity. The songs also allude to the religious aspect of women's economic life, in particular to the important role song magic plays in their productive activity. Although big women never attain positions equal in power and status to those of big men, the Rauto recognize nonetheless that

the power of a big woman approximates that of a big man. Female puberty ritual provides the most cogent formal expression of this notion. However, this is not really what is most significant about the ritual. What is, is what the ritual does not say, or rather what it does not *explicitly* say about women's power and religious or mythic identity. The ritual implies more often than it elaborates meaning. The meaning it implies provides as strong a statement of women's cultural centrality as does the rite itself.

The Presentation of the Menstrual Skirts

Both male and female puberty rituals among the Rauto are really part of a cycle of ceremonies, most of them achievement ceremonies, that parents arrange for their children a few years before or after puberty. What distinguishes Rauto puberty ritual from these achievement ceremonies is its aim of celebrating and cultivating the physical attractiveness of adolescents. In fact, some informants said that puberty rituals could be considered forms of "love magic" since one of their primary aims was to make the initiate attractive to members of his or her opposite sex.

By all accounts, menarcheal ritual is and always was a more central part of Rauto religious life than male initiation. A number of Rauto even said it was the most important of all their ceremonies. When I asked one of them to explain this statement, he said simply that the ceremony was something his people "could never give up" however much social change might alter the tenor of life. I took this to mean that the rite provided a particularly compelling statement about identity, one that, according to some, could not be dispensed with.

The menarcheal rites cannot begin until the girl's family has amassed sufficient wealth in the form of pigs, taro, and shell valuables to pay for the ritual services that will be provided. On the one hand, therefore, the rites may not take place until several years after a girl's first menses; on the other, they may be performed before the onset of menstruation if the family has accumulated the necessary wealth.

The major part of the ritual is directed by two "sisters" of the girl's father—either his true siblings or parallel cousins—assisted usually by the girl's maternal uncle. The night before the ritual proper, these officiants take the girl to a menstrual hut located on the outskirts of the hamlet settlement or, in coastal Rauto villages, on the edge of the sea. Throughout the night, these aunts and cousins bring the girl food and drink and they provide her with a special skirt to wear while she sleeps. This skirt, called the *agosgoso,* is made from the colorful leaves of a wild banana. More of these leaves are placed between her legs "to absorb her menstrual blood."

The next morning, at sunrise, the two aunts remove the skirt from around the girl's waist and throw it into the ocean or, if the ceremony is performed in a bush village, into the forest at the outskirts of the hamlet. In company with any other initiates, the girl then is led into the men's house of her father's extended family, where the two aunts scrape coconut meat and rub the extracted oil onto her breasts so that her skin will appear shiny and attractive.

The ritual I attended began when two aunts, officiating for two initiates, began to paint the girls' bodies. Red ocher was brushed onto their hair, and their faces were painted with red and white marks called *tinga tinga.* Next, the girls were taken to the center of the men's house, where their aunts presented each of them with a second, newly made menstrual skirt and a skirt the Rauto call *yaoli.* The aunts painted the skirts with red ocher and then informed the girls that the yaoli were "their own grass skirts," which they should wear until the end of their lives. The plants from which they were made, the girls were told, represented their personal finery, which they should use to decorate their bodies whenever they worked in their gardens or attended song festivals. The two aunts then pointed out and individually named each of the plants making up the yaoli. The aromatic scent of the plants and the burning and effervescent quality of their sap are thought to stimulate the girls' skin and thereby promote their physical growth. The implicit message of the aunts' instruction was that these

important materials are controlled by women and their care and reproduction is a woman's privilege.

The girls were then shown and told the names of important plants that they should plant or harvest: these included a taro corn and stalk, two kinds of yam, amaranth, and sugar cane. The youngsters also were shown and told the names of the tobacco plant and the vine on which the betel pepper grows. They were instructed in the proper way to cut the taro corn from its stalk with a clam shell cutter, and told that if a nontraditional object such as a knife were used, the taro stalk would produce no food.

Finally, songs for the new menstrual skirts were performed. Like the menstrual skirts that were tossed into the sea, these ceremonial menstrual skirts are made predominantly from dark purple, bright red, and yellow wild banana leaves. The two aunts opened one up and then, holding a hemp tie each, brought it up to one of the girls' waists and began to swing it back and forth against her backside as they sang the song for the skirt:

Lelme, ngapapenwo lelme	Swing the skirt
lelme, lelme,	back and forth,
lelme, ngapapenwo lelme	back and forth.
Lelme lelme.	

After a few minutes of song, the menstrual skirt was fastened around the girl's waist and the act repeated for the second girl. The yaoli were raised up and fastened above the girls' waists, some of the leaves being slipped inside the menstrual skirt, between their legs. As this operation was performed, the women all sang the song for the yaoli:

Yaoli a yao a	The yaoli skirt, yaoli.
yaoli a yao a	You put it on thus
a komela aupua.	(it is yours now).

The significance of these first few activities in the puberty ritual lies in their relation of a system of aesthetics to notions of physical development and bodily health. Informants told me that painting and anointing the girls' bodies makes them healthy and their skin attractive. The scent of the yaoli plants and the bright colors of the other skirts also are said to promote growth and health because they are pleasing to the senses. The same was said of the senior women's singing, but these women told me that the songs also "moved their hearts" and sometimes made them cry by causing them to remember those who had sung the songs for them when they were young girls. The songs allow elders to remember the poignancy of their own pasts at the very moment that they invest their spiritual power in the next generation. These statements made it clear to me that these first few rites are meant both to impart physical sensation and to elicit sentiment from the girls and the other ritual participants, and so sensitize and prepare the girls' minds and bodies for the instruction to come.

Rauto women told me that the most important part of this first phase of the puberty ritual was the girls' investiture with the women's skirts. With these presentations, they begin to acquire the outward signs of a new status. The skirts, especially the yaoli, signify a woman's acquisition of new duties and privileges. But what was fascinating to me was the way their presentation was related to a complex set of ideas about menstrual blood and the girls' developing power.

Almost all of the plants from which the skirts are made, and in the cultivation of which the girls are instructed, are also used in gardening rituals to promote the healthy development of a taro crop. It seems, then, that the grass skirts, most especially the yaoli, are not only meant to make the girls grow well but are also a visual sign that they are acquiring a greater ability to produce food. Yet the skirts are, at least during the puberty ritual, "menstrual" skirts. They denote the presence of menstrual blood, which paradoxically is usually thought harmful to the growth and health of humans, animals, and plants.

A girl's first menses thus marks the fact that she now possesses a dangerous and sometimes destructive power. Yet the Rauto choose to mark this event by celebrating her constructive economic, social, and moral influence. One might argue that this paradox expresses the idea that women are influential partly because they are dangerous, especially to men. But this does not satisfactorily explain why, in the context of puberty ritual, menstrual blood signifies an increase in a woman's personal power while, in other contexts, it is thought to lessen her productive powers and diminish rather than augment her other abilities.

I would point out, however, that it is men, not women, who most often voice fears about the polluting power of menstrual blood. Moreover, women certainly do not feel that menstruation places them at the periphery of social and cultural life. Rather, female puberty ritual suggests that the nature of women is partly defined by the fact of their menstruation, and women seize this opportunity to place themselves at the mythic center of Rauto life and draw strength from it.

The ritual itself does not reveal the mythic character of the menstrual skirts and indeed of female identity. The myth that tells of the origins of these skirts, of menstruation, of women's objects and activities, indeed of the origins of the female sex, provides a more rounded understanding of the meaning of female identity and even, in fact, of female ethos than does the simple presentation described here. The story reveals how woman's possession of menstrual skirts and of female dress was her first gesture of assertion and female personhood. The myth reveals that woman had literally to wrest her gender from man:

> Men were not originally men. They followed women's ways. They carried around with them and used all the things that women now have: their oven stones, their oven tongs, their clam shell cutters for harvesting taro, their taro shell scrapers. They menstruated as women do and, as women, when they did menstruate, they left their garden work exclaiming, "Oh! I can't work now, I have my period. I'll have to rest." As women, they would comb the reefs for crustaceans and small fish and they would also collect freshwater snails. Then one day one of these

supposed women came upon a real woman, and this real woman called out: "Hey you really large woman over there, where are you going?" And she answered, "I'm just going to comb the reefs for some small fish, although I wish I didn't have to do it all by myself. It's just that all my friends have their periods now and they are all much too exhausted to help me out. Do you see them over there resting on the verandas of their houses?" "Never mind them," said the real woman. "Come over here and let me get a good look at you," she said, eyeing this supposed woman suspiciously. "You know I don't think you're really a woman." As she said this, she lifted up the other woman's skirt, and after seeing what was hidden by the skirt exclaimed, "Hey, you're not a woman. Is a woman so big as you? You don't even have breasts. And your genitals are hanging down there. You are a man. Give me my woman's skirt, give me my menstrual skirt, give me my woman's fishing net, my oven stones, my taro scraper, my taro cutter. And give me my menstruation." And then the real woman gathered up the things that were given to her, and she put on her female dress and her menstrual skirts. She then told the man about the objects that rightfully belonged to him, and she pointed them out to him. "There, there are your fishing and hunting nets, and your fishing spears—and there is the men's house. Go there now and give me my things. And menstruation, that belongs to me so leave it alone." And so the woman gathered up her things and the man gathered up his.

We have two images before us then. That evoked by the puberty rite presents a naturalistic scene and an obvious meaning; it pictures the initiates being given their adult women's dress, their menstrual skirts, and a number of objects this culture associates with women. The images and acts of this opening phase suggest that women simply and naturally come to possess these objects at the time of their puberty.

The mythic narrative belies this suggestion. It indicates that woman's first act of au-

thentic personhood consisted in taking her menstruation, her women's objects, and her dress from men. The moment when she does this portrays her immediate assumption of female identity. We see here a Rauto myth of identity (Leenhardt 1947/1979, p. 23). Though this myth seems a living part of the Rauto present, it contains a sense of the past. It was not always so, it seems to say. Identity had to be won through a gesture of assertion rather than simply put on, as a menstrual skirt is put on.

The myth expresses this insight as much by its psychological character and humorous tone as by the sequence of events it outlines. The opening sequences that describe men following woman's life-way, carrying out woman's everyday tasks, and experiencing the state of menstruation, seem to parody female personhood rather than provide an authentic mimesis of it. The "she-males" portrayed seem grossly effeminate, frivolous, and clumsy as they comb the reefs for food, run from their gardens at the slightest hint of menstrual blood, and collapse exhausted on the verandas of their family houses during their menstruation.

In contrast, the narrator's portrait of the one woman of the myth seems an example of authentic personhood. This character quickly sends the man on his way by pointing him to his own sphere of activity with absolute certainty. She assumes her own identity and asserts her claim to her woman's objects with as much certainty. These are my things, she seems to say, I will take them and be what I am.

A portrait of woman and of female ethos begins to emerge in the myth, one counterposed to the narrator's weak parody of female personhood. This ethos corresponds to the assertiveness seen in the puberty rite, yet it stands in contrast to the rite's first sublime and simple act—the presentation of the menstrual skirts. Or rather, the acts and images of the first presentations of the puberty ritual are given meaning by two different yet simultaneously experienced feelings. The sort of pride evident in the women's clowning and assertive, if ribald, celebration of the sexual parts of their bodies contrasts with the sublime remembrance that is evoked by the menstrual songs. The initiates seem the objects of these two emotions. In becoming these two emotions, they objectify two aspects of the female ethos—assertive strength and a sort of sublime emotionality. It seems that the initiates come to objectify memory, emotion, and aspects of the female ethos during this ritual.

REFERENCES

Leenhardt, M. (1947/1974). *Do kamo: Person and myth in the Melanesian world.* Chicago: University of Chicago Press.

Leenhardt, M. (1948). *L'arts de l'Oceanie.* Paris: Musee de l'Homme.

Maschio, T. (1994). *To remember the faces of the dead: The plenitude of memory in Southwestern New Britain.* Madison: University of Wisconsin Press.

THINKING CRITICALLY

1. One of the purposes of the Rauto puberty rituals is "celebrating and cultivating the physical attractiveness of adolescents." How do industrialized societies celebrate the physical attractiveness of adolescents?

2. People in many cultures view menstrual blood with ambivalence, that is, as both positive and negative, as a source of fertility and creative power as well as potentially dangerous. How is this ambivalence evident in the practices of the Rauto?

3. How does the myth described in this reading show that Rauto adolescent girls are taught to view menstruation as a source of status and power even though it may sometimes limit what they can do?

Effects of the Timing of Puberty

The most frequently studied topic with regard to puberty has been the effects of the timing of puberty, that is, the effects of beginning the physical changes of puberty earlier than peers, later than peers, or "on time." One reason for the focus on this topic is that the timing of puberty has often been found to have a wide-ranging effect on development during adolescence, especially for early-maturing girls. In studying this topic, researchers hope to provide information that will help ameliorate the problems that may result from off-time pubertal maturation; note the researchers' suggestions at the end of this reading.

Reading 2.2

Is Psychopathology Associated With the Timing of Pubertal Development?

J. A. Graber, P. M. Lewinsohn, J. R. Seeley, and J. Brooks-Gunn

Recent epidemiological studies have begun to document the extent to which psychopathology occurs during adolescence (Bird et al., 1988; Lewinsohn, Hops, Roberts, Seeley, & Andrews, 1993; McGee et al., 1990). Embedded in developmental studies of psychopathology has been the hypothesis that the experience of pubertal development shapes and interacts with other transitions in ways that impact adolescent mental health (Brooks-Gunn, Graber, & Paikoff, 1994). The timing of the pubertal transition (compared with one's peers) has been considered most salient for determining whether or not pubertal development is associated with psychopathology. The earliest-maturing girls begin puberty when no other children are experiencing these events; hence, these girls have been hypothesized to be at risk for psychopath-

ology or lesser problems perhaps because they are less well-prepared for the physical, psychological, and social challenges posed by puberty and the entry into adolescence (Brooks-Gunn, Peterson, & Eichorn, 1985). Conversely, late-maturing boys begin (and complete) puberty after all other adolescents have already passed these events and may experience psychosocial problems or feelings of inferiority due to less mature appearance and poorer athletic ability in comparison with peers (Jones, 1965).

Research consistent with the "off-time" hypothesis has shown that girls who are early maturers are more likely than other girls to exhibit depressive, eating, and delinquent symptoms as well as general behavior problems (Attie and Brooks-Gunn, 1989; Caspi & Moffitt, 1991; Graber, Brooks-Gunn, Paikoff, & Warren,

Graber, J. A., Lewinsohn, P. M., Seeley, J. R., & Brooks-Gunn, J. (1997). Is psychopathology associated with the timing of pubertal development? *Journal of the American Academy of Child and Adolescent Psychiatry, 36,* 1768–1776. Copyright © 1997 by Lippincott Williams & Wilkins. Reprinted by permission.

1994; Hayward et al., 1997; Petersen, Sarigiani, & Kennedy, 1991; Simmons & Blyth, 1987), with late-maturing girls showing no consistent pattern of adjustment problems in comparison with on-time maturers across these same studies. For boys, Andersson and Magnusson (1990) report that both early- and late-maturing boys began to drink alcohol earlier than their peers and that late-maturing boys may be more likely to develop an alcohol abuse problem in young adulthood. No studies to date have examined pubertal timing and disorders in both boys and girls.

In this article, we examine whether self-reported pubertal timing is associated with concurrent and prior episodes of psychopathology (symptoms and disorders) in boys and girls. We are able to test for associations of pubertal timing effects across a wide range of disorders including major depression, anxiety, disruptive behavior, substance use, and eating disorders. Because timing effects have been demonstrated over a range of subclinical problems, we also examine several dimensions of psychosocial dysfunction. On the basis of the previous literature, it is hypothesized that for girls early maturation will be associated with psychopathology, whereas for boys late maturation will be associated with psychopathology.

Method

Participants

Three cohorts of adolescents were drawn from nine senior high schools in urban and rural western Oregon (total population of 10,200 students). Sampling within schools was proportional to size of school, size of grade within school, and proportion of boys and girls within grade to obtain a final sample of 1,709 adolescents that was representative of the larger population of students.

The demographic characteristics of the sample were as follows: mean age was 16.6 years (SD = 1.2); 52% were girls; 9% were nonwhite; 71% lived with two parents; 53% lived with both biological parents; 15% were in 9th, 27% were in 10th, 26% were in 11th, and 32% were in 12th grade, and 12% had repeated a grade. Parents' occupational status consisted of 3% unskilled, 8% semiskilled, 21% skilled, 58% minor professional, and 10% professional.

Diagnostic Interview

Adolescents were interviewed with the Schedule for Affective Disorders and Schizophrenia for School-Age Children (K-SADS). Items were added to derive diagnoses of past and current psychiatric disorders as outlined in *DSM-III-R* (American Psychiatric Association, 1987), the version of the *DSM* in usage at the time of assessment. Interviewer reliability as indicated by the x statistic was substantial to nearly perfect (Landis and Koch, 1977), with most equal to or greater than .80 with the exception of a few diagnoses (Lewinsohn et al., 1993).

Diagnoses were collapsed into five primary categories of disorder: (1) major depressive disorder; (2) anxiety, which was composed of panic disorder, agoraphobia, social phobia, simple phobia, obsessive-compulsive disorder, separation anxiety, and overanxious disorder; (3) disruptive behavior, which was composed of attention-deficit hyperactivity, conduct, and oppositional disorders; (4) substance use, which was composed of substance abuse and dependence disorders; and (5) eating disorder, which included anorexia and bulimia nervosa.

Psychosocial Constructs

An extensive questionnaire battery tapping all psychosocial variables known or hypothesized to be related to depression was administered (materials available upon request). Measures were shortened for administration (Andrews, Lewinsohn, Hops, & Roberts, 1993) and reduced to 20 composite scores (see Lewinsohn et al., 1993, for details). All variables were scored such that higher values indicated more problematic functioning.

Stress: Daily Hassles consisted of 20 items from the Unpleasant Events Schedule (Lewinsohn, Mermelstein, Alexander, & MacPhillamy, 1985).

Stress: Major Life Events consisted of 14 events from the Schedule of Recent Experiences (Holmes & Rahe, 1967) and the Life Events Schedule (Sandler & Block, 1979).

Current Depression consisted of the 20-item Center for Epidemiologic Studies-Depression Scale (Radloff, 1977); the 21-item Beck Depression Inventory (Beck, Ward, Mendelson, Mock, & Erbaugh, 1961); a single item assessing depression level during the preceding week; and the interviewer-rated 14-item Hamilton Rating Scale for Depression (Hamilton, 1960).

Internalizing Behavior Problems assessed the tendency to worry (5 items; Maudsley Obsessional Compulsive Inventory) (Hodgson & Rachman, 1977); hypomanic behavior (12 items; General Behavior Inventory) (Depue et al., 1981); State Anxiety (10 items) (Spielberger, Gorsuch, & Lushene, 1970); sleep patterns (8 items); and hypochondriasis (8 items) (Pilowsky, 1967).

Externalizing Behavior Problems consisted of current K-SADS symptoms for attention-deficit hyperactivity (15 items), conduct (17 items), and oppositional disorders (11 items) and an unpublished scale assessing conduct problems (6 items).

Depressotypic Negative Cognitions consisted of the Frequency of Self Reinforcement Attitude Questionnaire (10 items) (Heiby, 1982); the Subjective Probability Questionnaire (5 items) (Mufloz & Lewinsohn, n.d.); the Dysfunctional Attitude Scale (9 items) (Weissman & Beck, 1978); and perceived control over one's life (3 items) (Pearlin & Schooler, 1978).

Depressotypic Attributional Style consisted of the Kastan Attributional Style Questionnaire for Children (48 items) (Kaslow, Tannenbaum, & Seligman, 1978).

Self-Consciousness consisted of the Self-Consciousness Scale (nine items) (Fenigstein, Scheier, & Buss, 1975).

Self-Esteem consisted of the Body Parts Satisfaction Scale (three items) (Berscheid, Walster, & Bohrnstedt, 1973); the Physical Appearance Evaluation Subscale (three items) (Winstead & Cash, n.d.); and the Rosenberg Self-Esteem Scale (three items) (Rosenberg, 1965).

Self-Rated Social Competence consisted of the Social Subscale of the Perceived Competence Scale (five items) (Harter, 1982) and seven additional items (Lewinsohn et al., 1980).

Emotional Reliance consisted of the Emotional Reliance Scale (10 items) (Hirschfeld, Klerman, Chodoff, Korchin, & Barrett, 1976) assessing interpersonal sensitivity and the desire for support and approval from others.

Future Goals were assessed in three domains—Family (five items); Occupational (three items); and Academic (five items) using an adapted form of the Importance Placed on Life Goals Scale (Bachman, Johnston, & O'Malley, 1985).

Coping Skills consisted of 17 items from the Self-Control Scale (Rosenbaum, 1980), the Antidepressive Activity Questionnaire (Rippere, 1977), and the Ways of Coping Questionnaire (Folkman & Lazarus, 1980).

Social Support: Family consisted of the Conflict Behavior Questionnaire (11 items) (Prinz, Foster, Kent, & O'Leary, 1979); the Parent Attitude Research Instrument (6 items) (Schaefer, 1965); the Cohesion subscale of the Family Environment Scale (3 items) (Moos, 1974); the Competence scale of the Youth Self-Report (2 items) (Achenbach & Edelbrock, 1987); and an adaptation of the Arizona Social Support Interview Schedule (Barrera, 1986).

Social Support: Friends consisted of the Social Competence Scale (two items) (Harter, 1982); the UCLA Loneliness Scale (eight items) (Russell, Peplau, & Cutrona, 1980); the Competence scale of the Youth Self-Report (three items); and the number of friends providing social support (from the Arizona Social Support Interview Schedule).

Interpersonal: Conflict With Parents was based on occurrence and intensity of conflicts in the preceding 2 weeks using the Issues Checklist (45 items) (Robin & Weiss, 1980).

Interpersonal: Attractiveness consisted of the interviewer-rated Interpersonal Attraction Measure (17 items) (McCroskey & McCain, 1974).

Physical Illness consisted of number of visits to a physician, days spent in bed as a result of illness, and the occurrence of 88 physical symptoms in the previous year.

Miscellaneous Measures. Single-item measures of self-reported academic performance included grade point average (GPA), satisfaction with GPA, perceived parental satisfaction with GPA, number of missed school days in the previous 6 weeks, number of times late for school in the previous 6 weeks, frequency of failure to complete homework, and repeated a grade in school. Two health measures were included: self-rated health (4-point scale) and the lifetime occurrence of 88 physical symptoms. Finally, three K-SADS items were included: ever used tobacco (yes or no), current rate of tobacco use (6-point scale), and ever attempted suicide (yes or no).

Physical Maturation. Adolescents reported their height and weight and completed an adapted version of the Pubertal Development Scale (Petersen, Crockett, Richards, & Boxer, 1988). As adolescents were in senior high school (14 through 18 years of age), most reported pubertal development that was at the mid to advanced level. Adolescents also indicated whether their physical growth and development was early, on time, or late in comparison with that of most teenagers their age ($n = 1,669$).

Results

Reliability of Perceived Pubertal Timing

A series of analyses examined the reliability and validity of the self-reported pubertal timing measure. Analyses first tested the consistency of self-reported pubertal timing with self-reported weight and height. Weight was associated with gender ($F[1, 1,657] = 371.11, p < .001$) and perceived pubertal timing ($F[2, 1,657] = 31.78, p < .001$) such that boys were heavier than girls and early maturers were heavier than late maturers; on-time maturers reported weights between the other two timing groups (comparing within gender) as would be expected. There was a gender by timing group interaction for

height ($F[2, 1,657] = 3.90, p < .05$), along with main effects for gender ($F[1, 1,657] = 1,094.99, p < .001$) and pubertal timing ($F[2, 1,657] = 16.48, p < .001$). Again, as would be expected, boys were significantly taller than girls. The interaction effect occurred because there were differences in height by timing group for boys but not for girls such that early and on-time-maturing boys were significantly taller than late-maturing boys. These findings are in line with the literature on pubertal development in that girls complete growth spurt in height earlier than boys and have growth in height slightly earlier than growth in weight (e.g., Marshall & Tanner, 1986). Overall, results suggested reasonable confidence in the validity and reliability of self-reported pubertal timing.

Demographic Characteristics

Differences between the three pubertal timing groups with regard to gender, age, ethnicity, parental education, and whether the adolescent resided with both biological parents were examined. A statistically significant difference was obtained for gender ($X^2[2, N = 1,669] = 25.28, p < .001$); the proportions within the early, on-time, and late groups were 20%, 71%, and 9% for girls and 14%, 70%, and 16%, for boys, respectively. Previous research has also found that about two thirds of adolescents perceive themselves to be on time in their pubertal development (Dubas, Graber, & Petersen, 1991b), although gender differences in perceptions of pubertal timing have not been previously reported. None of the other demographic measures differed significantly between the three timing groups.

Association Between Pubertal Timing and Psychiatric Disorders

The associations between the three perceived pubertal timing groups and the lifetime and current prevalence rates of major depression, anxiety, substance abuse/dependence, disruptive behavior disorders, and any disorder were examined using contingency table analysis and logistic regression. In addition, the association between the pubertal timing groups and the

lifetime prevalence of eating disorders was examined for girls; the current prevalence rate of
eating disorders among girls was too low ($n = 3$),
as was the lifetime prevalence among boys ($n =
1$), to make group comparisons. Given the inter-
est in gender-specific associations, all analyses
were conducted separately for girls and boys. For
each analysis, two planned contrasts were tested:
(1) the early group versus the on-time group and
(2) the late group versus the on-time group.
Adolescent's age was entered as a covariate in
the logistic regression analyses.

The lifetime and current rates of psychiatric disorders for the three pubertal timing
groups by gender are shown in Table 2.2.1.
Compared with on-time girls, early-maturing
girls had significantly elevated lifetime rates
of major depression (30.2% versus 22.1%),
substance abuse/dependence (14.5% versus
6.7%), disruptive behavior disorders (9.9% versus 3.0%), eating disorders (3.5% versus 0.8%),
and any psychiatric disorder (52.9% versus
37.8%). Notably, early-maturing girls had a lifetime history of substance abuse and disruptive
behavior disorders at twice the rate experienced by either on-time or late-maturing girls.
Late-maturing girls also had a significantly elevated lifetime rate of major depression compared with the on-time girls (33.8% versus
22.1%). With regard to current diagnoses,
early-maturing girls had a significantly higher
rate of disruptive behavior disorders compared
with their on-time counterparts (2.9% versus
0.5%). For boys, the only significant contrast
was obtained for the lifetime rate of substance
abuse/dependence; late-maturing boys had significantly lower rates than did on-time boys
(3.2% versus 8.4%).

Association Between Pubertal Timing and Psychosocial Measures

The associations between the three pubertal
timing groups and the psychosocial measures
were examined separately by gender using
analysis of covariance (controlling for age)
for continuous variables and logistic regression analysis for the dichotomous measures.
Planned contrasts between the on-time group

versus the early and late groups were conducted. Standardized scores (with mean = 0
and SD = 1.0) were computed within gender
for the numeric measures.

For the 35 psychosocial measures, 12
(34%) significant associations ($p < .05$) were obtained for the contrasts between early-maturing
and on-time girls. Compared with on-time girls,
early-maturing girls reported significantly elevated levels of depression symptoms, externalizing behavior problems, and depressotypic
attributional style; had lower self-esteem, poorer
coping skills, and less support from family and
friends; had more days missed at school, poorer
self-rated health, and higher rates of ever having
used tobacco and current tobacco use; and had a
higher rate of suicide attempts. Only 3 (9%) of
the planned contrasts between late-maturing and
on-time girls were significant. Late-maturing girls
reported more self-consciousness, higher future
academic goals, and more conflict with parents.

For boys, 8 (23%) significant associations
were obtained for the contrasts between early-
maturing and on-time boys. Compared with on-
time boys, early-maturing boys reported more
major life events, a higher level of depression,
more emotional reliance on others, higher future family goals, more physical illness, an elevated hypomanic personality style, a greater
lifetime number of physical symptoms, and a
higher current rate of tobacco use. In contrast,
13 (37%) significant associations were obtained
for the contrasts between late-maturing and on-
time boys. Late-maturing boys reported more
daily hassles, higher level of depression, more
internalizing behavior problems, more negative
cognitions, more depressotypic attributional
style, more self-consciousness, more emotional
reliance on others, poorer coping skills, more
conflict with parents, elevated hypomanic personality style, more parental dissatisfaction with
grades, more tardiness at school, and lower
homework completion.

Discussion

To our knowledge, this is one of the first epidemiological investigations of adolescent psychopathology to examine links between timing

TABLE 2.2.1 Pubertal Timing Group Rates of Psychiatric Disorders Separately for Girls and Boys

| | GIRLS | | | | | BOYS | | | | |
| | Group | | | Planned Contrasts | | Group | | | Planned Contrasts | |
DISORDER	Early (n = 172)	On Time (n = 629)	Late (n = 77)	Early vs. On Time	Late vs. On Time	Early (n = 108)	On Time (n = 559)	Late (n = 124)	Early vs On Time	Late vs. On Time
Lifetime (%)										
Major depression	30.2	22.1	33.8	5.01*	4.71*	13.0	10.0	13.7	0.95	0.94
Anxiety	14.5	10.3	9.1	2.35	0.11	5.6	5.7	5.6	0.00	0.05
Substance use	14.5	6.7	5.2	10.42**	0.27	10.2	8.4	3.2	0.47	4.47*
Disruptive behavior	9.9	3.0	5.2	13.18****	1.04	11.1	9.5	9.7	0.27	0.00
Eating	3.5	0.8	1.3	6.09*	0.18	—	—	—	—	0.00
Any	52.9	37.8	49.4	12.69***	3.52	36.1	29.7	31.5	1.93	0.02
Current (%)										
Major depression	2.3	3.5	3.9	0.59	0.04	2.8	1.6	0.8	0.72	0.50
Anxiety	4.7	4.0	3.9	0.14	0.00	0.9	1.4	2.4	0.14	0.30
Substance use	1.7	1.9	3.9	0.02	1.29	3.7	2.1	1.6	1.04	0.30
Disruptive behavior	2.9	0.5	1.3	5.95*	0.80	3.7	2.5	1.6	0.46	0.26
Any	13.4	10.2	13.0	1.38	0.63	9.3	7.3	6.5	0.53	0.23

Note: Age-adjusted Wald tests via logistic regression analysis are reported for the planned contrasts. The lifetime prevalence of eating disorders among male subjects (n = 1) was too low for analysis.
*p < .05; **p < .01; ***p < .001

of puberty and psychological disorders. This investigation addressed the magnitude and pervasiveness of the effects of the timing of puberty on psychopathology during this period of life. As hypothesized, adolescents' perception that their pubertal development was off-time in comparison with peers (i.e., early for girls or late for boys) was associated with serious mental health outcomes during adolescence. Furthermore, early-maturing girls had the poorest current and lifetime history of adjustment problems. A range of psychopathologies, but especially depression, may be related to earlier or later maturation. These findings emphasize the importance of including information about pubertal timing in clinical assessments with adolescents and may serve as one form of screening device for early detection of psychopathology. Knowledge of this aspect of development should help in understanding the context in which the problems occur and may have direct implications for treatment in that off-time maturers may need to cope with the unique developmental challenges facing them (e.g., Brooks-Gunn et al., 1985).

Our findings confirm previous findings on subclinical symptoms and correlates of psychopathology for girls (Caspi & Moffitt, 1991; Graber et al., 1994; Stattin & Magnusson, 1990) and extend the risk to encompass the upper range of the continuum of psychopathology as suggested by recent work by Hayward et al. (1997). As gender differences in depression emerge in adolescence (12 through 14 years of age), the identification of early pubertal development as a source of individual differences within girls is particularly important for understanding girls' mental health. Early maturation was also associated with lifetime history of eating disorders, again in line with prior studies on eating symptoms (Attie & Brooks-Gunn, 1989; Graber et al., 1994).

Of note is the risk for not only internalizing (i.e., depression and anxiety) but also externalizing behaviors that is conferred to girls via early maturation. Rates of current and lifetime disruptive behavior disorders and lifetime substance abuse for these girls were comparable with the rates experienced by boys. Perhaps most alarming was the finding that early-maturing girls were the most likely to have attempted suicide. The finding of significantly poorer concurrent coping skills for early-maturing girls lends support to the hypothesis that they not only were less able to meet the challenges placed on them during puberty but that they still have deficits in coping that have not been ameliorated in the recent postpubertal years. Cultural pressures for thinness may be particularly strong for early-maturing girls because they gain weight when other girls are still thin. Societal definitions of appropriate adult behavior may also place pressure on these girls to engage in behaviors appropriate to their appearance rather than to their levels of emotional and cognitive maturity.

Altering school environments may help combat cultural and societal pressures on early-maturing girls. Prior research has suggested that single-gender schools reduce conduct problems for early-maturing girls (Caspi, Lynam, Moffitt, & Silva, 1993) and that fewer school changes (e.g., staying in the same school from kindergarten through eighth grade) may promote better self-esteem for these girls (Simmons & Blyth, 1987). An alternative approach to restructuring schools would be better educational programs for parents and children such that families receive more comprehensive information about pubertal development. It is unlikely that parents are aware of the risks of early maturation for girls and that they are prepared to assist their daughters in regulating the emotional and social demands conveyed on them through their maturation and younger involvement with boys (Stattin & Magnusson, 1990). That boys who developed off time also exhibited some psychopathology further suggests that many adolescents and families would benefit from such public health information.

For boys, early and late maturation conferred several similar adjustment problems such as higher levels of current depression symptoms, higher emotional reliance on others, and more hypomanic personality style than on-time maturers. Fewer studies have examined pubertal timing in boys than in girls. Prior research identified positive effects of early maturation for boys in social interactions (Jones, 1965) but did not examine psychopathology as extensively as our investigation. Thus, negative effects of early maturation for boys may be the result of different methodologies or historical change; this investigation cannot address these possibilities.

Late-maturing boys reported greater self-consciousness, more conflict with parents, and more trouble in school as indicated by parental dissatisfaction over grades. Our findings are consistent with prior studies that have linked late maturation in boys with less social competence, more internalizing tendencies, and more problems around school (Dubas, Graber, & Petersen, 1991a; Jones, 1965). In contrast, late-maturing girls actually seemed to be doing better in school. It has been suggested that these girls may spend more time studying to compensate for fewer social activities (Dubas et al., 1991a).

Because our investigation was cross-sectional, we are unable to consider whether these associations have implications for psychopathology in adolescence only or for longer-term adjustment. It could be argued that off-time adolescents experienced severe disturbance that was confined to the pubertal period and that present elevated symptoms merely indicate that they have not fully recovered. The participants in the study are being recontacted for a follow-up study of mental health in young adulthood (age 24) at which time some of these issues can be clarified.

The relationship between pubertal timing and psychopathology needs further investigation. Prospective, longitudinal studies that begin before children enter puberty and follow them through adolescence are needed to understand how off-time development confers risk to youth for psychiatric and developmental problems. Recent reports of racial differences in pubertal timing among girls (NHLBI Growth and Health Study Research Group, 1992) also suggest that future studies should consider whether pubertal timing is experienced similarly across subgroups of adolescents.

REFERENCES

Achenbach, T. M., & Edelbrock, C. S. (1987). *Manual for the Youth Self-Report and Profile.* Burlington: University of Vermont Department of Psychiatry.

American Psychiatric Association. (1987). *Diagnostic and Statistical Manual of Mental Disorders, 3rd edition—revised (DSM-III-R).* Washington, DC: American Psychiatric Association.

Andersson, T., & Magnusson, D. (1990). Biological maturation in adolescence and the development of drinking habits and alcohol abuse among young males: A prospective longitudinal study. *Journal of Youth and Adolescence, 19,* 33–41.

Andrews, J. A., Lewinsohn, P. M., Hops, H., & Roberts, R. E. (1993). Psychometric properties of scales for the measurement of psychosocial variables associated with depression in adolescence. *Psychology Report, 73,* 1019–1046.

Attie, I., & Brooks-Gunn, J. (1989). Development of eating problems in adolescent girls: A longitudinal study. *Developmental Psychology, 25,* 70–79.

Bachman, J. G., Johnston, J., & O'Malley, P. M. (1985). *Some recent trends in the aspirations, concerns, and behaviors of American young people.* Paper presented at the 40th annual conference of the American Association for Public Opinion Research, McAfee, NJ.

Barrera, M., Jr. (1986). Distinctions between social support concepts, measures, and models. *American Journal of Community Psychology, 14,* 413–445.

Beck, A. T., Ward, C. H., Mendelson, M., Mock, J., & Erbaugh, J. (1961). An inventory for measuring depression. *Archives of General Psychiatry, 4,* 561–571.

Berscheid, E., Walster, E., & Bohrnstedt, G. (1973). The happy American body: A survey report. *Psychology Today, 7,* 119–131.

Bird, H. R., Canino, G., Rubio-Stipec, M., et al. (1988). Estimates of the prevalence of childhood maladjustment in a community survey in Puerto Rico: The use of combined measures. *Archives of General Psychiatry, 45,* 1120–1126.

Brooks-Gunn, J., Graber, J. A., & Paikoff, R. L. (1994). Studying links between hormones and negative affect: Models and measures. *Journal of Research on Adolescence, 4,* 469–486.

Brooks-Gunn, J., Petersen, A. C., & Eichorn, D. (1985). The study of maturational timing effects in adolescence. *Journal of Youth and Adolescence, 14,* 149–161.

Caspi, A., Lynam, D., Moffitt, T. E., & Silva, P. A. (1993). Unraveling girls' delinquency: Biological, dispositional, and contextual contributions to adolescent behavior. *Developmental Psychology, 29,* 19–30.

Caspi, A., & Moffitt, T. E. (1991). Individual differences are accentuated during periods of social change: The sample case of girls at puberty. *Journal of Personality and Social Psychology, 61,* 157–168.

Depue, R. A., Slater, J. F., Wolfsetter-Kausch, H., Klein, D., Goplerud, E., & Farr, D. (1981). A behavioral paradigm for identifying persons at risk for bipolar depressive disorder: A conceptual framework and five validation studies. *Journal of Abnormal Psychology, 90,* 381–437.

Dubas, J. S., Graber, J. A., & Petersen, A. C. (1991a). The effects of pubertal development on achievement during adolescence. *American Journal of Education, 99,* 444–460.

Dubas, J. S., Graber, J. A., & Petersen, A. C. (1991b). A longitudinal investigation of adolescents' changing perceptions of pubertal timing. *Developmental Psychology, 27,* 580–586.

Fenigstein, A., Scheier, M. F., & Buss, A. H. (1975). Public and private self-consciousness: Assessment and theory. *Journal of Consultant and Clinical Psychology, 43,* 522–527.

Folkman, S., & Lazarus, R. S. (1980). An analysis of coping in a middle-aged community sample. *Journal of Health and Social Behavior, 21,* 219–239.

Graber, J. A., Brooks-Gunn, J., Paikoff, R. L., & Warren, M. P. (1994). Prediction of eating problems: An eight year study of adolescent girls. *Developmental Psychology, 30,* 823–834.

Hamilton, M. (1960). A rating scale for depression. *Journal of Neurology and Neurosurgery, 23,* 56–61.

Harter, S. (1982). The perceived competence scale for children. *Child Development, 53,* 87–97.

Hayward, C., Killen, J. D., Wilson, D. M., et al. (1997). Psychiatric risk associated with early puberty in adolescent girls. *Journal of American Academy of Child and Adolescent Psychiatry, 36,* 255–262.

Heiby, E. M. (1982). A self-reinforcement questionnaire. *Behavioral Research and Theory, 20,* 397–401.

Hirschfeld, R. M. A., Klerman, G. L., Chodoff, P., Korchin, S., & Barrett, J. (1976). Dependency, self-esteem, and clinical depression. *Journal of American Academy of Psychoanalysis, 4,* 373–388.

Hodgson, R. J., & Rachman, S. (1977). Obsessional-compulsive complaints. *Behavioral Research and Theory, 15,* 389–395.

Holmes, T. H., & Rahe, R. H. (1967). *Schedule of recent experiences.* Seattle: University of Washington School of Medicine.

Jones, M. C. (1965). Psychological correlates of somatic development. *Child Development, 56,* 899–911.

Kaslow, N., Tannenbaum, R., Seligman, M. (1978). *The KASTAN: A children's attributional style questionnaire.* Philadelphia: University of Pennsylvania Press.

Landis, J. R., & Koch, G. G. (1977). The measurement of observer agreement of categorical data. *Biometrics, 33,* 159–174.

Lewinsohn, P. M., Hops, H., Roberts, R. E., Seeley, J. R., & Andrews, J. A. (1993). Adolescent psychopathology, I: Prevalence and incidence of depression and other DSM-III-R disorders in high school students. *Journal of Abnormal Psychology, 102,* 133–144.

Lewinsohn, P. M., Mermelstein, R. M., Alexander, C., & MacPhillamy D. (1985). The Unpleasant Events Schedule: A scale for the measurement of aversive events. *Journal of Clinical Psychology, 41,* 483–498.

Marshall, W. A., & Tanner, J. M. (1986). Puberty. In F. Falkner & J. M. Tanner (Eds.), *Human growth, Vol. 2: Postnatal growth neurobiology* (pp. 171–209). New York: Plenum.

McCroskey, J. C., & McCain, T. A. (1974). The measurement of interpersonal attraction. *Speech Monographs, 41,* 261–266.

McGee, R., Feehan, M., Williams, S., Partridge, F., Silva, P. A., & Kelly, J. (1990). DSM-III disorders in a large sample of adolescents. *Journal of American Academy of Child and Adolescent Psychiatry, 29,* 611–619.

Moos, R. H. (1974). *Family environment scale.* Palo Alto: CA: Consulting Psychologists Press.

NHLBI Growth and Health Study Research Group. (1992). Obesity and cardiovascular disease risk factors in black and white girls: the NHLBI Growth and Health Study. *American Journal of Public Health, 82,* 1613–1620.

Pearlin, L. I., & Schooler, C. (1978). The structure of coping. *Journal of Health and Social Behavior, 19,* 2–21.

Petersen, A. C., Crockett, L., Richards, M., & Boxer A. (1988). A self-report measure of pubertal status: Reliability, validity, and initial norms. *Journal of Youth and Adolescence, 17,* 117–133.

Petersen, A. C., Sarigiani, P. A., & Kennedy, R. E. (1991). Adolescent depression: Why more girls? *Journal of Youth and Adolescence, 20,* 247–271.

Pilowsky, I. (1967). Dimensions of hypochondriasis. *British Journal of Psychiatry, 113,* 89–93.

Prinz, R. J., Foster, S., Kent, R. N., & O'Leary, K. D. (1979). Multivariate assessment of conflict in distressed and nondistressed mother-adolescent dyads. *Journal of Applied Behavioral Analysis, 12,* 691–700.

Radloff, L. S. (1977). The CES-D Scale: A self-report depression scale for research in the general population. *Applied Psychology Measures, 1,* 385–401.

Rippere, V. (1977). Some cognitive dimensions of antidepressive behavior. *Behavioral Research and Theory, 15,* 57–63.

Robin, A. L., & Weiss, J. G. (1980). Criterion-related validity of behavioral and self-report measures of problem-solving communication skills in distressed and nondistressed parent-adolescent dyads. *Behavioral Assessment, 2,* 339–352.

Rosenbaum, M. (1980). A schedule for assessing self-control behaviors: Preliminary findings. *Behavioral Theory, 11,* 109–121.

Rosenberg, M. (1965). *Society and the adolescent self-image.* Princeton, NJ: Princeton University Press.

Russell, D., Peplau, L. A., & Cutrona, C. E. (1980). The Revised UCLA Loneliness Scale: Concurrent and discriminant validity evidence. *Journal of Personality and Social Psychology, 39,* 472–480.

Sandler, I. M., & Block, M. (1979). Life stress and maladaptation of children. American Journal of Community Psychology, 7, 425–439.

Schaefer, E. S. (1965). Children's report of parental behavior: An inventory. *Child Development, 36,* 413–424.

Simmons, R. G., & Blyth, D. A. (1987). *Moving into adolescence: The impact of pubertal change and school context.* New York: Aldine.

Spielberger, C. D., Gorsuch, R. L., & Lushene, R. E. (1970). *Manual for the State-Trait Anxiety Inventory.* Palo Alto, CA: Consulting Psychologists Press.

Stattin, H., & Magnusson, D. (1990). *Pubertal maturation in female development.* Hillsdale, NJ: Erlbaum.

Weissman, A. N., & Beck, A. T. (1978). *Development and validation of the Dysfunctional Attitude Scale.* Presented at the Annual Meeting of the Association for the Advancement of Behavior Therapy, Chicago.

THINKING CRITICALLY

1. The authors state that this is the first study to examine the relation between pubertal timing and disorders in both boys and girls. What practical reasons may other researchers have had for focusing only on either boys or girls? What are the advantages of including both boys and girls in a single study?

2. Why do you think the researchers often included several questionnaires for each area they wished to investigate, rather than just one?

3. The authors reported that early-maturing girls were especially likely to experience problems, especially depression, but they did not to attempt to explain why. What explanation would you suggest for why maturing earlier than peers would often be difficult for girls? Why would it be less difficult for boys?

4. The authors offer suggestions to address the frequent problems of early-maturing girls. What would you suggest to address the problems late-maturing boys frequently have?

Cognitive Foundations

Understanding Deception
and Sarcasm

The cognitive advances that take place in adolescence include improvement in social cognition, which refers to our understanding of the nature and meaning of social relationships and social interactions. This reading examines how our understanding of deception and sarcasm changes with age, as we gradually learn that people do not always mean what they say or say what they mean.

Reading **3.1**

Words Speak Louder Than Actions:
Understanding Deliberately False Remarks

A. Demorest, C. Meyer, E. Phelps, H. Gardner, and E. Winner

Demorest, A., Meyer, C., Phelps, E., Gardner, H., & Winner, E. (1984). Words speak louder than actions: Understanding deliberately false remarks. *Child Development, 55,* 1527–1534. Reprinted by permission from the Society for Research in Child Development.

To understand the full meaning of a speaker's message, a listener must be sensitive to the speaker's belief and purpose (Grice, 1975; Searle, 1979). People usually say what they believe. However, this conversational postulate of sincerity may be broken for various purposes.

Consider a situation in which a swimmer, upon diving into a pool, surfaces and calls out to a reluctant friend: "C'mon in! The water's warm." This statement may be sincere or deliberately false. To distinguish between these two possibilities, the listener must determine the facts (whether the water is warm or cold) and the speaker's belief about the facts. If the speaker's belief is in accord with the statement, the remark is sincere. If not, it is deliberately false. In uttering a deliberate falsehood, the speaker may or may not want the listener to believe his statement. If the speaker tries to conceal his true beliefs so that the listener will take his words literally, the remark is deceptive. If he tries to signal to the listener that the statement is false, the remark is sarcastic. Thus, discriminating among sincere, deceptive, and sarcastic remarks requires more than the ability to decode syntactic and semantic information. For, as the above example illustrates, the same statement may be sincere, deceptive, or sarcastic depending on the speaker's belief and communicative purpose.

Recently, researchers have begun to investigate children's emerging ability to distinguish between sincere and deliberately false utterances (Ackerman, 1981, 1983; Demorest, Silberstein, Gardner, & Winner, 1983; DePaulo, Jordan, Irvine, & Laser, 1982; Wimmer & Perner, 1983). This distinction rests on the ability to appreciate whether or not a speaker's belief is congruent with his statement. These studies have documented that young children tend to interpret intentionally false utterances as sincere. When confronted by the discrepancy between a speaker's statement and the facts of the situation, children either discount the facts and take the remark as sincere and correct (Ackerman, 1981; Demorest et al., 1983), or they assume that the speaker is not aware of the facts and that his remark is sincere but wrong (Demorest et al., 1983).

The distinction between different types of deliberately false remarks (deception vs. sar-

casm) rests on the ability to appreciate whether or not the speaker's communicative purpose is congruent with his statement, once discrepant belief is appreciated. With deceptive remarks, the speaker wants the listener to believe his statement, whereas with sarcastic remarks he does not. No research has yet addressed children's ability to discriminate between these two types of purpose. Ackerman (1981) found no difference in children's ability to appreciate deceptive and sarcastic remarks as deliberately false, but did not assess children's understanding of speaker purpose. In a study of sarcasm, Demorest et al. (1983) found that children tend to mistake sarcasm as deception, thus indicating that they misread the speaker's purpose. However, this study did not examine children's understanding of deception as well, nor did it directly tease out understanding of speaker belief from communicative purpose.

The purpose of this study was to test the following hypothesis about the developmental ordering of the distinctions children make among sincere, deceptive, and sarcastic remarks. In line with the earlier research, three steps in understanding are predicted. First, children assume that the speaker's belief and communicative purpose are both in line with his statement; all remarks are taken as sincere. Next, children appreciate that a speaker's belief may be inconsistent with his statement, but still assume that the speaker wants his listener to believe the statement; both types of deliberately false remark are taken as deceptive. Finally, children recognize that a speaker can both not believe his statement and not want his listener to believe it; deception and sarcasm are accurately discriminated.

To test this hypothesized sequence, we assessed children's ability to identify speaker belief and communicative purpose in sincere, deceptive, and sarcastic remarks. In addition, subjects were asked about the evidence they used to infer the speaker's belief and purpose (e.g., the facts of the situation, the statement made, the speaker's tone of voice, and the speaker's behavior, such as gestures or facial expressions). While the facts of the situation are always the best evidence for judging speaker belief, different cues may be used to judge speaker purpose reliably in the case of sincere, deceptive, and sarcastic remarks. With sincerity and deception, the speaker's statement, behavior, and intonation are congruent, and each may be used to judge communicative purpose. However, in the case of sarcasm, the speaker's statement is out of line with his behavior and intonation, and only the latter two cues may be used to accurately assess his purpose.

Method

Subjects

The subjects were 32 children at each of ages 6 (16 males, 16 females), 9 (16 males, 16 females), and 13 (17 males, 15 females), and 13 adults (6 males, 7 females). The children were drawn from three middle-class public schools and were randomly selected from their classrooms. The adults were college undergraduates who agreed to participate in the study.

Materials

Twelve brief stories involving an interaction between two same-sex peers were tape-recorded. Half of the items involved male peers, half involved females. Each story contained 10 sentences and included a description of the facts of the situation (two sentences) and a description of the gestures and other nonverbal behaviors of the speaker (one or two sentences). The final remark was seven or eight words long. A 9 × 12-inch colored picture illustrating the context and characters was presented with each story. The pictures were used only to hold the subject's attention and revealed no specific cues (e.g., facial expressions) by which the final remark could be interpreted.

Four versions of each story were constructed by varying the facts of the situation and the speaker's intonation and nonverbal behavior such that the final remark was either sincere, deceptive, sarcastic, or neutral. Neutral remarks were clearly false but could be taken as having either deceptive or sarcastic purpose. Sincere, deceptive, and sarcastic remarks were delivered with appropriate intonation and were described as accompanied by appropriate gestures. Neutral remarks were delivered with flat intonation and uninformative gestures. Neutral items were included to determine whether, given a false remark, children are more likely to assume that it is deceptive or sarcastic. A sample story in all four versions is presented in Table 3.1.1. Four tapes were constructed, each containing 12 randomly ordered stories, equally divided among sincere, deceptive, sarcastic, and neutral types.

Procedure

Subjects were randomly assigned to one of the four tapes and were seen individually for two half-hour sessions. After each story, subjects were posed a set of questions. The questions

TABLE 3.1.1 The Four Versions of the Haircut Story

Sincere: Jay needed to get his hair cut. A new barbershop had just opened in town. Jay went to the new barbershop for a haircut. *Jay got the best haircut he had ever had. It was just the right length.* Jay walked home from the barbershop. He saw Mike walking down the street. Mike noticed Jay's new haircut. **He crossed the street to speak to Jay.** Mike said to Jay, "That new haircut you got looks terrific."

Deceptive: *Jay got the worst haircut he had ever had. It was so short that his ears seemed to stick out.* **He [Mike] put his arm around Jay's shoulder and smiled at Jay.**

Sarcastic: *Jay got the worst haircut he had ever had. It was so short that his ears seemed to stick out.* **He [Mike] laughed and pointed to Jay's head.**

Neutral: *Jay got the worst haircut he had ever had. It was so short that his ears seemed to stick out.* **He [Mike] crossed the street to speak to Jay.**

Note. The factors (besides intonation) that were varied across versions are in italics and boldface. Statements about the facts of the situation appear in italics. Descriptions of nonverbal behavior are in boldface.

for the Haircut Story presented in Table 3.1.1 are given below:

> Question 1 (to assess story recall) "What happened in the story?"
>
> Question 2 (to assess understanding of the facts of the situation): "Was Jay's haircut good or bad?"
>
> Question 3 (to assess knowledge of speaker belief): "Did Mike think Jay's haircut was bad or good?" (Order of mention of terms such as good and bad was counterbalanced across questions and stories.)
>
> Question 4 (to determine the evidence cited by subjects as indicative of speaker belief): "How do you know?"
>
> Question 5 (to assess understanding of speaker purpose): "Did Mike want Jay to think his haircut was good or bad?"
>
> Question 6 (to determine the evidence cited by subjects as indicative of speaker purpose): "How can you tell he wanted Jay to think that?"

Scoring

Utterance Interpretation. The interpretation of each utterance was determined by collating responses to Questions 2 (story facts), 3 (speaker belief), and 5 (speaker purpose). As shown in Table 3.1.2, the pattern of responses across these three questions can be used to identify interpretations as "sincere-correct," "sincere-mistaken," "deceptive," and "sarcastic." With the exception of the neutral items, each remark was scored both for the type of interpretation given and for the accuracy of the interpretation. Thus, if a deceptive remark was taken as "sincere-correct," it was coded both as "sincere-correct" and as "inaccurate." Since neutral utterances were included only to determine whether they were more likely to be taken as deceptive or as sarcastic, and since neither interpretation is more accurate, these remarks were scored only for the type of interpretation given and not for accuracy. The use of these two scoring systems made it possible to deter-

TABLE 3.1.2 Response Patterns Indicating Interpretation of Remarks

	QUESTION		
INTERPRETATION	(2) Do facts accord with statement? (Was Jay's haircut good or bad?)	(3) Does speaker believe statement? (Did Mike think Jay's haircut was bad or good?)	(5) Does speaker want listener to believe statement? (Did Mike want Jay to think his haircut was good or bad?)
Sincere-correct	Facts accord. (good)	Speaker believes statement. (good)	Speaker wants listener to believe statement. (good)
Sincere-wrong	Facts do not accord. (bad)	Speaker believes statement. (good)	Speaker wants listener to believe statement. (good)
Deceptive	Facts do not accord. (bad)	Speaker does not believe statement. (bad)	Speaker wants listener to believe statement. (good)
Sarcastic	Facts do not accord. (bad)	Speaker does not believe statement. (bad)	Speaker does not want listener to believe statement. (bad)

Note. Sample questions followed the haircut story from Table 3.1.1.

mine the relative difficulty of sincere, deceptive, and sarcastic utterances as well as the patterns of misinterpretation for all four types of remark.

Evidence Drawn Upon. Question 4 assessed the kind of evidence that subjects used (or believed they used) to identify speaker belief, and Question 6 assessed the kind of evidence used to determine speaker purpose. The four major scoring categories (used for both questions) are as follows:

> (A) Statement (e.g., You can tell Mike thinks it's a good haircut "because he says it is").
> (B) Facts (e.g., You can tell Mike thinks Jay's haircut is bad "because the story says it is").
> (C) Behavior (e.g., You can tell Mike thinks Jay's haircut is bad "because Mike laughs and points at Jay's head").
> (D) Intonation (e.g. You can tell Mike thinks Jay's haircut is bad "because he sounded funny").

Two raters scored one-third of the responses at each age and achieved 94% inter-rater reliability. The remaining responses were then scored by one of the raters.

Results

To test the hypothesis proposed above, two ANOVAs were performed, the first using number of correct interpretations as the dependent variable, the second using types of interpretation as the dependent variable. Pairwise comparisons were then performed with Tukey tests. The first analysis was a mixed-model ANOVA with two between-subjects factors, age (4) and sex (2), and one repeated measure, utterance type (sincere, deceptive, sarcastic). This ANOVA revealed main effects for utterance type, $F(2, 202) = 363.27$, $p < .001$, and for age, $F(3, 101) = 21.29$, $p < .001$, and an age X utterance type interaction, $F(6, 202) = 8.89$, $p < .001$. As can be seen in Figure 3.1.1, sincere utterances were understood most often, and sarcastic remarks proved more difficult than deceptive ones ($p < .01$). The frequency of accurate interpretations increased from each age to the next ($p < .05$). The interaction occurred because, while sincere remarks posed no difficulty at any age, comprehension of deceptive

FIGURE 3.1.1 Mean percentage of correct interpretations at each age for sincere, deceptive, and sarcastic remarks.

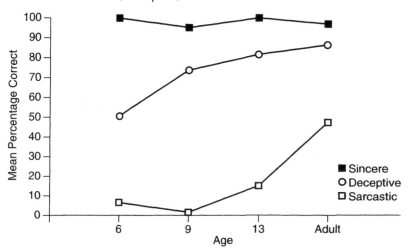

remarks improved between ages 6 and 13 ($p < .05$), and understanding of sarcasm improved only between age 13 and adulthood ($p < .01$). Sarcasm was rarely understood by the three younger age groups, and adults interpreted such remarks accurately only about half of the time. No effects of sex were found in this or any other of the analyses.

The results of the above analysis lend support to the three-step hypothesis proposed. To provide a more direct test of the hypothesis, it is necessary to determine the kinds of misinterpretations given for each kind of remark at each age. Thus, a second mixed-model ANOVA was performed with two between-subjects factors, age (4) and sex (2), and two repeated measures, utterance type (sincere, deceptive, sarcastic, neutral) and interpretation (sincere-correct, sincere-mistaken, deceptive, sarcastic). (Only those results involving interactions with utterance type are informative, and thus only these are reported.) This analysis revealed an interaction of interpretation and utterance type, $F(9, 909) = 300.49$, $p < .001$, and an interaction of age, interpretation, and utterance type, $F(27, 909) = 5.52$, $p < .001$. While sincere remarks were most often seen as sincere-correct (94%; $p < .01$) and deceptive remarks most often taken as deceptive (72%; $p < .01$), sarcastic remarks were most frequently interpreted as deceptive as well (65%; $p < .01$). This bias toward interpreting false remarks as deceptive appeared also for neutral remarks, which were taken as deceptive more often than as sarcastic (76% vs. 4%; $p < .01$).

In analyzing the three-way interaction, sincere-correct and sincere-mistaken interpretations were combined in order to compare interpretations of speaker belief as sincere versus deliberately false. (Sincere-correct always outnumbered sincere-mistaken interpretations for all false remarks.) At age 6, sincere remarks were most often seen as sincere (98%; $p < .01$), and deceptive remarks were interpreted as sincere and deceptive equally often (46% vs. 50%), while sarcastic remarks were more frequently taken as deceptive than as sincere (58% vs. 36%; $p < .01$). By ages 9 and 13, decep-

tive and sarcastic remarks both were seen predominantly as deceptive (9-year-olds: 72% and 84%, respectively; 13-year-olds: 80% and 71%, respectively). Finally, adults interpreted sincerity as sincerity (92%) and deception as deception (84%), and viewed sarcastic remarks as sarcasm as often as they took them as deceptive (46% in each case).

These findings support the hypothesized three steps in understanding, showing that 6-year-olds often interpret deliberately false remarks as sincere, 9- and 13-year-olds tend to see deliberately false remarks as deceptive, and adults can with some frequency discriminate sarcasm from deception. However, the fact that 6-year-olds also often interpreted deceptive and sarcastic remarks as deception indicates that by 6, children are beginning to appreciate the speaker's disbelief in deliberately false remarks. Furthermore, 6-year-olds interpreted sarcastic remarks as deliberately false more often than they interpreted deceptive remarks as deliberately false. This indicates that children are able to recognize the speaker's disbelief more easily in the case of sarcasm than in the case of deception.

Evidence Used to Determine Speaker Belief and Purpose

To examine developmental differences in the kinds of evidence used to judge speaker belief and purpose, responses to Questions 4 and 6 were tabulated. There were two major findings of interest. First, subjects at all ages used better, more reliable cues to judge speaker belief than to judge speaker purpose. To determine speaker belief (and hence distinguish between sincere and intentionally false utterances), the facts of the situation are the most informative cue, and this was the most common cue cited at all ages (44%, 48%, 50%, 58%, at each age, respectively). To determine speaker purpose (and hence distinguish between sarcasm and deception), the most reliable cues are the speaker's behavior and tone of voice. Instead of relying on these cues, subjects at all ages were most likely to use the statement itself as evidence (37%, 67%, 74%, 63%). (Six-year-olds were unable to answer this question 54% of the time.) The fact that children used more reliable cues to judge belief than purpose is consistent with the finding that children are sooner able to distinguish sincerity from deliberate falsehood (and thus to judge belief accurately) than to make distinctions among deliberately false remarks (and thus to infer purpose accurately).

The second finding was that reliance on more informative cues increased with age. A series of one-way ANOVAs by age showed that in judging belief, appeals to the statement declined with age, $F(3, 105) = 4.165$, $p < .01$, while the use of behavior increased with age, $F(3, 105) = 4.723$, $p < .01$, as did the use of tone of voice, $F(3, 105) = 6.602$, $p < .001$. Likewise, in judging purpose, the use of these latter two cues increased with age: behavior, $F(3, 105) = 3.115$, $p < .05$; tone, $F(3, 105)$ 3.997, $p < .01$.

To investigate the evidence used to interpret the different kinds of remarks, responses were separated into those accompanying accurate and inaccurate interpretations. Because of the small number of accurate interpretations at the three youngest ages for sarcastic items, it was not possible to perform ANOVAs on these data. Thus the findings of interest are presented here in terms of percentages. Since sincere items were for the most part interpreted accurately and with appropriate cues, only deceptive and sarcastic items will be discussed.

Deception. To distinguish a deceptive remark from a sincere one, subjects must appreciate that the speaker's belief is inconsistent with his statement. Subjects who understood deception judged speaker belief correctly by relying on the facts of the story (88%, 88%, 85%, 76%). Thus, when faced with a discrepancy between the statement and the facts, they appropriately assigned greater weight to the facts. Subjects who misinterpreted deception misjudged the speaker's belief by relying on the statement, thus taking the remark as sincere (56%, 61%, 50% for 6-, 9-, and 13-year olds; adults rarely misinterpreted deception).

Recognizing the speaker's purpose does not distinguish deceptive from sincere remarks because in both cases the speaker wants the listener to believe what is said. Indeed, it is not surprising that in judging purpose, subjects who accurately interpreted deception used the same cues as those who misinterpreted deception; both referred predominantly to the statement (accurate: 43%, 58%, 59%, 53%; inaccurate: 37%, 67%, 48%, 43%).

Sarcasm. The critical task to distinguish sarcasm from deception is to identify the speaker's purpose; the speaker's belief is the same for both utterance types. Thus it is not surprising that subjects who misinterpreted sarcasm judged belief by cues as valid as those used by adults to interpret sarcasm accurately. Subjects who misunderstood sarcasm judged belief by behavior (21%, 37%, 49%, 41%) or facts (36%, 40%, 26%, 33%), while adults who interpreted such remarks accurately relied for the most part on behavior (46%).

It was in judging the speaker's purpose that accurate and inaccurate interpreters of sarcasm used different cues. Those adults who understood sarcasm relied most often on behavior (52%), an informative cue revealing the speaker's purpose; those subjects who misunderstood sarcasm relied on the uninformative cue of the statement (40%, 69%, 85%, 96%). Thus, while subjects who misunderstood sarcasm used behavioral cues to determine that the speaker's belief was inconsistent with the statement, they were unable to use these same cues to recognize that the speaker's purpose deviated from his statement.

Discussion

The results of this study reveal three developmental steps in the understanding of deliberately false remarks. The first step is shown here by many 6-year-olds (and may well be more prevalent among even younger children). Six-year-olds tend to take remarks as sincere by assuming that a speaker's belief and purpose are both in line with his statement. These subjects rely on the speaker's statement as evidence of his belief and purpose.

Next, by 9 years of age, children are able to appreciate deliberate falsehood by relying on the facts of the situation and the speaker's behavior when these cues are inconsistent with the statement. However, they maintain their bias toward viewing the speaker's purpose as congruent with his statement: both sarcasm and deception are seen as deceptive. These children still use the speaker's statement as evidence for his purpose.

Finally, sometime between age 13 and adulthood, people become better able to appreciate that a speaker's purpose may also be out of line with his statement: sarcasm and deception are discriminated. When sarcastic purpose is recognized, listeners give more weight to the speaker's behavior than to his statement in judging what he wants the listener to believe.

It should be noted that in the stimuli used here, the discrepancy of the final statement may be underscored by the brevity of the stories and the clear contradictions of the final remark with story facts and speaker behavior. Thus this study may have demonstrated understanding of deliberately false remarks at a younger age than occurs in ordinary discourse.

Two somewhat puzzling findings arise from this study. First, even though 6-year-olds misinterpret sarcastic remarks more frequently than deceptive ones, children of this age are more likely to recognize sarcasm as deliberately false (mistaking it for deception) than they are to recognize deception as deliberately false. The explanation for this may be found in the evidence used to judge speaker belief. With sarcasm, a speaker's behavior is inconsistent with his statement, and children are able to use this cue to judge speaker belief. Deceptive remarks are not accompanied by behavior and intonation cues discrepant from the statement; the speaker's false belief is therefore less obvious. Thus, appreciation of deliberate falsehood may be facilitated by the greater number of cues indicating false belief in sarcasm than in deception.

The second intriguing finding was that, in the case of sarcasm, subjects were able to rec-

ognize the speaker's behavior as discrepant from his statement and to rely on this to judge speaker belief, but they did not rely on behavior to judge speaker purpose. In contrast, in the case of deceptive remarks, in which the speaker's behavior is consistent with this statement, subjects did use behavior as evidence of speaker purpose. Thus, when a speaker's behavior is inconsistent with his statement, children are apt to see this behavior as evidence of his belief, but not as an intentionally manipulated cue to signal disbelief to the listener. Children assume instead that the speaker's statement reflects his purpose; his behavior is unintentional. It appears that children feel that a speaker's words are more under his control than is his behavior.

We have pointed to the tendency to rely on the statement rather than discrepant cues as cause for an initial bias to interpret sarcasm as deception. However, this bias may also result from children's difficulty in understanding the motives for being sarcastic versus deceiving. Past work in social cognition has demonstrated that with age, children are increasingly able to attribute underlying motivations to people in order to resolve incongruities (Coie & Pennington, 1976; Flavell, 1977; Peevers & Secord, 1973; Whiteman, Brook, & Gordon, 1977). The motives behind deception are obvious, and may account for the prevalence of deception across diverse settings. The motives for sarcasm may be less clear, as sarcasm involves not only social aims but also linguistic play. Because social aims achieved through sarcasm can also be achieved by speaking sincerely, the purpose for speaking sarcastically must also include a desire to play with language and to be contradictory. For example, sarcasm can be employed to insult (e.g., "That's a terrific haircut"), but an insult could also be made by speaking sincerely (e.g., "That's an awful haircut"). Thus sarcasm is used not only to insult but also to convey this insult more cleverly or forcefully by stating one thing but signaling its opposite with behavior or tone. Perhaps children interpret all false remarks as deceptive because the purposes served by deception seem so much more self-evident and important than those served by sarcasm.

REFERENCES

Ackerman, B. (1981). Young children's understanding of a speaker's intentional use of a false utterance. *Developmental Psychology, 17,* 472–480.

Ackerman, B. (1983). Form and function in children's understanding of ironic utterances. *Journal of Experimental Child Psychology, 35,* 487–508.

Coie, J. D., & Pennington, B. (1976). Children's perceptions of deviance and disorder. *Child Development, 47,* 407–413.

Demorest, A., Silberstein, L., Gardner, H., & Winner, E. (1983). Telling it as it isn't: Children's understanding of figurative language. *British Journal of Developmental Psychology, 1,* 121–130.

DePaulo, B., Jordan, A., Irvine, A., & Laser, P. (1982). Age changes in the detection of deception. *Child Development, 53,* 701–709.

Flavell, J. H. (1977). *Cognitive development.* Englewood Cliffs, NJ: Prentice Hall.

Grice, P. (1975). Logic and conversation. In R. Cole & J. Morgan (Eds.), *Syntax and semantics: Speech acts.* New York: Academic Press.

Peevers, B. H., & Secord, P. F. (1973). Developmental changes in attribution of descriptive concepts to persons. *Journal of Personality and Social Psychology, 27,* 120–128.

Searle, J. (1979). *Expression and meaning: Studies in the theory of speech acts.* Cambridge: Cambridge University Press.

Whiteman, M., Brook, J., & Gordon, A. (1977). Perceived intention and behavioral incongruity. *Child Development, 48,* 1133–1136.

Wimmer, H., & Perner, J. (1983). Beliefs about beliefs: Representation and the constraining function of wrong beliefs in children's understanding of deception. *Cognition, 13,* 103–128.

THINKING CRITICALLY

1. Although understanding of sarcastic remarks improved with age, even the college students understood the sarcastic remarks only about half the time. Is that because sarcastic remarks are inherently ambiguous? Or is it because hearing and seeing someone make a sarcastic remark are much different from listening to a recorded story about a sarcastic remark?

2. The "adults" in this study are actually emerging adults (i.e., college students). Do you think that the performance of adults older than age 30 would have exceeded the performance of the college students in this study? Why or why not?

3. Not much research has been conducted on this topic since this study was published in 1984. What study would you design to build on the findings of this one and learn more about this topic?

The Development of Social Cognition

Part of social cognition is our perception of what other people are like and why they behave the way they do. Important changes in this aspect of social cognition take place in adolescence. Adolescents tend to be more reflective than children are, and they reflect on their own identities as well as the characteristics of others. Although the study described in this reading was conducted in the early 1970s, it remains one of the best studies charting the development of social cognition from middle childhood through adolescence and emerging adulthood. Social cognition is a field of study that has developed fairly recently, so the authors of this reading do not use the term, but instead call their study an investigation of "person perception."

Reading 3.2

Cognitive Theory and the Developmental Psychology of Impression Formation

W. J. Livesley and D. B. Bromley

This reading deals with some further qualitative and theoretical aspects of the developmental psychology of person perception in relation to the cognitive processes underlying the complex and subtle changes in conceptualization and language.

Although 7-year-old children can make categorical classifications of persons, frequently they fail to do so and produce descriptions which contain no reference to personal qualities—descriptions which are extremely stereotyped, consisting of a string of physical characteristics together with statements about personal identity and family relationships. Consider the following examples.

A boy aged 7,10 describes a boy he dislikes:

He is very tall. He has dark brown hair, he goes to our school. I don't think he has any brothers or sisters. He is in our class. Today he has a dark orange jumper and gray trousers and brown shoes.

A girl aged 7,6 describes a boy she likes:

Max sits next to me, his eyes are hazel and he is tall. He hasn't got a very big head, he's got a big pointed nose.

A girl aged 7,8 describes a man she dislikes:

He is six feet tall. He isn't very well dressed. He has two sons, Peter and William. They can afford a car. Peter and William got a tractor each for Christmas. William has two bicycles. Their dad has blue eyes, black trousers, and a green jumper. They have hens and a cat and dog and a budgie. Their telephone is . . .

A girl aged 7,11 describes a woman she likes:

She is very nice because she gives my
friends and me toffee. She lives by the
main road. She has fair hair and she
wears glasses. She is 47 years old. She has
an anniversary today. She has been married since she was 21 years old. She sometimes gives us flowers. She has a very nice
garden and house. We only go in the
weekend and have a talk with her.

The child's concept of the other incorporates his family, physical surroundings and even
his possessions, so much so that the person is
held responsible for the actions of his family
and pets. A good example of this is given by a
boy who wrote, "I used to like her but I don't
now because her dog bit me."

The young child's concept of another
person is diffuse, that is, fragmented, unstable
and lacking focus. This is to be understood
in part as a consequence of his egocentrism,
his inability to decenter, his simplicity and
the syncretic nature of his reasoning, as described by Piaget. In syncretic thinking, a mul-
titude of diverse things are chaotically but
intimately related within a global scheme;
thus, everything the child knows about a
person becomes relevant, and no logical
framework exists by means of which he can sys-
tematize his knowledge. Instead, items are juxtaposed by simple "and" connections rather
than by causal and organizing statements. The
resulting description is, as we have seen, a
string of unrelated statements lacking coherence and organization.

Gradually, egocentrism declines as cognitive and social skills develop. The child learns
to take into account things other than a person's appearance, identity and possessions. He
applies his growing powers of abstraction and
generalization and goes beyond the immediate
stimulus situation to infer stable and constant
features in a person's behavior, referring to
them in terms of trait names and general
habits.

The incidence of descriptions referring
to personal qualities increased considerably
from the age of 7 to the age of 8 years; in fact,

this change is almost as great as that between
8 and 15 years. The concepts used by 7- and
8-year-old children to refer to personal qualities seemed to be vague, diffuse and at a low
level of abstraction; even so, they mark a considerable advance in cognitive development,
since they reveal some ability to abstract a
common feature from a number of positive
instances, and they reveal some ability to
combine or group together a variety of stimuli
into a single class. The organization of experience in terms of conceptual categories like
"traits" and "habits" means that the subject can
construe the stimulus person separately, as it
were, from specific stimulus situations; and this
enables him to make predictions based on his
general impressions.

Although egocentrism declines from
about the age of 7, it continues to color the
child's impressions for several years. Most of
the terms used by 7-, 8- or 9-year-old children
indicated that the child was not so much describing the stimulus person as describing his
own reaction to the stimulus person and the
way that person's behavior affected him. The
child describes the other person as "kind" because "he gives me sweets," or "bad tempered"
because "he shouts at me." Egocentrism is
never completely outgrown; even as adults it
colors our perceptions of other people and
shapes our reactions to their behavior. The
adolescent's developmental achievement is to
recognize the limitations of one's personal
point of view.

Descriptions containing a string of personality terms intermingled with details of appearance and other concrete details occurred
quite frequently up to the age of 10, as in the
following example.

A boy aged 9,11 describes a boy he dislikes:

He smells very much and is very nasty. He
has no sense of humor and is very dull.
He is always fighting and he is cruel. He
does silly things and is very stupid. He
has brown hair and cruel eyes. He is sulky
and 11 years old and has lots of sisters. I
think he is the most horrible boy in the
class. He has a croaky voice and always

chews his pencil and picks his teeth and I think he is disgusting.

Descriptions such as this are considerably more sophisticated in content than those of 7-year-old children but are little better organized. Almost no attempt is made to sharpen the information through the use of qualifying and organizing words and phrases, thus making some items more precise or salient than others. One exception is the use of qualifiers that intensify the impression, such as "very." This is undoubtedly a product of the child's tendency to emphasize personally relevant features of his social environment; not that the child is sure about what features are relevant or irrelevant—equal emphasis is often placed upon details of behavior, mannerisms and appearance.

The list of characteristics frequently contains opposites; the child apparently is unaware of the conflict and inconsistency in his account. Descriptions of this sort make up approximately 10% of the total in children between the ages of 8 and 10 years, which suggests that the simple impressions of early childhood are giving way to more realistic and complex impressions. Thus *absolute invariance* gives way to an *intermediate stage,* in that the child begins to take into account more than one feature of a person's behavior and to integrate experience over longer intervals of time. He becomes aware that the same person may exhibit both positive and negative qualities. He notices that a person can be kind on some occasions but mean on others, sometimes good tempered and sometimes bad tempered. Thus a person may be described as both "nice" and "not nice," "good" and "bad," "good tempered" and "bad tempered," as in the following example.

A girl aged 9,8 describes a boy she likes:

Charles is a sort of cousin of mine. He likes watching television and riding his bicycle. He lives in Preston. His behavior is sometimes good and sometimes it is bad. He likes watching television and eating sweets.

It is probable that at first the child is not aware of the conflict in his impressions, since his beliefs about people are too chaotic or syncretic. At the same time he lacks the intellectual maturity, concepts and experiences needed to integrate his impressions. He cannot discern the common intention underlying diverse actions; to him the actions appear inconsistent and puzzling. The concept of intention is not one that he has so far acquired.

Another reason why the child in middle childhood cannot resolve apparent inconsistencies in the behavior of the stimulus person is that he is unable to take account of the way human action is influenced by the stimulus situation and by the residues of past experience. Between 8 and 12 years of age the child's concept of personality is more narrowly defined (focused) than that of the younger child; he makes less frequent reference to concrete situational factors, possessions and family. The descriptive material tends to be confined to the "person himself," and this is an important developmental advance leading the child to focus on invariances "within the person" or in his behavior, that is he focuses on stable inner-personal processes and regularities in behavior. But in one sense the child goes too far, in that he neglects important environmental influences and historical factors. This leaves him at a temporary disadvantage in that he cannot resolve the inconsistencies he observes in a person's action, and hence cannot predict his behavior very accurately. Nevertheless, the older child's emphasis on the "person himself" paves the way for insights and a better understanding of personality and behavior. Subsequently, his concept of personality is extended so as to embrace more than mere coincidental and contiguous situational factors, to include more pertinent circumstantial determinants.

As the system becomes better organized—through the development of networks of trait implications and through the development of beliefs about the connections between a person's actions and his past and present circumstances—the individual reaches the final stage of *integrated invariance.* Before this stage, the child can identify and isolate variances—in-

ternal dispositions and regular patterns of behavior—but he is unable to relate them to one
another or to see that the various dispositions
and behavioral regularities are parts of an overall system (an achievement marking the final
stage of the development of the concept of psychological invariance). There are, of course,
occasions when older subjects are unable to
deal with puzzles and inconsistencies in their
beliefs about others, either because they lack
ability or experience or because the information about the stimulus person is in fact inadequate or "inexplicable." At a commonsense
level, when this happens one uses a variety of
terms like "strange," "peculiar," and "funny,"
which have the effect of excluding the stimulus
person from the normal range of convenience
of everyday concepts of human behavior.

The final stage is reached when the child
grasps the idea that the behavior of persons,
like the behavior of things, is "lawful" and recognizes that many of the laws, or rules, are
complex and far from explicit. Prediction and
explanation are not only possible but also reasonably successful much of the time. If they
were not, interpersonal relationships would be
far less satisfactory, and social interactions
would be much less smooth and effective.

The Transition to an Adult Level of Impression Formation

A. Adolescence

The changes that take place in personality descriptions after the age of 13 years are clearly
demonstrated by the following examples.

A girl aged 14,3 describes a boy she dislikes:

I dislike this boy because he is very rude,
ignorant, cheeky and thinks he is the
best. Although he can sometimes be very
nice, his poorer qualities outnumber his
better qualities which are not very good
to start with. He is very rude to his friend
who is nice and this leads to an argument. I think he is very ignorant by the
way he ignores things when he wants to.
He is exceptionally cheeky to his mother
when his friends are there especially.

A girl aged 14,1 describes a girl she likes:

This girl is not in my form she is just in
the same division as me. She is very quiet
and only talks when she knows a person
very well. She is clever in one sense, she
comes top of her form. She is very reserved but once you get to know her she
is exactly the opposite. It is very unusual
to see her not attending the lessons. At
sometime or other all our minds wander
but hers never seems to do so. One of the
things I admire in her is she is very tidy.

A boy aged 15,8 describes a boy he likes:

Andy is very modest. He is even shyer
than I am when near strangers and yet is
very talkative with people he knows and
likes. He always seems good tempered
and I have never seen him in a bad tem-
per. He tends to degrade other people's
achievements, and yet never praises his
own. He does not seem to voice his opinions to anyone. He easily gets nervous.

These descriptions amply illustrate the
"qualitative" difference between younger children and those over 13 years of age. There is a
considerable increase and shift in the range of
ideas, and in the qualities assigned to the other
person; there is greater flexibility in selecting
from and dealing with these ideas. The older
child is not so greatly misled by irrelevant de-
tail; he attempts to show how the person's behavior and inner personal states can be related
to historical, biological and social factors. He is
aware (implicitly) that behavior is a function of
the total situation. Older subjects select some
of the more salient or interesting aspects of the
stimulus person and present the relevant evidence in a fairly organized way. Integration and
organization are achieved through the use of
qualifying and organizing statements. The qualifying statements are not used in the simple way
that young children use terms like "very," but
in a more constructive way to integrate one
quality with another or with the rest of the impression, or to suggest that one quality is more
salient or important than another, as in the following examples.

A girl aged 14,4 describes a girl she likes:

She is very kind and friendly. She is always very sensible and willing to help people. Sometimes she gets a bit cross but that doesn't last long and soon she is her normal self.

Integration is also achieved through the use of organizing words and phrases, for example, in distinguishing between real and apparent qualities.

A girl aged 14,3 describes a girl she dislikes:

Although she professes to be your friend, when you are ill she does not come to visit you.

A girl aged 14,1 describes a girl she likes:

She is very reserved but once you get to know her she is exactly the opposite.

Some of the older subjects attempted to explain a person's actions and personal qualities by searching for underlying motives, dispositions, or situational factors.

A boy aged 15,5 describes a man he dislikes:

He is very shy. He does not know how to answer snap questions. He does not talk very much. He always obeys his wife to the letter and never thinks for himself. He fusses over his wife but does not stay in all the time he is off work. There is a greater pull on him from his mother who is a hypochondriac. He very often visits her.

This adolescent is probably no longer relying only on personal observation and experience as the sources of his ideas about people. Instead, he is making use of indirect evidence, and information supplied by others; he is using more advanced concepts about behavior and psychological processes, and he is capable of relating evidence and inference in order to read stability and organization into a person's actions and qualities; thus the descriptions tend to become focused and hierarchically organized through selection, differential emphasis and interconnection. Subjects producing these organized and integrated descriptions usually need to make the important distinction between observation and inference. They must realize that information about a person is to some extent ambiguous in the sense that it can be construed in several ways; hence they try to justify their interpretation or construction by introducing supporting evidence and by illustrative examples. They go to some lengths to verify and amplify the internal consistency of their argument. These subjects have become capable of dealing rationally with systems of psychological ideas; their thinking about other people has become flexible and capable of self-correction; their ideas about other people are functional in the sense that they are connected with the facts of observation and with the demands of personal adjustment.

B. Early Adulthood

Several hundred free descriptions have been written as class exercises by day students and evening students taking courses in psychology. It was assumed that their accounts would approach the upper limits of conceptual development, and provide a sort of "baseline" for the measurement of developmental level. Surprisingly, perhaps, their reports show little evidence of technical, that is "professional" or "scientific," psychological concepts.

The conditions under which the young adults' free descriptions were collected were too diverse to justify exact quantitative analysis, or to justify exact comparisons with the children's descriptions. They were written as class exercises, and were used to obtain clinical impressions about the content and organization of adult conceptions of personality. The systems of classification used in the main developmental study took account of the sorts of ideas produced by those adults.

Some of the categories frequently used by young adults overlap considerably with the categories used by the children. General Personality Attributes and Specific Behavioral Consistencies are frequently used by both young adults and children. Appearance is prominent in the reports of the young adults and occurs in the children's reports in spite of the instructions to exclude such information. Appearance, evidently, plays an important role in our impressions of other people in spite of the fact that appearance is often quite unrelated to psychological qualities. Statements about appearance serve to introduce and identify the person.

Descriptions including Motivation and Arousal occurred with moderate frequency in the young adult reports but were largely absent from the children's descriptions. An explanation for these apparent differences is that intelligent young adults with an interest in human behavior can be expected to have the abilities needed to handle motivational concepts. Children, in contrast, can do little more than report what they observe or believe; hence their descriptions are usually unorganized collections of items of information about overt behavior or circumstances.

The difference between the children and the young adults is not merely one of vocabulary or experience but also one of conceptual level or "attitude." For example, General Information was used by both children and adults, but whereas the children are usually content simply to *mention* facts, the young adults are usually concerned to *relate* the facts to other items of information and interpretation.

One obvious and important developmental change is a vast increase in the range of available ideas coupled with a much greater flexibility in selecting from and dealing with these ideas. The descriptions given by children are, by and large, limited in content and in focus of interest, so that an investigator can easily compile a "typical" description. The descriptions given by young adults however, are diverse—they range freely over all the categories and introduce all kinds of points of interest. Young adults select some of the more salient or interesting aspects of their case and present the relevant evidence in a fairly organized way, whereas younger children soon exhaust their limited ideas and are not greatly concerned with the organization of the material.

Another obvious developmental change is the appearance of a variety of words and phrases which young adults use to "shape" the material

to get greater coherence in, and more effective presentation of, the information. As we have seen, there are terms which say something about the intensity, frequency, duration and variety of the stimulus person's characteristics, for example, terms like "very," "occasionally," "persistently." Examples or definitions of the characteristic may be given. Then there are ways of selecting and emphasizing, that is sharpening, the stimulus person's characteristics—even to the point of caricature. In contrast, there are ways of counteracting the primacy effect in communication and presenting a "balanced account" of the person's qualities by introducing further information beginning with terms like, "on the other hand," "but,'" or "although." Adults frequently make distinctions between the real and the apparent characteristics of the stimulus person and between earlier and later impressions, for example, "Outwardly he seems easy going, but he is really very aggressive," or "At first he's shy, but when you get to know him he's great fun." Adults sense that particular psychological characteristics are a function of circumstances or of other psychological factors.

Adults, more so than children, recognize that their descriptions are personal viewpoints liable to differ from the viewpoints of other observers and liable to be modified. It seemed likely, too, as we have seen, that our opinions of others provide useful outlets for, and are distorted by, our personal feelings. Terms expressing ethical evaluation are commonly found in descriptions by adults.

Unlike the descriptions of younger children, adult descriptions tend not to be confined to statements about the concrete here-and-now situation. They contain statements pointing to the past and others pointing to the future, as well as to the present; they contain statements about what is probable or possible, as well as to what is actually the case. Naturally, descriptions contain many faults and inadequacies.

The following complete examples, from young adult descriptions, illustrate some aspects of the previous analysis, namely, the use of qualifiers, selection and emphasis, balancing, real versus apparent characteristics, the effects of circumstances, and psychodynamic explanation.

Julia

On first acquaintance Julia is a quiet and rather nondescript looking person with pale coloring and fair hair. She is not very pretty, taken feature by feature, but she can look attractive when she is happy. She is the only child of wealthy parents and has everything she wants in the way of clothes, personal belongings and spending money. Her parents are very fond of her and she is very fond of them.

Julia's main trouble is that she has no self-assurance socially. In mixed company, she regards herself as utterly unattractive. Following one or two dances when she has not enjoyed herself much, she absolutely refuses to go to another. She can be witty and humorous in company, but with boys she often seems to overdo this and never gets beyond a teasing slanging relationship.

She seems to have reached a stage now, through her feelings of inferiority, that she will not go anywhere or plan anything where she may be the odd girl out and not enjoy herself. She retires more into her shell with periods of depression and harbors romantic illusions about various inaccessible men. She recently canceled her birthday party because she did not want to invite her friends from home in case the party was not a success. Her real trouble seems to be that she admires some inaccessible man who does not notice her at all, and then assumes that no one likes her, although she has plenty of female friends.

Enid

Enid is all right really, although most people think she is very bad tempered because she goes around looking as if everyone and everything irritates her. In fact, she is quite easily irritated and does not get on very well with people she does not know well. She expects people to adapt themselves to her ways.

Her natural expression is, however, often very deceiving and may arise from the fact that she easily detaches herself from everyday life and is often thinking of things quite different from those which occupy other people's attention. She has a very great love of animals especially horses, and often attributes human characteristics to them that few others would think of.

She is remarkably indifferent to her parents or to any other authority. The only adult she seems to respect is her brother. Nevertheless she enjoys arguing with him—"Just to show we are still alive" as she says. Once she knows you well and feels you are "on her wavelength," she is a very generous person and willing to help. Her vagueness is a source of great amusement to others which she finds difficult to understand.

Briefly, then, the more obvious developmental changes in the way we conceptualize persons include the following:

a. An increase in the number of descriptive categories.
b. Greater flexibility and precision in the use of these categories.
c. An increase in the selectivity, coherence, complexity and organization of information and ideas.
d. An increase in the use of subtle qualifying and connecting terms.
e. An increased ability to analyze and interpret the person's behavior.
f. An increased concern with the presentation of the material, to make it a convincing communication.

By the time we have reached adulthood, we have become capable of formal operations with systems of psychological ideas. We understand the "grammar" of human behavior. We are capable of coordinating observation with reason, and our thinking about other people has become flexible and capable of self-correction.

It must be stated clearly, however, that not all adults are as capable as this; individual differences are considerable. Adult life, moreover, is associated with further "developmental" or "aging" effects that can be expected to influence impression formation.

THINKING CRITICALLY

1. The authors observe that egocentrism is never outgrown, even in adulthood. What examples could you give of egocentrism among emerging adults or older adults?

2. How would you summarize, in your own words, the changes that take place in person perception from middle childhood to adolescence?

3. The emerging adults (or "young adults") in this study were college students in psychology classes. In what ways might the person perceptions of such students be different from those of other emerging adults and therefore not be representative of emerging adults more generally?

4. Write a brief description of a person you know. How does it reflect the characteristics described in this reading as typical of college students' person perceptions?

Cultural Beliefs Among Immigrant Adolescents

In recent decades there has been a surge of immigration into the United States, especially from Asia and Latin America. Western European countries have also experienced increased immigration, from many parts of the world but especially from Eastern Europe. Often these immigrants come from cultures with values that tend to be collectivistic, in contrast to the individualistic values of the Western countries they are entering. This reading examines the values of adolescents in immigrant families who have come to the United States from three cultures. Their values are compared with their parents' values and with the values of adolescents and their parents in nonimmigrant European American and African American families.

Reading 4.1

Cultural Values and Intergenerational Value Discrepancies in Immigrant and Non-Immigrant Families

J. S. Phinney, A. Ong, and T. Madden

From Phinney, J. S., Ong, A., & Madden, T. (2000). Cultural values and intergenerational value discrepancies in immigrant and non-immigrant families. *Child Development, 71,* 528–539. Reprinted by permission from the Society for Research in Child Development.

Recent increases in the proportion of immigrants in the U.S. population (Portes & Rumbaut, 1990; Schoeni, McCarthy, & Vernez, 1996; Smith & Edmonston, 1997) provide valuable opportunities for understanding processes of psychological change in individuals and groups across cultural contexts (Rogler, 1994). Yet mainstream American psychology has not dealt extensively with immigration, perhaps because, like the study of culture (Shweder, 1990), it poses challenges to the search for universals in human behavior and development. Researchers concerned with development within immigrant families are faced with questions about the level of generality of their models and findings: What processes are unique to particular immigrant groups? What generalizations are possible across immigrant groups? What developmental processes are common across both immigrant and non-immigrant groups?

Researchers interested in immigration must also deal with the fact that adaptation among immigrant families in the United States is a complex, multidimensional process (Portes, 1997). In place of the generally uniform assimilation process assumed for earlier immigrants, more recent immigrants show diverse patterns of adaptation within and across groups (Rumbaut, 1994; Zhou, 1997). The children of immigrants in particular differ widely in the extent to which they show positive developmental outcomes in the United States (Zhou, 1997).

Adolescent children of immigrants face especially complex issues, as they must deal with exposure to possibly conflicting sets of cultural values while simultaneously negotiating the developmental transition to adulthood (Chiu, Feldman, & Rosenthal, 1992). Because the rates of adaptation following immigration may vary between parents and adolescents (Portes, 1997), intergenerational discrepancies in cultural values may increase. To understand the processes of adaptation for these adolescents, we must take into consideration their different contexts: those related to belonging to a particular ethnic group, those associated with being an immigrant, and those pertaining to adolescent development generally (Garcia Coll et al., 1996; Szapocznik & Kurtines, 1993). An approach that considers different levels of analysis can lead to a better comprehension of the generality of processes of adaptation across diverse immigrant groups and also across immigrants and non-immigrants. The present study used such a multilevel approach in a study of cultural values and intergenerational value discrepancies from 3 immigrant groups (Vietnamese, Armenian, and Mexican) and 2 non-immigrant groups (European American and African American) in Southern California.

Values represent central or desirable goals that serve as standards to guide the selection or evaluation of behavior, people, and events (Smith & Schwartz, 1997). The values of the society in which children are raised provide a framework that shapes parental behaviors and interactions with children and the resulting developmental outcomes (Kagitcibasi, 1996; Super & Harkness, 1997). Within all cultures, parents engage in practices aimed at socializing the child to become a responsible adult member of the society (Whiting & Whiting, 1975). Yet the patterning of values varies widely across cultural groups (Kluckhohn & Strodtbeck, 1961). Two fundamental values that have been shown to differentiate European American culture from most non-Western cultures are individualism and collectivism (Hofstede, 1980; Kagitcibasi, 1996, 1997; Kim, Triandis, Kagitcibasi, Choi, & Yoon, 1994). These underlying values shape the processes of development through the ways in which parents socialize their children (Greenfield & Cocking, 1994).

Collectivism can be defined by an emphasis on group interdependence, harmony in interpersonal relations, and conformity to group norms (Triandis, 1990, 1995). Collectivist values are characteristic of the cultures of the 3 immigrant groups studied in the current research, Vietnamese, Armenian, and Mexican. Vietnamese culture, based in Confucian and Buddhist roots, is strongly collectivist; the family structure is typically patriarchal, and children are expected to obey their parents and fulfill their obligations within the family (Matsuoka, 1990; Nguyen & Williams, 1989;

Rosenthal, Ranieri, & Klimidis, 1996). Adult children are expected to remain at home until they marry and to follow the advice of their elders in matters of dating, marriage, and career choice; individual autonomy is subordinated to the needs of the family. For example, in a study of Vietnamese immigrants in the United States, Nguyen and Williams (1989) found that Vietnamese Americans endorsed conforming to parental authority more and were less supportive of adolescent autonomy than were their European American counterparts. Zhou and Bankston (1994) found that Vietnamese immigrant parents emphasized obedience, industriousness, respect for elders, and helping others.

Armenian culture is similarly characterized by a traditional family structure that includes clear parental authority, strong family ties among extended family members, and a sense of obligation to the family (Bakalian, 1993; Bamberger, 1986–87). Children are typically expected to live at home until they marry, and there is pressure to marry within the ethnic group. Although their collectivist cultural values in some ways parallel those found in Vietnamese families, the Armenian immigration experience differs substantially, characterized by a lower proportion of refugees and a higher socioeconomic status.

Mexican Americans come from a predominantly Catholic culture that is considered to be collectivist (Delgado-Gaitan, 1994; Hofstede, 1980). They have been described as having a strong emphasis on family interdependence and reliance on an extended family system (Marin & Marin, 1991; Sabogal, Marin, Otero-Sabogal, Marin, & Perez-Stable, 1987). The family is hierarchical, with the father assuming the dominant role (Ramirez, 1989; Rueschenberg & Buriel, 1989). Okagaki and Sternberg (1993) found that Mexican parents valued conforming behaviors in their children more than did European American parents. Chia et al. (1994) showed that Mexican college students valued family cohesion more than autonomy.

When families from these backgrounds immigrate to the United States, they are confronted with a culture with very different attitudes about the obligations of children toward their parents (Fuligni, Tseng, & Lam, 1999). European American adolescents hold values reflecting the greater individualism of American culture. Although they also have obligations to their parents and families, they expect greater equality with their parents and less emphasis on obedience. Young people typically move away from home at the end of adolescence, and there is less expectation that grown children will physically care for elderly parents. In keeping with these expectations, European American parents encourage less interdependence in their children than do parents in collectivist cultures (Greenfield & Cocking, 1994; Okagaki & Sternberg, 1993).

It is interesting to note that African American families occupy a position that shares some characteristics with both immigrants and European Americans. As a result of their many generations in the United States, African Americans have been exposed to the individualistic values of the dominant culture. Harrison, Wilson, Pine, Chan, and Buriel (1990), however, argue that African Americans, like other ethnic groups of color in the United States, have stressed collective values and group solidarity as a response to exploitation and blocked opportunities. Parents emphasize interdependence and sharing as socialization goals for children. This observation is consistent with the finding that African American children are more willing to share within a group (Sims, 1979), and that African American college students score higher on collectivism than do European Americans (Gaines et al., 1997). Close ties with the extended family are important (Hatchett & Jackson, 1993; White & Parham, 1990). Thus, in comparison to the other groups of interest, African Americans may possess intermediate values, sharing individualistic attitudes with the larger society and collectivist attitudes with recent immigrants.

Differences between the values of the culture of origin of immigrant families and those of the larger society provide an ideal opportunity to study the generality of processes of change that occur with acculturation (Greenfield & Cocking, 1994; Rogler, 1994). Such changes may be attributed to a number of factors, including place of birth, age at migration, and length of time in the new culture. Immigrants who arrive as adults have been socialized into the culture of origin throughout their early life. As a result, they hold on to their cultural values and practices more strongly than do their children (Liebkind, 1992; Rosenthal et al., 1996; Szapocznik & Kurtines, 1993). Immigrant parents have more difficulty in learning a new language than do their children (Portes & Schauffler, 1994). Within their home and community, they typically have less contact with the larger society than do children, who are exposed to new values in school and among peers from other backgrounds. As a result, adults adapt to American culture at a slower rate than those who arrive as children or who are born in the United States, a pattern that Portes (1997) calls "dissonant acculturation." This pattern can be seen in a study of immigrant Vietnamese adolescents and their parents by Nguyen and Williams (1989), who found that Vietnamese parents endorsed traditional cultural values significantly more strongly than did their adolescent children.

In addition to differences between adolescents and their parents, there are likely to be differences among adolescents in relation to their place of birth. Foreign-born (first generation) immigrants have been found to endorse family obligations more strongly than do those born in the United States (second generation) (Sabogal et al., 1987). Those born outside the United States, even if they arrived at an early age, have a self-identification based on their country of origin, for example, Mexican or Vietnamese. In contrast, their U.S.-born peers more often have a compound identity, for example, Mexican American, or simply American (Rumbaut, 1997). The identity of foreign-born Americans of Mexican descent is more strongly linked to the culture of origin than is the identity of those born in the United States (Gurin, Hurtado, & Peng, 1994). In comparison, adolescents born in the United States are likely to feel more American and may, in turn, develop attitudes and expectations closer to those of their non-immigrant peers.

In addition to the acculturation process, adolescents in immigrant families are experiencing a transition to adulthood. A central feature of adolescent development in Western and economically developed countries is the process of individuation and increasing autonomy (Grotevant & Cooper, 1985; Hauser, Powers, & Noam, 1991; Steinberg, 1990). Individuation involves the young person's developing awareness of his or her own attitudes, opinions, and identity as distinct from those of his or her parents. This process is linked to disagreements with parents, as adolescents establish areas of personal jurisdiction (Laursen & Collins, 1994; Smetana & Asquith, 1994).

The process of individuation has been studied largely with European American families, and it may occur differently in other cultures (e.g., Kurtz, 1992). Kagitcibasi (1996) suggests that as collectivist cultures develop economically and are exposed to Western values of individualism, family members may become more financially independent, yet remain interdependent emotionally. In a study of adolescents in Hong Kong, a society which is economically developed but rooted in Chinese culture, Yau and Smetana (1996) found that adolescent-parent disagreements occur as a part of development. They suggest that such disagreements serve an individuating function; however, the ways they are expressed are influenced by the cultural context (see also Wainryb & Turiel, 1994). Fuligni and colleagues (1999) found no differences between immigrant and non-immigrant adolescents in the United States in their perceptions of disagreements with parents. If parents and adolescents independently report their values, however, discrepancies may be found even if there are not open disagreements.

In summary, the goal of the present study was to examine intergenerational value discrepancies in families from 3 immigrant groups and from a comparison sample from 2 nonimmigrant groups. In contrast to studies that have relied on adolescents' reports of parental values (Feldman, Mont-Reynaud, & Rosenthal, 1992; Fuligni et al., 1999), the present study independently assessed both adolescent and parent endorsements of values. Our first question was whether value discrepancies in immigrant families increase over time in the United States as a result of the more rapid acculturation of adolescents. Our second question was whether this process is general across the 3 immigrant groups. Our final question was whether intergenerational value discrepancies in immigrant families are greater than those in non-immigrant families.

Method

Participants

The participants were 701 families, including adolescents (263 males and 438 females) and their parents, from five ethnic groups: Armenian ($n = 197$), Vietnamese ($n = 103$), Mexican/Mexican American ($n = 171$), African American ($n = 95$), and European American ($n = 135$). Participants were from middle- and working-class communities in the Los Angeles area. Socioeconomic status (SES) was calculated from the parents' report of each parent's education and occupation, and participants were assigned to one of four categories. Parent respondents reported the educational and occupational level for each parent on a 4-point scale. Educational and occupational level were then averaged and four categories were created for the purposes of analysis. Adolescents' report of parental occupation was used when parental data were missing (see Table 4.1.1).

SES categories differed significantly among ethnic groups, chi-square (12, $N = 701$) = 304.3, $p < .001$. A majority of the European American, African American, and Armenian families were middle class, whereas for the Vietnamese and Mexican families, a majority were working class. Because of these differences, SES was included in the analyses. Demographic characteristics of the sample are shown in Table 4.1.1.

Procedures

Middle schools and high schools were identified in which at least two of the five ethnic groups were represented and no single group predominated. Of the 12 schools contacted, two declined to participate due to testing schedules. Research assistants visited randomly selected 8th and 10th grade classrooms and informed students about the study. About three quarters of the students in all classes expressed interest in the study; in virtually all classes, girls were more responsive than boys. The proportions of girls were virtually identical across ethnic groups, however. Interested students were given a demographic screening form on which they reported their age and gender, their own and their parents' ethnicity, their place of birth, their length of residence in the United States, and their ability to read English.

All students who submitted screening forms and who met the criteria were invited to participate. Participants were from one of the five groups of interest, with both parents from the same group. For the three immigrant groups, all parents were foreign-born, and adolescents had at least four years of schooling in the United States and rated themselves as able to read English quite well or very well. The latter criteria were based on our goal of focusing on the experience of adolescents with substantial exposure to U.S. culture and schools, rather than on the more immediate problems of recent immigration. All parents of adolescents from the two non-immigrant groups (African American and European American) were born in the United States. Students took home parent consent forms and parent questionnaires in English and in their ethnic language. A few days later, during a free period or lunch, the adolescent questionnaire was completed by all those who returned the parent consent form and parent questionnaire. About 75% of those given the forms completed the questionnaire. This proportion did not differ significantly across ethnic groups. Adolescents were paid $5.00 for their participation.

Adolescent Measures

The measures used in this study are part of a larger study (Berry et al., 1995). Adolescents completed the questionnaire in English.

Family Obligations. The initial measure consisted of 14 items assessing family relation-

TABLE 4.1.1 Characteristics of Sample, by Ethnic Group

	ARMENIAN (n = 197)	VIETNAMESE (n = 103)	MEXICAN (n = 171)	AFRICAN AMERICAN (n = 95)	EUROPEAN AMERICAN (n = 135)
Adolescents					
Age, years: *mean (range)*	14.4 (12–17)	14.9 (13–18)	14.6 (13–18)	14.7 (13–18)	14.6 (12–18)
Gender					
Male	77 (39%)	41 (39%)	68 (40%)	31 (32%)	46 (35%)
Female	120 (61%)	62 (61%)	103 (60%)	64 (68%)	89 (65%)
Parental SES					
Unskilled work and/or little education beyond elementary	16 (8.3%)	40 (38.5%)	86 (52.8%)	1 (1.1%)	2 (1.4%)
Skilled work and/or some secondary education	45 (23.3%)	28 (30.4%)	58 (35.6%)	13 (14.3%)	23 (16.9%)
White-collar work and/or some college education	85 (44.0%)	18 (19.6%)	15 (9.2%)	40 (44.0%)	46 (33.8%)
Professional work and/or college or graduate education	47 (24.4%)	5 (5.4%)	4 (2.5%)	36 (39.6%)	65 (47.8%)
Parental marital status					
Married	172 (88.2%)	87 (85.3%)	124 (72.9%)	36 (40.9%)	96 (70.1%)
Divorced/other	23 (11.8%)	15 (14.7%)	46 (27.1%)	52 (59.1%)	41 (29.9%)
Neighborhood ethnicity					
Nearly all from different groups	32 (16.5%)	15 (15.0%)	19 (11.3%)	15 (16.7%)	20 (14.8%)
Mostly from different groups	15 (7.7%)	30 (30.0%)	28 (16.7%)	14 (15.6%)	24 (17.8%)
About equal, own and other groups	73 (37.6%)	42 (42.0%)	70 (41.7%)	25 (27.8%)	34 (25.2%)
Mostly from own group	60 (30.9%)	9 (9.0%)	38 (22.6%)	26 (28.9%)	34 (25.2%)
Nearly all from own group	14 (7.2%)	4 (4.0%)	13 (7.7%)	10 (11.1%)	23 (17.0%)
Father's reason for immigrating					
Improve life	91 (51.7%)	35 (38.5%)	132 (92.3%)		
Refugee	57 (32.4%)	54 (59.3%)	1 (0.7%)		
Other	28 (16.0%)	2 (2.2%)	10 (7.0%)		

Note: Numbers for breakdowns may not add up to total for sample because of missing data.

ships. The items were based on scales that have been used in prior research with collectivist cultures (Georgas, 1989; Georgas, Berry, Shaw, Christakopoulou, & Mylonas, 1996; Nguyen & Williams, 1989). The items were modified with input based on the experience of a team of cross-cultural researchers from diverse cultures (Berry et al., 1995). A pilot study was conducted to determine the structure and reliability of the measure. The participants were 105 adolescents (*M* age = 16.1 years) and their foreign-born parents from immigrant families in the United States (50 Armenian and 55 Vietnamese). Adolescents and their parents completed the measure. Based on an exploratory factor analysis, eight items were selected that had a coherent factor structure and acceptable internal consistency for both adolescents and parents (Cronbach's α = .77 for adolescents, .70 for parents). The measure was termed "family obligations" (see Table 4.1.2).

Demographic Variables. The adolescents reported their gender, age, and place of birth (whether United States or foreign), and age of arrival in the United States if foreign-born. English and ethnic language proficiency were assessed with four items each (ability to under-

TABLE 4.1.2 Measure of Children's Obligations to Parents (Family Obligations)

Respondents indicated agreement (from Strongly disagree to Strongly agree) to the following statements:

1. Children should obey their parents.
2. Children should not talk back to their parents.
3. It is a child's responsibility to look after the parents when they need help.
4. Girls should share in the work at home without payment.
5. Parents always know what is best.
6. Boys should share in the work at home without payment.
7. Girls should live at home until they get married.
8. Boys should live at home until they get married.

stand, speak, read, and write), using a rating scale from 1 (not at all) to 5 (very well). The ethnic composition of their neighborhood and their in-group social interaction were also reported on 5-point scales.

Parent Measures

The immigrant parents were given questionnaires in both English and the language of their country of origin (Armenian, Vietnamese, or Spanish) and had the option of answering in either language. Ethnic language versions were translated into English, checked against the original, and revised as necessary. Because of ethnic differences in both family structure and parental roles across ethnic groups, parents were given the option of having either parent (or both together) complete the questionnaire. Overall, questionnaires were completed by the mother (46%), by the father (14%), by both together (27%), or by another relative (e.g., grandparent, guardian; 3%); data were missing in 10% of the cases. As expected, the respondents differed significantly by ethnic group, χ^2 (12, N = 671) = 62.23, p < .001. The number of mothers completing the survey was higher than average in the African American and European American families; the number of fathers was higher in Vietnamese families, and joint completion was higher in the Armenian families. Separate analyses of variance carried out for each group showed no significant differences in parental endorsement of family obligations based on who completed the questionnaire (mother, father, or both).

Family Obligations. Parents completed the same eight items as the adolescents (see Table 4.1.2). The internal consistency, assessed by Cronbach's α, was .74.

Parent Demographic Variables. Ethnicity, age, country of birth, education, occupation, and marital status were reported for both mother and father. Immigrant parents reported their length of residence in the United States, their reason for immigrating, and their English and ethnic language proficiency.

Results

Differences in Value Discrepancies in Immigrant Families by Cohort and Ethnicity

Our first question concerned differences in value discrepancies in immigrant families by cohort and ethnicity. Two cohorts were defined. Cohort 1 consisted of those with a U.S.-born adolescent and parents with longer residence in the United States ($n = 208$); cohort 2 included those with a foreign-born adolescent and parents with shorter residence in the United States ($n = 263$). The cohorts differed in a number of ways, as would be expected from their immigration history (see Table 4.1.3).

Preliminary analyses in the immigrant families revealed no gender differences in values or value discrepancies and no interaction of gender and ethnicity. Therefore, gender was not included in further analyses.

Our expectation of cohort differences in value discrepancies was based on the assumption that endorsement of family obligations would differ between cohorts for the adolescents but not for the parents. A 2×3 (Cohort $\times$ Ethnicity) analysis of variance of family obligations, with SES as a covariate, showed no cohort

effect for parents, as expected. There were significant differences by ethnicity, with Armenian and Vietnamese parents scoring higher than Mexican parents. There was no effect of SES (see Table 4.1.4).

A similar analysis of variance for adolescents' scores on family obligations showed, as expected, that adolescents in cohort 2 (foreign-born) endorsed family obligations more strongly than did adolescents in cohort 1 (U.S.-born), $F(1, 469) = 10.19$, $p < .01$. There was a significant difference by ethnicity, $F(2, 469) = 4.21$, $p < .02$; Armenian adolescents had higher scores than did Vietnamese and Mexicans. There was a significant interaction of ethnicity and birthplace, $F(2, 469) = 3.61$, $p < .05$, such that the Armenian and Vietnamese adolescents in cohort 2 endorsed family obligations more strongly than did those in cohort 1, but this finding did not hold for Mexican adolescents. There was no SES effect (see Table 4.1.4).

We expected that the discrepancy between adolescents and parents would be greater in cohort 1 than in cohort 2. A 2×3 (Cohort $\times$ Ethnicity) analysis of variance of the discrepancy scores, with SES as a covariate, showed a significant effect of cohort, $F(1, 469) = 4.78$, $p < .05$. As expected, cohort 1 families

TABLE 4.1.3 Characteristics of Two Cohorts of Immigrant Families and Cohort Differences

	ARMENIAN		VIETNAMESE		MEXICAN AMERICAN	
	Cohort 2 ($n = 148$)	Cohort 1 ($n = 49$)	Cohort 2 ($n = 59$)	Cohort 1 ($n = 44$)	Cohort 2 ($n = 56$)	Cohort 1 ($n = 115$)
Adolescents						
Mean years in United States	7.42	—	10.26	—	8.64	—
Ethnic language proficiency	4.12	3.60***	3.10	2.60*	4.46	4.06**
English language proficiency	4.88	4.91	4.53	4.88***	4.49	4.77***
In-group social interaction	4.25	3.50***	3.31	3.04	4.06	4.05
Parents						
Father's age at immigration	36.11	32.95*	33.90	29.92*	29.41	21.26***
Father's years in the United States	10.13	12.79*	12.20	14.05	12.71	22.86***
Ethnic language proficiency	4.88	4.93	4.76	4.80	4.78	4.79
English language proficiency	3.54	3.70	3.58	3.59	2.15	2.98***

Note: Cohort 1 = Families with a U.S.-born adolescent; cohort 2 = Families with a foreign-born adolescent. Significant differences between cohorts (within each ethnic group): *$p < .05$; **$p < .01$; ***$p < .001$.

TABLE 4.1.4 Means and Standard Deviations for Family Obligations and Discrepancies in Immigrant Families, With Effects for Birth and Ethnicity

| | ARMENIAN | | VIETNAMESE | | MEXICAN AMERICAN | | F VALUES | |
	Cohort 2 ($n = 148$)	Cohort 1 ($n = 49$)	Cohort 2 ($n = 59$)	Cohort 1 ($n = 46$)	Cohort 2 ($n = 56$)	Cohort 1 ($n = 116$)	Cohort	Ethnicity
Parents	4.39	4.26	4.36	4.21	4.03	4.03	1.31	11.18***
	(.51)	(.63)	(.45)	(.59)	(.54)	(.64)		
Adolescents	4.09	3.80	3.86	3.45	3.84	3.87	10.19**	4.21*
	(.67)	(.72)	(.66)	(.70)	(.78)	(.70)		
Discrepancy	.29	.44	.49	.73	.17	.17	4.78*	6.73***
	(.72)	(.66)	(.64)	(.95)	(.90)	(.81)		

Note: Cohort 1 = U.S.-born adolescent, longer residence in the United States; cohort 2 = foreigh-born adolescent, shorter residence in the United States. Discrepancy score equals parent score minus adolescent score. Because of missing values in some calculations, discrepancy values are not always the exact difference between the reported means. Standard deviations are in parentheses.
*$p < .05$; ** $p < .01$; *** $p < .001$.

(with a U.S.-born adolescent) had higher discrepancy scores than cohort 2 families (with a foreign-born adolescent).

The analysis also addressed our second question, concerning the generality of the cohort differences across ethnic groups. There were significant ethnic differences, $F(2, 469) = 6.73$, $p < .001$, and a significant interaction, $F(2, 469) = 3.44$, $p < .05$. The means in Table 3 show that for the Armenian and Vietnamese families, cohort 1 had higher discrepancy scores than did cohort 2; in the Mexican families, there was no cohort difference. SES was not significant.

Differences in Value Discrepancies Between Immigrant and Non-Immigrant Families

Before examining differences in value discrepancies, we analyzed parent and adolescent value scores across the 5 groups. A 5 × 2 (Ethnicity × Sex) analysis of variance of parents' scores on family obligations, with SES as a covariate, showed the expected ethnic group differences, $F(10, 697) = 59.32$, $p < .001$. Post-hoc analyses showed that Armenian and Vietnamese parents scored highest, followed (with significant differences in each case) by Mexican, African American, and European Ameri-

can parents. There were no SES or gender effects. The means are shown in Table 4.1.5.

A similar analysis of the adolescents' scores on family obligations showed a significant effect for ethnicity, $F(10, 696) = 31.99$, $p < .001$; there were no SES or gender effects. Post-hoc comparisons showed that Armenian adolescents scored highest, followed by Mexican and Vietnamese, and then by African American and European American adolescents. For both parents and adolescents, family obligation scores of African Americans were in between those of the immigrant families and the European American families (see Table 4.1.5).

To investigate our final question, the extent to which value discrepancies are associated with the immigration experience, we examined the discrepancy between parents and adolescents across the five ethnic groups. For all ethnic groups, parents endorsed family obligations more strongly than did their adolescent children. This intergenerational difference was significant within each ethnic group: Armenians, $t(192) = 6.23$, $p < .001$; Vietnamese, $t(91) = 6.80$, $p < .001$; Mexicans, $t(162) = 2.45$, $p < .02$; African Americans, $t(90) = 4.61$, $p < .001$; and European Americans, $t(135) = 3.48$, p < .001.

A 5 × 2 (Ethnicity × Gender) analysis of variance of the discrepancy score was carried out with SES as a covariate, followed by post-hoc

TABLE 4.1.5 Means and Standard Deviations for Family Obligations and Discrepancies for All Groups, With Effects for Ethnicity

	ARMENIAN (N = 197)	VIETNAMESE (N =105)	MEXICAN AMERICAN (N = 172)	AFRICAN AMERICAN (N = 92)	EUROPEAN AMERICAN (N =137)	F	ETHNIC EFFECTS
Parents	4.36 (.54)	4.29 (.53)	4.03 (.61)	3.63 (.61)	3.39 (.65)	54.99***	A, V > M > AA > E
Adolescents	4.02 (.69)	3.67 (.70)	3.86 (.72)	3.33 (.66)	3.11 (.69)	34.29***	A > M, V > AA, E
Discrepancy	.33 (.70)	.60 (.81)	.17 (.84)	.38 (.73)	.24 (.77)	3.48***	V > A, M, E

Note: Significant differences between means are shown by ">". A = Armenian; B = African American; M = Mexican American; V = Vietnamese; E = European American. Discrepancy score equals parent score minus adolescent score. Because of missing values in some calculations, discrepancy values are not always the exact difference between the reported means. Standard deviations are in parentheses.
*** $p < .001$.

comparisons. The discrepancy score differed significantly by ethnicity, $F(10, 696) = 3.51, p < .001$. However, the discrepancies were not necessarily greater in the immigrant families. Discrepancy scores for the Vietnamese families were significantly higher than for the Armenian, Mexican, and European American families, but the latter three groups did not differ among themselves. The African American discrepancy score was between the Vietnamese and the other three groups but did not differ significantly from any other group. SES and gender were not significant in any of the analyses (see Table 4.1.5).

To illustrate the differences in absolute value levels and in the discrepancy between parents and adolescents, Figure 4.1.1 shows parents' and adolescents' endorsement of family obligations by ethnic group and, for the immigrant families, by cohort. The figure provides graphic evidence that immigrants and non-immigrants differ in the absolute levels of the values. However, the discrepancy between parents and adolescents, although differing by ethnicity, is unrelated to whether the groups are immigrants or non-immigrants.

Discussion

The study of immigration, like the study of culture generally, presents unique challenges to developmental researchers, as they attempt to understand developmental processes associated with distinct cultural groups and processes that are common across groups. The present study demonstrates the importance of considering processes associated with immigration at different levels of analysis. Immigrant families need to be understood in terms of their unique history and culture, the immigration experience, and adolescent development generally.

The focus of the study was on value discrepancies between adolescents and children over issues of family obligations. Acculturation theory (Berry & Sam, 1997) and prior research (Nguyen & Williams, 1989) led to the prediction of gradual change of immigrant values toward the values of the dominant group. However, because of dissonant acculturation (Portes, 1997), that is, more rapid change among adolescents than among their parents, value discrepancies in immigrant families were

FIGURE 4.1.1   Endorsement of family obligations by parents and adolescents, by ethnicity and cohort (Co 1: Cohort 1, longer residence in the United States, U.S.-born adolescent; Co 2: Cohort 2, shorter residence in the United States, foreign-born adolescent).

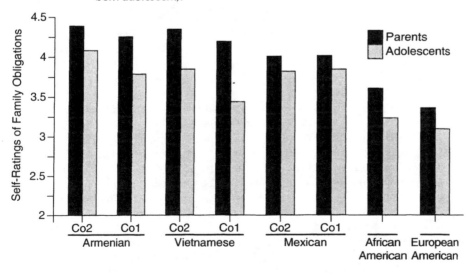

expected to increase over time. Our results with the Armenian and Vietnamese families showed this effect; the intergenerational discrepancy was greater in cohort 1 families, who had longer residence and a U.S.-born adolescent, than in cohort 2 families, with shorter residence and a foreign-born adolescent. This increase in value discrepancies is a potential source of difficulty in the acculturation process (Szapocznik & Kurtines, 1993).

The observed patterns do not necessarily apply to all the groups; in addition to the broad patterns they have in common, there are unique aspects that differentiate immigrant groups. The Vietnamese were similar to the other immigrant groups in the absolute level of endorsement of values. They were similar to the Armenians in showing a significant difference in value discrepancy between cohorts. However, they showed the largest intergenerational discrepancy compared to the other immigrant groups. It is important, therefore, to consider their particular situation. The Vietnamese families sampled in this study live in communities in which Vietnamese are a relatively smaller proportion of the population. Although there are Vietnamese institutions and businesses, such enterprises lack the density and coherence found in Armenian and Mexican communities. These factors may explain the lower levels of ethnic language proficiency and in-group social interaction among the Vietnamese, compared to other groups (Table 4.1.3). It is likely that less in-group and more out-group experience among these youth leads to greater questioning of their cultural values.

The Mexican families also show a unique pattern. In contrast to the Vietnamese and Armenians, the Mexican families did not show the expected cohort differences in intergenerational discrepancies in family obligations. The two cohorts of Mexican families were very similar in their values, even though there were greater demographic differences between the two cohorts of Mexican parents than between the two cohorts of the other immigrant families (for example, a greater difference in father's age of immigration and years in the United States). The explanation may lie in the particular experience of Mexican immigrants in the United States

(Suarez-Orozco & Suarez-Orozco, 1995). Mexican Americans have a lengthy history in the region, extending back to periods of Spanish and Mexican control. Currently, people of Mexican descent represent close to half the population in many areas of Southern California, in contrast to the small proportion of Vietnamese and Armenians (under 2% of the population in the area; Portes & Rumbaut, 1990; Schoeni et al., 1996). Furthermore, the proximity of Mexico makes for a bidirectional influence between Mexico and the United States, with Mexicans likely to be exposed to American values before coming to the United States. Under these circumstances, differences between the Mexican and U.S. cultures are likely to be less apparent, and the generational discrepancy between cohorts may thus be reduced.

Furthermore, contrary to previous research and theory suggesting that such intergenerational discrepancies are greater in immigrant families than among non-immigrants (Rosenthal et al., 1996; Szapocznik & Kurtines, 1993), we found that European American and African American families did not differ from Armenian or Mexican families. These results suggest that discrepancies in values between parents and adolescents are not necessarily related to the immigrant experience. In all ethnic groups, parents expressed more support for family obligations than did their adolescent children. This finding may reflect a near universal situation in modern societies, in which the parental generation seeks to maintain the existing norms and expectations, whereas adolescents question the obligations expected of them (Steinberg, 1990; Yau & Smetana, 1996). As a result of this process, adolescents, regardless of their cultural background, value family obligations less than do their parents.

Nevertheless, the discrepancy may have different implications for immigrant and non-immigrant families. In U.S. society generally, differences between parents and adolescents may be seen as part of a normal developmental process. Within immigrant groups, however, with a norm of greater respect for elders and obedience to authority, intergenerational differences may be less accepted. When it occurs, intergenerational conflict may be more disruptive

(Szapocznik & Kurtines, 1993; Williams & Westermeyer, 1993). Value discrepancies have been shown to be related to lower life satisfaction among adolescents in immigrant families (Phinney & Ong, 2000). Consequently, people who work with immigrant families should be sensitive to the possibility of intergenerational discrepancies but also attentive to the unique factors that shape the experience of each group.

There are a number of limitations that should be kept in mind in evaluating the results of this research. First, Southern California has the highest rate of immigration in the country and therefore cannot be taken as representative of the United States. (Schoeni et al., 1996; U.S. Bureau of the Census, 1992). However, issues similar to those faced in Southern California are likely to be faced increasingly in other regions of the country as they become increasingly diverse. Second, social class indicators differed across the groups. Yet socioeconomic status showed virtually no effect on the values studied. Kagitcibasi (1996) suggests that as collectivist cultures experience increasing prosperity, there may be a decline in material interdependence, while emotional interdependence remains strong. Our results indicate that the importance attached to family obligations is rooted in cultural values that transcend socioeconomic status.

Finally, the sample involved adolescents and parents who were willing to be involved in research. Participation required active consent and completion of questionnaires by both adolescents and parents. Across all five groups, about a quarter of the families who met the criteria did not complete the questionnaire. Schwarz, Groves, and Schumann (1998) point out that nonresponse does not indicate a bias unless there are systematic differences between respondents and nonrespondents. We have no data on possible differences, but subsequent interviews and focus group discussions with other families from the same immigrant backgrounds suggest that nonparticipation might result from privacy concerns and distrust of institutions supporting research. Such attitudes are likely to be linked to less contact with the larger society and lower levels of acculturation. Thus, participants may have been more acculturated than nonparticipants. If so, cohort differences and differences between non-immigrants and immigrants would have been even greater with a less acculturated sample, but the direction of effect would not be altered. In addition, more girls than boys participated, perhaps because girls are generally more adept at verbal tasks. There were, however, no gender differences in any of the analyses, and there is no reason to assume that gender introduced a systematic bias.

In summary, the results suggest that to understand the role immigration plays in adolescent development one must consider the different levels at which generalizations can be made. Immigrant families share with all families the need to deal with the adolescent transition to adulthood. Immigration may complicate this process, when adolescents are exposed to values that differ substantially from those of their parents. However, the impact of this process on the family will depend in important ways on the particular ethnic group. With the ongoing changes in the demographics of American society, there is a continuing need for studies that will examine psychological processes that influence developmental outcomes among immigrant groups. Such studies will be most effective if they consider processes unique to each group, processes associated with the immigration process generally, and developmental processes common across families in the United States.

REFERENCES

Bakalian, A. (1993). *Armenian-Americans.* New Brunswick, NJ: Transaction Publishers.

Bamberger, J. (1986–87). Family and kinship in an Armenian-American community. *Journal of Armenian Studies, 3,* 77–86.

Berry, J., Kwak, K., Liebkind, K., Phinney, J., Sabatier, C., Sam, D., Virta, E., & Westin, C. (1995). *The ICSEY Ques-* *tionnaire.* Working document of the International Comparative Study of Ethnocultural Youth.

Berry, J., & Sam, D. (1997). Acculturation and adaptation. In J. Berry, M. Segall, & C. Kagitcibasi (Eds.), *Handbook of cross-cultural psychology: Vol. 3. Social behavior and applications* (2nd ed.). Boston: Allyn and Bacon.

Chia, R., Wuensch, K., Childers, J., Chuang, C., Cheng, B., Cesar-Romero, J., & Nava, S. (1994). A comparison of family values among Chinese, Mexican, and American college students. *Journal of Social Behavior and Personality, 9,* 249–258.

Chiu, M., Feldman, S., & Rosenthal, D. (1992). The influence of immigration on parental behavior and adolescent distress in Chinese families residing in two Western nations. *Journal of Research on Adolescence, 2,* 205–239.

Delgado-Gaitan, C. (1994). Socializing young children in Mexican-American families: An intergenerational perspective. In P. Greenfield & R. Cocking (Eds.), *Cross-cultural roots of minority child development* (pp. 55–86). Mahwah, NJ: Erlbaum.

Feldman, S., Mont-Reynaud, R., & Rosenthal, D. (1992). When East moves West: The acculturation of values of Chinese adolescents in the U.S. and Australia. *Journal of Research on Adolescence, 2,* 147–173.

Fuligni, A., Tseng, V., & Lam, M. (1999). Attitudes towards family obligations among American adolescents with Asian, Latin American, and European backgrounds. *Child Development, 70,* 1030–1044.

Gaines, S., Jr., Marelich, W., Bledose, K., Steers, W., Henderson, M., Granrose, C., Barajas, L., Hicks, D., Lyde, M., Yum, N., Riso, D., Garcia, B., Farris, K., & Page, M. (1997). Links between race/ethnicity and cultural values as mediated by racial/ethnic identity and moderated by gender. *Journal of Personality and Social Psychology, 72,* 1460–1476.

Garcia Coll, C., Lamberty, G., Jenkins, R., McAdoo, H., Crnic, H., Wasik, B., & Garcia, H. (1996). An integrative model for the study of developmental competencies in minority children. *Child Development, 67,* 1891–1914.

Georgas, J. (1989). Changing family values in Greece: From collectivist to individualist. *Journal of Cross-Cultural Psychology, 20,* 80–91.

Georgas, J., Berry, J., Shaw, A., Christakopoulou, S., & Mylonas, K. (1996). Acculturation of Greek family values. *Journal of Cross-Cultural Psychology, 20,* 80–91.

Greenfield, P., & Cocking, R. (Eds.), (1994). *Cross-cultural roots of minority child development.* Hillsdale, NJ: Erlbaum.

Grotevant, H., & Cooper, C. (1985). Patterns of interaction in family relationships and the development of identity exploration in adolescence. *Child Development, 56,* 415–428.

Gurin, P., Hurtado, A., & Peng, T. (1994). Group contacts and ethnicity in the social identities of Mexicanos and Chicanos. *Personality and Social Psychology Bulletin, 20,* 521–532.

Harrison, A., Wilson, M., Pine, C., Chan, S., & Buriel, R. (1990). Family ecologies of ethnic minority children. *Child Development, 61,* 347–362.

Hatchett, S., & Jackson, J. (1993). African American extended kin systems. In H. McAdoo (Ed.), *Family ethnicity: Strength in diversity.* Thousand Oaks, CA: Sage.

Hauser, S., Powers, S., & Noam, G. (1991). *Adolescents and their families: Paths of ego development.* New York: Free Press.

Hofstede, G. (1980). *Culture's consequences: International differences in work-related values.* Thousand Oaks, CA: Sage.

Kagitcibasi, C. (1996). *Family and human development across cultures.* Mahwah, NJ: Erlbaum.

Kagitcibasi, C. (1997). Individualism and collectivism. In J. Berry, M. Segall, & C. Kagitcibasi (Eds.), *Handbook of cross-cultural psychology: Vol. 3. Social behavior and applications* (2nd ed.). Boston: Allyn and Bacon.

Kim, U., Triandis, H., Kagitcibasi, C., Choi, S., & Yoon, G. (1994). *Individualism and collectivism: Theory, methods, and applications.* Thousand Oaks, CA: Sage.

Kluckhohn, F., & Strodtbeck, F. (1961). *Variations in value orientations.* Evanston, IL: Row, Peterson.

Kurtz, S. (1992). *All the mothers are one.* New York: Columbia University Press.

Laursen, B., & Collins, W. (1994). Interpersonal conflict during adolescence. *Psychological Bulletin, 115,* 197–209.

Liebkind, L. (1992). Refugee mental health and cultural identity. *Psychiatria Fennica, 23,* 47–58.

Marin, G., & Marin, B. (1991). *Research with Hispanic populations.* Newbury Park, CA: Sage.

Marin, G., Sabogal, F., Marin, B., Otero-Sabogal, R., & Perez-Stable, E. (1987). Development of a short acculturation scale for Hispanics. *Hispanic Journal of Behavioral Sciences, 9,* 183–205.

Matsuoka, J. (1990). Differential acculturation among Vietnamese refugees. *Social Work, 35,* 341–345.

Nguyen, N., & Williams, H. (1989). Transition from East to West: Vietnamese adolescents and their parents. *Journal of the American Academy of Child and Adolescent Psychiatry, 28,* 505–515.

Okagaki, L., & Sternberg, R. (1993). Parental beliefs and children's school performance. *Child Development, 64,* 35–56.

Phinney, J., & Ong, A. (2000). *Family obligation and life satisfaction among adolescents from immigrant and non-immigrant families: Direct and moderated effects.* Manuscript submitted for publication.

Portes, A. (1997). Immigration theory for a new century: Some problems and opportunities. *International Migration Review, 31,* 799–825.

Portes, A., & Rumbaut, R. (1990). *Immigrant American: A portrait.* Berkeley: University of California Press.

Portes, A., & Schauffler, R. (1994). Language and the second generation: Bilingualism yesterday and today. *International Migration Review, 28,* 640–661.

Ramirez, O. (1989). Mexican American children and adolescents. In J. Gibbs & L. Huang (Eds.), *Children of color: Psychological interventions with minority youth* (pp. 224–250). San Francisco: Jossey-Bass.

Rogler, L. (1994). International migrations: A framework for directing research. *American Psychologist, 49,* 701–708.

Rosenthal, D., Ranieri, N., & Klimidis, S. (1996). Vietnamese adolescents in Australia: Relationships between perceptions of self and parental values, intergenerational conflict, and gender dissatisfaction. *International Journal of Psychology, 31,* 81–91.

Rueschenberg, E., & Buriel, R. (1989). Mexican-American family functioning and acculturation: A family system perspective. *Hispanic Journal of Behavioral Sciences, 11,* 232–244.

Rumbaut, R. (1994). The crucible within: Ethnic identity, self-esteem, and segmented assimilation among children of immigrants. *International Migration Review, 28,* 748–794.

Rumbaut, R. (1997). Assimilation and its discontents: Between rhetoric and reality. *International Migration Review, 31,* 923–960.

Sabogal, F., Marin, G., Otero-Sabogal, R., Marin, B., & Perez-Stable, E. (1987). Hispanic familism and acculturation: What changes and what doesn't? *Hispanic Journal of Behavioral Sciences, 9,* 397–412.

Schoeni, R., McCarthy, K., & Vernez, G. (1996). *The mixed economic progress of immigrants.* Santa Monica, CA: Rand.

Schwarz, N., Groves, R., & Schumann, H. (1998). In D. Gilbert, S. Fiske, & G. Lindzey (Eds.), *The handbook of social psychology* (4th ed.) (pp. 143–179). New York: McGraw-Hill.

Shweder, R. (1990). Cultural psychology—What is it? In J. Stigler, R. Shweder, & G. Herdt (Eds.), *Cultural psychology: Essays on comparative human development.* New York: Cambridge University Press.

Sims, S. A. (1979). Sharing in black children: The impact of reference group appeals and other environmental factors. In A. Boykin, A. Franklin, & J. Yates (Eds.), *Research directions of black psychologists* (pp. 146–162). New York: Russell Sage.

Smetana, J., & Asquith, P. (1994). Adolescents' and parents' conceptions of parental authority and personal autonomy. *Child Development, 67,* 1262–1275.

Smith, J., & Edmonston, B. (Eds.). (1997). *The new Americans.* Washington, DC: National Academy Press.

Smith, P., & Schwartz, S. (1997). Values. In J. Berry, M. Segall, & C. Kagitcibasi (Eds.), *Handbook of cross-cultural psychology: Vol. 3. Social behavior and applications* (2nd ed.). Boston, Allyn and Bacon.

Steinberg, L. (1990). Autonomy, conflict, and harmony in the family relationship. In S. Feldman & G. Elliott (Eds.), *At the threshold: The developing adolescent* (pp. 255–276). Cambridge, MA: Harvard University Press.

Suarez-Orozco, C., & Suarez-Orozco, M. (1995). *Transformations: Immigration, family life, and achievement motivation among Latino adolescents.* Stanford, CA: Stanford University Press.

Super, C., & Harkness, S. (1997). The cultural structuring of child development. In J. Berry, P. Dasen, & T. Saraswathi (Eds.), *Handbook of cross-cultural psychology, Vol. 2. Basic process and human development* (2nd ed.) (pp. 1–39). Boston: Allyn and Bacon.

Szapocznik, J., & Kurtines, W. (1993). Family psychology and cultural diversity. *American Psychologist, 48,* 400–407.

Triandis, H. (1990). Cross-cultural studies of individualism and collectivism. In J. Berman (Ed.), *Nebraska Symposium of Motivation: Vol. 37. Cross-cultural perspectives* (pp. 41–133). Lincoln: University of Nebraska Press.

Triandis, H. (1995). *Individualism and collectivism.* Boulder, CO: Westview.

U.S. Bureau of the Census. (1992). *Census of the population: 1990.* Washington, DC: U.S. Government Printing Office.

Wainryb, C., & Turiel, E. (1994). Dominance, subordination, and concepts of personal entitlements in cultural contexts. *Child Development, 65,* 1701–1722.

White, J., & Parham, T. (1990). *The psychology of blacks: An African American perspective.* Englewood Cliffs, NJ: Prentice Hall.

Whiting, B., & Whiting, J. (1975). *Children of six cultures: A psychocultural analysis.* Cambridge, MA: Harvard University Press.

Williams, C., & Westermeyer, J. (1993). Psychiatric problems among Southeast Asian refugees. *Journal of Nervous Mental Disorders, 171,* 79–85.

Yau, J., & Smetana, J. (1996). Adolescent-parent conflict among Chinese Adolescents in Hong Kong. *Child Development, 67,* 1262–1275.

Zhou, M. (1997). Segmented assimilation: Issues, controversies, and recent research on the new second generation. *International Migration Review, 31,* 923–960.

Zhou, M., & Bankston, C. (1994). Social capital and the adaptation of the second generation: The case of Vietnamese youth in New Orleans. *International Migration Review, 28,* 821–845.

THINKING CRITICALLY

1. How do the authors explain the finding that adolescents in all the cultures studied favored values supporting family obligations less than their parents did? How would you explain it?

2. How might influences outside the family lead immigrant adolescents to have values that are different than their parents' values? Consider peers, school, and media.

3. What is meant by "dissonant acculturation"? Was support for this concept found in this reading?

Religious Beliefs in Emerging Adulthood

In American society, as in many other societies, cultural beliefs often take the form of religious beliefs. Americans tend to be more religious than people in most other industrialized countries, but emerging adulthood is the period of life when religious participation in the United States tends to be at its lowest. This reading explores various aspects of emerging adults' religious beliefs and locates the relatively low religious involvement of emerging adults in a collision between the demands of religious beliefs and emerging adults' focus on learning to think for themselves.

Reading 4.2

A Congregation of One: Individualized Religious Beliefs Among Emerging Adults

J. J. Arnett and L. A. Jensen

It is well established that the late teens and early twenties are ages of relatively low religious participation in American society. Even if they attended religious services frequently as children and adolescents, in their late teens and twenties many young people fall off in their religious participation (Gallup & Castelli, 1989; Gallup & Lindsay, 1999; Hoge, Dinges, Johnson, & Gonzales, 1998a; 1998b; Hoge, Johnson, & Luidens, 1993). Most young people leave home after high school (Goldscheider & Goldscheider, 1999), and the change of residence often breaks the tie to the religious institution they had attended while growing up (Hoge et al. 1993). Leaving home also removes the encouragement and perhaps the coercion of parents to attend religious services.

Other reasons for the drop off in religious participation in the late teens and early twenties include becoming busy with other activities, doubting previously held beliefs, and simply losing interest (Hoge et al., 1998a, 1998b). However, religious participation tends to rise in the late twenties, as young people marry, have children, settle down personally and geographically and express an increased spiritual need for religious involvement (Gallup & Castelli, 1989; Hoge et al., 1998a, 1998b; Hoge et al., 1993; Stolzenberg, Blair-Loy, & Waite, 1995; Wilson & Sandomirsky, 1991).

Most studies on the religiosity of young people in their late teens and twenties have focused on this issue of why their religious participation tends to fall and then rise again. Here, we focus more directly on the religious beliefs and attitudes of young people. How important a part does religion play in their lives? Do they value religious beliefs differently than religious participation? What do they actually believe,

Arnett, J. J., & Jensen, L. A. (2001). *A congregation of one: Individualized religious beliefs among emerging adults.* Manuscript submitted for publication.

with regard to religion? How do they view religious institutions?

The conceptual framework used here for understanding young people's religious beliefs is the concept of *emerging adulthood*. Emerging adulthood has been proposed as a term for the new period that has opened up in the life course of people in industrialized societies during the past half-century, bridging adolescence and young adulthood (Arnett, 1998, 2000a, 2000b). During recent decades the median ages of marriage and first birth in the United States have risen to unprecedented levels, into the late twenties (Arnett, 2000a). Similarly, rates of participation in higher education following secondary school have steadily increased, so that by now a majority of young Americans obtain at least some higher education (Bianchi & Spain, 1996). As a consequence of these changes, the late teens and early twenties are no longer a period of intensive preparation for and entry into stable and enduring adult roles but are more typically a period of exploring various life possibilities while postponing role transitions into the mid-to-late twenties (Arnett, 1998; 2000a; 2000b).

Exploration is a key part of emerging adulthood. In areas such as love, work, and ideology, many emerging adults explore diverse possibilities. The focus during emerging adulthood tends to be on self-development, and on becoming independent and self-sufficient (Arnett, 1998). Part of this process, in the view of most emerging adults, is forming a distinctive set of beliefs about religious issues. Several studies have indicated that deciding on one's own beliefs and values is one of the criteria young people view as most important to becoming an adult (Arnett, 1997, 1998; Greene, Wheatley, & Aldara, 1992).

Not only is emerging adulthood an especially self-focused period of the life course, but today's emerging adults are coming of age in an especially individualistic period in American society (Alwin, 1988; Bellah, Madsen, Sullivan, Swidler, & Tipton, 1985; Jensen, 1995). In the course of the 20th century, the qualities American parents most desired to teach their children changed from obedience and respect for others

to independence and self-esteem (Alwin, 1988). With regard to religious beliefs in particular, surveys indicate that a strong majority of Americans agree that individuals should form their religious beliefs independently of religious institutions (Gallup & Castelli, 1989).

In the present study the goal was to explore the content of emerging adults' religious beliefs. Based on previous studies and on the nature of emerging adulthood as a time of focusing on self-development and self-sufficiency, we expected emerging adults to emphasize forming their own beliefs independently of their parents. Specifically, we expected to find only a weak relationship between childhood religious socialization and religious beliefs in emerging adulthood. We also expected emerging adults to have only a tenuous tie to religious institutions, even when they had been raised in a particular religious tradition, because institutional membership would be viewed as a compromise of their individuality. Furthermore, we expected their religious beliefs to be highly diverse, as they draw from a variety of cultural sources in the course of constructing their own distinctive beliefs.

Method

Participants

The participants were 140 persons aged 20–28. General characteristics of the sample are shown in Table 4.2.1. Close to half of the participants were married, and about one-fourth had at least one child. Two-thirds of the participants were employed full-time, and one-fourth part-time. Twenty-eight percent were in school full-time, 8% part-time. "Some college" was the modal level of education, indicated by 52% of the participants. There was a broad range of variability in the social class of the participants' families of origin, as indicated by father's and mother's education.

Procedure

The data presented here were collected as part of a larger study on emerging adults in their twenties. The study took place in a medium-sized city

TABLE 4.2.1 Background Characteristics of the Sample

Gender	Percent	Employment	Percent
male	53	full	67
female	47	part	24
Ethnicity		none	9
white	94	*Marital status*	
black	5	married	60
other	1	single	40
Current educational status		*Number of children*	
in school full-time	28	none	73
in school part-time	8	one	14
not in school	65	two or more	13
Mother's education		*Father's education*	
less than h.s. degree	8	less than h.s.	8
high school degree	23	high school degree	24
some college	23	some college	15
college degree	27	college degree	24
some grad. school or		some grad. school or	
grad. school degree	19	grad. school degree	30

in the Midwest. Potential participants were identified through enrollment lists from the two local high schools for the previous 3–10 years. All persons on the enrollment lists who had a current address in the area that could be identified through phone book listings or through contacting their parents were sent a letter describing the study, then contacted by phone. Seventy-two percent of the persons contacted agreed to participate in the study. Data collection took place in the first author's office or the participant's home, depending on the participant's preference.

Measures

The study included an interview and a questionnaire. Six items on the questionnaire pertained to religion, and concerned religious attendance, the importance ascribed to religion, the certainty of the participant's beliefs, and belief in God (Table 4.2.2). Two questions in the interview pertained to religion, specifically participants' childhood exposure to religion and participants' current religious beliefs (Table 4.2.3).

Coding categories for each interview question were developed from reading through the interviews and identifying common themes.

The two authors independently coded all participants' responses to the two interview questions. Rate of agreement was over 80% for each question.

The full text of the interview question on childhood exposure to religious socialization was "Were you brought up to believe any particular set of religious beliefs, or did your parents more or less leave it up to you?" The categories for the coding of this interview question were:

- *Low exposure.* Parents rarely or never took children to church; religion clearly was not important to them.
- *Moderate exposure.* Parents made some effort to take children to church, expose them to religious ideas, but not on a regular basis and/or parents did not attend themselves and/or religion did not seem very important to parents. Parents may have taken children to church now and then in a perfunctory way.
- *High exposure.* Parents took children to church on a regular and fairly frequent basis, clearly regarded religion as important.

The full text of the question on current religious beliefs was "What are your religious or

TABLE 4.2.2 Religiosity of Emerging Adults, Questionnaire Items

	PERCENT
How often do you attend religious services?	
About 3–4 ×/mo.	19
About 1–2 ×/mo.	10
Once every few months	20
About 1–2 ×/yr. or less	50
How important is it to you to attend religious services?	
Very important	16
Quite important	11
Somewhat important	24
Not at all important	50
How important to you are your religious beliefs?	
Very important	30
Quite important	22
Somewhat important	30
Not at all important	18
How important is religious faith in your daily life?	
Very important	27
Quite important	20
Somewhat important	21
Not at all important	32
How certain are you about your religious beliefs?	
Very certain	38
Quite certain	33
Somewhat uncertain	21
Very uncertain	8
To what extent do you believe that God or some higher power watches over you and guides your life?	
Strongly believe this	52
Somewhat believe this	22
Somewhat skeptical of this	16
Definitely do not believe this	10

TABLE 4.2.3 Religious Socialization and Beliefs, Coded Interview Questions

	PERCENT
Were you brought up to believe any particular set of religious beliefs, or did your parents more or less leave it up to you?	
High exposure	64
Moderate exposure	13
Low exposure	23
What are your religious or spiritual beliefs now, if any?	
Agnostic/atheist	24
Deist	29
Liberal Christian	26
Conservative Christian	22

spiritual beliefs now, if any?" The categories for the coding of this question were:

- *Agnostic/atheist.* Person explicitly rejects any belief in religion or declares uncertainty about what they believe and/or they do not believe it is possible to know anything about God.
- *Deist.* Person declares a general belief in God or "spirituality," but only in a general sense, not in the context of any religious tradition. Person may refer to self as "Christian," but beliefs do not reflect traditional Christian dogma, and may even explicitly reject parts of it. May also reject organized religion generally. May include idiosyncratic personal elements drawn from various sources, for example, Eastern religions, extra-terrestrials, witchcraft.
- *Liberal Christian.* Person describes self as Christian (or as adherent of particular denomination, e.g., Methodist, Lutheran, Catholic). However, person may express skepticism about the institution of the church and/or about some aspects of Christian dogma, for example, the idea that Christianity is the only true set of beliefs. May express favorable or at least tolerant view of beliefs of other (non-Christian) faiths.
- *Conservative Christian.* Person expresses belief in traditional Christian dogma, for example, that Jesus is the son of God and the only way to salvation. Person may mention being saved, or refer to afterlife of heaven and hell. Person may mention that Christianity is the only true faith.

Only one participant in the study had a Jewish background, and his response was coded as "deist."

Results

First the quantitative results are presented, then qualitative results from the interviews.

Quantitative Results

The emerging adults in this study were highly diverse in their religious beliefs, attitudes, and practices, as shown in Tables 4.2.2 and 4.2.3. Half reported rarely or never attending religious services, but the other half attended occasionally or regularly, with nearly one-fifth attending 3–4 times per month. Similarly, half reported that it was not at all important to them to attend religious services, whereas for the other half the importance of attendance varied from somewhat important to very important.

Religious beliefs were more likely to be important to them than attendance at religious services. Although 50% indicated that it was "not at all important" to attend religious services, only 18% indicated that their religious beliefs were "not at all important" to them. Also, 47% reported that religious faith was "quite" or "very" important in their daily lives, compared to 27% for whom attendance at religious services was "quite" or "very" important. Participants also varied in the degree of certainty they expressed about their religious beliefs, but over 70% were "very" or "quite" certain. Over half (52%) indicated that they strongly believed that "God or some higher power" watches over them and guides their lives, but the views of the other participants varied from somewhat believing this to definitely not believing it.

Nearly two-thirds of participants were coded as having had high exposure to religious socialization, from their response to the interview question about whether or not their parents had brought them up to believe any particular set of religious beliefs (Table 4.2.3). In terms of their current beliefs, participants were spread more or less evenly among the four categories: agnostic/atheist, deist, liberal Christian, and conservative Christian (Table 4.2.3).

Childhood religious socialization (the coded question from the interview) was ana-lyzed in chi-square tests in relation to current religious attendance (the questionnaire item) and religious views (the coded interview question and the five questionnaire items on religious views). There was no relationship between childhood religious socialization and current religious attendance, nor between childhood religious socialization and any of the six items on religious views.

Age, marital status, parenthood status, educational attainment, mother's education, and father's education were all analyzed in relation to the variables concerning religious attendance and religious views. Chi-square tests were used for the analyses involving marital status (married vs. unmarried) and parenthood status (no children vs. one or more children). Bivariate correlations were used for the analyses involving age, educational attainment, mother's education, and father's education.

Age and educational attainment were unrelated to any of the religious variables. Marital status was related to religious beliefs (the coded interview question), with married persons more likely to be conservative and single persons more likely to be deists ($chi\text{-}square$ (3, 122) = 11.79, $p < .01$). Married persons were also more likely than single persons to attend religious services ($chi\text{-}square$ (3, 116) = 11.34, $p < .05$), to indicate that it is important to them to attend religious services ($chi\text{-}square$ (3, 116) = 8.52, $p < .05$), and to indicate that religious beliefs are important to them ($chi\text{-}square$ (3, 136) = 11.10, $p < .05$).

Parenthood status was also related to the religious variables. Persons with children were more likely than those without children to be religiously conservative, and less likely to be agnostics or deists ($chi\text{-}square$ (3, 125) = 16.64, $p < .001$). Persons with children were also more likely than those without children to attend religious services ($chi\text{-}square$ (3, 119) = 11.00, $p < .05$), to indicate that it is important to them to attend religious services ($chi\text{-}square$ (3, 119) = 11.34, $p < .05$), to indicate that religious beliefs are important to them ($chi\text{-}square$ (3, 136), $p < .05$), to indicate that religious beliefs are important in their daily lives ($chi\text{-}square$ (3, 94) = 9.58, $p < .05$), and to believe that God or some higher power watches over them and guides their lives (*chi-square* (3, 119) = 15.67, $p < .01$).

Mother's education was inversely related to several religious variables, with persons with mothers who had relatively lower education being more likely to indicate that religious beliefs are important to them ($r = .22$, $p < .05$), that religious beliefs are important in their daily lives ($r = .24$, $p < .05$), and that they believe God or some higher power watches over them and guides their lives ($r = .21$, $p < .05$). Similarly, father's education was inversely related to believing it is important to attend religious services ($r = .22$, $p < .05$), to indicating that religious beliefs are important to them ($r = .22$, $p < .05$), and to believing that God or some higher power watches over them and guides their lives ($r = .21$, $p < .05$).

Qualitative Results

In addition to the quantitative results presented above, the interview responses contained qualitative information about emerging adults' beliefs that provides important insights into their views on religious issues. Four main themes were identified from the interview responses: the high degree of individualization of their beliefs, skepticism about religious institutions, the dubious meaning of denominational affiliation, and the lack of relation between childhood religious socialization and current religious beliefs. In the sections below, qualitative responses illustrating the first three themes were taken from the interview question about current beliefs, and qualitative responses illustrating the fourth theme were taken from the interview question about childhood religious socialization.

Emerging Adults' Beliefs Are Highly Individualized. As noted in the quantitative results, emerging adults' religious beliefs were found to be diverse, falling into four more or less equal categories: agnostic/atheist, deist, liberal, and conservative. However, these four categories are only a rough approximation of the diversity of their beliefs. Within many of these categories, concepts and practices from differ-

ent religious and non-religious traditions were combined in unique and fascinating ways.

One reason their beliefs were highly individualized was that the emerging adults expressed a high value on thinking for themselves with regard to religious questions, and on forming a unique set of religious beliefs rather than accepting a ready-made dogma. For example, Ted described himself as a Christian, but he also said he believed that "You don't have to be one religion. Take a look at all of them, see if there is something in them you like—almost like an *a la carte* belief system. I think all religions have things that are good about them." Janie said "I was raised Catholic . . . and I guess if I had to consider myself anything I would consider myself Catholic," but she also said "I don't have any really strong beliefs because I believe that whatever you feel, it's personal. . . . Everybody has their own idea of God and what God is, and because you go to a church doesn't define it any better because you still have your own personal beliefs of how you feel about it and what's right for you personally."

In forming their individualized beliefs, emerging adults often combined Christian beliefs with Eastern ideas such as reincarnation or with ideas taken from popular culture. Jenny's father was a minister in a Disciple of Christ church and she went to church every Sunday growing up, but at age 23 her beliefs had become a singular pastiche of New Age, Eastern, and Christian notions. "A lot of my beliefs border on what would be labeled as witchcraft," she said. "I believe that objects can capture energy and hold it. . . . I do believe it's possible to communicate with people who have died. . . . I do believe in reincarnation. . . . I believe I've had past lives. . . . I am what I would label a 'guardian angel,' and there are certain people that I'm supposed to help out." Lenny described himself as a Christian, but he also said "I feel that there is kind of more like the Star Wars thing, 'The Force,' there's just this kind of planetary aura, that everyone's thoughts and actions and feelings generate this energy. . . . That's what influences other things around the universe."

Sam also drew his religious beliefs from popular culture. "There's a movie with Albert

Brooks, *Defending Your Life,* and it was great. He goes up to heaven and he has to defend all his actions throughout the course of his life. And after I saw this, I wondered how I would do in that situation. . . . I really like the idea that it's psychological in the way that [heaven] goes by whatever your perception of reality is at that point in time. So like, if medieval guys went to heaven, maybe there was a big omnipotent God being, but now if we go to heaven there's George Burns or whatever. I wouldn't mind that."

Emerging Adults Are Skeptical of Religious Institutions.   Many emerging adults expressed skepticism about the value of religious institutions. This skepticism was sometimes based on negative experiences with religious institutions or religious believers. Such experiences had led some of them to view religious institutions as bastions of corruption and hypocrisy. Tracy had been disillusioned about organized religion because of "hypocritical things in Christians that I knew." She gave as an example her grandmother, who "only reads the Bible and has it in her lap every day," yet freely casts racist aspersions on Black people. Vicky described herself as "brought up Baptist" and said she "still believes in God," but she also says she rarely attends church. "I don't feel that going to church every Sunday makes you a good Christian. You can go to church every Sunday and be a hypocritical asshole, as far as I'm concerned." Ray was skeptical of religious institutions more generally. "I don't think that organized religion as a whole is a good thing, I really don't. . . . I just think that having an organized religion is like having a gang. It's your beliefs against their beliefs, and whoever is left standing at the end is the one whose beliefs are the best."

Terry had negative memories of her church experiences in childhood. "I remember going to church [as a child] and being bored, and seeing everybody around me being bored." By emerging adulthood she had rejected the Catholicism of her youth because of "the guilt. I got so sick of feeling guilty all the time. And, oh God, 'lust is so awful.' I really feel like there

are things that are natural to us, because I really believe that yes, we are human, but we also still have animal tendencies, and you can't guilt those out of people. And I decided that yes, I did have an animal in me and I wasn't going to guilt my animal any more because it made me unhappy. So I gave up being Catholic."

Another reason for their skepticism about religious institutions was that they tended to view participation in any institution as a compromise of their individuality. As Jerry said, "I'm just not real big on the church thing. I think that's a manmade thing. I don't need anyone telling me what's right or wrong. I know what's right and wrong." Similarly, Chris viewed clerical exhortations as a threat to his individual autonomy. "I believe in God, I just don't necessarily believe in an organized religion. . . . Jesus was probably an actual thing, but I don't think you have to go to church to worship God and his teachings. I think God is in here, in how you feel, and not what somebody at the pulpit's telling you God is."

Many expressed the view that they could be religious or "spiritual" on their own, without institutional membership. In John's view, "Just being outside is more spiritual to me than going in and sitting in a church with a bunch of people and somebody preaching from the Bible. I think it's almost more religious and more spiritual for me to go out in the woods by myself or go fishing. . . . I kind of like to be independent and free to think on my own. I don't want to inherit my spiritual values like so many kids do." Similarly, Joanne observed, "I'm the kind of person that feels that you don't have to go to church to be religious. I mean, it's just something that you do for yourself. It's not necessary to be in a certain place to be religious."

Denominational Affiliation Means Little.   Many emerging adults identified themselves as being part of a particular denomination. If asked to specify their denominational affiliation on a questionnaire or in a telephone survey, they would have a ready answer. However, when they described their beliefs in the interview format it often became clear that their beliefs bore little similarity to the traditions of their supposed denomination. For example, Leanne described herself as a Catholic and said that she attended mass weekly. However, her beliefs sounded more Unitarian than Catholic: "Religion is like a shoe that fits everyone differently, and there isn't one good or bad religion. In fact, if you look at it, everybody worships the same god, whether they call him 'Buddha' or whatever." Ken said he was raised Methodist and called himself "a good Christian." Yet he also said, "I believe in God, but not fanatically. I mean, I also believe in aliens. Actually, there are two theories that I believe in. One is that aliens came down here and they had their way with some monkeys, and slowly things changed. Or that we just evolved."

Charles said he "was brought up Episcopalian . . . and if I still went to church regularly I would still go to the Episcopal church." Yet he also said, "As far as God and is there a God, I don't know." His identification of himself as a Christian was equally equivocal: "I think I'm a Christian—not in the classic sense of the word, but I believe in Christ and I believe there was some person who said they were the savior and professed to die for somebody else's sins. Whether it was a divine thing, I don't know."

Childhood Religious Socialization Has Limited Effects.

As noted in the section on quantitative results, childhood religious socialization did not significantly predict religious attendance or beliefs in emerging adulthood, even though nearly two-thirds of the participants had high exposure to religious socialization during childhood. Although this may seem odd, it is easier to understand after examining the qualitative results. Like so many aspects of their religious beliefs, the lack of association between their childhood religious beliefs and their current beliefs was a reflection of their individualism, of their resolve to think for themselves and form their own beliefs.

Jim said he was a "full-blown Catholic" as a child, but when he was 17 years old "I just flat told Mom I wasn't going to go any more. It was a waste of time. I didn't like it. I went because I was under Mom and Dad's rules. I did what

they said to do, went to Sunday school and stuff like that. [But] I can go to church all you want, and I'm still going to believe what I believe. You're not going to change me." Trudy said she and her husband were "exploring churches right now. I think we're still trying to find out exactly what we believe, and not just what we were brought up to believe."

The typical pattern was that they attended church throughout childhood, but stopped going as soon as parental encouragement or coercion eased, usually during adolescence. Steve said "I had my 'perfect attendance' pins for the Methodist Sunday school up until the day I was confirmed, and then they said it was up to me whether or not I go to church and I haven't been back since. . . . It's kind of hard to smoke pot until four o'clock in the morning and get up at seven and go sing 'Amazing Grace' or whatever. . . . I guess I would still consider myself Methodist, but in all honesty I'd probably have to say that I'm agnostic." Lisa said "I made a deal with my mom in high school that if I got confirmed I would never have to go to church again. And she said okay, so after I was confirmed I didn't have to get up on Sunday mornings any more and I didn't have to fight with her about 'I don't want to go to church.'"

Often, the disparity between their religious socialization as children and their current beliefs was sharp and striking. Tom said "I was brought up as a Christian. I was baptized when I was seven years old, went to church every Wednesday, every Sunday, and Sunday night. I had to go for years and years in a row. . . . I'm surprised I'm not a complete saint right now, as much church as I was subjected to." Now, however, he says, "I'm not religious at all. Zero. I question the credibility of religion now. I can't say for sure if I believe there is a supreme being out there or not. I just don't know." Kurt said that he "went to church every Sunday until I was 16." By now, however, he has decided "I'm an atheist. . . . I look at the Bible as just being a myth. It doesn't make any sense. I don't see how there can be a God, with the condition of the world. Especially not an all-knowing, all-powerful God."

However, emerging adults' religious development was not always away from religious institutions. Sara said "My parents were atheists. They didn't believe in God." Now, in emerging adulthood, she attends an evangelical church and says her own beliefs are "definitely that there's a God, and that he controls every part of your life, of everyone's life. I believe in the Bible." For her, church involvement was a refuge from "all this gloom that I had in my home life. . . . It was a wonderful influence, and I am so close to some families at church that just really helped me out. They give this unconditional love. That's something I still don't understand, how people that barely knew me could give me unconditional love because of Jesus, more so than my own parents."

Furthermore, not all parents' attempts at religious socialization had come to naught. Ray was raised in a family where "our faith was certainly present in the home," and said that "I still believe in the principles and doctrines taught by our church." Karen said "I was brought up Presbyterian, and I belong to the same church I've gone to since I was a child." Pete was brought up in the conservative Lutheran–Missouri Synod church, and described his current beliefs as "essentially the same." But generally, emerging adults formed their own beliefs independently of the religious socialization provided by their parents, and overall there was no correlation between childhood religious socialization and current beliefs.

For the one-fourth of persons in the study who had children, parenthood had inspired some of them to resume church attendance. As noted in the quantitative results, parents were more likely than non-parents to attend religious services, and more religious in other respects as well. For example, Karen and her husband had recently begun attending church with their four-year-old daughter, because "we both decided that we better start going because we have a child now and we need to give her some type of feeling of church." Some parents viewed religious socialization as part of their children's moral socialization. Tim said he and his wife planned to begin attending with their young daughters, be-

cause "I think religion has a lot to do with ethics and morals and values. . . . I think it has a lot to do with teaching them right from wrong."

Discussion

What do emerging adults in American society believe about religious issues? "Whatever they choose" might be a concise summary of the study presented here. The salient impression of the results is that emerging adults form their beliefs independently, with little influence from their parents or religious institutions. Consequently, their beliefs are extremely diverse, as they form unique combinations of beliefs from various religious traditions and from other sources as well, including popular culture. It is not just that religious traditions have become "symbolic toolboxes" (Hervieu-Leger, 1993, p. 141) from which young people can draw freely, but that these traditions are only one source among many from which young people construct their religious beliefs.

Overall, their beliefs fell more or less evenly into four categories: agnostic/atheist, deist, liberal Christian, and conservative Christian. Within these categories, there was also considerable diversity. The diversity of religious beliefs among the emerging adults' in this study reflects the fact that they have grown up in a pluralistic society. No matter what religious socialization they have received in their families, they have also been exposed to diverse influences from friends, school, and popular culture. Out of these diverse materials, they construct their own beliefs by the time they reach emerging adulthood. Often, the beliefs they form bear little or no resemblance to what their parents believed and taught them to believe (Hoge et al., 1998b; Hoge et al., 1993).

Perhaps it should not be so surprising that there is little relationship between childhood religious socialization and religious beliefs in emerging adulthood. As young people grow beyond childhood into adolescence and emerging adulthood, the strength of family socialization wanes while the influence of socialization sources outside the family increases

(Arnett, 1995; Larson, Richards, Moneta, Holmbeck, & Duckett, 1996). Because young people view it as both their right and their responsibility to form their beliefs and values independently of their parents (Arnett, 1997, 1998), they pick and choose from the ideas they discover as they go along, and combine them to form their own unique, individualized set of beliefs, "an *a la carte* belief system."

Emerging adults view their independence from their parents' beliefs as a good and necessary thing. In their view, simply to accept what their parents have taught them about religion and carry on the same religious tradition as their parents would represent a kind of failure, an abdication of their responsibility to think for themselves, become independent from their parents, and decide on their own beliefs. Quite consciously and deliberately, they seek to form a set of beliefs about religious questions that will be distinctly their own.

This emphasis on individualism also underlies their rejection of religious institutions. Just as it would be wrong in their eyes for them to accept wholesale the beliefs of their parents, so many of them view participation in religious institutions as an intolerable compromise of their individuality. Participating in a religious institution inherently means subscribing to a common set of beliefs, declaring that you hold certain beliefs that other members of the institution also hold. To the majority of emerging adults, this is anathema. They prefer to think of their beliefs as unique, the product of their own individual questioning and exploring.

Will they return to religious institutions as they grow beyond emerging adulthood? Other studies have indicated that young people often return to religious participation once they marry and have children (Gallup & Castelli, 1989; Hoge et al., 1998a, 1998b; Hoge et al., 1993; Stolzenberg, Blair-Loy, & Waite, 1995; Wilson & Sandomirsky, 1991). In the present study, too, being married and having children were both related to higher likelihood of religious participation. Thus it appears that for some members of the current cohort of young people, as in previous cohorts, their departure from religious participation is temporary, to be resumed once they enter adult roles of marriage and parenthood. However, like the Baby Boomers before them, they may retain the individualism of their beliefs even as they (and their children) return to religious institutions (Roof, 1993).

As a consequence of their individualism, their beliefs may not fit neatly into denominational categories even when they attend services regularly. Indeed, an especially interesting and surprising finding of the study was the lack of validity of denominational affiliation. For decades, national surveys have included questions about denomination affiliation (e.g., Gallup & Castelli, 1989; Gallup & Lindsay, 1999). On the basis of these stated affiliations, relationships have been drawn to a wide range of variables, such as social class and political views. However, the results of the present study suggest that conclusions based on denominational affiliation should be made with caution, at least where emerging adults are concerned. That is, people may state in response to a simple question about denominational affiliation that they are Catholic, or Presbyterian, or Episcopal, but further questions about their actual religious beliefs may show that their beliefs bear little or no resemblance to anything that would be recognized as part of these religious traditions. For emerging adults, statements about denominational affiliation often appear to be based on childhood religious socialization rather on their current beliefs.

Even for emerging adults who are not currently involved in religious institutions, it is not as if they are uninterested in religious issues. On the contrary, their responses in the interviews show that they have given religious issues much thought. Also, their responses to the questionnaire items indicated that religious beliefs are important to many of them for whom religious participation is not. However, for the most part they have concluded that at this time of their lives their beliefs are best observed not through regular participation in a religious institution with other, like-minded believers, but by themselves, in the privacy of their own hearts and minds, in a congregation of one.

REFERENCES

Alwin, D. F. (1988). From obedience to autonomy: Changes in traits desired in children, 1924–1978. *Public Opinion Quarterly, 52,* 33–52.

Arnett, J. J. (1995). Broad and narrow socialization: The family in the context of a cultural theory. *Journal of Marriage and the Family, 57,* 617–628.

Arnett, J. J. (1997). Young people's conceptions of the transition to adulthood. *Youth and Society, 29,* 1–23.

Arnett, J. J. (1998). Learning to stand alone: The contemporary American transition to adulthood in cultural and historical context. *Human Development, 41,* 295–315.

Arnett, J. J. (2000a). Emerging adulthood: A theory of development from the late teens through the twenties. *American Psychologist, 55,* 469–480.

Arnett, J. J. (2000b). High hopes in a grim world: Emerging adults' views of their futures and of "Generation X." *Youth and Society, 31,* 267–286.

Bellah, R. N., Madsen, R., Sullivan, W. M., Swidler, A., & Tipton, S. M. (1985). *Habits of the heart: Individualism and commitment in American life.* New York: Harper & Row.

Bianchi, S. M., & Spain, D. (1996). Women, work, and family in America *Population Bulletin, 51(3),* 1–48.

Gallup, G., Jr., & Castelli, J. (1989). *The people's religion: American faith in the '90s.* New York: MacMillan.

Gallup, G., Jr., & Lindsay, D. M. (1999). *Surveying the religious landscape: Trends in U.S. beliefs.* Harrisburg, PA: Morehouse.

Goldscheider, F., & Goldscheider, C. (1999). *The changing transition to adulthood: Leaving and returning home.* Thousand Oaks, CA: Sage.

Greene, A. L., Wheatley, S. M., & Aldava J. F., IV. (1992). Stages on life's way: Adolescents' implicit theories of the life course. *Journal of Adolescent Research, 7,* 364–381.

Hervieu-Leger, D. (1993). Present-day emotional renewals: The end of secularization or the end of religion? In W. H. Swatos (Ed.), *A future for religion? New paradigms for social analysis.* Thousand Oaks, CA: Sage.

Hoge, D., Dinges, W., Johnson, M., & Gonzales, J. (1998a, November). *Religious beliefs and practices of American young adult Catholics.* Paper presented at the annual meeting of the Religious Research Association, Montreal, Canada.

Hoge, D., Dinges, W., Johnson, M., & Gonzales, J. (1998b, November). *Young adult Catholics: Family and religious history and institutional identity.* Paper presented at the annual meeting of the Religious Research Association, Montreal, Canada.

Hoge, D., Johnson, B., & Luidens, D. A. (1993). Determinants of church involvement of young adults who grew up in Presbyterian churches. *Journal of the Scientific Study of Religion, 32,* 242–255.

Jensen, L. A. (1995). Habits of the heart revisited: Autonomy, community, and divinity in adults' moral language. *Qualitative Sociology, 18,* 71–86.

Larson, R. W., Richards, M. H., Moneta, G., Holmbeck, G., & Duckett, E. (1996). Changes in adolescents' daily interactions with their families from ages 10 to 18: Disengagement and transformation. *Developmental Psychology, 32,* 744–754.

Roof, W. C. (1993). *A generation of seekers.* New York: HarperCollins.

Stolzenberg, R. M., Blair-Loy, M., & Waite, L. J. (1995). Religious participation in early adulthood: Age and family life cycle effects on church membership. *American Sociological Review, 60,* 84–103.

Wilson, J., & Sandomirsky, S. (1991). Religious affiliation and the family. *Sociological Forum, 6,* 289–309.

THINKING CRITICALLY

1. Emerging adults were more likely to view their religious beliefs as important than to view attendance at religious services as important. How does this reflect their individualism?

2. Why is there so little relationship between childhood religious socialization and current religious beliefs and practices? Looking at the qualitative results, does that mean that parents' attempts to shape their children's religious views are invariably ineffective?

3. How is the individualism of the religious views of the persons in this study related to their developmental status as emerging adults? That is, what is it about emerging adulthood that promotes individualism in religious beliefs as well as in other areas of life?

PART V Gender

Requirements for Manhood in an East African Culture

For a girl in a traditional culture, menarche, her first menstrual period, is often recognized with cultural rituals that signify her entrance into puberty and her approaching womanhood. For boys, there is no comparable biological event that marks the beginning of puberty and the approach of manhood. Instead, to be considered worthy of manhood, boys in traditional cultures are often expected to demonstrate specific capacities for providing, protecting, and procreating. In this reading, the expectations and rituals that structure adolescent boys' entrance into manhood are described as they take place among the Samburu, an East African tribe.

Reading 5.1

Markers to Manhood: Samburu

D. Gilmore

"Markers to Manhood: Samburu," in D. Gilmore (1990), *Manhood in the Making: Cultural Concepts of Masculinity,* pp. 123–145. Reprinted by permission from Yale University Press.

A number of traditional societies provide collective rites of passage that usher youths through sequential stages to an unequivocal manhood. Such rites dramatize the masculine transition through a clear-cut process of ritual investiture, culminating in the public conferral of an adult status that equals manhood. The basis for interpreting these male rituals of initiation was provided long ago by Arnold van Gennep in his classic *The Rites of Passage* (1960), first published in 1908. The underlying theme of such passage rites, according to van Gennep, is a change in status and identity: the boy "dies" and is "reborn" a man, each stage accompanied by appropriate symbolization. For van Gennep, rites of passage represent the death of childhood. Van Gennep claimed that this death-rebirth theme is played out in three stages: separation, transition, and incorporation. During the first stage, the boy severs relations with childhood by renouncing the mother or being forcibly taken away from her. In the transition stage, he is sent away to a new place in the bush or is otherwise isolated where he remains in limbo, a "liminal" (or transitional) status when he is neither boy nor man but something in-between. Finally, he emerges a "man," through the vigorous exit ceremonies such as those we will examine here among the Samburu.

A Structured Ascension to Manhood

The Samburu are a black pastoral people who live in an upland plateau between Lake Rudolf and the Uaso Ngiro river in northern Kenya. They were colonized like many of their neighboring tribes by the British at the turn of the century but not so severely treated or forcibly acculturated as some other tribes. Like these other pastoral tribes, the Samburu still live mainly off their herds of cattle, sheep, goats, plus a few donkeys, as their ancestors did, using everything but the squeal. It is upon the value of cattle in particular that the emphasis is squarely placed in traditional Samburu culture, at times almost to the exclusion of small stock. Possession of cattle here is the mark of a man of substance, a "big man." A man who has cattle is important, they say. He has many wives and

many sons to look after his herds. Cattle represent both the principal source of nourishment and the main trade item; they are the central cultural value, aside from wives and children. It should therefore come as no surprise that their manhood imagery revolves around competence in dealing with herds.

In the Samburu culture, cattle represent liquid wealth—an all-purpose currency for trading and for thus acquiring other good things. The most deeply held ideal among the Samburu is that each man should have his own herd and ultimately manage it independently and see to its increase. The key term in this equation is independent, meaning both economic and social freedom: no debts, no lords, no masters. But aside from possession, a man must also be in full, uncompromised control of his stock; he must be viewed as an autonomous entrepreneur of herds, exercising administrative control, without even a whiff of dependency about him. The Samburu are insistent upon this point, regarding independent animal care and ownership as the very basis of adult male status.

Accumulated wealth in the form of meat, managed and augmented through careful and unencumbered stock-breeding, allows a man to marry often in this polygynous society and to achieve the coveted status of "worthy man" by adding wives, wealth, and children to his lineage. A man rich in cattle is a worthy elder and "a man of respect," but only if he is also generous to the point of self denial. That is, Samburu men accumulate herds so that, bursting with pride, they can give them away, engaging in a "battle" of generosity in the tribal competition to distribute food to the people. To manage this greedy generosity, a man must be free to trade and breed cattle and to slaughter on his own initiative.

In the past, before the British came in the early years of the 20th century, the Samburu were courageous warriors as well as stockmen, but warfare has virtually ceased since the arrival of the Pax Britannica. One of the main goals of East African warfare and raiding formerly was to capture cattle, and the Samburu warriors ranged far and wide, battling and raiding neighboring tribes in order to build up their herds. In return, they were raided and preyed upon by their equally opportunistic neighbors. Accordingly, the principal way for a Samburu youth to garner approval was to kill people of other tribes and to steal their stock for prestige. In turn, they were attacked by others, so every Samburu man was expected to be a brave warrior. The survival of the tribe depended upon it.

It appears, then, that warfare had an economic as well as prestige motivation. When all this abruptly ceased after the imposition of peace by the British, the Samburu were not to be denied, and they continued to engage in small-scale skirmishing with the purpose not so much of killing but of rustling cattle, as did their neighbors. Because cattle rustling is the easiest and most expeditious means of acquiring stock and of increasing herd size in a short time, it remains a critical coefficient of male social value. Manhood thus retains a military quality, and all "worthy" men are expected to engage in successful marauding, for otherwise they cannot be rich and cannot sponsor the festivals and feasts that nourish and enrich the tribe. So previously, while the youths engaged in warfare to promote the survival of the tribe, today, with the tribe's survival no longer at stake, the main context for the display of courage and manly virtue is in the accumulation of stock through raiding. Especially for young men (called moran, an important term we will return to shortly), who have little other opportunity to amass animals for breeder stock, raiding and rustling represent the principal means of achieving manhood and all its social rewards: respect, honor, wives, children. The only way to win a wife is by showing one's potential as a herdsman to potential parents-in-law.

An institutionalized competition of tribal generosity spurs men to try to best each other in giving away meat. At every feast, each man tries to give the most and take the least. According to Spencer (1965), "At most feasts, for instance, younger men would insist on giving their seniors the best pieces of meat. . . . Even among age mates, whose equality was beyond

question, there was a continual battle of politeness in which the man who seemed to eat the least and encourage his neighbors to eat the most was the moral victor, the truly worthy man" (p. 26). A selfish man, an "eater" of his own herds, is described as *laroi*—a term used among the Samburu for small, paltry things, undersized or fragile objects, and for tools that do not work effectively, like a leaky water bucket. The *laroi* man, then, is childlike (undersized), mean, deficient, wasteful, inefficient. He takes more than he gives, and is despised on this account. This dislike can amount to an "unvoiced curse bringing with it disaster" upon his useless person (Spencer, 1965, p. 28). Conversely, the Samburu sense of masculinity is a kind of moral invisible hand that guides the activities of self-respecting individuals toward the collective end of capital accumulation. The goal is to become a tribal patron, creating dependencies in others, involving oneself in battles of generosity with other men in which everyone indirectly benefits.

Age-Sets

What makes the Samburu famous in the ethnographic literature is their system of age-sets and colorful attendant rituals by which the male life cycle is advanced and celebrated. In this, they are similar to their related East African tribes, but because of Spencer's (1965) superb documentation they serve as an exemplar of the ritualized masculine transition common to all. Samburu males must pass through a complicated series of age-sets and age-grades by which their growing maturity and responsibility as men in the light of these tribal values are publicly acknowledged. Basically, there are three main age-grades, which are subdivided into a number of chronological age sets. These main groupings, the age grades, are first, boy; then *moran*, or adolescent/young adult; and finally elder.

A celebrated feature of East African cattle societies, the special status of moran is a long, drawn-out transitional period of testing; it is the one with which I am most concerned here. Previously adapted toward preparing boys for a stoic warrior's life, and today for success in rustling, moranhood begins at about age 14 or 15 and lasts for about 12 years. It is initiated by a circumcision procedure described later, which begins the separation stage.

After passing the test of circumcision, the initiates are spatially isolated as a group, being removed from the confines of the village to a preselected place in the bush where they will live for the next decade or so, perfecting their skills and functions as elders. In addition, during moranhood there are a number of subsidiary rituals and tests that each youth must perform. The most important of these are the arrow ceremony, the naming ceremony, and, finally, the bull ceremony, all involving tests of skill, endurance, or competence. The bull ceremony involves the boy's first sacrifice of his own ox and the distribution of its meat. This represents the exit ceremony of moranhood, eventually ushering the young man into full status as *lee,* or worthy man, corresponding to van Gennep's incorporation stage. But no moran may marry or father children until he kills his first ox, so everything, again, revolves around the moran's ability to acquire and provide meat. Reflecting this, the ritualization of manhood culminates in a very specific act of tribal generosity indicating a future of successful industry. Rather than describing all the minor details of the age-grade series, which the reader may find clearly elaborated in Spencer's classic studies (1965, 1973), I will only point out the main features of this transitional period as they relate to the question of the meaning of manhood.

Moranhood

The first test for the boys entering moranhood is that of the traumatic circumcision procedure. A trial of bravery and stoicism, the operation is intensely painful, and no anesthetic is used, nor is anything done to lessen the anticipatory terror of the initiate, suggesting that the purpose is specifically one of testing. Each youth, placed on view before his male relatives and prospective in-laws, must remain motionless and silent during the cutting, which may last four minutes or more. Even an involuntary

twitch would be interpreted as a sign of fear. If the boy makes the slightest movement or sound, there is a collective gasp of shock and dismay; he is forever shamed as a coward and will be excluded from joining his age-set in the march toward adult status. No other initiate would want to form an age-mate relationship with a boy who "runs," for this boy will bear a stigma of inferiority for the rest of his life. Besides being cruelly ostracized himself, he brings ruin upon his entire lineage forever. In the Samburu proverb, all of his people must publicly "eat their respect" because one of their boys has run.

Following the rite of circumcision during the early stages of the moranhood, the young novice must ritually pass by his own mother's hut for the last time. At this dramatic and stylized juncture, he swears publicly before those assembled that he will no longer eat any meat seen by a married woman. Furthermore, the boy swears to refrain from drinking milk from any source inside the village settlement, and he also forswears drinking milk altogether if it has been produced by certain categories of people related to the women he may later marry. This self-denial is important because milk, either alone or mixed with cow's blood, is a major source of food for the Samburu. A much loved delicacy in all its forms, it is hard to resist. Giving it up is a real sacrifice. Doing so demonstrates maturity of resolve that amounts to a symbolic disavowal of dependency. These frustrating food taboos are of major cultural significance to the Samburu; they see the capacity for self-denial as one of the determining criteria of moranhood.

Aside from food and ritual taboos, the main ideal of moranhood has to do with acquiring cattle, which, as we have seen, is the main source of tribal wealth. Much of moranhood is spent in learning how to manage a herd and how to procure cattle, as this skill will enable a moran to create and sustain a new homestead. This entails mainly raiding and stealing, which in turn demand raw courage and steely fortitude. Rustlers may be captured, beaten, jailed, or even killed, but, if successful, rustling bestows manhood on the young moran. This naturally makes him attractive to the girls, who find such exploits manly.

Sexual Magnetism

The way the Samburu moran impress their objects of desire through running risks seems to conform to a virtually global strategy of courting. Sexual magnetism is often inspired by demonstrations of courage, as though virility were itself a matter of braving danger. Among the Samburu, the context for this heroic theme is the tribal dance. Fabulous entertainments bring youths and maidens together in their finery. These are main times for sexual dalliance. During these exuberant affairs, in which all the young people participate eagerly as a preliminary to trysting, the nubile girls, standing on the sidelines, sing lilting songs that taunt those moran who have never been on a stock raid. In their finery they chant their lyrics, making galling insinuations of cowardice. Moved by the beauty and challenge of the girls, the boys are whipped into a frenzy of desire. Driven to try their hand at rustling without delay, they impulsively take up the challenge. Spencer observes: "That the taunts of the girls help to maintain this ideal and induce the moran to steal may be judged from this description by one moran. 'You are standing there in the dance, and a girl starts to sing. She raises her chin high and you see her throat. And then you want to go and steal some cattle for yourself. You start to shiver. You leave the dance and stride into the night, afraid of nothing and only conscious of the fact that you are going to steal a cow' " (1965, p. 127).

Aroused by the girl's taunts, the youthful swain decides he must make his mark to impress her. Ostentatiously "afraid of nothing," he strides out of the settlement into the dark night of danger to prove himself by filching cattle-wealth. His objective, consciously stated, is to pass dangers in order to gain the laurels that win a woman. The link between cattle rustling and sexual conquest is linguistically recognized in the Samburu language, for, interestingly, the word *apurr* ("to steal") can also mean "to seduce" when applied to a woman.

In the passage just quoted, the fleeting mention of "shivering" merits a note as well. A traditional muscular discharge of tension among the East African warriors preparatory to battle in precontact days, this shivering forms part of the manly code of the modern Samburu cattle rustler. The Samburu moran do a "shaking" or palpitating in which they say they are "angry" and about to perform noteworthy deeds of bravery. The body movements indicate a total lack of fear, a contempt of bodily danger, a willingness to expend their blood—their lives if necessary. According to Spencer's account (1965, p. 264), the Samburu regard this muscular phenomenon as a sign of "manliness, an indication of the assertive qualities expected of the moran." So when the men "shiver" they are again publicly communicating their courage in the face of death, their commitment to be men, to meet the demands made upon them by their culture.

The conjunction of moral and gender images shows that the requisite character traits of the moran—assertiveness, productivity, fearlessness—serve as proofs not only of Samburu manhood but also of worthiness and rectitude more inclusively, and, one may also say, of practical utility. The code of the moran creates at the same time respectability and gender-identity, which are again equated in manly images; so the ritual cycle that makes men from boys is a kind of structural transformation by which children are changed into adults, narcissistic passivity is changed into selfless agency, and the raw protoplasm of nature is changed into finished culture.

There could be no purer exponents of grace under pressure than these virile Africans. But what of the youths who fail the test of manliness? These black African youths are accused of a failure to grow. Spencer notes that any failure of the moran's code of behavior is met with immediate accusations not so much of deviance or immorality as of "immaturity," of "behaving like a child" (1965, p. 87), which is worse. This type of criticism bites deeply enough to force the necessary reforms, since the accusation of retrogression is the most humiliating of taunts. Like the mockery of the pretty girls who during the tribal dances show their throats and demand a cow in return for their affections, the charge of being childish

strikes a mortal blow to the progress of the moran toward the status of manhood, the goal of his ten-year apprenticeship.

REFERENCES

van Gennep, A. (1960). *The rites of passage.* Trans. Monika B. Vizedom & Gabrielle L. Caffe. Chicago: University of Chicago Press.

Spencer, P. (1965). *The Samburu: A study of gerontacracy in a nomadic tribe.* Berkeley: University of California Press.

Spencer, P. (1973). *Nomads in alliance: Symbiosis and growth among the Rendille and Samburu of Kenya.* London: Oxford University Press.

THINKING CRITICALLY

1. Elsewhere in the book from which this reading is taken, Gilmore specifies *provide, protect,* and *procreate* as the three challenges that adolescent boys must learn to be considered worthy of becoming a man. Describe the form these three challenges take among the Samburu.

2. Gilmore also says elsewhere in his book that in many cultures there is a concept of a "failed man," someone who fails to measure up to the requirements of manhood. What is the nature of that concept among the Samburu? Is there such a concept in your own culture?

3. Tribal cultures such as the Samburu are usually assumed to have collectivistic values, but collectivism and individualism are often intermingled in cultures' belief systems. What evidence of collectivism and individualism do you find in this reading?

Gender Socialization in Girls' Teen Magazines

Teen magazines have long been popular with adolescent girls in the United States. The over-arching theme of these magazines is gender socialization, as they provide girls with information on how a girl is supposed to look, dress, smell, feel, and act toward boys. This reading explores issues of gender socialization in girls' teen magazines, with a focus on how the magazines represent sexuality.

Reading 5.2

Dilemmas of Desire: Representations of Sexuality in Two Teen Magazines

M. G. Durham

In this article, I engage questions of gender socialization with the ideological analysis of representations of sexuality in contemporary American adolescent popular culture. Specifically, I interrogate the symbolic construction of sex and desire in two top-circulating "teen" magazines with a view to understanding more about the strategies deployed in the mediated construction of girls' sexuality and their relation to social conditions for girls coming of age in America.

Mass Media and Adolescent Girls

In recent years, media scholars have focused a fair amount of attention on the content of magazines aimed at teenage girls. Most of these analyses have found that texts relating to the construction of gender are limited and rigidly stereotypical in these publications.

McRobbie's (1983) pathbreaking analysis of the British teen magazine *Jackie* found a system of messages that promoted severely restrictive ideologies of femininity in which heterosexual romance was explicitly defined as the central goal for adolescent girls and according to which girls were expected to submit—or even aspire—to male domination. McRobbie followed up her initial work more than a decade later by studying other British girls' magazines and reported the situation to be considerably improved. In 1994, she found that these magazines were addressing new modes of femininity; they no longer constructed girls as "slaves to love" and had abandoned their formerly patronizing editorial tone for a more emancipated view of girls as strong and autonomous subjects (McRobbie, 1994).

Changing social conditions and new gender dynamics are not similarly reflected in U.S. media aimed at adolescent girls. Pierce's (1990,

1993) analyses of *Seventeen* reveal portrayals of girls as neurotic, helpless, and timid beings who must rely on external sources, usually men, to make sense of their lives. Evans, Rutberg, Sather, and Turner's (1991) content analysis of *Sassy, Seventeen,* and *YM* concludes that these publications "reinforced an underlying value that the road to happiness is attracting males for successful heterosexual life by way of physical beautification" (p. 110). Duffy and Gotcher (1996) found that the teen magazine *YM* constructs a world in which

> young women must attempt to discern the minds and desires of young men in order to attract them. It is a place where they must costume and beautify themselves to achieve the almost impossible physical beauty ideal. And it is a place where sexuality is both a means and an objective, where the pursuit of males is almost the sole focus of life. (p. 43)

They concluded that *YM* presents "a dangerous and impoverished range of scripts for female teens to consult when attempting to find meaning in the world around them" (p. 46).

In general, ample empirical evidence exists to show that magazines for teenage girls overtly sustain mainstream ideologies of gender with an emphasis on the centrality of heterosexual relationships and the need to achieve stereotypical norms of physical attractiveness through the consumption of products such as cosmetics, fashionable clothing, and diet aids. However, there is a need for further interrogation of the construction of female heterosexuality in teen magazines, focusing specifically on how girls' desires are conceptualized and on what the implications of the discourse about sexuality might be. This article seeks to advance the research in that direction.

This research is significant in light of the role that mass media play in gender socialization. Lafky, Duffy, Steinmaus, and Berkowitz (1996) found that gender role stereotyping in advertisements reinforced viewers' stereotypes about gender roles. Many girls respond to mass media according to what Hall (1980) might

term a "dominant reading" of a media message, that is, by agreeing with and accepting the ideology of the message. This pattern of acceptance of the dominant discourse of femininity has aroused deep concern among those who care about girls' psychological and social development.

Sexuality, in particular, presents a conundrum for teenage girls. Orenstein (1994) notes how girls' self-confidence deteriorates as they learn the contradictory and confining rules of female sexuality. Girls learn "to look sexy, but say 'no'; to be feminine, but not sexual; to attract boys' desire, but never to respond with one's own" (p. 63). Culture imbues sexuality with meaning, and the patterns of sexual socialization are striking because of their widespread occurrence among girls of various racial, ethnic, and class backgrounds. For example, Lees's (1993) ethnographic study of adolescents uncovered the paradoxes of sexuality in girls' lives; girls, she found, had to walk a narrow line between being sexually desirable and sexually active, a situation that held true for girls from various racial, ethnic, and socioeconomic groups. Lees notes, "Girls' identities are fractured by the widespread depiction of them as sex objects, yet indications of sexual desire on their part can render them as 'whores,' 'good-time girls,' or 'slags.' Adolescent socialization for girls is fraught with discontinuity and conflict" (p. 261). Tolman (1994) observes,

> As the unmistakable contours of a female body emerge, a girl's body becomes defined in cultural terms as an object of men's fantasies and desires. When breasts grow and hips form, girls' bodies are rendered sexual, and the relationship between internal and external, the subjective experience of desire and the objective experience of finding oneself objectified, is essentially confusing and problematic for girls. (p. 251)

In light of the connections between the social construction of gendered ideologies and their maintenance in mass media aimed at adolescent girls, it is relevant to ask whether teen magazines' editorial content reinforces these sexual discontinuities and conflicts. This study examines representations of girls' sexuality in *YM* and *Seventeen* in an effort to explore to what degree paradoxical conventions of sexuality are reproduced and sustained through the cultural mechanism of the teen consumer magazine.

Method

YM and *Seventeen* are generally acknowledged to be the two top-selling magazines in the teen magazine market in the United States; *YM* has a base circulation of about 1.98 million, and *Seventeen*'s is estimated at 2.3 million (Audit Bureau of Circulations, 1996). Both magazines enjoy high popularity and credibility among adolescent girls. According to Duffy and Gotcher (1996), 67% of teenage girls surveyed by *YM*'s competitor, *Seventeen*, agreed with the statement, "This magazine [*YM*] seems to really understand me; its articles often are about things which concern me" (p. 34). In the same survey, 62% of the respondents said they trusted *YM* and 72% said it was their favorite magazine. *Seventeen*, according to its editorial statement in a prominent advertising rate book, "is a young woman's first fashion and beauty magazine. Tailored for young women in their teens and early twenties, *Seventeen* covers fashion, beauty, health, fitness, food, cars, college, careers, talent, entertainment, fiction, plus crucial personal and global issues" (Standard Rate and Data Service, 1996). *Seventeen* is a "perennial leader" in terms of sales in the teen market and enjoys a reputation for excellence (Rubin, 1993, p. 48). "We're in every school library in the U.S.," according to *Seventeen*'s editor-in-chief, Midge Richardson. "That's a franchise we don't want to lose" (quoted in Rubin, 1993, p. 48).

That these magazines are trusted and widely read by adolescent girls positions them as powerful discursive mechanisms in girls' lives, which is the primary reason I chose to examine them for this analysis. To track the current discourses of sexuality in the two teen magazines, I examined every issue of both *YM* and *Seventeen* from January through November 1996. This yielded 11 issues of *Seventeen* and 10

of *YM* (which published a combined June/July issue in 1996).

The method of analysis involved, first, a close textual reading of all written texts—features, department page articles, photo captions, letters from readers, advertising copy, and any other written content—overtly relating to sex or sexuality. Much of this content was accompanied by images explicitly illustrating the message embodied in the written text, and these are included in the analysis. The images were analyzed according to a series of visual codes generated for an earlier study (Durham, 1995). The visual codes used to identify sexualized representations of women in this analysis were as follows:

- The representation of girls as sexual objects of the male gaze;
- The costuming of girls such that their nudity is emphasized and their vulnerability is increased;
- Sexual explicitness through the exposure of girls' breasts, buttocks, and genitals;
- The arrangement of girls' bodies in positions of sexual submission—lying down, kneeling, or reclining;
- The feminine self-touch, in which girls are shown caressing or touching themselves; and
- Facial expressions of coyness, seduction, or sexual ecstasy.

For the written text, the analytic method I used was a variant of domain analysis. "Analysis of this general sort draws on the cultural significance of linguistic symbols to create and maintain shared meaning" (Coffey & Atkinson, 1996, p. 89). The aim of this analytic strategy is to explore the linguistic terms used by the magazines to construct their discourses of sexuality: "The overall goal is to be able to identify categories of expression and gain an overview of the social or cultural scene being studied through the linguistic domains and classifications used" (p. 91).

In addition to the analysis of texts specifically relating to sexuality, the ideological context of these texts was studied more broadly. My strategy of analysis was loosely based on Frye's (1990) conceptualization of feminist epistemology:

> Our process has been one of discovering, recognizing, and creating patterns. . . . Pattern recognition/construction opens fields of meaning and generates new interpretive possibilities. . . . Instead of drawing conclusions from observations, it generates observations. . . . What we do is sketch a schema within which certain meanings are sustained. (p. 179)

In this study, I used a combination of these techniques to uncover discursive patterns in the representation of adolescent girls' sexuality in the selected magazines.

The Discourses of Sexuality

The patterns that emerged in the two magazines revealed specific tensions in the construction of girls' sexuality that centered on sexual decision making versus sexual signification via costuming, cosmetics, and body image. These themes are organized in this analysis with reference to (a) the symbolic representation of sexuality, (b) the rhetorical imperative of defending girls' virtue, and (c) the trope of romantic love.

Symbols of Sexuality

Both *Seventeen* and *YM* covered fashion and beauty extensively, and these were conceptualized somewhat differently in the two publications. The discursive construction of beauty in *YM* centered exclusively on heterosexual desirability. *YM*'s presentation of fashion, beauty, and fitness information emphasized the heteroerotic rewards for consuming featured products. These texts played up words such as "hot" "sexy," "touchable," and "kissable" to characterize the appeal of the commodities they were promoting. Accompanying photographic representations of girls were highly erotic and consistently conformed to one or more of the six visual codes for sexualized representations of women. For instance, a fashion feature in the May 1996 *YM* featured flowered clothing with the promise that "These flirty floral fashions

will make your friendship bloom into romance" and showed a picture of a girl in a sports bra and low-cut flowered pants lying on a bed, her legs intertwined with those of a teenage boy ("Best Buds," 1996). Similarly: "Warm his heart in the softest, sexiest knits around" urged the subheading of the article "Sweet Sweaters" (1996). Three of the six images in the article showed girls in submissive, off-balance positions, and two showed girls physically subordinate to boys. The boys in the photographs were standing firmly upright and were in clear attitudes of power over the women in both instances.

Of the 10 issues of *YM* examined, 6 used the word "hot" on the cover in reference to articles about beauty, fashion, and exercise, making the point that exercising or clothing oneself is done solely to attract sexual attention (presumably male). Examples included "How to look hot in a bikini" (*YM*, May 1996, front cover) and "The hot bod workout" (*YM*, August 1996, front cover). "Get a crazy sexy cool stomach!" exhorted the headline to a piece on abdominal exercise ("Fitness Info," 1996, p. 28); later in the year, the magazine touted "the only three exercises you need to look great from behind" ("Kick Butt," 1996, p. 38).

By comparison, the discourse of fashion and beauty in *Seventeen* contained more internal contradictions and inconsistencies than that in *YM*. The framework was less monolithic but more problematic in many ways. The verbal texts on fashion and beauty, examined in isolation from the rest of the magazine, were not transparently focused on attracting male desire. On the contrary, many of *Seventeen*'s fashion pieces used active verbs and emphasized girls' pleasure independently of boys' pleasure; for example, "The newest fruit hues—lemon, lime, and tangy tangerine—pack a major punch!" exclaimed one headline for a fashion layout featuring citrus-colored clothing ("Citrus," 1996, p. 116). "With sneakers by day and satin by night, this little denim dress really gets around," noted another ("Dress It Up" 1996, p. 24). Both of these layouts contained photographs of girls on their own; boys were not used as markers of the clothes' viability. Yet, closer analysis of the photos in the former article evidenced repeated use of the visual codes of sexualized representation, particularly the use of submissive body postures, the feminine self-touch, and coy facial expressions.

In other *Seventeen* fashion features, the verbal texts remained asexual, whereas the visual texts located girls as sexual objects; in a fashion spread about "hippie" styles, the text focused on "offbeat" and "earthy" clothes, whereas the photographs featured semi-clad girls posed in attitudes of vulnerability and seductiveness ("Free Spirit," 1996). A few of *Seventeen*'s fashion features were actually overt about emphasizing the use of clothing as a means of attracting male desire. In the July 1996 issue, the fashion article "Seaworthy" (1996) featured "nautical-inspired" clothes (including skimpy swimsuits), accompanied by the captions "When I told him my only sailing experience was *Love Boat* reruns, he offered to show me the ropes" and "I learned how to tie a mean slipknot. After that it was nothing but smooth sailing." The photographic images that went with these captions showed partially dressed adolescent girls as objects of the admiring gaze or grasp of young men nearby.

In addition, it is important to examine text in relation to context. The fashion and beauty layouts in *Seventeen* appeared in the context of an enforced discursive feminine heterosexuality. *Seventeen*'s covers prominently displayed headlines such as "Love and jealousy: What guys think" (*Seventeen*, March 1996, front cover), "Bikinis he'll love" (*Seventeen*, May 1996, front cover), "The deal on dating older guys" (*Seventeen*, November 1996, front cover), and "Crush-crazed: Obsessed with getting a guy?" (*Seventeen*, August 1996, front cover). The monthly quizzes are a standard part of the cover design, and the quiz topics almost invariably created a negative frame for femininity such as "Quiz: Are you insecure?" (*Seventeen*, October 1996, front cover), "Quiz: Are you too possessive?" (*Seventeen*, December 1996, front cover), and "Quiz: Is he using you?" (*Seventeen*, Feburary 1996, front cover).

Finally, the advertisements in *Seventeen* (which also appeared in *YM* during the calendar year examined in this study) located girls within linguistic and visual domains geared to patriarchal norms of femininity and sexuality. Notable were perfume ads for products such as "Cherish" or "Raw Vanilla" that almost inevitably pictured women and men in close embraces; an ad for Lee jeans that showed a young man gazing at a teenage girl's derriere with the caption, "He said the first thing he noticed was your great personality. He lied. Lee: The brand that fits"; a 16-page special advertising section on clothes for college, titled "Campus Close-Up" (1996), which ran in the September 1996 issue of *Seventeen* and began with a photo of a young man embracing a young woman with text that read "Q: What *won't* you learn in class that you need to know to survive at school? A: What college guys—and relationships with them—are all about!"; and finally, the frequent ads for a product called "Curves," which are silicon pads made to be inserted into a brassiere. "Think of it as breast implants without the surgery," suggests the ad copy aimed at teenage girls. Together, the advertising in *Seventeen* created a frame for the editorial copy that subscribed to the goal of heterosexual success via socially normative standards of femininity and sexuality.

Defending One's Virtue

The goal of heterosexual success in these magazines hinges on girls' ability to induce desire in men/boys within a problematic construction of sexuality: Girls' sexuality is negatively constructed, whereas boys' sexuality has a positive construction. For instance, the year began for *Seventeen* readers with a cover line asking "Sex: How do you know if you're ready?" juxtaposed with one that announced pictures of "17 hot new guys!" (*Seventeen*, January 1996, front cover). The feature story on sex (Barry, 1996) promised to "help you keep your cool" and then ran through a list of "common" reasons girls gave for becoming sexually active including "I don't know how to say no," "I don't want to ruin the moment," and "I want to, but I'm afraid other people will think I'm a slut" (pp. 118–121). The article noted, "If a guy is pressuring you to have sex and you feel that doing it with him would mean 'giving in'—wait!" This article clearly advocated that girls should try to refrain from sexual activity—advice based on the assumption that girls are generally coerced into having sex. The same issue of *Seventeen* urged girls to buy the "hot" clothes on its "Scoop" department page: "With their superstitched pockets and skintight fit, designer jeans are as hot as they were in the '80s" ran the caption to a photo of an African American teenager clad in a revealing top and tight-fitting jeans, bending over with a hand resting provocatively on her buttocks ("Hot Stuff," January 1996, p. 26).

Both *YM* and *Seventeen* consistently offered readers sexual advice and information while exhorting girls to present themselves as sexually desirable. The sex advice was rendered in intimate and helpful tones that worked to create "a privatized subcultural space" for teenage girls (McCracken, 1993, p. 141). *YM*'s February 1996 issue contained a "top-secret sealed section" on love and sex. This included "The Ultimate Sex Checklist" for which the subheading read, "Don't even think about saying yes to him unless you can say yes to these 8 questions" (Nelson, 1996, p. 42). "Are you ready for sex?" the article began. "Yeah, we know *he* is, but . . . is it right for you?" The text of the article urged girls to withstand boys' sexual pressure and engage in sex only after careful deliberation. This article was confusingly accompanied by three photographs of a young girl, clad only in a bra and panties, posed provocatively on a bed—sitting, reclining, and ultimately curling up and covering her breasts with a pillow. In two of the pictures, her expression was coy and seductive; in one, her eyes were closed and she was smiling in eroticized ecstasy. The very same issue of *YM* advised girls on how to acquire "sexy hair" ("Red Alert," 1996, p. 20) and featured "soft, easy clothes for when it's just you and him. . . . You can keep each other warm" ("Home Alone," 1996, pp. 70–75). This contradiction between the cautionary tone of the sexual advice doled out in print versus every other construction of girls' sexuality was manifested throughout all issues of both magazines. The April 1996 issue of *YM*

flaunted a cover line that read, "7 ways to make him want you bad" (*YM*, April 1996, front cover). But the same issue elsewhere urged girls to "reduce date rape risk": "If a guy wants more than you're willing to give, tell him to stop—firmly. If he doesn't, leave pronto" (Bonner, 1996, p. 90).

These contradictory patterns were, in fact, unvarying. Apart from the articles specifically designated as containing sexual advice, every other reference to sex or sexuality unproblematically endorsed the intensification of girls' erotic appeal to boys or men.

Of the 10 issues of *YM* examined, 9 had cover stories focusing on strategies for girls to attract male sexual attention with cover lines such as "Guy-snagging moves that really work" (*YM*, May 1996, front cover) and "Love secrets: How he wants to be kissed" (*YM*, August 1996, front cover). In addition, 2 of the 10 offered sex advice on the covers, and both of these cover lines stressed the necessity for secrecy in discussing girls' sexuality; one advertised a "special sealed section" on sex (*YM*, February 1996, front cover), whereas the other read, "Top-secret sex stuff: Your questions answered" (*YM*, October 1996, front cover). In *YM*, male desire was unproblematized and a given; female desire was secret, taboo, and ultimately proscribed.

Readers of both magazines appeared to subscribe to the sexual ideologies presented by them—or, rather, the magazines printed letters from readers who located themselves in the mainstream of their declared sexual advice policy. In response to *Seventeen*'s "Sex Talk" (1996) story, readers wrote the following:

> I am so glad you printed "Are You Ready for Sex?" I'd been battling the question for a while, and just when I thought I was ready, thanks to you, I realized I wasn't. You saved me from making what could have been the worst decision of my whole life!

and

> "Are You Ready for Sex?" was really helpful for those like me who have had sex and regret it. I was 15 at the time and a bit disillusioned. Now, two years later, I

am proud to declare myself a born-again virgin. However much I regret having had sex, I don't hate myself, and I'm ready to move on. (p. 10)

The Trope of Romantic Love

In *Seventeen*, the discontinuities were more complex with regard to the urgent message for girls to attract male attention and the magazine's editorial position of discouraging girls from premature sexual activity. The word "hot" on *Seventeen* covers was used only in reference to adolescent male celebrities such as "Starwatch: 17 hot new guys" (*Seventeen*, January 1996, front cover), "Boywatch: 30 hot new guys" (*Seventeen*, August 1996, front cover), and "Red hot Jeremy London" (*Seventeen*, February 1996, front cover). On the other hand, "real" boys—boys whom the female readers might actually encounter in their daily lives—were idealized as romantic, never sexual, beings. The implication was that sexual feelings could be safely expressed only with regard to males with whom no contact was actually possible; embodied sexual feelings in real life were thus rendered explicitly taboo. On the covers of *Seventeen* as well as inside, when real-life relationships with boys were at issue, love was emphasized and any notion of sex was completely absent, with the sole exception of the January 1996 cover, which asked, "Sex: How do you know if you're ready?" and focused inside on the need to cool girls' passion (Barry, 1996, p. 121). In general, love/romance was the goal of interaction with members of the male sex. The monthly section on "Guys" carried articles such as "Love Him or Leave Him?" (McCarthy, 1996, p. 94), which, on the way to suggesting that girls leave boyfriends who "aren't right for them," contained lines such as "Everyone knows that the wrong boyfriend is better than—perish the thought—no boyfriend at all" (p. 94). "Best Friend to Boyfriend" provided details of how "real-life couples" moved from being friends to falling in love; sex did not enter the picture in any of the vignettes (Livers, 1996, p. 78).

Attracting the attention of boys was the plainly expressed motif of almost all of *Seventeen*'s cover lines. The articles corresponding to these cover lines provided girls with strategies for entering into romantic relationships with boys. Yet, in the content of the stories, these strategies often involved attracting boys' sexual attention; for example, in "How to Make the First Move," Carreño (1996) suggested that girls "make a coy remark," "get him to console you," or "get away from it all," which exhorts girls to "get boys alone": "maybe you're in the car, where he's close, he's trapped—very romantic" (p. 61). In the approved context of romance, the goal for girls was to induce sexual desire in their boys of choice.

Conclusions

The foregoing analysis uncovered a representation of sexuality that parallels sociocultural norms in teen magazines' characterizations of girls' desire. This must be considered in light of Hall's (1982) assertion that media do not simply reflect or express an already achieved social consensus; instead, they reinscribe the conditions that legitimate existing power structures (p. 66). The social construction of girls' sexuality that simultaneously requires them to be sexually alluring and devoted to sexual "responsibility" or even chastity has multiple implications in girls' lives. On the most obvious level, this construction channels girls' energies into a struggle to attain the norms of physical attractiveness that are equated with sexual desirability, and the rigid requirements of these norms are known to result in girls' experiencing severe physical and emotional distress (Bordo, 1993; Wolf, 1991).

Through hetero-eroticized beauty ideals, girls are encouraged to cast themselves as objects of male desire while being admonished never to succumb to that desire or to acknowledge their own. Instead, their primary sexual role is culturally defined as bearing the burden of rejecting or accepting male advances without any interrogation or analysis of those advances. Male sexuality is unproblematized; it is represented as being naturally and transparently aggressive. This emphasis on girls' sense of "choice" in relation to male sexual ardor is celebrated as being empowering for girls. On closer inspection, it becomes apparent that this sexual ideology denies the possibility of sexual negotiation, of a more equitable sexual dialogue between boys and girls. "It reminds [girls] that they are defined by their bodies. . . . It confirms their belief that boys' sexuality is uncontrollable while their own must remain in check" (Orenstein, 1994, p. 117). Whatley (1994) links this construction of adolescent sexuality with the high incidence of date rape among adolescents.

In reinscribing these dilemmas of desire in the construction of adolescent girls' sexuality, teen magazines sustain and support the social power dynamics that keep girls sexually subordinated and constrained. The missing discourses in teen magazines—the absence of a recognition of the validity of girls' sexual feelings apart from male sexual aggression, of alternative sexual orientations, of the possibility of pleasurable sex that is not related to succumbing or not succumbing to male desire—uphold patriarchal articulations of girls' sexuality. These mediated texts have no potential for contesting or changing gendered social relations and, indeed, actually contribute to the patriarchal control of girls' sexual lives.

REFERENCES

Audit Bureau of Circulations. (1996, June 30). *Fas-Fax: Magazine, farm and religious publications' circulation averages.* Schaumburg, IL: Author.

Barry, R. (1996, January). Are you ready for sex? *Seventeen,* pp. 118–121.

Berger, J. (1972). *Ways of seeing.* London: British Broadcasting Corporation.

Best buds. (1996, May). *YM,* pp. 72–77.

Bonner, S. (1996, April). Don't be a victim! *YM,* p. 90.

Bordo, S. (1993). *Unbearable weight: Feminism, Western culture, and the body.* Berkeley: University of California Press.

Carreño, C. (1996, June). How to make the first move. *Seventeen,* p. 61.

Citrus. (1996, February). *Seventeen,* pp. 116–121.

Coffey, A., & Atkinson, P. (1996). *Making sense of qualitative data: Complementary research strategies.* Thousand Oaks, CA: Sage.

Dress it up. (1996, January). *Seventeen,* p. 24.

Duffy, M., & Gotcher, J. M. (1996). Crucial advice on how to get the guy: The rhetorical vision of power and seduction in the teen magazine *YM. Journal of Communication Inquiry, 20,* 32–48.

Durham, M. G. (1995, May). *Decoding the visual grammar of pornography: A comparison of softcore pornography with women's fashion magazines.* Paper presented at the annual meeting of the International Communication Association, Albuquerque, NM.

Evans, D., Rutberg, J., Sather, C., & Turner, C. (1991). Content analysis of contemporary teen magazines for adolescent females. *Youth and Society, 23,* 99–120.

Fitness info: Get a sexy stomach now! (1996, April). *YM,* p. 6.

Free spirit. (1996, July). *Seventeen,* pp. 100–105.

Frye, M. (1990). The possibility of feminist theory. In D. L. Rhode (Ed.), *Theoretical perspectives on sexual difference* (pp. 173–184). New Haven, CT: Yale University Press.

Hall, S. (1980). Encoding/decoding. In S. Hall (Ed.), *Culture, media, language* (pp. 128–138). London: Hutchinson.

Hall, S. (1982). The rediscovery of ideology: The return of the repressed in media studies. In M. Gurevitch, J. Curran, T. Bennett, & J. Woollacott (Eds.), *Culture, society, and media* (pp. 56–90). London: Methuen.

Home alone (well, not completely alone). (1996, February). *YM,* pp. 70–75.

Hot stuff. (1996, January). *Seventeen,* p. 26.

Kick butt. (1996, September). *YM,* p. 38.

Lafky, S., Duffy, M., Steinmaus, M., & Berkowitz, D. (1996). Looking through gendered lenses: Female stereotyping in advertisements and gender role expectations. *Journalism Quarterly, 73,* 379–388.

Lees, S. (1993). *Sugar and spice: Sexuality and adolescent girls.* London: Penguin.

Livers, E. (1996, October). Best friend to boyfriend. *Seventeen,* pp. 78–80.

McCarthy, J. (1996, April). Love him or leave him? *Seventeen,* pp. 94–96.

McCracken, E. (1993). *Decoding women's magazines: From Mademoiselle to Ms.* New York: St. Martin's.

McRobbie, A. (1983). *Jackie*: An ideology of adolescent femininity. In E. Martella, D. C. Whitney, & S. Windhal (Eds.), *Mass communication review yearbook* (Vol. 4, pp. 251–271). Beverly Hills, CA: Sage.

McRobbie, A. (1994). Shut up and dance: Youth culture and changing modes of femininity. In A. McRobbie (Ed.), *Postmodernism and popular culture* (pp. 155–176). London: Routledge.

Nelson, S. (1996, February). The ultimate sex checklist. *YM,* pp. 42–43.

Orenstein, P. (1994). *Schoolgirls: Young women, self-esteem, and the confidence gap.* New York: Anchor.

Pierce, K. (1990). A feminist theoretical perspective on the socialization of teenage girls through *Seventeen* magazine. *Sex Roles, 23,* 491–500.

Pierce, K. (1993). Socialization of teenage girls through teenage magazine fiction: The making of a new woman or an old lady? *Sex Roles, 29,* 59–68.

Red alert. (1996, February). *YM,* p. 20.

Rubin, H. (1993, February). Teen idol. *Folio,* p. 48.

Seaworthy. (1996, July). *Seventeen,* pp. 90–97.

Sex talk. (1996, April). *Seventeen,* p. 10.

Standard Rate and Data Service. (1996, June). *Consumer Magazine and Agri-Media Source* (Wilmette, IL).

Sweet sweaters. (1996, October). *YM*, pp. 80–85.

Tolman, D. L. (1994). Daring to desire: Culture and bodies of adolescent girls. In J. Irvine (Ed.), *Sexual cultures and the construction of adolescent identities* (pp. 250–284). Philadelphia: Temple University Press.

Whatley, M. H. (1994). Keeping adolescents in the picture: Construction of adolescent sexuality in textbook images and popular films. In J. Irvine (Ed.), *Sexual cultures and the construction of adolescent identities* (pp. 183–205). Philadelphia: Temple University Press.

Wolf, N. (1991). *The beauty myth: How images of beauty are used against women.* New York: Doubleday.

THINKING CRITICALLY

1. Magazines of the kind described in this reading—focusing on how to be sexually attractive—are bought solely by adolescent girls. No comparable magazines exist for adolescent boys. How would you explain that?

2. If the format of adolescent girls' magazines changed to include a more open encouragement of girls' sexual desires, do you think it would be welcomed by girls? Would parents and other adults protest?

3. Do magazines such as the ones described in this reading simply reflect cultural beliefs about gender roles, or do they also help create and maintain those beliefs?

4. Research indicates that girls generally report more regret and less satisfaction than boys following their first episodes of sexual intercourse. In what ways is this research finding reflected in the magazines described in this reading?

PART VI The Self

The Complexity of the Self in Adolescence

Research on self-concept in adolescence has gone beyond simply examining overall self-esteem and now explores a variety of aspects of the complexity of the self in adolescence. Susan Harter of the University of Denver has long been a leader in research on self-concept in adolescence. In this reading, she and her colleagues describe a number of their ideas in this area, including contradictions between different self-attributes, variations in presentations of the self to different people, and the development of the false self.

Reading 6.1

The Development of Multiple Role-Related Selves During Adolescence

S. Harter, S. Bresnick, H. A. Bouchey, and N. R. Whitesell

"The Development of Multiple Role-Related Selves During Adolescence" by S. Harter, S. Bresnick, H. A. Bouchey, and N. R. Whitesell (1997). From *Development and Psychopathology, 9,* 835–853. Reprinted with the permission of Cambridge University Press.

The study of the self-system has witnessed a number of shifts within the last two decades (see Harter, in press). Of particular relevance to this article is the shift from a focus on more global representations of the self to a multidimensional framework. Earlier theorists (e.g., Coopersmith, 1967; Rosenberg, 1979) emphasized constructs such as global self-esteem, namely the individual's overall sense of worth as a person. However, such an approach has been challenged on the grounds that it masks important evaluative distinctions that individuals, beginning in middle childhood, make about their adequacy in different domains of their lives. The prevailing zeitgeist, supported by extensive data, underscores the fact that multidimensional models of self far more adequately describe the phenomenology of self-evaluations than do unidimensional models (see Bracken, 1996; Damon & Hart, 1988; Harter, 1982, 1990, 1993; Hattie, 1992; Marsh, 1987, 1989; Mullener & Laird, 1971; Oosterwegel & Oppenheimer, 1993; Shavelson & Marsh, 1986). Moreover, differentiation increases with age, such that the number of domains that can be evaluated increases across the periods of childhood, adolescence, and adulthood.

Differentiation of Multiple Selves During Adolescence

From a developmental perspective, there is considerable evidence that the self becomes increasingly differentiated. Findings reveal that during adolescence there is a proliferation of selves that vary as a function of social context. These include self with father, mother, close friend, romantic partner, peers, as well as the self in the role of student, on the job, and as athlete (Bresnick, 1986, 1995; Gecas, 1972; Griffin, Chassin, & Young, 1981; Hart, 1988; Harter & Monsour, 1992; Smollar & Youniss, 1985). For example, the adolescent may be depressed and sarcastic with parents, caring and rowdy with friends, curious and attentive as a student, and flirtatious but also self-conscious with someone in whom one is romantically interested. A critical developmental task of adolescence, therefore, is the construction of multiple selves in different roles and relationships.

Developmentalists highlight both cognitive and social processes that contribute to this proliferation of selves. Cognitive-developmental advances allow the adolescent to make greater differentiations among role-related attributes (see Fischer, 1980; Fischer & Canfield, 1986; Harter, 1990; Harter & Monsour, 1992; Keating, 1990). Moreover, these advances conspire with socialization pressures, leading to the emergence of different selves in different relational contexts (see Erikson, 1959, 1968; Grotevant & Cooper, 1983, 1986; Hill & Holmbeck, 1986; Rosenberg, 1986). For example, bids for autonomy from parents make it important to define oneself differently with peers in contrast to parents (see also Steinberg & Silverberg, 1986; White, Speisman, & Costos, 1983). Rosenberg (1986) points to another component of the differentiation process in observing that as one moves through adolescence, one is more likely to be treated differently by those in different relational contexts. Such differentiation should produce less overlap in those role-related attributes that are identified as salient self-descriptors, which is precisely what our research reveals. In two studies from our own laboratory (Harter & Monsour, 1992; Bresnick, 1986) we have found that the percentage of overlap in self-attributes generated for different social contexts decreases during adolescence, from 25% to 30% for young adolescents to a low of approximately 10% among older teenagers.

Contradictions and Conflict Between Attributes

The fact that adolescents perceive themselves differently in different relational contexts sets the stage for attributes to be considered contradictory. Indeed, the possibility of a "conflict of the different Me's" would appear to be particularly salient during adolescence. A certain level of intrapsychic conflict over opposing attributes in the adolescent self-portrait would appear to be normative. However, excessive conflict experienced by particular individuals may put one at psychological risk (as will become more evident later in this article).

There has been little in the way of systematic, empirical efforts that explore the extent to which opposing role-related attributes provoke conflict in the developing adolescent. Thus, we have embarked upon a program of research to address these issues. In an initial study from our laboratory (Harter & Monsour, 1992) we focused on the phenomenological conflict provoked by the identification of opposing or contradictory role-related attributes (e.g., cheerful vs. depressed, rowdy vs. calm, studious vs. lazy, at ease vs. self-conscious) within the adolescent self-portrait. Adolescents at three grade levels (7th, 9th, and 11th) first generated lists of self-descriptors for four roles: self with friends, with parents, in romantic relationships, and in the classroom. They then transferred each attribute to a large circle, which allowed for a spatial representation of their self-portrait. They were asked to arrange their attributes in one of three concentric circles (center, intermediate, and outer) corresponding to importance of each attribute. They were then asked to identify pairs of attributes that represented *opposing* characteristics, as well as which of these opposites they experienced as conflicting or clashing.

Across five converging indices (mean number of opposites, mean number of conflicts, percent of opposites in conflict, percent of subjects reporting that at least one opposite caused conflict, and percent of subjects reporting that opposites made them feel confused), the same pattern emerged. Attributes identified as contradictory and experienced as conflicting did not appear with great frequency among young adolescents. However, they peaked for those in midadolescence, and then showed a slight decline for older adolescents. Examples of conflicting attributes included being serious at school but fun-loving with friends, being happy with friends but depressed with family, being caring with family but inconsiderate with peers, being talkative as well as shy in romantic relationships, and being both attentive and lazy at school.

From a cognitive-developmental perspective, how might an increase in contradictions

and conflict within the adolescents' self-portraits be explained? Why do their self-theories not meet the criterion of *internal consistency* (Epstein, 1973)? Those of a Piagetian persuasion would argue that with the advent of formal operations in early adolescence, one should have the cognitive tools necessary to construct an integrated theory in which the postulates are internally consistent, and therefore not troublesome. However, our findings critically challenge such an expectation, and therefore demand an explanation that moves beyond classic Piagetian theory.

Thus, in interpreting the developmental data, we initially turned to Fischer's neo-Piagetian cognitive-developmental theory (Fischer, 1980; Fischer & Lamborn, 1989). Unlike classic Piagetian theory which posits the single stage of formal operations for the period of adolescence and beyond, Fischer identifies four stages through which development proceeds, beginning in early adolescence. Moreover, there are liabilities associated with the stage observed in midadolescence. According to this formulation, early adolescent thought is characterized by "single abstractions" in which one can construct rudimentary, abstract self-descriptors, for example, self-conscious, at-ease, awesome, dorky, cheerful, depressed, and so on. However, young adolescents do not yet have the cognitive ability to simultaneously compare these abstractions to one another, and therefore they tend not to detect, or be concerned over, self-attributes that are potential opposites (e.g., self-conscious vs. at ease). As one young adolescent put it, when confronted with the fact that he had indicated that he was both "nice" and "mean," "Well, you are nice to your friends and then mean to people who don't treat you nicely; there's no problem. I guess I just think about one thing about myself at a time and don't think about the other until the next day." When another young adolescent was asked why opposing attributes did not bother her, she succinctly exclaimed: "That's a stupid question, I don't fight with myself!"

During midadolescence, the cognitive skills (namely, "abstract mappings") necessary to compare single abstractions begin to emerge. This particular substage should usher in the need to integrate multiple attributes into a theory of one's personality that is coherent and unified. However, the ability to "map" constructs about the self onto one another for the purposes of comparison also represents a liability since the adolescent does not yet possess the ability to integrate seemingly opposing postulates (e.g., depressed and cheerful). As a result, they are experienced as contradictions with the self-system that may also provoke intrapsychic conflict. As one 14-year-old put it, "I really think I am a happy person and I want to be that way with everyone but I get depressed with my family and it really bugs me because that's not what I want to be like." Another 15-year-old, in describing a conflict within her romantic relationships, exclaimed, "I hate the fact that I get so nervous! I wish I wasn't so inhibited. The real me is talkative, I just want to be natural but I can't." Another 15-year-old girl explained that, "I really think of myself as friendly and open to people, but the way the other girls act, they force me to become an introvert, even though I know I'm not." In exasperation, one ninth grader observed of the self-portrait she had constructed, "It's not right, it should all fit together into one piece!"

According to Fischer's theory, consolidation and coordination should be more likely in later adolescence, with the emergence of "abstract systems," since they allow one to integrate or resolve seeming contradictions within the self-theory. For example, the tendency to be both cheerful and depressed can be coordinated under higher order abstractions such as "moody" or "temperamental." As one older adolescent explained, "Sometimes I'm really happy and sometimes I get depressed, I'm just a moody person." Older adolescents also can and do (Harter & Monsour, 1992) normalize or find value in seeming inconsistency, suggesting that it would be unnatural if not weird to act similarly with everyone. Rather, they report that it is desirable to be different across relational contexts. One teenager indicated that, "You can be shy on a date, and then outgoing with friends because you are just different with different people; you can't always be the same

person and probably shouldn't be." As another older adolescent put it, "There's a time you should listen and a time you should talk. You can do both."

The major developmental differences, therefore, reflect an increase in the detection of opposing attributes and the associated phenomenological experience of conflict associated with multiple role-related selves, particularly as individuals move from early to midadolescence. Such a developmental shift can be interpreted within neo-Piagetian models that identify cognitive advances and liabilities that reflect substages during the period of adolescence. For those older adolescents who can normalize seeming contradictions or integrate them at more abstract levels of thought, there may be some reduction in the conflict experienced, although these processes can be expected to continue well into adulthood.

Are there more contradictions across or within roles? We have also extended our analysis to parameters of the conflict experienced between opposing attributes that go beyond cognitive-developmental explanations. Thus, we were curious about whether there are more opposing attributes and associated conflict within particular roles (e.g., rowdy vs. quiet with friends) or across different roles (e.g., tense with a romantic other but relaxed with friends). This issue has been briefly addressed in the adult (although not the adolescent) literature. Among those social psychologists who have focused on the adult self, it has been argued that consistency within a particular relationship is critical; therefore, perceived violations of this consistency ethic, where one displays opposing attributes within the same role, should be particularly discomforting to the individual (Gergen, 1968; Vallacher, 1980). According to these theorists, the adoption of different behaviors in different roles should be less problematic or conflictual for adults, since they represent an appropriate adaptation to different relational contexts rather than inconsistency.

From a developmental perspective, we did not expect these particular processes to be in place during adolescence. Adolescents are actively concerned with creating, defining, and differentiating role-related selves. As reported earlier, this preoccupation results in relatively little overlap in the self-attributes associated with different roles, particularly as one moves through adolescence. As our cognitive-developmental analysis indicated, perceived opposition between differing attributes across relational contexts should become more marked or salient, beginning in mid-adolescence when teenagers develop the cognitive ability to detect seeming contradictions. Thus, the salience of these differences should cause adolescents to identify more opposing attributes across roles than within roles. Perceived conflict caused by opposing attributes should also be greater across roles, particularly with the onset of mid-adolescence, when teenagers can begin to compare characteristics across such roles but cannot integrate these salient and seemingly contradictory self-attributes.

Findings from two different studies conducted in our laboratory (Bresnick, 1986, 1995) confirmed these expectations in that there were significantly more opposing attributes and a greater percentage of opposing attributes in conflict identified across, compared to within, roles. In the first study, which included six different roles (self with mother, father, friends, in the classroom, in romantic

relationships, and on the job), across-role opposing attributes were more frequent (M = 3.68) than were within-role opposites (M = 1.56). This pattern was confirmed in a second study which included five roles, all of which represented interpersonal relationships (self with mother, father, best friend, a group of friends, and a romantic interest) as opposed to more general contexts such as the classroom or on the job. In this second study, opposing attributes across roles (M = 2.72) were significantly more frequent than were within-role contradictions (M = .50). Those opposing attributes experienced as in conflict followed the same pattern. Figure 6.1.1 presents the data for opposing attributes both across- and within-roles as a function of developmental level. Consistent with our earlier work (Harter & Monsour, 1992), young adolescents reported fewer opposing attributes than either those in mid- or late adolescence. However, the slight decline in opposing attributes and conflicts found for older adolescents in the earlier study was only obtained for the within-role characteristics. As can be seen in Figure 6.1.1, for those across-role attributes, there was a systematic developmental increase in opposing attributes, particularly noteworthy between early and midadolescence.

FIGURE 6.1.1 Mean number of opposing attributes across and within roles at three periods of adolescence.

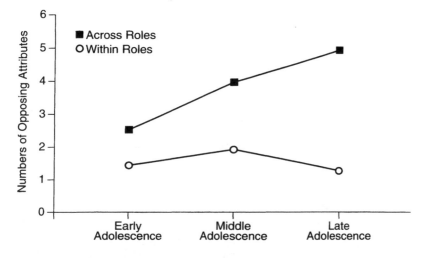

True Versus False Self-Behavior

The construction of multiple selves in which different attributes are perceived as contradictory should understandably provoke some concern over which of the opposing attributes in a given pair reflects one's "true self." Our own work has revealed that this proliferation of selves does engender problematic questions for adolescents about which is "the real me," particularly when attributes in different roles appear contradictory (e.g., cheerful with friends but depressed with parents). During our multiple-selves procedure, a number of adolescents spontaneously agonized over which of the attributes represented their "true self." The salience of this issue has been further documented by our subsequent findings demonstrating that adolescents can readily distinguish true and false self-behaviors.

When asked to define true self-behavior, adolescents' descriptions include the "real me inside," "saying what you really think," "expressing your opinion." In contrast, false self-behavior is defined as "being phony," "not stating your true opinion," "saying what you think others want to hear" (Harter, Marold, Whitesell, & Cobbs, 1996). These observations converge with what Gilligan and colleagues (Gilligan, 1982, 1993; Gilligan, Lyons, & Hammer, 1989) have referred to as "loss of voice," namely the suppression of one's thoughts and opinions. In developing questionnaires that specifically address the extent to which adolescents engage in false self-behavior, we have found that many sixth graders do not embrace this concept. They will inquire into what it means, or state that it doesn't make sense because they are always their true selves. The distinction between true and false self-behavior is, however, well understood by seventh graders, and becomes increasingly salient among those in midadolescence and beyond.

Our contextual approach to adolescent self-processes has prompted us to inquire, in recent studies of the multiple selves that adolescents construct, whether they display more false self-attributes in some contexts compared to others. Across these studies, each of which has addressed slightly different roles, there is a general pattern. The highest levels of false self-behavior (30% to 40% of attributes) are displayed with one's father and (for female adolescents from an all-girls school environment) with boys in social situations (Johnson, 1995). (We have not yet asked male adolescents to report on females in social situations.) Lower levels of false self-behavior (20–25%) are reported with classmates, teachers, and one's mother. The least false self-behavior is reported in relationships with close friends (10–15%). A similar pattern is obtained in our studies of the extent to which adolescents are able to voice their opinions (Harter et al., in press).

We have also, in some studies, inquired into the *reasons* that adolescents report for why opposing attributes cause conflict, and these reasons parallel the findings cited above. In two such studies (Bresnick, 1986; Harter & Monsour, 1992) the largest reason category included explanations in which a behavior violated the adolescent's perception of who he/she was or wanted to be (53% and 44% of all reasons, respectively). As one adolescent put it, "I really think of myself as a happy person and I want to be that way with everyone because I think that's my true self, but I get depressed with my family and it bugs me because that's not what I want to be like or who I am." Another observed: "I am a patient person, particularly with friends, and want to be, but then I get impatient with my mom." In these reasons it would appear that the conflicts represent a behavior experienced as "false," which clashes with an attribute that is perceived to reflect more true self-behavior.

A second category of reasons offered for conflict seems to reflect opposing attributes where each member of the pair represents true self-behaviors; the frequency across the same two studies was 36% and 29%, respectively. As one adolescent explained, "I'm close with my family and fun-loving with my friends, and that's how I want to be, but sometimes these work against each other." Another observed, "I'm glad I can be emotional with my mother but I'm more naturally reserved with my father."

A third category of reasons offered for why opposing attributes conflict is that the significant others in each relational context expect or elicit different behaviors (11% and 20%, respectively). For example, one adolescent noted that "My teachers expect me to be serious but my friends want me to be rowdy." Another explained how "On a date I get withdrawn and self-conscious and just the opposite with my friends where I can get very sarcastic, but I don't like being either way, that's not me." Although adolescents providing such reasons do not always explicitly indicate that each opposing attribute represents a form of false self-behavior, the implication in their explanations is that they are behaving in ways that others call for, rather than how they feel they really are, or would prefer to act.

Self-Organization During Adolescence: Normative and Pathological Implications

A certain level of conflict among self-attributes is normative, particularly during midadolescence. That is, teenagers at this level of development do not yet possess the skills necessary to integrate those opposing attributes that come to define the loose confederation of multiple selves that have proliferated. However, certain individuals, as well as subgroups, may be more vulnerable to conflict. For example, we have identified a subset of girls, namely those with a feminine gender orientation, that are more prone to conflict, particularly among attributes that are displayed in public arenas such as in the classroom, as well as with boys in social situations.

The challenges posed by the need to create different selves are also exacerbated for ethnic minority youth in this country who must bridge "multiple worlds," as Cooper and her colleagues point out (Cooper, in press; Cooper, Jackson, Azmitia, Lopez, & Dunbar, 1995). Minority youth must move between multiple contexts, some of which may be with members of their own ethnic group, including family and friends, and some of which may be populated by the majority culture, including teachers, classmates, and other peers who may not share the values of their family of origin. Rather than

assume that all ethnic minority youth will react similarly to the need to cope with such multiple worlds, Cooper and colleagues have highlighted several different patterns of adjustment. Some youth are able to move easily across the borders of their multiple worlds, in large part because the values of the family, teachers, and peers are relatively similar. Others, for whom there is less congruence in values across contexts, adopt a bicultural stance, adapting to the world of family, as well as to that of the larger community. Others find the transition across these psychological borders more difficult, and some find it totally unmanageable. Particularly interesting is the role that certain parents play in helping adolescents navigate these contextual waters, leading to more successful adaptations for some than others.

The differentiation of multiple selves will be of particular concern to developmental psychopathologists to the extent that it is associated with a number of negative correlates and outcomes. These include excessive conflict between attributes in multiple roles, high levels of false self-behavior, and the devaluation of those characteristics that define one's role-related behavior. Moreover, each of these variables is, in turn, associated with lower levels of social support as well as low relational self-esteem in the corresponding context. In addition, we know from previous studies (see Harter, in press; Harter et al., 1996) that low self-esteem and high levels of false self-behavior are predictive of depressive reactions including depressed affect, low energy level, and hopelessness. The perception that certain self-attributes are false would seem to be very central to this constellation of liabilities.

A basic claim of theorists concerned with false self-behavior is that lack of authenticity has negative outcomes or correlates. Gilligan and colleagues (Gilligan et al., 1989; Gilligan, 1993), as well as others (see Jordan, 1991; Jordan, Kaplan, Miller, Stiver, & Surrey, 1991; Lerner, 1993; Miller, 1986, 1991) observe that suppression of the self leads to lack of zest which, in the extreme form, will be manifest as depressive symptoms and associated liabilities such as low self-esteem. In our own studies of self-reported level of false self-behavior (e.g., Harter et al., 1996), we have demonstrated that adolescents highest in false self-behavior reported the lowest level of global self-esteem and were the most likely to report depressive affect. Moreover, they acknowledged that they were much less likely to be in touch with their true self-attributes. With adults, we have demonstrated that those reporting lack of authenticity with a spouse or partner also report lower self-esteem and more depressed affect than those who were able to be their true selves (Harter, Waters, Pettitt, et al. 1997). Thus, the pattern reveals that those who experience greater levels of false self-behavior are at risk for negative outcomes that can be quite debilitating, from a mental health perspective.

In summary, the period of adolescence represents normative challenges to the harmonious organization and integration of self-constructs. However, with increasing development, further skills emerge which equip the individual with strategies that normalize the construction of multiple selves, that allow one to selectively occupy those contexts in which self-evaluations are more favorable, and that provide for a sense of unity through the construction of a meaningful narrative of one's life story.

REFERENCES

Bracken, B. (1996). Clinical applications of a context-dependent multidimensional model of self-concept. In B. Bracken (Ed.), *Handbook of self-concept* (pp. 463–505).

Bresnick, S. (1986). *Conflict in the adolescent self-theory.* Unpublished honors thesis, University of Denver, Denver, CO.

Bresnick, S. (1995). *Developmental and gender differences in role-related opposing attributes within the adolescent self-portrait.* Unpublished doctoral dissertation, University of Denver, Denver, CO.

Cooper, C. (in press). *The weaving of maturity: Cultural perspectives on adolescent development.* New York: Oxford University Press.

Cooper, C. R., Jackson, J. F., Azmitia, M., Lopez, E., & Dunbar, N. (1995). Bridging students' multiple worlds: African American and Latino youth in academic outreach programs. In R. F. Macias & R. G. Garcia-Ramos (Eds.), *Changing schools for changing students: An anthology of research on language minorities* (pp. 211–234). Santa Barbara, CA: University of California Linguistic Minority Research Institute.

Coopersmith, S. (1967). *The antecedents of self-esteem.* San Francisco: W. H. Freeman.

Damon, W., & Hart, D. (1988). *Self-understanding in childhood and adolescence.* New York: Cambridge University Press.

Epstein, S. (1973). The self-concept revisited. *American Psychologist, 28,* 405–416.

Erikson, E. (1959). Identity and the life cycle. *Psychological Issues, 1,* 18–164.

Erikson, E. (1968). *Identity, youth, and crisis.* New York: Norton.

Fischer, K. F. (1980). A theory of cognitive development: The control and construction of hierarchies of skills. *Psychological Review, 87,* 477–531.

Fischer, K. W., & Canfield, R. (1986). The ambiguity of stage and structure in behavior: Person and environment in the development of psychological structure. In I. Levin (Ed.), *Stage and structure: Reopening the debate* (pp. 246–267). New York: Plenum.

Fischer, K. W., & Lamborn, S. (1989). Mechanisms of variation in developmental levels: Cognitive and emotional transitions during adolescence. In A. de Ribaupierre (Ed.), *Transition mechanisms in child development: The longitudinal perspective* (pp. 37–61). Cambridge: Cambridge University Press.

Gecas, V. (1972). Parental behavior and contextual variations in adolescent self-esteem. *Sociometry, 35,* 332–345.

Gergen, K. J. (1968). Personal consistency and the presentation of self. In C. Gordon & K. J. Gergen (Eds.), *The self in social interaction* (pp. 30–326). New York: Wiley.

Gilligan, C. (1982). *In a different voice.* Cambridge, MA: Harvard University Press.

Gilligan, C. (1993). Joining the resistance: Psychology, politics, girls, and women. In l. Weis & M. Fine (Eds.), *Beyond silenced voices* (pp. 143–168). Albany, NY: State University of New York Press.

Gilligan, C., Lyons, N., & Hammer, T. J. (1989). *Making connections.* Cambridge, MA: Harvard University Press.

Griffin, N., Chassin, L., & Young, R. D. (1981). Measurement of global self-concept versus multiple role-specific self-concepts in adolescents. *Adolescence, 16,* 49–56.

Grotevant, H. D., & Cooper, C. R. (1983). *Adolescent development in the family: New directions for child development.* San Francisco, CA: Jossey-Bass.

Grotevant, H. D., & Cooper, C. R. (1986). Individuation in family relationships. *Human Development, 29,* 83–100.

Hart, D. (1988). The adolescent self-concept in social context. In D. K. Lapsley & F. C. Power (Eds.), *Self, ego, and identity* (pp. 71–90). New York: Springer-Verlag.

Harter, S. (1982). The perceived competence scale for children. *Child Development, 53,* 87–97.

Harter, S. (1990). Causes, correlates and the functional role of global self-worth: A life-span perspective. In J. Kolligian & R. Sternberg (Eds.), *Perceptions of competence and incompetence across the lifespan* (pp. 67–98). New Haven, CT: Yale University Press.

Harter, S. (1993). Causes and consequences of low self-esteem in children and adolescents. In R. F. Baumeister (Ed.), *Self-esteem: The puzzle of low self-regard* (pp. 87–117). New York: Plenum.

Harter, S. (in press). The development of self-representations. In W. Damon (Series Ed.) & N. Eisenberg (Vol.

Ed.), *Handbook of child psychology: Vol. 3. Social, emotional, and personality development* (5th ed.). New York: Wiley.

Harter, S., Marold, D., Whitesell, N. R., & Cobbs, G. (1996). A model of the effects of parent and peer support on adolescent false self behavior. *Child Development, 67,* 360–374.

Harter, S., & Monsour, A. (1992). Developmental analysis of conflict caused by opposing attributes in the adolescent self-portrait. *Developmental Psychology, 28* (2), 251–260.

Harter, S., Waters, P. L., Pettitt, L. M., Whitesell, N., Kofkin, J., & Jordan, J. (1997). Autonomy and connectedness as dimensions of relationship styles in men and women. *Journal of Social and Personality Relationships, 14,* 147–164.

Harter, S., Waters, P., & Whitesell, N. R. (in press). Relational self-esteem: Differences in perceived worth as a person across interpersonal contexts. *Child Development.*

Hattie, J. (1992). *Self-concept.* Hillsdale, NJ: Erlbaum.

Hill, J. P., & Holmbeck, G. N. (1986). Attachment and autonomy during adolescence. In G. J. Whitehurst (Ed.), *Annals of child development* (Vol. 3, pp. 145–189). Greenwich, CT: JAI Press.

Johnson, E. (1995). *The role of social support and gender orientation in adolescent female development.* Unpublished doctoral dissertation, University of Denver, CO.

Jordan, J. V. (1991). The relational self: A new perspective for understanding women's development. In J. Strauss and G. Goethals (Eds.), *The self: Interdisciplinary approaches* (pp. 136–149). New York: Springer-Verlag.

Jordan, J. V., Kaplan, A. G., Miller, J. B., Stiver, J. L., & Surrey, L. P., (Eds.) (1991). *Women's growth in connection.* New York: Guilford.

Keating, D. P. (1990). Cognitive processes in adolescence. In S. Feldman & G. Elliot (Eds.), *At the threshold: The developing adolescent* (pp. 54–89). Cambridge, MA: Harvard University Press.

Lerner, H. G. (1993). *The dance of deception.* New York: HarperCollins.

Marsh, H. W. (1987). The hierarchical structure of self-concept and the application of hierarchical confirmatory factor analysis. *Journal of Educational Measurement, 24,* 17–19.

Marsh, H. W. (1989). Age and sex effects in multiple dimensions of self-concept: Preadolescence to early adulthood. *Journal of Educational Psychology, 81,* 417–430.

Miller, J. B. (1986). *Toward a new psychology of women* (2nd ed.). Boston: Beacon Press.

Miller, J. B. (1991). The development of women's sense of self. In J. V. Jordan et al. (Eds.), *Women's growth and connection: Writing from the Stone Center* (pp. 11–26). New York: Guilford Press.

Mullener, N., & Laird, J. D. (1971). Some developmental changes in the organization of self-evaluations. *Developmental Psychology, 5,* 233–236.

Oosterwegel, A., & Oppenheimer, L. (1993). *The self-system: Developmental changes between and within self-concepts.* Hillsdale, NJ: Erlbaum.

Rosenberg, M. (1979). *Conceiving the self.* New York: Basic Books.

Rosenberg, M. (1986). Self-concept from middle childhood through adolescence. In J. Suls & A. G. Greenwald (Eds.), *Psychological perspective on the self* (Vol. 3, pp. 182–205). Hillsdale, NJ: Erlbaum.

Shavelson, R. J., & Marsh, H. W. (1986). On the structure of the self-concept. In R. Schwarzer (Ed.), *Anxiety and cognition* (pp. 283–310). Hillsdale, NJ: Erlbaum.

Smollar, J., & Youniss, J. (1985). Adolescent self-concept development. In R. H. Leary (Ed.), *The development of self* (pp. 247–266). New York: Academic Press.

Steinberg, L., & Silverberg, S. B. (1986). The vicissitudes of autonomy in early adolescence. *Child Development, 57,* 841–851.

Vallacher, R. R. (1980). An introduction to self theory. In D. M. Wegner & R. R. Vallacher (Eds.), *The self in social psychology* (pp. 3–30). New York: Oxford University Press.

White, K., Speisman, J., & Costos, D. (1983). Young adults and their parents: Individuation to mutuality. In H. D. Grotevant & C. R. Cooper (Eds.), *Adolescent development in the family: New directions for child development* (pp. 61–76). San Francisco: Jossey-Bass.

THINKING CRITICALLY

1. The authors discuss how conceptions of opposing self-attributes change from early to late adolescence. What further changes might you expect in emerging adulthood?

2. Why do you think adolescents are most likely to show a false self to their fathers and (for girls) potential romantic partners?

3. For minority adolescents, what factors do you think might explain why some are more successful than others at moving across their "multiple worlds"?

4. Most people exhibit false self-behavior occasionally, but relatively high levels of false self-behavior are related to problems such as depression. Why is some false self-behavior normal? Why is a relatively high degree of false self-behavior predictive of problems?

Variations in Ethnic Identity

All young people face the challenge of forming a coherent identity when they reach adolescence, but young people who are members of minority groups face the additional challenge of forming an ethnic identity. There are a variety of ways that young people respond to being part of an ethnic culture but also part of American society. In this reading, the authors describe some of those responses, focusing on African American and Mexican American adolescents.

Reading 6.2

Variations in Bicultural Identification Among African American and Mexican American Adolescents

J. S. Phinney and M. Devich-Navarro

Members of ethnic minority groups within a society are exposed to two cultures, their ethnic culture and the culture of the larger society. However, the ways in which they actually identify with and participate in these two cultures are far from clear. Although there has been a considerable amount of speculation and theorizing about biculturalism (Birman, 1994; LaFramboise, Coleman, & Gerton, 1993; Ramirez, 1984), there is little empirical evidence about how individuals from ethnic minority groups think about and handle their relationship with the two cultures in which they live.

The issue of cultural identification has particular relevance during adolescence when, as part of the identity formation process (Marcia, Waterman, Matteson, Archer, & Orlofsky, 1994), minority youths examine their ethnicity and its implications in their lives as they seek to establish a secure ethnic or racial identity (Helms, 1990; Phinney, 1989, 1993). In addition to examining their ethnicity, adolescents are likely to consider their role and position in the wider society. As they engage in this process, they are faced with the differing demands and possible conflicts among alternative cultural frames of reference, and the reality of minority status and discrimination (Fordham & Ogbu, 1986; Mendelberg, 1986). To gain understanding of this complex phenomenon, we sought in this study to examine the ways in which Mexican American and African American adolescents understand being part of two cultures.

To clarify different types of ethnic identity as a basis for this study, we present a diagram based on the models of Berry (1990),

Birman (1994), and LaFromboise et al. (1993). In the diagram (see Figure 6.2.1), the circles represent the two cultures as understood or experienced by a minority group member, and the "X" represents the individual's position with respect to the two cultures.

The top panel of Figure 6.2.1 illustrates the assimilation and fusion patterns. In *assimilation*, the individual gives up the ethnic culture and becomes part of the larger society (Berry, 1990). The ethnic culture may continue to exist, but the person is no longer part of it and does not value it. In the diagram, the cultures are separate, and the person is part of just the dominant culture. In contrast, in *fusion*, as described by LaFromboise et al. (1993), the two cultures are seen as fused to produce a new culture, and the individual is part of a combined culture. This pattern reflects the true "melting pot" concept, in that the two cultures are no longer distinguished. Thus, in the diagram, the two cultures are shown as completely overlapping.

The bottom panel in Figure 6.2.1 illustrates separation and marginalization. In both these cases, the individual sees the two cultures as distinct and incompatible. The differentiating factor is the position of the individual with

FIGURE 6.2.1 Identification patterns based on the individual's perception of American and ethnic cultures (represented by circles) as separated, combined, or overlapping, and his or her position relative to each culture (represented by "X").

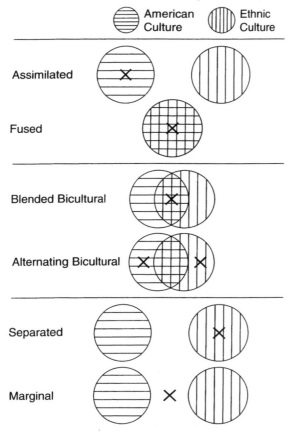

respect to the two cultures. *Separation* defines an individual who is embedded in the ethnic culture and not at all part of the larger society; *marginalization* refers to a person who is between two cultures and part of neither (Berry, 1990; Birman, 1994).

The middle panel of Figure 6.2.1 presents two possible types of biculturalism. In biculturalism, which is comparable to Berry's (1990) integration, the two cultures are perceived as overlapping to some extent, but not completely. Different models of biculturalism can then be represented in terms of the individual's position with respect to the two cultures. An individual who occupies primarily the area of overlap can be considered a *blended bicultural*, in Birman's (1994) terminology. The overlap allows for a new identity as a combination of both cultures. On the other hand, those who move between the two nonoverlapping areas can be considered *alternating biculturals* (LaFromboise et al., 1993). Obviously, these are not the only possibilities; there may be varying degrees of perceived overlap and also differing positions within the two cultures, thus suggesting other types of biculturalism. However, the diagram provides a starting point for conceptualizing the possible ways of being bicultural.

Although this diagram helps to organize the ways of thinking about biculturalism, the various types of biculturalism remain somewhat vague in the absence of concrete examples. It is not clear to what extent these models correspond to the actual experience of members of various ethnic minority groups. To understand the different types of biculturalism, it is necessary to examine the ways in which people actually understand and express their sense of being part of two cultures. It is important to examine biculturalism separately in different ethnic groups, taking into consideration their distinct histories and experiences.

In this study, we focus on adolescents from two American ethnic groups, African American and Mexican American. Both of these groups originate from a distinct cultural heritage (Greenfield & Cocking, 1994) and have a particular relationship with the larger society. Because of the substantial differences in the history and experience of these two groups, African Americans and Mexican Americans cannot readily be compared. The goal of this study was not to compare groups, but rather to understand the experiences of these adolescents on their own terms. Our emphasis was on variations in bicultural identification within and across ethnic groups, rather than on differences between groups.

Current evidence suggests that the experience of being part of two cultures is complex and multidimensional. The research that examines biculturalism is highly diverse; both ethnographic and survey methods have been used to explore this topic, but there have not been systematic studies that combine these two approaches. In this study, we incorporated these two methods to provide a fuller understanding of variation in biculturalism among adolescents from two ethnic groups. The study was carried out with adolescents who were American born and identified themselves and both parents as members of the same ethnic group, either African American or Mexican American; thus, they were clearly exposed to both cultures. We addressed the following questions: In what ways do these adolescents identify with their two cultures, and to what extent do their types of identification match models that have been proposed in the literature? Are differences in types of identification related to independent measures of ethnic and American identity and other characteristics? How is being part of two cultures experienced by minority youth?

Method

Participants

The participants were 52 African American and 46 Mexican American 10th- and 11th-grade high school students, with equal numbers of males and females in each ethnic group. Participants were selected on the basis of being American born and having both parents from the same ethnic group. The mean age for the African Americans was 16.1 years, and for the Mexican Americans, 15.7 years. All of the participants came from one of two public high schools whose ethnic compositions were predominantly African American and Mexican American, respectively. Both schools were located in a stable middle- and working-class suburb of Los Angeles. The African American adolescents, like most African Americans, had parents who were predominantly American born (for 92%, one or both parents were American born). The Mexican Americans were primarily from immigrant families, as is typical of Mexican Americans in the community (for 93%, one or both parents were foreign born).

All the 10th- and 11th-grade social studies classes of two teachers at each school were selected for recruitment. Social studies courses are required for all students; thus these classes represented all levels of proficiency. About a week prior to beginning the study, research assistants representing the two ethnic groups studied visited each class and explained the purpose of the research in very general terms (i.e., to learn more about what adolescents think about some of the current issues they face). The students were told that participation was voluntary. They were assured that their privacy would be protected and that neither teachers, school administrators, nor parents would know their responses. Student's were told that those who met the criteria and who completed the questionnaire and the interview would receive $5. In each class, one-third to one-half of the students expressed interest. All interested students were provided with a parental consent form and a student assent form that elicited basic demographic information on gender, age, and own and parental ethnicity. From among students who returned both forms, we selected as participants all those who met the criteria of being an American-born African American or Mexican American, with both parents from the same ethnic group.

Questionnaire

The questionnaire was administered in classroom settings before the interview and took about 20 minutes to complete. It included the following scales:

Ethnic identity. Ethnic identity was assessed using the 14-item Multigroup Ethnic Identity Measure (Phinney, 1992), which has a reliability of $\alpha = .81$ with high school students. It has three subscales that assess three aspects of ethnic identity: (1) sense of belonging to, and attitudes toward, one's ethnic group (5 items); (2) ethnic identity achievement, based on exploration and commitment (7 items); and (3) ethnic behaviors and customs (2 items). Items are rated on a 4-point scale ranging from 1 *(strongly disagree)* to 4 *(strongly agree)*. An ethnic identity score is derived by reversing negative items, summing across the 14 items, and obtaining a mean. A high score indicates a strong identification with one's ethnic group. Subscale scores can be calculated similarly for each of the three aspects of ethnic identity. The measure had a reliability of $\alpha = .75$ with this sample.

American identity. This measure was designed to determine the participant's sense of being American. It consisted of eight statements to which participants indicated agreement on a 4-point scale ranging from 1 *(strongly disagree)* to 4 *(strongly agree)*. Typical statements were: "I think of myself as being American," "I have a strong sense of being American," "I am proud of being American." The responses were summed and a mean score was obtained. A high score indicated a strong American identity. The measure had a reliability of Cronbach $\alpha = .88$ with this sample.

Other-group attitudes. Attitudes toward other groups were measured using a 6-item scale (Phinney, 1992), which has a reliability of .71 with high school students. Participants rate each item on a 4-point scale ranging from 1 *(strongly disagree)* to 4 *(strongly agree)*. It includes both positively and negatively worded items, such as, "I like meeting and getting to know people from ethnic groups other than my own," and "I sometimes feel it would be better if different ethnic groups didn't try to mix together." A score is derived by reversing negative items, summing across the items, and obtaining a mean. The measure had a reliability of $\alpha = .60$ with this sample.

Demographic information. The questionnaire included questions on the participants' gender, age, ethnicity, parents' ethnicity, parents' occupation, and self-report of academic grades.

Interview Procedures

After the questionnaire was completed, individual interviews of the participants were conducted by upper division or graduate students in psychology who were of the same ethnicity as the participant. The interviews were tape recorded and lasted 30 to 40 minutes. Upon completion, the respondents were given the opportunity to ask questions or add comments, and were paid $5 for their participation.

In the interview, the interviewer first elicited the adolescent's self-report of his or her ethnic or racial label (i.e., African American, Black, Mexican American, Latino, etc.). Because of the variation in use of self-labels, interviewers used the respondent's chosen self-label during the remainder of the interview (e.g., the term "Mexican American" in place of the term "ethnic" in the following examples). The interview included both closed and open-ended questions designed to determine the respondents' sense of being ethnic, American, and bicultural. Regarding their ethnicity, participants were asked questions about the meaning of their ethnic group membership and its impact on their lives. They were asked similar questions about being American, such as how American they felt, and what being American meant to them. They were then asked whether they saw themselves as more ethnic or more American, and this question was repeated with reference to specific settings, including home, school, and with their friends. They were next asked about their sense of being part of two cultures, including both the conflicting and the positive aspects of that experience and the ways in which they dealt with it. Finally, they were again asked whether they saw themselves as more ethnic or more American, and whether they dealt with the two cultures by combining them, keeping them separate, or deemphasizing the issue of culture. Tape-recorded interviews were transcribed for coding.

Results

The results are presented in three sections. The first section describes the types of identification patterns that we found. The next section presents quantitative analyses of differences among the types of identification, using the questionnaire data. Finally, the third section provides qualitative descriptions of the patterns, based on the interviews.

Patterns of Bicultural Identification

The first question that we addressed was: In what ways do minority adolescents identify themselves with reference to their two cultures, ethnic and American? Three types of responses were evident. One group of adolescents described themselves as equally American and ethnic, or, in a few cases, more American, without denying their ethnic background. They typically responded to the two questions concerning whether they were more ethnic (e.g., African American) or more American with reluctance to choose one or other. These students generally indicated that they dealt with the two cultures by combining them or deemphasizing cultural issues; none said that they kept the two cultures separate. These adolescents appear to fit the model of blended bicultural described by Birman (1994), and we therefore called this pattern *blended biculturalism.*

A second group of adolescents described themselves as more ethnic than American. They acknowledged being American, but the ethnic component was clearly the stronger influence. These students frequently mentioned situational differences in how they saw themselves; usually at school they felt more American, while at home and with friends they felt more ethnic. The students had a distinct identity as ethnic but functioned comfortably in both cultural settings. We used the term *alternating biculturalism* for this pattern.

A smaller group did not see themselves as bicultural. Like the alternating biculturals, they stated that they were more ethnic than American. However, they indicated further that they did not feel very American or, in some cases, rejected being American altogether. We labeled these adolescents as *separated*, defined as having a strong ethnic identification and a weak or nonexistent identification with the larger society. These adolescents could not be considered bicultural.

These identification patterns were defined precisely with reference to specific interview questions about being ethnic or American. In most cases, participants could be unambiguously assigned to one of the defined types on the basis of their responses to the specific closed-ended questions. In a few cases ($n = 11$) where participants did not fall clearly into one type, two independent coders reviewed the transcripts and made an assignment. In these cases, the two coders had an 82% agreement rate. Where there was disagreement, a third reader reviewed the transcript, and assignment was resolved by discussion.

Final categorization of participants revealed that among the African American adolescents, 28 (54%) were blended biculturals, 13 (25%) were alternating biculturals, and 9 (17%) were classified as separated. In the case of 2 African Americans, the responses were sufficiently inconsistent that no assignment could be made; these two cases were eliminated from the analyses.

Among the Mexican Americans, 16 (35%) were blended biculturals, 29 (63%) were alternating biculturals, and 1 Mexican American (2%) was separated. The single Mexican American separated adolescent was eliminated from the analyses, as a single case could not be analyzed statistically or be used as the basis of a qualitative description.

Quantitative Analyses: Differences Among Patterns

All analyses were carried out separately for each ethnic group. Preliminary log linear analyses were used to examine the association of socioeconomic status (SES) and gender with type of identification within each ethnic group separately. For both ethnic groups, there was no relation between type of identification and gender or SES, and no interaction of gender and SES. One-way analyses of variance (ANOVAs) were used to examine the relation of type of identification to age and academic grades for each ethnic group. These analyses showed no significant relation of age or academic grades to identification for either ethnic group.

Analyses were carried separately for each ethnic group to examine the relation of types of identification to independent measures of ethnic and American identity and to other measured variables.

Ethnic Identity. One-way ANOVAs of ethnic identity scores for each ethnic group showed no relation of the identification types to ethnic identity scores. Similar analyses carried out for each of the subscales of ethnic identity also showed no significant relation to identification in either ethnic group. However, the direction of difference was consistent with the greater emphasis on ethnicity reported in the interviews by the alternating biculturals; scores on each ethnic identity subscale were (nonsignificantly) higher for the alternating biculturals than for the blended biculturals in both the African American sample and the Mexican American sample.

American Identity. ANOVAs showed a significant relation of type of identification to American identity for each ethnic group. For the African Americans, the differences were significant overall, $F(2, 45) = 4.58$, $p < .02$, and paired comparisons showed that the blended biculturals scored significantly higher than the separated adolescents. For the Mexican Americans, there were significant overall differences by type, $F(1, 43) = 7.93$, $p < .01$; the blended biculturals scored significantly higher than the alternating biculturals.

Attitudes Toward Other Groups. ANOVAs by type of identification for each ethnic group showed that, among the Mexican Americans, attitudes toward other groups differed significantly, $F(1, 43) = 5.52$, $p < .05$; the blended biculturals had more positive attitudes toward other groups than did the alternating biculturals.

Correlations Among Measured Variables. A subsidiary question was whether ethnic and American identity are independent factors, as suggested by the two-dimensional model, or negatively correlated, as suggested by the one-dimensional model. Pearson product moment correlations were nonsignificant for each type of identification within each ethnic group.

In summary, the quantitative data support the identification patterns revealed in the interviews by adolescents from both ethnic groups. The blended biculturals, that is, those who described themselves as equally American and ethnic or as more American, had the highest American identity scores; and among the Mexican Americans they showed more positive attitudes toward other groups. The separated, who described themselves only as ethnic, had the lowest American identity scores, as well as the least positive attitudes toward other groups. The alternating biculturals tended to be intermediate between the other two types.

Qualitative Analyses: Descriptions of Patterns

Blended Biculturals. The interview comments of both the African American and the Mexican American blended bicultural students revealed a bicultural identity that was rooted in good feelings about being American, accompanied by a positive sense of their ethnicity. Being American carried distinct advantages for these adolescents. In America, they felt, you can do whatever you want, "without getting permission from other people." You can "express your feelings more here." These ideas of freedom were often contrasted with the lack of freedom elsewhere: "I like the freedom, the things you're able to do here that you are not able to do in other countries."

Related to these positive feelings was a sense of inclusion in American society. An African American student said, "As an American . . . you are one whole person, you are part of everything in American society." This sense of inclusion stemmed from a view of America as" a very diverse culture. . . . I do not think there is any true blood American; people have come from all different places." A Mexican American adolescent commented: "America has many different things . . . [they] don't exclude anybody . . . [they] don't segregate people here." Another stated, "The whole country was founded on togetherness."

Blended bicultural students from both ethnic groups affirmed their ethnicity, expressed pride in their background, and considered themselves equally ethnic and American. Among the African Americans, however, the comments conveyed a somewhat vague or impersonal sense of their ethnicity. Many of the African American blended biculturals expressed uncertainty about their culture: "We do not really have a culture," or "I do not know what African American really means." As a result, they were less likely to articulate specific attributes of their ethnic group. Being Black is "just a skin color; I don't think it is any more special than any other group." One of these students felt that, "Sometimes there is too much focus on being ethnic." Some of the African American blended biculturals expressed ambivalence about their ethnicity. One African American adolescent stated, "It is a good feeling that you are Black and not another color. . . . Sometimes you hate being Black because of what other people do . . . gangs, people who kill their own kind."

The blended bicultural Mexican American students also strongly affirmed their identity as Mexican American and their pride in the culture. However, the pride that they expressed appeared to be based on the accomplishments of their ethnic group rather than on an internalized or personal ethnic reality: "[Being Mexican American] makes me think of the people before me, who have come to this land and who have built from scratch all the things we see here." They also frequently referred to cultural characteristics such as history, music, and customs.

For both African American and Mexican American blended students, being bicultural was not seen as problematic, in part because there was little sense of differentiation and conflict between cultures. Many did not see a strong distinction between the two cultures and did not see themselves as caught between two cultures. Rather than seeing conflict between cultures, they felt that being bicultural was a either a neutral experience or a positive aspect of their lives. For some, it meant "having the best of both worlds. You have other roots you can draw from. . . . You can have a better understanding . . . of all points [of view]." Another felt that being bicultural meant being "a well-rounded person. . . . I think it benefits me to bring them together. I feel very lucky to be part of two cultures."

The blended biculturals mentioned conflict in one area. Compared to the other patterns, they were more likely to report pressure from peers to affirm their ethnicity or be more ethnic. African American students made comments such as: "When friends see themselves as more African American than me they call me a sell-out"; "They tell me not to talk White"; "They feel that I should cuss more and act more like them." Similarly, Mexican American students reported that "People tell me I should speak more Spanish"; "My friends say, 'aren't you a Mexican?' A lot of them wanted me to speak more Spanish, to listen to . . . Spanish music."

However, most of these blended bicultural adolescents comfortably incorporated both aspects of their identity: "I am both. . . . You have to look at everything." A Black student summed it up by saying, "Some people . . . think of themselves as just Black; I think of myself as Black American."

Alternating Biculturals. The alternating bicultural adolescents based their sense of being bicultural on strong personal feelings of closeness to their ethnic culture. These feelings of closeness were common across both ethnic groups, but African American and Mexican American youths varied in the ways in which the feelings were expressed.

Among African American alterating biculturals, there was a feeling of unity among Black people: "I like being Black. . . . We are more like a family. I feel like I belong to something." Another student stated, "I am proud to be Black because of the unity between Black people and what we do together as a people."

One girl added: "Black women are rising up, we are accomplishing a lot of things." Unlike the blended biculturals, these adolescents often talked about being Black in physical terms, and African Americans were described as beautiful: "I love the skin complexion and rough hair. I just love it. I would not want to change." These African American students were less likely to mention negative images of their ethnic group than were the blended bicultural adolescents. Problems in the African American community were acknowledged, but they were typically seen as coming from outside the group: "They" portray African Americans in a bad light; "White people" do not like African Americans.

Being bicultural was more problematic for the African American alternating adolescents than for the blended biculturals, and there was greater awareness of conflict. One African American student stated that having two cultures "is harder; you are not as American as another White person." School presented a situation that highlighted the differences: "At school I have to act a certain way. I can't talk like I want to. With my friends and at home, I talk like I want to." Even a student who stated that he had no difficulty in combining two cultures unconsciously made a distinction between the two: "I put myself as a mixture. It works as me accepting some of *their* culture and I keep *my* culture too" [emphasis added]. Thus, there appeared to be a clear sense of two distinct components to their identity. In contrast to the blended bicultural student who stressed being a "Black American," an alternating bicultural saw herself as "Black in America."

The Mexican American adolescents who showed the alternating bicultural pattern conveyed a strong sense of taking pleasure in their ethnicity: "I feel proud of being Mexican, I think I am lucky. I love it." Being ethnic was experienced internally and personally, as evidenced by their frequent use of first person statements: "I'm proud of it. . . . I like my race, I wouldn't want to be anything else"; "I think Hispanics have a real family. . . . We are more happy."

For these Mexican American alternating adolescents, being bicultural was discussed in positive tones. These adolescents were more aware than the blended biculturals of having two distinct cultures, and they mentioned their ability to speak two languages as the primary basis for the distinction. Although being bilingual was also mentioned by the blended students, it was stressed as a distinct advantage and was discussed at greater length by the alternating biculturals. Being bilingual meant greater job opportunities: "Since you can speak two languages, you can work in a lot of places." A number of students commented that being bilingual gave them "a better insight into the world," so that they could "learn to interact with all people." Thus for these alternating Mexican Americans, being bicultural was generally seen as an enriching experience because of the two languages, even though the American component was not a strong element in their identity.

Alternating bicultural adolescents from both ethnic groups acknowledged that they were Americans, mainly because they were born here and live here. They mentioned aspects of themselves that were American, such as "how I talk—I do not have an accent," but there was little sense of connection: "The American part—I do not feel much for it." America appeared to be an abstract idea which had little personal meaning for them. "I don't really understand what America represents." Several said that "being American is not important." For the Mexican American students, America was thought of mainly in contrast to the harder life in Mexico: "It gives me a freedom that I would not have if I were still where my parents are from." America is valued less for itself than for what it is not: "It is better here than to live somewhere else."

Separated Adolescents. The separated adolescents were distinguished by their assertion that they were not bicultural. Only one Mexican American showed the separated type of identification. The following description is therefore based on African American participants.

Like the alternating biculturals, the separated students had strong positive feelings about their ethnicity. "I would rather be Black than anything else." These students were the ones described by blended or alternating adolescents as exerting pressure to be more ethnic. Asked if he felt such pressure, a separated student stated, "I have said it to others. . . . I told them to act more Black . . . because they were acting White." These adolescents expressed a strong sense of the difference between Black and American culture. "You have to choose one or the other." "The other" meant White.

Although a few students from all patterns expressed the idea that "America" meant White, the separated adolescents made this point more often and more emphatically: "Everything is so White." "White is American to me, and no one in my family is White." Therefore, the adolescents could not see themselves as part of the larger society: "I'm not part of two cultures. I am just Black."

Furthermore, America was characterized by discrimination. While many of the African American students mentioned discrimination, it was described in particularly strong and personal terms by the separated adolescents: "In some places they can't stand you [African Americans]." As a result, these students had strongly negative feelings about their country: "I really don't believe in America"; "I wish it wasn't a thing called America . . . because it does not work."

Some of these separated adolescents seemed uncertain about how to deal with the uncomfortable feeling of being American: "I try to fit [the American part of me] in but it is hard." Yet most showed no inclination to try to fit into the larger society, in large part because society excluded them: "Some people see us as just Black. They do not include us in America." It was not seen as possible or desirable to combine the two worlds. "Most of the time we can't get along; we should just be separate, not talk to one another. It is like that for me now." For these students, being bicultural was not a viable option in a society that did not accept them.

Discussion

The results of this study provide evidence for wide variation among ethnic minority adolescents in the ways they identify with their ethnic culture and with the wider society. Differences among the types of identification were evident both in the adolescents' scores on questionnaire measures and in their interview comments about the meaning of being bicultural. Nearly 90% of the adolescents, all except the separated group, considered themselves to be bicultural, that is, both ethnic and American, but the meaning of being bicultural had qualitatively different meanings within and across ethnic groups. To identify adolescents simply as bicultural does not adequately address the complexity of their experiences.

The results suggest two bicultural patterns, blended biculturals and alternating biculturals, as well as a third pattern of separated adolescents who were not bicultural. For the blended bicultural adolescents, biculturalism was based on a strong sense of being American while affirming their ethnicity. The alternating bicultural adolescents, in contrast, described themselves as distinctly more ethnic than American. They acknowledge their American identity, but being American lacked a clear meaning for them, beyond the general idea of freedom. Finally, the third group, the separated adolescents, could not be considered bicultural. They strongly affirmed their ethnicity but they expressed little or no identification with America, which many saw as "White."

We found no evidence for the assimilated, fused, or marginal patterns. No adolescents indicated that they were American and not ethnic, that is, assimilated, and none said they felt they were neither American nor ethnic, that is, marginal. Finally, none suggested that the two cultures were indistinguishable, as would be expected from those with a fused identity. It is possible that the specific questions asked (i.e., whether the participants saw themselves as more ethnic or more American) influenced the patterns we found. This interpretation seems unlikely, as most of the respon-

dents rejected the two options by indicating that they were both, to varying degrees. We suggest that the assimilated, fused, and marginal patterns are all possible patterns that might be found in other regions of the country. For example, minority group members, such as those living in predominantly White areas where there is no ethnic community and little same-ethnic contact, may become assimilated (Tatum, 1987). Native Americans who have left a reservation and have not become part of the larger society have often been described as marginal (Berlin, 1987). The large number of blended and alternating bicultural students in our study may be due in part to the ethnically diverse school and neighborhood environments of these adolescents.

The current results demonstrate that in the process of balancing the two cultures, the sense of identification with American culture is a critical factor. American identification differed significantly by identification pattern, while ethnic identity scores did not differ and ethnicity was salient and positive for all the adolescents. As noted earlier, the topic of American identity has not been widely studied, but it is clearly a key component of being bicultural. Although most of the adolescents acknowledged being American, they differed in the extent to which they felt included in the larger society. In fact, a determining factor in one's cultural identification appears to be the individual's perception of society; to feel bicultural, one must see the larger society as inclusive. For some adolescents, mostly the blended biculturals, America signified diversity; thus, they could see themselves as part of it. The increasing diversity evident throughout Southern California, together with the increasing visibility of people of color in the media and in positions of authority, may allow these youths to see themselves as part of the larger whole. For other adolescents, especially the separated group, American meant White, and they were not part of it. For these students, as for many minority group members, the rejection they experience from members of the majority culture may be seen as limiting their participation in the mainstream (Anderson, 1991; Cose, 1993; Jones,

1988; Keefe, 1992). The attitudes of the larger society toward the ethnic group are clearly an important influence on the extent to which individuals feel bicultural (LaFromboise et al., 1993).

In summary, we found that most ethnic minority adolescents combine their sense of being ethnic and American and acknowledge being bicultural, but their sense of being bicultural varies widely, depending on how they perceive the two cultures and the way they identify with each. Being bicultural does not require a weakening of identification with one's ethnic culture; most of the participants felt identified with both cultures. Yet biculturalism is a complex and multidimensional phenomenon; there is not just one way of being bicultural. The patterns described, like any typologies, are oversimplifications; no doubt there is a range of possibilities for resolving the bicultural issue. However, the patterns provide a useful heuristic for future research. By recognizing these differences, research can gain greater insight into the ways in which ethnic minority adolescents develop in a multicultural society. Clearly, future research is needed to define these types more precisely and examine their relevance to other ethnic groups. A better understanding of these patterns might provide clinicians with insights that could help minority youth who are wrestling with bicultural conflicts, and could shed light on friction within ethnic groups, including the pressures some adolescents feel to be more or less ethnically identified.

REFERENCES

Anderson, L. (1991). Acculturative stress: A theory of relevance to Black Americans. *Clinical Psychology Review, 11,* 685–702.

Berlin, I. (1987). Effects of changing native American cultures on child development. *Journal of Community Psychology, 15,* 299–306.

Berry, J. (1990). Psychology of acculturation. In J. Berman (Ed.), *Cross-cultural perspectives: Nebraska symposium on motivation* (pp. 201–234). Lincoln: University of Nebraska Press.

Birman, D. (1994). Acculturation and human diversity in a multicultural society. In E. Trickett, R. Watts, & D. Birman (Eds.), *Human diversity: Perspective on people in context* (pp. 261–284). San Francisco: Jossey-Bass.

Cose, E. (1993). *The rage of a privileged class.* New York: HarperCollins.

Fordham, S., & Ogbu, J. (1986). Black students' school success: Coping with the burden of "Acting White." *The Urban Review, 18*(3), 176–206.

Greenfield, P., & Cocking, R. (1994). *Cross-cultural roots of minority child development.* Hillsdale, NJ: Erlbaum.

Helms, J. (1990). *Black and white racial identity: Theory, research, and practice.* New York: Greenwood.

Jones, J. (1988). Racism in Black and White: A bicultural model of reaction and evolution. In P. Katz & D. Taylor (Eds.), *Eliminating racism: Profiles in controversy* (pp. 137–157). New York: Plenum.

Keefe, S. (1992). Ethnic identity: The domain of perceptions of and attachment to ethnic groups and cultures. *Human Organizations, 51,* 35–43.

LaFromboise, T., Coleman, H., & Gerton, J. (1993). Psychological impact on biculturalism: Evidence and theory. *Psychological Bulletin, 114,* 395–412.

Marcia, J., Waterman, A., Matteson, D., Archer, S., & Orlofsky, J. (1994). *Ego identity: An handbook for psychosocial research.* New York: Springer-Verlag.

Mendelberg, H. (1986). Identity conflict in Mexican-American adolescents. *Adolescence, 21,* 215–222.

Phinney, J. (1989). Stages of ethnic identity development in minority group adolescents. *Journal of Early Adolescence, 9,* 34–49.

Phinney, J. (1992). The Multigroup Ethnic Identity Measure: A new scale for use with diverse groups. *Journal of Adolescent Research, 7,* 157–176.

Phinney, J. (1993). A three-stage model of ethnic identity development. In M. Bernal & G. Knight (Eds.), *Ethnic identity: Formation and transmission among Hispanics and other minorities* (pp. 61–79). Albany: State University of New York Press.

Ramirez, M. (1984). Assessing and understanding biculturalism-multiculturalism in Mexican-American adults. In J. Martinez & R. Mendoza (Eds.), *Chicano psychology* (pp. 77–94). Orlando, FL: Academic.

Tatum, B. (1987). *Assimilation blues: Black families in a white community.* Westport, CT: Greenwood.

THINKING CRITICALLY

1. The study in this reading includes African American adolescents and Mexican American adolescents. Based on the findings here for these two groups, what results would you hypothesize for Asian Americans?
2. How is having a blended bicultural identity different for African American and Mexican American adolescents? How would you explain this difference?
3. What is the difference between blended biculturals and alternating biculturals? Is one group more bicultural than the other?

PART
VII Family Relationships

Adolescents' Family Relationships in India

Americans sometimes assume that when children reach adolescence, it is inevitable that they will have more conflicts with their parents, become more distant from them, and be embarrassed to be seen with them, preferring to spend their leisure time with peers instead. Although these changes in family relations occur in many American families when children enter adolescence, this reading shows that the basis for these changes is cultural and that there is nothing inevitable or "natural" about them. The Indian adolescents described here maintain close, loving relationships with their parents. The authors of this reading compare the Indian eighth graders in their study with a comparable sample of American eighth graders, and the contrast is striking.

Reading 7.1

Adolescent's Family Relationships in India: The Daily Family Lives of Indian Middle Class Teenagers

R. Larson, S. Verma, and J. Dworkin

"Adolescents' Family Relationships in India: The Daily Lives of Indian Middle-Class Teenagers" by R. Larson, S. Verma, and J. Dworkin (March 2000). From a paper presented at the biennial meeting of the Society for Research on Adolescence, Chicago. Reprinted by permission from Reed Larson.

By comparison to other cultures, the Indian family is recognized to be strong and cohesive (Bharat, 1997). India is often identified as a prime example of a collectivistic culture, with collectivist values embodied in strong family ties (Sinha, 1988). What does this mean in terms of Indian adolescents' family experience? Many Westerners have a difficult time understanding that adolescents' family experiences could be any different than the combination of distancing, individuation, and renegotiation that characterizes parent-adolescent relationships in Western cultures. This chapter is aimed at describing Indian adolescence in its own right, but also at addressing this question: Do Indian adolescents really have a different kind of experience with their families than adolescents in individualistic Western societies?

As a means to these aims, we focus on the daily, hour-to-hour family experience reported by a sample of Indian middle class adolescents. How much time do teenagers in a collectivistic culture such as this spend with their families, and in what types of situations? Do Indian adolescents feel positive emotions during this family time, or do they feel an undercurrent of unhappiness, irritability, and anger?

We approach our topic with a posture of critical inquiry. Our data show that middle class Indian adolescents spend large amounts of their waking hours with their families, but we do not automatically assume that this is a positive experience. Is it possible that the traditional hierarchical nature of Indian families or tensions between spouses or in-laws make family members, though physically present, emotionally unresponsive to children? How much time do Indian adolescents actually spend talking to other family members? Do they experience other family members as responsive and friendly or as authoritarian? We also ask whether the ongoing socioeconomic changes in India toward two-parent employment and nuclear (as opposed to extended) households are related to changes in adolescents' family experience.

This chapter is written by two Americans and an Indian and attempts to weave together our different perspectives and insights. We have chosen to focus on the family experience of a sample of urban middle class Indian adolescents, a group that is experiencing (and initiating) dramatic cultural change. In some ways, this group is being influenced by Western culture, particularly in their material acquisitions and life style (e.g., drinking Coke and wearing Levis). However, much evidence suggests that adolescence in India is not converging with Western adolescence. Rather we see the evolution of an alternate conception of this life period, particularly in its orientation toward the family.

Culture and Family Experience

In the West, individuation from family is seen as a developmental task of adolescence (Havighurst, 1953), and the process of distancing or "breaking away" from family is endorsed by the cultural scripts of literature and films (Considine, 1985; Kiell, 1959). This does not necessarily mean rebellion and it certainly does not mean renouncing your family, but it does mean a mutual renegotiation of relationships with parents that grants adolescents more individual autonomy and brings them toward becoming independent adults who have a more peer-like relationship with their parents (Grotevant & Cooper, 1986; Hauser, 1991; Hill & Holmbeck, 1987).

In India, there is much reason to expect that the normative adolescent scenario will be different. We have already mentioned collectivist values that place the family at the center of people's lives (Bharat, 1997; Sinha, 1988). Far from romanticizing "breaking away," celebrated Indian epics such as the Ramayana and Mahabharata provide scripts of life-long devotion to parents, and traditional Indian values stress continuity rather than discontinuity in family ties from childhood to adulthood (Komar, 1993). In traditional Indian values it is a virtue to subordinate one's own individual needs to the interests of the kinship group (Saraswathi, 1999). Respect, trust, and deference to elders is taught to children from an early age and "behavior that threatens the cooperative spirit and unity [of the family] is discouraged from surfacing" (Bharat, 1997, p. 204). Independence is not valued in traditional Indian families and is equated with disobedience. Pursuit of individual autonomy occurs only among older adults (Mines, 1988).

Within the growing Indian urban middle and upper class, parents are becoming less authoritarian, more child-centered, and more responsive to children (Kashyap, 1993). As compared to traditional rural families, these parents give more weight to the psychological rather than economic value of children; they value children as a source of love and personal fulfillment (Srivastava, 1997). These changes, however, have not altered the strong Indian value on family cohesiveness and the continuity of family connections into adulthood. Parents still often choose careers for their children, and, in the great majority of cases, choose their children's spouses (Ramu, 1988). Adolescents and young adults, irrespective of educational level, generally accept that "parents know best" (Saraswathi, 1999). Strong ties to family continue into adulthood, with continued emotional dependence on family, particularly on mothers. What do these patterns mean in terms of the daily family experience of Indian middle class adolescents?

A Study of Indian Adolescents' Daily Lives

The sample for this study included 100 middle class 8th graders from Chandigarh, a city in northern India. This metropolitan area consists of about 1.2 million people and is recognized to be affluent and modern as compared to other Indian cities. Median family income in the study was in the range of U.S.$3600–4800. Parents were well-educated: 52 fathers and 49 mothers had graduate degrees. The participants included 51 girls and 49 boys, with a mean age of 13.2. All of these adolescents lived in two-parent families. Forty of the adolescents lived in households that included extended family relatives; the rest lived in nuclear households. In 40 households, the mothers were employed. Seventy of the families were Hindu and 30 were Sikh.

To study daily experience, we employed a procedure—the Experience Sampling Method (ESM)—that the first author has used in a number of studies with American adolescents. Participants carried alarm watches for one week and filled out self-reports on their experience each time they were signaled by the watches. Eight signals were sent at random times each day between 7:30 AM and 9:30 PM. The adolescents responded to an average of 86% of the signals, providing a total of 4,764 self-reports.

At the moment of each ESM signal, adolescents reported on their experience at that moment. First they reported on their objective situation: where were they, whom they were with, and what they were doing. In addition, participants rated their subjective states at the time of each signal on a series of rating scales. These dealt with their emotional experience, cognitive and motivational states, the social climate they experienced at the moment, and who they perceived to be the leader of the current interaction. For most analyses we use values for these scales that have been standardized to z-scores within the person, with negative values indicating responses below the person's norm and positive values indicating responses above the norm.

To provide cross-cultural comparisons, for several of the analyses we report data from a sample of middle class U.S. 8th graders studied with exactly the same procedures. This sample consisted of 84 adolescents, 41 boys and 43 girls, with a mean age of 13.2.

We will look first look at the quantity of time Indian adolescents spend with their families, then we will look at how they experience this time.

Quantities of Family Time

With Whom Do Indian Adolescents Spend Their Time?

Because the ESM signals occurred at random times, they provide a representative sample of how these Indian adolescents spent their waking hours. Figure 7.1.1 provides a pie chart of

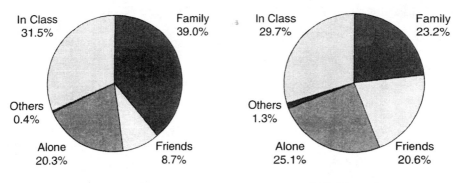

FIGURE 7.1.1 Whom adolescents spend time with.

how often these 8th graders reported being with different categories of companions. For comparison purposes, we have included a similar pie chart for the U.S. 8th graders. Since both groups of youth were studied for approximately 100 hours across the week, one percent of their self-reports is equivalent to approximately one hour per week.

To begin with, we can see that the two cultural groups spend quite similar amounts of time with classmates (in class) and Indian adolescents spend somewhat less time alone. The first author has demonstrated that time alone for American adolescents serves an important function, as a sanctuary for the development of a private autonomous self (Larson, 1990, 1997). Analyses performed with the Indian adolescents did not find evidence that it has a similar function for them. Indian adolescents who spent intermediate amounts of time alone were not better adjusted than those who were rarely alone.

The Indian 8th graders also spent much less time with friends than did the U.S. adolescents. In the U.S., friends accounted for a fifth of 8th graders' waking hours and reached a quarter of waking time by the high school years (Csikszentmihalyi & Larson, 1984; Richards, Crowe, Larson, & Swarr, 1998). For these Indian 8th graders, time with friends accounted for less than one eleventh of waking hours. This figure may not surprise Indian scholars, who have recognized the lesser importance of the peer group in India than in the West (Komar, 1993).

This is more true of girls than boys, however. Indian girls spent much less time with friends (6%) than Indian boys (11%, $t = 3.37$, $p < .001$), with this difference entirely attributable to girls spending less time with friends in public locations (2.8%) than boys (7.4%). Boys in India are given more freedom of movement; it is less acceptable for girls to be on their own away from home, family, and adult monitoring (Bharat, 1997; Saraswathi, 1999). For the U.S. data there was no gender difference in time with friends.

While spending less time alone and with friends, the Indian 8th graders reported spending much more time with their families. Their family time—accounting for close to 40% of their waking hours—was two thirds more than that of the American 8th graders. Time budget data from older Indian adolescents indicate that this large quantity does not diminish with age (Verma, 1995; Verma & Saraswathi, 1992). Indian girls spent more time with family (44%) than boys (35%; $t = 3.03$, $p < .01$), while there was no gender difference for the Americans. Yet for Indians of both genders, family is clearly a prominent part of daily life. They are not breaking away; they are not disengaging from daily interaction with their families.

What impressed us most were the responses of these Indian youth to a question in our follow-up questionnaire asking whom they would rather spend time with. In the U.S., by the 8th grade this type or question is almost always answered in favor of peers (Bowerman & Kinch, 1959). But 43 of our Indian adolescents named family members as their preference and only 29 said peers, with 9 saying alone and 19 saying family *and* friends. This suggests that the large amount of time they spend with their families is not simply a result of parental constraints. Family appears to be a high priority for many of these teenagers. We now turn to examining what goes on during Indian adolescents' time with family.

What Happens During Indian Adolescents' Family Time?

Does the large quantity of time that Indian youth spend with their families provide rich experiences? Might it be a developmental asset? As a first step toward approaching this question we asked where this family time takes place, who is present, and what activities occur. We first determined that the great majority of family time occurs at home. Eighty-six percent of all family time occurs at the family residence (vs. 78% for U.S. 8th graders). Schoolwork and preparation for competitive exams is a very high priority for Indian youth (Verma, Sharma, & Larson, 2000), and parents often gave that as

an explanation for engaging in few family outings. Compared to American parents, Indian parents also spend far less time in transportation with their 8th graders, driving them between one activity and another.

We next looked at which family members or groups of family members the adolescents were with during the ESM signals. We found that nuclear family members accounted for the great majority of family time (Table 7.1.1). Despite the importance given to the extended family in India (Biswas, 1992), amount of time with extended relatives was comparatively small, only 3.8% of all time (10% of family time). Of course, total time with extended family was greater for youth in extended households

Among nuclear family members, Indian adolescents spent most time with mothers and siblings. Fathers were secondary. Amount of time alone with mother was about twice the amount of time alone with father. The largest quantity of time with fathers occurred in family groups in which the mother was also present. This lesser involvement of fathers with adolescent children is common across most societies that have been studied (Collins & Russell,

TABLE 7.1.1 Division of Adolescents' Time With Family

	TOTAL	GIRLS	BOYS
Mother	**21.6**	**22.6**	**20.2**
mother only	12.6	14.2	10.4
mother and siblings	9.0	8.4	9.8
Father	**9.8**	**10.2**	**9.1**
father only	6.1	6.1	6.0
father and siblings	3.7	4.1	3.1
Mother and Father	**34.1**	**33.8**	**34.7**
parents only	8.2	9.0	7.2
parents and siblings	23.4	22.6	24.5
parents and others	2.5	2.2	3.0
Siblings	**24.4**	**22.5**	**27.0**
siblings only	24.4	22.5	27.0
Extended Relatives	**10.2**	**11.0**	**9.1**
uncles, aunts, and cousins	5.2	5.9	4.2
grandparents	2.6	2.3	3.0
grandparents and other relatives	2.4	2.8	1.9
	100.0	100.0	100.0

Note. The comparison between girls and boys is significant, χ^2 (10, $N = 1843$) = 19.7, $p = .032$

1991), including in our European American and African American data (Larson, 1993; Larson, Richards, Sims, & Dworkin, in press). Unlike in many groups, however, we found that the proportion of family time with mothers versus fathers did not differ markedly by gender of the child. While Western studies find a tendency for youth to spend more time with their same-gender parents (Collins & Russell, 1991; Youniss & Smoller, 1985), that was not evident for these Indian adolescents.

Lastly, we looked at what activities occurred during family time. We were particularly interested in how much time was spent talking with family, because this activity represents the most direct interaction. We found that the most frequent activities with family were watching TV (21% of family time), homework (19%), and eating (17%), with little difference by gender. Talking was the fourth most frequent activity, accounting for 13% of family time. This is about the same percentage as for our U.S. 8th graders, 11%, but given that Indian 8th graders spent much more time with their families, their net amount of time talking with family is substantially higher (5% vs. 2.6% of waking hours).

Perhaps the most notable finding regards how frequently fathers were conversation partners. In European American families, fathers are a less frequent companion in conversation than mothers, especially for adolescent daughters (Larson, Richards, Moneta, Holmbeck, & Duckett, 1996; Youniss & Smollar, 1985). Yet for these Indian 8th graders, the rate of talking with fathers did not differ greatly from the rate of talking with mothers, and girls talked as much if not more with their fathers than boys. In our interviews, one girl said, "I talk about everything with my father: politics, games, movies, friends, day's activities at school." Similarly, another girl said, "I talk about everything with my father, even about good-looking guys." This is consistent with the data we obtained from these fathers' ESM reports (Larson, Verma, & Dworkin, 2000) and with another study that found middle class Indian fathers to report equality in their treatment of sons and daughters (Srivastava, 1997). Indian fathers ap-

pear to do better than American fathers in engaging their children in conversation. Although the traditional Indian father has been portrayed as being on the periphery of the family, these middle class fathers appear to be comparatively engaged in the lives of their adolescent children of both genders.

To summarize, we have found that the large amount of time that Indian middle class 8th graders' spent with their families occurred mainly at home, in the company of nuclear family members, and involved a range of routine activities, from watching TV to homework to conversation. While fathers were less frequently present during these interactions than mothers, rates of conversation with fathers, including by daughters, were comparatively high.

Qualities of Family Time

Adolescents' Emotional States Across Contexts

Large amounts of family time may be meaningless or even detrimental if, beneath the surface, adolescents are filled with anger, worry, or unhappiness. What do Indian adolescents feel during this large volume of family time? Beneath their filial role of being a good child might there be undercurrents of negative feeling?

As a starting point, we looked at responses to a general index of emotional state. Eighth graders in both the Indian and U.S. samples rated their emotions or "affect" at each ESM signal on a scale summing responses to three semantic differential items (happy-unhappy, cheerful-irritable, friendly-angry) that represented how positive to negative their state was on a scale from +9 to -9. Youth in both countries reported a wide range of mostly positive but not infrequent negative states. In fact we were surprised to find that the distribution of hour-to-hour emotions on this scale was virtually identical for these middle class 8th graders living on opposite sides of the world. They differed, however, in when they most often experienced these positive and negative states.

In two contexts, there were no cultural differences. When they were in class and alone, the Indian and American youth reported remarkably similar states. Being in class was associated with average affect that was slightly above each person's mean in both countries. Being alone was associated with average affect that was markedly below each person's mean.

The big differences between Indian and U.S. 8th graders were in their emotional experience with friends and with family. Both groups reported favorable affect with their friends; this was the happiest segment of their daily lives. Indian adolescents, however, reported feeling somewhat less happy on average during this time. Compared to the Americans they had fewer times when they were at the extreme positive end of the scale (on the raw, non z-scored scale, they were above +7 for 20% of their reports with friends vs. 26% for the Americans); and they had slightly more times when they experienced negative emotions (7% vs. 5% for the Americans).

Indian adolescents, in contrast, reported feeling happier than Americans during time with their families. Whereas affect is below average for Americans during time with family, for Indians it is average—it is at the norm for the rest of their lives. The main reason for this is that the Indians had fewer occasions when they experienced negative emotions during time with family. They reported feeling irritable for 12% of these times, as compared to 20% for the Americans; and they reported feeling unhappy for 10%, versus 15% for the Americans. Indians are not without negative feelings in the presence of their families, but these kinds of feelings occur less often, and in fewer families. One girl said, "Anything that happens in the family makes me feel good; I know that someone cares."

Indian adolescents also rated the social climate when with their family as responsive and favorably disposed towards them. At each ESM report, they rated whether they rated the people they were with as helpful (vs. unhelpful) and friendly (vs. unfriendly), which we summed to create the social climate scale. For the U.S. 8th graders, means z-scores for these items were negative during family time; however, for Indians they were significantly positive. The Indian adolescents reported family members to be very friendly for 52% of the time, as compared to 40% for the Americans; and the Indians only reported family members to be unfriendly for 2% of the time, as compared to 6% for the Americans.

Lastly, we examined whom adolescents identified as the leader during these interactions. If Indian families are authoritarian, we would expect adolescents to experience their parents as being the leader for much of the time. In fact, the adolescents reported that there was no leader for 72% of the time. This is similar to the rate reported by the American 8th graders (62%). These rates indicate that these middle class Indian adolescents' experience of the family is anything but authoritarian.

Cultural Difference and Cultural Change

While our findings paint a positive picture of Indian adolescents' family lives, a number of Indian scholars have expressed alarm at the possibility that changes in the family may be moving India toward an American-like pattern in which adolescents spend less time with their families, experience less adult control, and manifest more problem behaviors. A common lament is that adolescents in nuclear family households do not get the benefits of the rich social support system provided by multiple adults in traditional joint households (Bharat, 1997). Concerns about mothers' employment have also been voiced.

As a means to evaluate these concerns, we examined whether the distinct patterns of adolescents' family relationships varied as a function of indicators of cultural change. Is time with family and affect with family less in nuclear households? In families where mothers are employed? In families whose parents have higher education and income? Tests of these comparisons suggested no weakening of the family related to these variables. Our findings do not support alarm about the average Indian middle class family. Indian adolescents' rich experience of high quantity and quality of time with their families does not appear to be threatened by changes in the family.

Conclusion

Indian adolescents' experience with their families, we conclude, is quite positive. Indian adolescents spend much more time with their families than European American adolescents and they generally feel positive about this time. They do have negative experiences. At one signal, a youth reported feeling "bored, my father was giving me a lecture." Another reported feeling lonely because "nobody loves me as they always criticize me." But they reported many more positive experiences, for example feeling "Excited; my uncle was coming to visit us this evening"; "Very happy, we just bought a gift for papa for his birthday."

What is striking to the American authors (but not surprising to the Indian author) is that we found little undercurrent of rebellion or distrust. In the interviews with these youth, very few admitted any significant conflict or difference of views with their parents. These adolescents seemed to genuinely like being with their families. They did not feel a cultural imperative to break away. One father reported that his daughter had asked him to memorize a set of facts about each of her friends, including their likes and dislikes, a request that would be unheard of in the U.S., especially between a daughter and father. The American phenomenon in which adolescents do not want to be seen in public with their families would, in turn, be very anomalous in India.

The large volume of time that Indian adolescents spend with their families may well be a developmental asset. The family is typically a context that reinforces adult values, promotes school success, and supports emotional security (Larson & Richards, 1991). Indian adolescents are undoubtedly getting a much bigger dose of these experiences. In addition to more time in the family's presence, Indian 8th graders were found to spend nearly twice as much time talking to their families as Americans, with much more time talking to their fathers. We believe that this larger diet of family interaction, especially given that it is experienced positively, is developmentally beneficial.

Yes, the Indian middle class family is changing, but we should not assume it is becoming Western. The hierarchical family relationships described in traditional Indian families is not highly evident here. Adolescents indicated that there was no leader during family interactions for the majority of times. Fathers were not feared. Furthermore, adolescents in families that were more "modern"—nuclear families and families where mothers were employed—did not spend less time with family members or have less positive experiences.

Students of cultural values have repeatedly come to the conclusion that the cluster of social changes sometimes called "modernization" or "globalization" does not inevitably mean adoption of individualism (Kagitçibasi, 1997; Malik, 1981; Smith & Schwartz, 1997). There is no reason to assume that social and technological change in India will alter adolescents' family relationships to include the processes of individuation, negative feeling, and daily disengagement that occurs in the West.

REFERENCES

Bharat, S. (1997). Family socialization of the Indian child. *Trends in Social Science Research, 4*(1), 201–216.

Biswas, P. C. (1992). Perception of parental behaviour and adolescents' frustration. *Indian Journal of Social Work, LIII*(4), 669–678.

Bowerman, C. E., & Kinch, J. W. (1959). Changes in family and peer orientation of children between the fourth and tenth grades. *Social Forces, 37*, 206–211.

Collins, W. A., & Russell, G. (1991). Mother-child and father-child relationships in middle childhood and adolescence: A developmental analysis. *Developmental Review, 11*, 99–136.

Considine, D. M. (1985). *The cinema of adolescence.* Jefferson, NC: McFarland.

Csikszentmihalyi, M., & Larson, R. (1984). *Being adolescent: Conflict and growth in the teenage years.* New York: Basic Books.

Grotevant, H. D., & Cooper, C. R. (1986). Individuation in family relationships: A perspective on individual differences in the development of identity and role-taking skill in adolescence. *Human Development, 29*, 82–100.

Hauser, S. T. (with Powers, S. I., & Noam, G. G.) (1991). *Adolescents and their families: Paths of ego development* (pp. 231–243). New York: The Free Press.

Havighurst, R. J. (1953). *Human development and education.* New York: McKay.

Hill, J., & Holmbeck, G. N. (1987). Familial adaptation to biological change during adolescence. In R. M. Lerner &

T. T. Foch (Eds.), *Biological-psychosocial interactions in early adolescence* (pp. 207–223). Hillsdale, NJ: Erlbaum.

Kagitçibasi, C. (1997). Individualism and collectivism. In J. W. Berry, M. H. Segall, & C. Kagitçibasi (Eds.), *Handbook of cross-cultural psychology: Social behavior and applications* (2nd ed., Vol. 3, pp. 1–49). Boston: Allyn and Bacon.

Kashyap, L. D. (1993). Adolescent/youth and family dynamics and development programmes. *Indian Journal of Social Work, LIV,* 94–107.

Kiell, N. (1959). *The adolescent through fiction.* New York: International Universities Press.

Komar, K. (1993). *Political agenda (?) of education: A study of colonialist and nationalist ideas.* New Delhi: Sage.

Larson, R. (1990). The solitary side of life: An examination of the time people spend alone from childhood to old age. *Developmental Review, 10,* 155–183.

Larson, R. (1993). Finding time for fatherhood: The emotional ecology of adolescent-father interactions. In S. Shulman and W. A. Collins (Eds.). *Father-adolescent relationships.* New Directions for Child Development, no. 62, pp. 7–18. San Francisco: Jossey-Bass.

Larson, R. (1997). The emergence of solitude as a constructive domain of experience in early adolescence. *Child Development, 68*(1), 80–93.

Larson, R., & Richards, M. H. (1991). Daily companionship in childhood and adolescence: Changing developmental contexts. *Child Development, 62*(2), 284–300.

Larson, R. W., Richards, M. H., Moneta, G., Holmbeck, G., & Duckett, E. (1996). Changes in adolescents' daily interactions with their families from ages 10 to 18: Disengagement and transformation. *Developmental Psychology, 32*(4), 744–754.

Larson, R., Richards, M. H., Sims, B., & Dworkin, J. (in press). How urban African American young adolescents spend their time: Time budgets for locations, activities, and companionship. *Journal of Community Psychology.*

Larson, R., Verma, S., & Dworkin, J. (2000). *Fathers' work and family lives in India: Daily ecology of time and emotion.* Manuscript submitted for publication.

Malik, S. M. (1981). *Psychological modernity: A comparative study of some African and American graduate students.* Ph.D. dissertation, University of Chicago.

Mines, M. (1988). Conceptualizing the present: Hierarchical society and individual autonomy in India. *American Anthropologist, 90,* 568–579.

Ramu, G. N. (1988). *Family structure and fertility.* New Delhi: Sage.

Richards, M., Crowe, P., Larson, R., & Swarr, A. (1998). Developmental patterns and gender differences in the experience of peer companionship during adolescence. *Child Development, 69* (1), 154–163.

Saraswathi, T. S. (1999). Adult-child continuity in India: Is adolescence a myth or an emerging reality? In T. S. Saraswathi (Ed.), *Culture, socialization, and human development.* New Delhi: Sage.

Sinha, D. (1988). Basic Indian values and behavior dispositions in the context of national development: An appraisal. In D. Sinha & H. S. R. Kao (Eds.), *Social values and development: Asian perspectives.* New Delhi: Sage.

Smith, P. B., & Schwartz, S. H. (1997). Values. In J. W. Berry, M. H. Segall, & C Kagitçibasi (Eds.), *Handbook of cross-cultural psychology: Social behavior and applications* (2nd ed., Vol. 3, pp. 77–118). Boston: Allyn and Bacon.

Srivastava, A. K. (1997). The changing place of child in Indian families: A cross-generational study. Trends in *Social Science Research, 4,* 191–200.

Verma, S. (1995). *Expanding time awareness: A longitudinal intervention study on time sensitization in Indian youth.* Zurich: The Johann Jacobs Foundation.

Verma, S., & Saraswathi, T. S. (1992). *At the crossroads: Time use by university students.* [A report submitted to the International Development Research Centre.] New Delhi: International Development Research Centre.

Verma, S., Sharma, D., & Larson, R. (2000). *School stress in India: Effects on time and daily emotions.* Manuscript submitted for publication.

Whiting, B., & Edwards, C. (1988). *Children of different worlds: The formation of social behavior.* Cambridge, MA: Harvard University Press.

Youniss, J., & Smollar, J. (1985). *Adolescent relations with mothers, fathers, and friends.* Chicago: University of Chicago Press.

THINKING CRITICALLY

1. The authors observe that for adolescents in Western countries, "the process of distancing or 'breaking away' from family is endorsed by the cultural scripts of literature and films." Can you think of examples?

2. Indian parents often choose their children's occupations and spouses. What do you see as the potential positive and negative consequences of these practices?

3. The authors refer to collectivism and individualism in this reading, but they did not ask questions directly about values. How do the results presented here reflect collectivist values in India and individualistic values in the United States?

4. The authors conclude that Indian adolescents' relationships with their parents constitute a "developmental asset." Explain what is meant by this term, as it is used here.

How Leaving Home Influences Relations With Parents

Most young people in American society leave home by age 18 or 19. Unlike in childhood and adolescence, when daily contact with parents is inevitable as a consequence of living in the same household, in emerging adulthood contact with parents becomes one reflection of one's relationships with them. Here, the authors present a study that examined young people's relationships with parents at age 14, 16, and 25, with a focus on relationships at age 25. The authors emphasize the importance of a balance of autonomy *and* relatedness *in relationships with parents at all ages and explore how this balance is related to contact with parents and satisfaction in relationships with parents at age 25.*

Reading 7.2

Adolescent-Parent Relationships and Leaving Home in Young Adulthood

T. G. O'Connor, J. P. Allen, K. L. Bell, and S. T. Hauser

In this chapter, we examine the transition to young adulthood as it affects the nature of parent-adult child relationships. We have two aims. The first is to outline a developmental model of parent-adult child relationships based on the constructs of autonomy and relatedness (Allen, Hauser, Bell, & O'Connor, 1994), and to present supporting findings from recent studies. The second is to link the dynamics of autonomy and relatedness in adolescent-parent interactions to the process of leaving home in a longitudinal study tracking individuals from midadolescence into young adulthood.

Autonomy and Relatedness in Parent-Child Relationships

A dynamic that consistently surfaces in theoretical and empirical analyses of the parent-child relationship throughout the first two decades concerns variations on themes of autonomy and relatedness (Grotevant & Cooper, 1985; Frank, Avery, & Laman, 1988; Mahler, Pine, & Bergman, 1975; Moore, 1987; Murphey, Silber, Coelho, Hamburg, & Greenberg, 1963; Ryan & Lynch, 1989; White, Speisman, & Costos, 1983). Researchers are increasingly documenting that children and adolescents who appear most au-

Adolescent-parent relationships and leaving home in young adulthood by T. G. O'Connor, J. P. Allen, K. L. Bell, and S. T. Hauser (1996). From *New Directions for Child Development, 71*, pp. 39–52. Copyright © 1996. Reprinted by permission of Jossey-Bass, Inc., a subsidiary of John Wiley & Sons, Inc.

tonomous and self-reliant report close, affectionate parental relationships (Allen, Hauser, Bell, & O'Connor, 1994; Ryan & Lynch, 1989). Thus autonomy, an independence of thought and behavior, and relatedness, an involvement with and support or connectedness to others, are not opposing dynamics. Indeed, for theoretical and empirical reasons, we focus on *autonomous-relatedness*, a relationship dynamic originally described by Bowlby (Allen, Hauser, Bell, & O'Connor, 1994; Bowlby, 1982; Murphey et al., 1963).

In previous studies, Allen and colleagues described how adolescents and parents negotiate changes in autonomy and relatedness in family interactions (Allen, Hauser, O'Connor, Bell, & Eickholt, 1993; Allen et al., 1994). One interesting finding from these studies is that a subset of adolescents was observed to gain pseudoindependence in parent-adolescent interactions at the expense of a positive, supportive relationship with their parents. Adolescents who undermined autonomy in interactions with their parents at age 14 were observed to compensate for their lack of autonomy by emotionally distancing themselves from parents at age 16. Other studies similarly document that an imbalance in the dynamic between autonomy and relatedness—either an emotionally detached or an enmeshed relationship—is often associated with poor concurrent and longitudinal adjustment (Frank et al., 1988; Moore, 1987; Ryan & Lynch, 1989). Allen and colleagues noted that adolescents who displayed comparatively low levels of autonomy and relatedness also exhibited low levels of ego development and self-esteem.

In a second set of studies, autonomy and relatedness in adolescent-parent interactions have been linked to several important indices of adjustment in young adulthood, including educational and occupational attainment (Bell, Allen, Hauser, & O'Connor, 1996), psychopathology and drug use (Allen, 1995), and attachment security and coherence of mind in attachment relationships (Allen & Hauser, 1994). These studies' findings support the hypothesis that successfully negotiating a stage-salient task of adolescence—establishing autonomy while maintaining a close, affectionate relationship with parents—has important implications not only for concurrent adjustment but also for successful resolution of later developmental tasks.

These findings also set a context for understanding the trajectory of parent-child relationships into young adulthood. In many ways, the increased autonomy demands in parent-adolescent relationships parallel the increased autonomy demands in parent–young adult relationships. Consequently, difficulty in establishing autonomy and relatedness with parents in adolescence may forecast difficulty in maintaining the autonomy and relatedness dynamic with parents in adulthood. In adolescence, difficulty establishing autonomy and relatedness with parents may manifest as conflict (Allen et al., 1993). In young adulthood, difficulty handling separation or individuation may manifest as a problem in setting the appropriate degree of involvement and contact. Contact, at this stage, is a new dimension in the parent-child relations as young adults have a greater power to regulate it.

Parent-Child Relationships in the Third Decade

Relatively few studies track the quality and correlates of parent-child relationships through young adulthood (Frank et al., 1988; Moore, 1987). Consequently, little is known about the longitudinal predictors of parent–adult child relationships or how these relationships are transformed as young adults leave the home. To date, available research on the relationship between parents and their young adult offspring relies heavily on two variables: amount of contact and overall satisfaction (Cooney, 1994; Lawton, Silverstein, & Bengtson, 1994).

Contact

Research findings indicate that young adults generally stay in close contact with their parents (Umberson, 1992; Rossi & Rossi, 1990) but that the amount of contact varies as a function of several demographic variables. For example, girls and young adults from nondivorced families appear to have the highest rates of contact (Aquilino, 1994; Frank et al., 1988). Furthermore, young adults who have started their own families tend to report higher rates of contact (Frank et al., 1988; Umberson, 1992; White et al., 1983), but young adults whose parents have divorced and remarried report comparatively less contact (Umberson, 1992; Aquilino, 1994; Cooney, 1994). This is particularly so in relation to noncustodial fathers. Although geographical proximity has also been related to more frequent contact with parents (Aquilino, 1994; Rossi & Rossi, 1990), several researchers have suggested that physical distance may be a consequence, rather than a cause, of the quality and intensity of the adult child-parent relationships (Lawton et al., 1994).

The sociodemographic factors that influence the frequency of adult child–parent contact are beginning to be understood, but there is relatively little discussion regarding the meaning of young adults' frequency of contact with parents or regarding the relationship dynamics that underlie the amount of contact. Available findings offer little guidance. In this chapter, we examine the meaning and the developmental significance of frequency of adult child–parent contact within an autonomy-relatedness framework.

Satisfaction

As in the case of frequency of contact, research findings point to several demographic correlates of young adults' satisfaction with their relationships with parents. Divorce history is perhaps the most consistent negative predictor of relationship satisfaction in young adulthood and may represent a continuation of the conflict that immediately followed, and most likely preceded, the divorce (Aquilino, 1994; Hetherington & Clingempeel, 1992). However, custodial status of the parent, parent gender, and parental remarriage significantly complicate this general finding (Aquilino, 1994; Cooney, 1994). Gender differences in satisfaction with parent–adult child relationships, especially regarding same-sex relationships, have been suggested but are inconsistently reported (Aquilino, 1994; Frank et al., 1988). Available findings also suggest that young adults' satisfaction with their relationship with parents is positively associated with their own level of adjustment (Rossi & Rossi, 1990, Umberson, 1992)

Remarkably little is known about the longitudinal predictors of young adults' satisfaction with their relationships with parents, especially how the quality of parent-adolescent relationships may influence later satisfaction. The studies cited above on the importance of autonomy and relatedness in adolescence suggest that satisfaction with parents may be predicted from the quality of parent-adolescent relationships.

We examined three hypotheses that expand previous research on parent-adult child relationships and further examined the hypothesis that establishing autonomy while maintaining relatedness with parents is a stage-salient task of adolescence. First, we hypothesized a significant positive relationship between satisfaction with parents and young-adult adjustment. Second, we hypothesized that compared to adolescents who display autonomy-relatedness with parents, adolescents who display imbalances in autonomy and relatedness would have greater difficulty separating from parents in young adulthood. Third, based on previous research, we hypothesized that men and adult children from families that have experienced divorce in which fathers left home would report less contact and less satisfaction with their parents in young adulthood.

Methods

The sample consisted of a subset of a larger sample of 146 adolescents and their families initially studied when the adolescents were approximately fourteen years old (Hauser, Powers, & Noam, 1991). To assess a broad range of psychosocial and family functioning, we initially selected one-half of the adolescents from the ninth grade. The other one-half of the subjects were selected from a psychiatric hospital and had diagnoses of mood or conduct disorders. Families in the study were white and predominantly middle and upper middle class. Adolescents in both sample groups were similar in age, gender composition, and number of siblings. However, families with hospitalized adolescents were slightly but significantly lower in social class and, at the time of the age 25 assessment, were more likely to have experienced a divorce.

Procedures

The current study includes data collected when the subjects were, on average, 14, 16, and 25 years old. At the age 14 and age 16 assessments, adolescents and their mothers and fathers (if applicable) participated in a revealed differences interaction task (Strodtbeck, 1951) using Kohlberg moral dilemmas. Families were asked to discuss and, if possible, resolve three disagreements among family members based on the moral dilemmas (Allen et al., 1994). When subjects were twenty-five, they were asked to complete a variety of questionnaire measures. In addition, a *Q*-sort rating of personality and adjustment was obtained from a peer whom the target young adult named as knowing well.

Autonomy and Relatedness Coding System. The Autonomy and Relatedness Coding System (Allen, Hauser, Borman, & Worrell, 1991) was used to code adolescent-family interactions. The coding system combines micro- and macroanalytic strategies of classifying behaviors into three categories: *exhibiting autonomous-relatedness* (behaviors reflecting differentiation of thought and opinion in the context of interest and engagement in others' thoughts); *undermining autonomy* (behaviors that make it difficult to reason or disagree or that personalize a disagreement); and *undermining relatedness* (behaviors that are critical, hostile, or that otherwise discourage affectionate, accepting interactions). Previous research has demonstrated the validity and reliability of the system (Allen et al., 1994). Observational data were available

on 79 mother-adolescent pairs. Data on only 51 father-adolescent pairs were available because some families were single mother families, and in some nondivorced families the father did not participate in the observational task.

Contact With Mother and Father. At age 25, young adults were asked to rate how often they had phone contact and how often they had personal contact with their mothers and fathers on a 6-point scale (1 = not at all, 6 = more than once a week). The items are comparable to other studies (Cooney, 1994). Young adults whose mothers (*N* = 7) or fathers (*N* = 12) were deceased were excluded from analyses.

Satisfaction With Relationship with Mother and Father. Also at age 25, young adults were asked to rate how satisfied they were with their relationships with mothers and fathers on a 5-point scale (1 = not at all, 5 = extremely). As with the contact measures, this measure is comparable to other studies assessing relationship satisfaction (Aquilino, 1994).

Psychosocial Adjustment in Young Adulthood. At age 25, young adults were asked to complete a battery of measures assessing overall adjustment. *Self-worth* and *social competence* are subscales taken from the Harter Self-Perception Profile (Harter, 1988). The Hopkins Symptom Checklist (HSCL) is a widely used and well-validated self-report measure of general symptomatology; only the global scale is examined in this report (Derogatis 1983). *Ego undercontrol* and *ego resiliency* are based on one of the young adult designated friend's California *Q*-sort ratings of the target young adult (Block & Block, 1980).

Results

The initial analyses tested whether gender or history of psychiatric hospitalization were associated with young adults' contact with parents. No gender differences were found in the adolescent-parent interaction behaviors, age 25 adjustment variables, or contact and satisfaction measures with parents in young adulthood. History of psychiatric hospitalization was not significantly related to frequency or quality of contact with parents at age 25; however, adolescents with a history of psychiatric hospitalization exhibited significantly lower levels of autonomous-relatedness to both mothers and fathers (Allen et al., 1994).

Contact and Satisfaction

There was a close correspondence between young adults' contact with both mothers and fathers by phone and in person (for mothers, $r = .64$, $p < .001$; for fathers, $r = .77$, $p < .001$). Given the high correlation between these variables and the tendency for previous research to combine measures of personal and phone contact (Aquilino, 1994; Cooney, 1994), these two measures were averaged in analyses.

The frequencies of visits and phone contacts with parents suggested that most of the young adults had regular contact with one or both parents, while one subset had either no or rare contact, and another subset had contact more than once a week. For example, slightly over 50 percent of the sample reported at least weekly contact with their mothers; 43 percent of the sample had weekly contact with their fathers.

Young adults' frequency of contact was positively related to satisfaction with the relationship (for mothers, $r = 38$, $p < .001$; for fathers, $r = .54$, $p < .001$). The magnitude of this correlation did not vary significantly by gender or divorce history (but see Cooney, 1994).

Correlates and Predictors of Young Adult–Parent Relationships

Frequency of contact with either mother or father showed no consistent link with young-adult adjustment. Correlations between relationship satisfaction and measures of adjustment were generally moderate in magnitude and differed in many cases, depending on whether the parental relationship was with mothers or fathers. Relationship satisfaction was significantly correlated in expected directions with ego undercontrol and ego resiliency (mothers), psychopathological symptoms (fathers), self-worth (mothers and fathers), and social competence (mothers and fathers) (see Table 7.2.1).

Correlations between parent-adolescent interactions at ages 14 and 16 and relationship variables at age 25 are displayed in Table 7.2.2. Of the family interactions variables, adolescents' autonomous-relatedness was strongly negatively correlated with frequency of contact in their relationships with their parents ten years later; this relationship was slightly stronger at age sixteen than at age fourteen, especially regarding fathers.

With one exception, neither undermining autonomy nor undermining relatedness was correlated with frequency of contact at age twenty-five. The one exception was a significant positive correlation between adolescents inhibiting autonomy toward mothers and more frequent contact with mothers ten years later ($r = .19$, $p < .05$). Interestingly, none of the adolescent interaction variables were significantly

TABLE 7.2.1 Correlations Between Adult Child–Parent Relationship Variables and Young-Adult Adjustment

ADJUSTMENT	FREQUENCY OF CONTACT		RELATIONSHIP SATISFACTION	
	Mother	Father	Mother	Father
Self-worth	.03	−.01	.23**	.20*
Social competence	−.03	−.07	.32**	.20*
Psychological symptoms	.12	−.02	−.11	−.24**
Ego control	.24*	−.11	.21*	−.14
Ego resiliency	.01	.11	.27**	.07

Note. N's for correlations range from 102 to 125.
*$p < .05$; **$p < .01$.

TABLE 7.2.2 Correlations Between Adolescent-Parent Interactions at Ages Fourteen and Sixteen and Adult Child–Parent Relationship Variables

	1	2	3	4
1. Autonomous relatedness (14)	—	.57**	−.15	.15
2. Autonomous relatedness (16)	.61**	—	−.51**	.09
3. Frequency of contact	−.25**	−.31**	—	.55**
4. Relationship satisfaction	.02	.05	.38**	—

Note. Correlations above the diagonal pertain to fathers; correlations below the diagonal pertain to mothers. N's for correlations range from 51 to 125; all available data were used, i.e., a pairwise deletion was used (see Methods section in this chapter for an explanation).
**p < .01

correlated with satisfaction with maternal or paternal relationships at age 25.

Correlations between parents' behavior toward their adolescents and adolescents' frequency of contact and satisfaction with parental relationships as young adults were also examined. The pattern of findings is almost identical to those found with adolescents' behavior. Specifically, the most robust correlations were found between parents' autonomous-relatedness in interactions and a decreased frequency of later contact (for fathers' behavior, $r = -.34$, $p < .05$; for mothers' behavior, $r = -.37, p < .05$).

Regression analyses were examined to determine the combined prediction of adolescent relationship and demographic variables for the frequency of contact and relationship satisfaction with parents in young adulthood. Demographic variables were entered first and were followed by adolescent behaviors at age 16 (Table 7.2.3). Only the age 16 variables were used in regression analyses because of the high correlation between the interaction variables at age 14 and 16 and because relating the later interactions to age 25 would be a more direct examination of the pre- and postseparation process.

For contact with mothers, only autonomous-relatedness made a significant contribution. In contrast, autonomous-relatedness and the gender X autonomous-relatedness interaction were significant predictors of contact with fathers, accounting for approximately 38 percent of the variance. Follow-up analyses of the interaction indicated that the link between autonomous-relatedness and contact with fathers was stronger for males than for females.

An inspection of the scatter plot helps clarify the nature of the negative relationship between autonomous-relatedness in adolescent-parent interactions and frequency of contact with parents ten years later. Almost without exception, adolescents who displayed the lowest levels of autonomous-relatedness with mothers and fathers maintained very close contact with parents as young adults. In contrast, adolescents who displayed middle to high levels of autonomous-relatedness appeared neither especially likely nor especially unlikely to maintain close contact with parents.

Regression analyses predicting satisfaction in adult child–parent relationships were similar for mothers and fathers (Table 7.2.3). In both cases, young adults reported less satisfaction with their relationships with both mothers and fathers if the family had experienced a divorce; only for fathers did autonomous-relatedness positively predict relationship satisfaction.

Discussion

The goals of this chapter have been first, to outline a theory of adolescent development emphasizing the stage-salient task of developing autonomy while maintaining close, affectionate attachments with parents, and second, to merge current findings with previous findings

TABLE 7.2.3 Hierarchical Regression Analyses Predicting Frequency of Contact and Relationship Satisfaction

| | FREQUENCY OF CONTACT | | | | RELATIONSHIP SATISFACTION | | | |
| | Mother (N = 83) | | Father (N = 51) | | Mother (N = 83) | | Father (N = 51) | |
	β	R^2	β	R^2	β	R^2	β	R^2
Step 1								
Gender	−.08		−.06		.02		−.06	
Psychological history	.04		−.02		.05		.00	
Statistics for step		.03		.05		.01		.02
Step 2								
Divorce history	−.04		−.19		−.25*		−.43**	
Statistics for step		.05		.13+		.05		.18*
Step 3								
Autonomous-relatedness (16)	−.28*		−.45**		.11		.13	
Statistics for step		.11+		.31**		.06		.20*
Step 4								
Autonomous-relatedness X Gender	—		.27*		—		—	
Total R^2		.11+		.38***		.06		.20*

Note: Beta coefficients reported are those obtained from the final model.
+ $p < .1$; * $p < .05$; ** $p < .01$; *** $p < .001$.

reported by Allen and colleagues, which document concurrent and longitudinal results of the relative success or failure in developing autonomous-relatedness in parent-adolescent relationships.

Moderate associations between the quality of parent–adult child relationships and several indices of young-adult adjustment were obtained. These findings are in general agreement with other studies that have examined the developmental significance of positive adult child–parent relationships (Rossi & Rossi, 1990; Seltzer, 1994; Umberson, 1992). The finding that some adjustment measures were related to relationship satisfaction with mothers, whereas other measures were related to satisfaction with fathers or with both parents, requires further inquiry.

Consistent with previous research (Aquilino, 1994; Cooney, 1994) a history of divorce in the family was found to be negatively related to relationship satisfaction in adult child–parent re-

lationships. As other researchers have suggested (Aquilino, 1994), this finding may be a continuation of the well-documented negative effects of divorce on parent-child relationships in adolescence (Hetherington & Clingempeel, 1992). It is significant to note that the negative effects of divorce on parent-child relationships continue into adulthood despite a major transformation in the nature of the parental relationship. In the current study, small sample sizes precluded tests of whether remarriage, the age of target children at the time of divorce (or remarriage), or the number of marital transitions would modify this finding (Aquilino, 1994).

The novel finding in this study is that the failure to establish autonomy and relatedness in adolescence predicts difficulty separating from parents in young adulthood. Virtually all of the adolescents who displayed low levels of autonomous-relatedness with their parents tended to stay in close contact with them as young adults approximately ten years later. A focus on autonomy as a central dynamic underlying this process is supported by the finding that adolescents who actively inhibit autonomy from mothers reported increased contact a decade later.

A high level of contact with parents in young adulthood is not necessarily believed to represent a developmental failure. Indeed, amount of contact was unrelated to several indices of adult adjustment. However, the uniformity with which adolescents low in autonomous-relatedness maintain close parental contacts, compared to the wide variability in contact frequency among young adults with moderate to high levels of autonomous-relatedness as adolescents, is striking in its apparent consistency. These individuals may illustrate one strategy for managing the stress associated with separation.

It is somewhat surprising that the quality of parent-adolescent relationships was more closely related to later contact than to later relationship satisfaction. These findings support Lawton and colleagues' suggestion that distance from, and by extension contact with, parents is more than a demographic variable. It may actually reflect underlying dynamic parent-child relational processes, especially regarding separation. In this vein, it is interesting to note that other patterns of leaving home and separating from parents have been described within this general framework. Aro and Palosaari's report (1992) of marriage to an undesirable partner as a method for leaving home may be another dysfunctional strategy.

Despite the conceptual appeal of transitions or stages of development in adulthood (Levinson, 1978), their significance past adolescence has received relatively little empirical attention. Even scarcer are data linking continuities of adaptation across developmental stages. In this chapter, we offer evidence suggesting that a developmental task of young adulthood, leaving home, is parallel to, and may evoke a model of adaptation that resembles, the manner in which an individual negotiated the task of developing autonomy while maintaining relatedness to parents in adolescence. We hope that these data spur additional efforts to connect patterns of adaptation across developmental transitions.

REFERENCES

Allen, J. P. & Hauser, S. T. (1994). *Autonomy and relatedness in adolescent-family interactions as predictors of young adults' states of mind regarding attachment.* Unpublished manuscript.

Allen, J. P., Hauser, S. T., Bell, K. L., & O'Connor, T. G. (1994). Longitudinal assessment of autonomy and relatedness in adolescent-family interactions as predictors of adolescent ego development and self-esteem. *Child Development, 65*(1), 179–194.

Allen, J. P., Hauser, S. T., Borman, E., & Worrell, C. M. (1991). *The autonomy and relatedness coding system: A scoring manual.* Unpublished manuscript, University of Virginia.

Allen, J. P., Hauser, S. T., Eickholt, C. E., Bell, K. L., & O'Connor, T. G. (1995). Autonomy and relatedness in family interaction as predictors of expressions of negative adolescent affect. *Journal of Research on Adolescence, 4,* 535–552.

Allen, J. P., Hauser, S. T., O'Connor, T. G., & Bell, K. L., & Eickholt, C. E. (1993). *The connection of the observed hostile family conflict to adolescents' developing autonomy and relatedness with parents.* Unpublished manuscript, University of Virginia.

Aquilino, W. S. (1994). Impact of childhood disruption on young adults' relationship with parents. *Journal of Marriage and the Family, 56,* 295–313.

Aro, H. M., & Palosaari, U. K. (1992). Parental divorce, adolescence, and the transition to young adulthood: A follow-up study. *American Journal of Orthopsychiatry, 62,* 421–429.

Bell, K. L., Allen, J. P., Hauser, S. T., & O'Connor, T. G. (1996). Family factors and young adult transitions: Educational attainment and occupational prestige. In J. Graber, J. Brooks-Gunn, & A. C. Petersen (Eds.), *Transitions through adolescence.* Hillsdale, NJ: Erlbaum.

Block, J. H., & Block, J. (1980). The role of ego-control and ego-resiliency in the organization of behavior. In W. A. Collins (Ed.), *The Minnesota Symposia on Child Psychology, Vol. 13.* Hillsdale, NJ: Erlbaum.

Bowlby, J. (1982). Attachment and loss (2nd ed.). New York: Basic Books.

Cooney, T. M. (1994). Young adults' relations with parents: The influence of recent parental divorce. *Journal of Marriage and the Family, 56* (1), 45–56.

Derogatis, L. R. (1983). *Description and bibliography for the SCL-90-R and other instruments of the psychopathology rating scale series.* Baltimore, MD: Johns Hopkins University School of Medicine.

Frank, S. J., Avery, C. B., & Laman, M. S. (1988). Young adults' perceptions of the relationships with their parents: Individual differences in connectedness, competence, and emotional autonomy. *Developmental Psychology, 24*(5), 729–737.

Grotevant, H. D., & Cooper, C. R. (1985). Patterns of interaction in family relationships and the development of identity exploration in adolescence. *Child Development, 56*(2), 415–428.

Harter, S. (1988). *The self-perception profile for adolescents.* Unpublished manuscript, University of Denver.

Hauser, S. T., Powers, S. I., & Noam, G. G. (1991). *Adolescents and their families: Paths of ego development.* New York: Free Press.

Hetherington, E. M., & Clingempeel, W. G. (1992). Coping with marital transitions: A family systems perspective. *Monographs of the Society for Research in Child Development, 57,* 2–3 (Serial no. 227).

Lawton, L., Silverstein, M., & Bengston, V. (1994). Affection, social contact, and geographic distance between adult children and their parents. *Journal of Marriage and the Family, 56*(1), 57–68.

Levinson, D. J. (1978). *The seasons of a man's life.* New York: Knopf.

Mahler, M., Pine, F., & Bergman, A. (1975). *The psychological birth of the human infant: Symbiosis and individuation.* New York: Basic Books.

Moore, D. (1987). Parent-adolescent separation: The construction of adulthood by late adolescence. *Development Psychology, 23*(2), 298–307.

Murphey, E. B., Silber, E., Coelho, G. V., Hamburg, D. A., & Greenberg, I. (1963). Development of autonomy and parent-child interactions in late adolescence. *American Journal of Orthopsychiatry, 33,* 643–652.

Rossi, A. S., & Rossi, P. H. (1990). *Of human bonding: Parent-child relations across the life course.* Hawthorne, NJ: Aldine.

Ryan, R. M., & Lynch, J. H. (1989). Emotional autonomy versus detachment: Revisiting the vicissitudes of adolescence and young adulthood. *Child Development, 60,* 340–356.

Strodtbeck, F. (1951). Husband-wife interactions over revealed differences. *American Sociological Review, 16,* 463–473.

Umberson, D. (1992). Relationships between adult children and their parents: Psychological consequences for both generations. *Journal of Marriage and the Family, 54,* 664–674.

White, K. M., Speisman, J. C., & Costos, D. (1983). Young adults and their parents: Individuation to mutuality. In H. Grotevant and C. Cooper (Eds.), *Adolescent development in the family.* New Directions for Child Development, no. 22. San Francisco: Jossey-Bass.

THINKING CRITICALLY

1. The authors emphasize that autonomy and relatedness are complementary rather than opposing dimensions of relationships with parents. Explain, in your own words, how that could be true.

2. In many cultures, young people typically live at home until marriage. To what extent do you think the findings here would apply to young people in such cultures?

3. Parents' divorce was related to lower relationship satisfaction between young adults and *both* their parents. Why do you think that would be so?

VIII Friends and Peers

Popularity and Unpopularity in Middle School

Researchers often obtain information through questionnaires and interviews, but in studies such as the one presented in this reading, researchers use a method called participant observation *in which they spend a great deal of time among the people they wish to study and record their observations during this time. Here, the author and her assistants describe the results of their participant observation among adolescents in an American middle school. As you will see, the research method of participant observation allowed them to obtain a vivid picture of the social world of the middle school and the way early adolescents rank themselves and others in a status hierarchy.*

Reading 8.1

Segregating the Popular From the Unpopular

D. Eder

The students who attended this school did not regard each other as equals. Within days of being in the school, it was evident to us that certain groups had more status than did others, especially in the seventh and eighth grades. The higher-status groups were generally the larger ones, and their members were often the topic of conversation by others in the school. In seventh grade, there were two separate popular groups, one made up only of boys, the other of girls. By eighth grade, these two groups had merged to some degree, so that many of the popular boys and girls now sat together at a row of tables at one end of the cafeteria.

Although it was evident from the start that these students were more popular than others, it took us well into the first year of the study to understand what popularity meant at Woodview. Studies of elementary students imply that the popular students are the best-liked. This was definitely not the case in this school. Instead, we were told that popular people were the most *visible in* the school; they were the students most people knew by name. According to some girls who were not as visible, the nice part about being popular is that "everybody knows you." Students who were more visible explained to us that "the good part [about popularity] is that you get a lot of attention," whereas those who lacked visibility felt that they and their achievements were generally ignored by others. Given Woodview's large size, it would be impossible for all the students to know each other by name. Thus, in many ways it makes sense that being well known would make some people stand out.

In sixth grade there were few ways for students to gain visibility. Two of the more attractive girls in the grade were talked about as being popular, but no elite groups existed at this grade level. Instead, there was a greater sense of equality among all students. When cheerleading and athletic teams were formed in seventh grade there was a basis for some people to gain greater visibility than their peers. Certain athletic games were considered important events and were widely attended by students outside the athletic sphere. This made participants in these events highly visible to the entire student body.

The interest shown by the larger community and the student body in the interscholastic competition of the male athletic teams at Woodview reflects this activity's cultural importance. Crowds for football games ranged from two hundred to five hundred people. Wrestling matches and basketball games did not match these attendance figures but did attract in excess of one hundred persons regularly. Informal groups discussed upcoming games and made plans to attend together, meet at the games, or socialize after the games. Even the athletic players seemed to have more interest in planning postgame activities with friends than in the games themselves.

Participants understood that their identities as team members increased their prestige, and they therefore actively attempted to make this identity more visible. Wearing uniforms was a major source of pride for team members. Being allowed to wear their team jerseys in school was a reward coaches granted players for exceptional effort and performance. Athletes also approved of the official team dress code, which some coaches enforced on game days.

The high status of boys' sports activities was evident in the fact that one had to be an athlete to be a member of the popular group. Self-identification as an athlete was enhanced by associating only with other athletes. Identity as a team member was further enhanced in informal talk by focusing on team activities as topics of conversation.

The high level of interest surrounding boys' athletic events was not present for girls' athletic competition. This was in part because boys' athletic events have a longer history in secondary schools and have gained considerable community support over the years. Woodview helped promote greater interest in boys' athletic events by holding school rallies. Furthermore, some of the male coaches were openly critical of attempts by female coaches to enhance the visibility of female athletics. The lack of faculty and administrative support for female athletics limited their cultural significance in the school. There were never more than twenty-five students at a girls' athletic event, and usually there were ten or fewer. As a result of this low visibility, female athletics did not provide girls with an avenue for peer status.

Instead, since boys' athletic activities were the most important and most highly attended events in the school, cheerleaders had considerable visibility among their classmates. Not only did the cheerleaders get to be seen by large numbers of students at male basketball and football games, they also performed for the entire student body at pep rallies and other school activities. In addition, the fact that there were only seven or eight cheerleaders per grade served to heighten their visibility further.

As a result, cheerleading was a highly valued activity, especially among the younger girls. Many of the sixth-grade girls told us they hoped to be cheerleaders next year, and some told us they wanted to be professional cheerleaders when they grew up. A large percentage of the girls in the school went to cheerleading tryout practices; forty-four girls tried out for the sixteen available positions. While practices for cheerleading tryouts were going on, many of the sixth-grade girls spent their lunch period practicing cheers. Girls who were not planning to try out would join in. Even many girls who were not going out for cheerleading knew all the cheers and could do them.

Some boys imitated cheers as a way of mocking this high-status female activity. Even a male coach was observed mocking cheerleaders on one occasion. He told the football players that he'd get them skirts if they wanted to cheer instead of practicing harder. Then he went on to act like a cheerleader with a pom-pom, saying "Go team go" in a falsetto voice.

Among the girls, there was more agreement about the high status of cheerleaders. In seventh and eighth grades, the popular groups consisted of all or most of the cheerleaders and their friends. Girls were aware that being cheerleaders enhanced their popularity, and they sought to make their cheerleading identity even more visible. For example, on the days of the boys' basketball games, many of the cheer-

leaders who were on the gymnastic team would skip practice and get dressed in their cheerleading uniforms in order to present themselves in the role of cheerleader for as long a period as possible. The cheerleaders also wore their cheerleading shirts to school on certain special occasions, and some even had T-shirts made with the word *cheerleader* printed on the back. In contrast, when the volleyball team members were allowed to wear their volleyball shirts to school on the day of a game, one of the members, who was also a member of the popular group, did not wear her shirt. It appeared that she did not want to endanger her position in the popular group by making her association with the volleyball team too visible.

Differing Views on Social Rankings

As students experienced this new, more complex level of social ranking, they expressed a range of views about its legitimacy. Although boys disagreed with each other to some degree, most were accepting of the use of athletic ability to determine one's athletic opportunities, such as making a particular team or being part of the starting lineup. For example, one day a group of football players was discussing whether it was fair that the second- and third-string football players usually did not get to play. Initially, some boys felt that their lack of playing caused the non-starters to perform more poorly than the starting lineup. This viewpoint was challenged by others, who felt that these boys lacked the ability and effort to play better, justifying the legitimacy of the sports' hierarchy.

> This became a discussion of how bad the second and third stringers were. There was somewhat of an ideological debate of how good they should be. George's and Ron's opinion seemed to be that they never get to play and that's why they are no good. Tony, Bryan, and to a certain degree, Chris, said the reason that they don't get to play is that they are no good. Bryan was sort of the spokesman for this group and even stood up while he made his point, saying, "Well, those guys

shouldn't be messin' around in practice. They oughta be at practice learnin' so they can play instead of standin' around pickin' their butt. They just stand around and do nothin' and when they get the chance they go in there and act like dummies." Everybody agreed with this and they mentioned somebody named Jack Nelson in particular. They got down on this guy quite a bit. [Steve's notes]

Whether or not these boys were correct in their belief that sports activities represent a true meritocracy, it had important implications for their general acceptance of social hierarchies. Since all the boys in the popular group were members of athletic teams and thus perceived to have strong athletic skills, few boys questioned the legitimacy of the male social rankings. Demonstration of other strengths, such as physical and verbal fighting skills, use of humor, and willingness to be daring and defy politeness norms, further enhanced the likelihood of being in the top group. Again, the sense that certain boys had strengths that others lacked tended to limit the degree of resentment expressed toward popular boys.

Girls were much more likely to express dissatisfaction with social rankings, and especially with the popular girls. Only a small proportion of the student body had the opportunity to participate in the elite activity of cheerleading. Cheerleading selection itself was not considered as clear-cut as athletic competition. Some girls expressed confusion about why certain cheerleaders were selected. Others were very critical of those girls who were selected, commenting negatively on their appearance as well as their performance.

The fact that the rest of the top group consisted primarily of friends of cheerleaders made the social hierarchy seem even more arbitrary. When some eighth-grade girls in a medium high-status group were asked about factors that influenced popularity, they expressed their confusion to us by saying "We're nice and we wear nice clothes, so how come we're not more popular?" Since these girls relied so much on the friendliness of popular girls to gain higher status, they were often ex-

tremely upset when they were ignored by one of these girls. In addition, cheerleaders were often viewed as being snobs because some cheerleaders abandoned former friends to join the popular group.

While most viewed popular girls as being stuck-up, occasionally the snobbishness of these girls was the subject of open debate. For example, one day the name of a cheerleader came up in a conversation of sixth-graders, and immediately someone called her a snob. When Natalie disagreed with this assessment, Andrea went on to give a more extended explanation of why some people might consider this particular girl to be stuck-up.

Andrea: I don't—I just can't believe it. I mean usually she's sittin' with Jane May and those guys you know. [Brief discussion to identify who she is referring to.]
Stephanie: Where's Jane May? [They point to her.]
Laura: [Unclear] she's a snob.
Natalie: I don't think she's a snob.
Andrea: Huh?
Natalie: I don't think she's a snob.
Andrea: I don't think she's a snob either. It's just I don't like her. [Laughs.]
Laura: [Unclear] I don't care if other people like her, I just—it's my opinion.
Andrea: The thing that uhm the thing that people are jealous of her—other girls are jealous of her. They say, you know, like, they don't like her because she's pretty and all the boys like her and they think that she's stuck-up. She's really not. She's really very nice.

Andrea believed that this girl was being labeled a snob because others were jealous of her, not because of her actual behavior. This shows that some popular girls might be unfairly judged as a result of general resentment about the status hierarchy.

High-status girls talked to us about the disadvantages of being in a popular group. One girl reported that because popular girls are viewed as being stuck-up, other kids are "kind of scared of them and they don't know their real personality." Other cheerleaders told us they felt it was unfair that they were labeled stuck-up, whereas popular boys were liked by everyone. Although these girls did not consider themselves stuck-up, they later expressed an unwillingness to associate with lower-status people.

> One thing that came up right away was that they said that since they became cheerleaders (or popular—the two words are practically synonymous to them) that a lot of girls were jealous and that they were called "stuck-up" or "Little Miss Priss" a lot. Carrie said that people had gone so far as to make up and spread rumors about her that weren't true. Darlene brought up the point that it wasn't fair because it was the popular girls who were treated like this and the popular boys were not, that people simply liked them. . . . The bell rang and I asked if I could sit with them at lunch sometime and they said yes. I asked where they usually sat, if it was usually on the gym side of the cafeteria. They said, "Oh we *never* sit on the other side." I asked why not and they said, "That's where all *the grits* sit." [Cathy's notes]

In general, the greater association between popularity and friendship among girls made popularity appear more arbitrary and less merited. This contributed to much greater resentment among the girls, leading to the beginning of a reverse status hierarchy in which high-status girls are disliked almost as much as low-status girls.

The Complex Dynamics of Social Class

The social ranking that developed within this school was influenced largely by the extracurricular activities, but in complex ways it was also related to the students' social class backgrounds. Many of the students came from middle-class and upper-working-class backgrounds. Others came from lower-working-class, often rural, backgrounds and were negatively referred to as the "grits" (a reference to being tough and "gritty"). Although a few lower-working-class boys were on the football team and oc-

casionally sat with the popular group, most lower-working-class students sat on the opposite side of the cafeteria, especially in the seventh and eighth grade.

In many ways *grit* was a label by default. Students viewed as deviant by certain popular students were considered grits. For example, if a boy was not involved in sports he lacked an important basis for participating in conversations in the high-status groups. Other students were viewed as deviant because they displayed a lack of concern with school officials and values or because of their physical appearance and dress. The "grit" label generally implied the person was a loser in the struggle for social status. Certain boys might be feared because of their propensity toward violence, but they were not respected. Many people who sat on the same side of the cafeteria as the most popular students viewed everyone on the other side of the cafeteria as being grits. People on the low-status side did not necessarily give themselves this label, however, and instead referred only to certain people as grits. For example, one girl told us that a grit was "somebody who smokes marijuana and sleeps with just about any boy."

At the same time, some people who sat on the low-status side viewed all of the people on the other side as being stuck-up. The same process that took place among girls regarding the members of the popular group also seemed to take place among girls regarding the two different sides of the cafeteria. No one explained precisely why some people sat on one side rather than the other, but it seemed to be due in part to a sense that people from certain social class backgrounds wanted to avoid contact with lower-class people. In return, lower-class people wanted to avoid people they believed to be stuck-up.

Eighth-Grade Interview with Donna

Julie: And those kids who are poor and can't afford expensive clothes sit over there. [Points to the other side of the cafeteria]

Donna: How does that get started? How does it get started that certain people sit over there and certain people sit at this table?

Bonnie: Like if there's a gross dirty kid that came and sat by this girl that was real clean and everything she'd go, "Oh, gross. You smell," or something like that. So they'd get up and go over there and most of those guys over there think that everybody over here is a snob and they don't want to sit by them.

Julie: Most of them are.

The fear of being ridiculed or mistreated by high-status students was incredibly strong for some students, who were willing to do anything to avoid having to associate with them. This suggests that the general social ranking within the school was extremely rigid. As one girl put it, "It's like segregation of unpopular people and popular people."

Despite the strong influence of social class on social rankings within the school, students' views on the legitimacy of class stratification differed and were quite complex. It is clear from some of the preceding discussion that some people assumed that social class was a legitimate basis for discriminating against others—that it was normal not to want to sit near grits or someone who didn't wear the same type of clothes or was perceived to have a different standard of cleanliness. At the same time, it is also clear that many of the lower-status students resented their higher-status classmates and referred to them as being snobbish. This resentment indicates that people who were at the other end of this hierarchy did not see social class as a legitimate or fair basis for social ranking because it was something over which they have little control.

Not only low-status but high-status students were often openly critical of students they perceived as being elitist or upper class. In one group, the student from the wealthiest background had trouble making any friends because others were always commenting on her family background. In the group of popular boys, the heaviest teasing that went on during the course of the entire year was based on one member's perceived snobbishness when he moved from the locker he was sharing with a group member to another locker.

I was greeted by Joe as I sat down. As soon as I sat down they started talking about how Mike was too upper class to sit with them. Joe was the most active in this. He asked Mike if he was sure he didn't mind "all us grits" sitting with him. When he said this he was laughing a lot, as was Eric. Mike sat in silence and looked like he didn't want to have to deal with this. This went on a while and I finally asked how come they were blowing Mike so much grief. Mike said that it started when he moved out of the locker he was sharing with Joe. Joe said it was because he thought he was too good for him while Mike said it had something to do with the location of the locker. . . . Eric started talking about all the "Polo" stuff that Mike had. I don't ever remember Mike wearing much designer stuff but I just listened. Eric said that Mike wore "Polo" socks and underwear and "Polo" garters to hold up his socks. . . . Eric started talking about the mansion Mike lived in and Mike denied it was a mansion, saying it wasn't even as big as the two-story house that Eric had.

Since Mike was not responding playfully, the teasing escalated into ridicule and continued for much of the lunch period, until finally Mike became so upset he resorted to physical aggression.

Joe kept talking about how upper class Mike was and finally Mike reached over the table and swung at him two or three times. He hit him in the chest but not hard enough to cause any damage. When this happened I noticed that everyone within twenty-five feet of our table was watching to see what would happen next. Mike sat back down and told Joe he was going to kick his ass. He was real upset, and Hank asked if he was going to cry. Mike said no, and I don't think he was, but he was real upset. He broke a pencil into three of four pieces. [Steve's notes]

This incident reflects a negative orientation toward people who act as if they are better than others, in this case by wearing designer clothes or refusing to associate with people with less money. Mike's background was not that different from other group members and, as he tried to explain, his background had nothing to do with his desire to change lockers. Yet, he was extremely sensitive to the accusation of elitism and, while he could handle some other types of teasing by these boys, he lost control of his anger when accused of snobbishness.

This example indicates a complex attitude toward social class among some of the youth at this school. Although an elitist attitude toward lower-working-class and rural students was so ingrained that it was not even recognized by many students, these same students often accused their classmates of having elitist attitudes. This suggests that social class has a complex effect on students' attitudes regarding hierarchies, so that students tend to view their own position as being a legitimate one, but view those above them as having unfair advantages.

The Dynamics of Race

Social class was much more closely related to status processes in this school than was race, in part because only a small number of African-American students attended the school. They came from different social class backgrounds and were as likely as Euro-American students to participate in cheerleading and athletics. Thus, African-American students were found at every level of the status hierarchy, except for the very lowest level, which happened to be entirely Euro-American.

Even though racial discrimination in the community and larger society was not directly reflected in the social rankings at Woodview, it was evident at times in the peer activities of students. Boys on the low-status side of the cafeteria often told racist jokes and occasionally targeted particular black students in their parodies. In the incident described here a group of boys began to mock a classmate's hairstyle after someone realized his hair was standing up in a fashion similar to that of a black girl in the school.

Andrea came up and said hello to everyone and rubbed Jeff's hair so it all stood up. Walter laughed, and Jeff, realizing how it looked, stood up and said, "My name is Karla West. Look at me. My name is Karla West." He said it loud enough for a lot of people to hear, and I noticed that people from a couple of different tables were laughing. Then Walter pointed to the end of our table and said that Karla was sitting down there. I looked and figured out who she was. All the girls she was with were laughing, and so was she. For the rest of the lunch period Jeff would stand up and do this every so often, and by the end of the period it had regressed toward racial overtones. He started using more of a black dialect when he did it, and Ken, Jack, and Walter started to tell racist jokes. . . . A black guy walked by, and Walter started calling him Sambo. The guy turned and looked but kept walking. Walter said that if Karla were taller she could mop the ceiling. Finally, some food started being thrown from our area to the area Karla was in. I was embarrassed but stayed. Tracy [a black cheerleader] was with Karla's group and told Jeff to quit making such a fool of himself. Jeff laughed at this and acted more like a fool by talking funny and addressing nonsensical comments toward Tracy. [Steve's notes]

The parody of Karla began with a simple imitation of her hairstyle. It is interesting, and revealing of how racial attitudes become normalized, that everyone found this initial parody humorous. It is not clear how Karla really felt, but she, too, went along with it at first. Not until the incident became more explicitly racist was it challenged by another black student. Her position as a cheerleader gave her considerable status over this group of lower-status males. Her challenge was not enough to completely stop their behavior, but it did defuse it.

Incidents such as this were relatively rare at Woodview, but a black student who attended another middle school in the same community told us that she and her sister faced racial insults on almost a daily basis. These insults ranged from explicit comments about their skin color to negative labels such as "porch monkey" and "nigger." The relatively greater frequency of such insults in this school may be due to the more isolated status of these two students, who described themselves as being very shy, and/or the absence of adult researchers.

In general, their vulnerable position as outsiders meant that African-American students had to work to maintain group acceptance. None of these students was among the smallest percentage of students who had no friends or group affiliation, but they were clearly aware of the negative experience of those students. In fact, when two researchers (Cathy and I) started coming to the lunchroom, African-American students were among the first to invite us to join their groups. Being on the outside themselves, they seemed particularly aware of the importance of finding some way to fit in with a group and avoid the ridicule encountered by isolates.

Targeting the Low End of the Hierarchy

The students who most dramatically felt the negative impact of the school status hierarchy were those at the very bottom. At each grade level, three to five students became identified as having characteristics with which most students wanted to avoid being associated. Often these characteristics reflected gender concerns such as perceived unattractiveness in girls and atypical gender behavior in both boys and girls. Other undesirable factors were perceived low intelligence and unusual behavior; this made special education students more likely candidates for social isolation.

Students often deal with their insecurities by scapegoating others whom they view as being even more deficient than themselves. By creating a group of isolates at the bottom of the status continuum, most students at least have the assurance that they are not as unpopular or as abnormal as some of their classmates. Like the popular students, isolates also become highly visible in the school setting. For them, however, visibility is painful and often embarrassing—a source of unwanted negative attention rather than the positive attention and esteem received by their popular peers.

Many isolates were also subject to some form of sexual ridicule. The most common

form of sexual insulting or ridicule in this school was the use of homosexual labels such as *faggot* and *queer*. Since many youth have some anxiety about homosexuality, one way to deal with this anxiety is to attach the homosexual label to students they consider to be least like themselves, that is, isolates.

> Ted pointed to a girl in line and said she was in Special Ed and that she was always getting picked on. As I saw her in line I noticed three or four people circled around her. They were laughing and exchanging comments, but the girl in the middle did not appear to be enjoying herself. Ted said her problem was that she liked girls. "You know, one of those kinds." When I asked what kind he said, "You know, kind of queer." [Steve's notes]

By ridiculing isolates in this manner, students ensured that homosexuality became more solidly associated with social rejection. This in turn very likely increased the degree of homophobia among the students.

Students also ridiculed female isolates by making fun of their perceived unattractiveness, in particular, their lack of sexual attractiveness to boys. A common way to do this was for boys to convey their romantic interest in a particular isolate and then make fun if she took it seriously. This type of ridicule extended to accusations that isolates had slept with particular boys, or even gotten pregnant by them.

> Several students said to Theresa, "Theresa, did you have a baby with Donnie?" Theresa just smiled and shook her head, and I looked over and sort of smiled at her. Then Sharon explained to me that this is the same Donnie that she had gone with and he had asked Theresa to go with him as a joke, but she had taken it seriously. She said that now they really make fun of her and that she's easy to make fun of because she'll start to cry. Sharon said if she doesn't watch out, Theresa's going to be loony when she gets out of here. [Stephanie's notes]

Theresa was initially ridiculed because she was considered unattractive, not because of an emotional handicap. Here a student expresses concern that Theresa might *become* loony as a result of the ridicule she faced at school. There is increasing awareness in the popular press that ridicule of isolates is extremely damaging to their psychological well-being, sometimes leading to suicide. By scapegoating these isolates, the anxiety of the general student population is focused on a few students who end up experiencing very high levels of social distress.

One might think that students who experience ridicule would be less inclined to make fun of others, but this does not seem to be the case. Although Billy was ridiculed and pushed around by his peers, he himself made fun of certain isolates, such as Jenny. In the following instance, Billy at first defended Jenny's intelligence, but then, in an attempt to be included in group camaraderie, he joined in the gossip by derisively imitating her.

> Pat told me a story about how someone in her group had hit a girl and then she pointed out the girl, who was Jenny. She said that she was "retarded." Billy said, "She can't be too retarded, she reads books." Pat replied, "She's pretty retarded." Then Billy started giving his imitation of a retarded person, acting like he was asking questions about how to get around in the school, acted really stupid, sort of stuttered his words. [Cathy's notes]

By joining the group's ridicule of Jenny, Billy was able both to redirect his own insecurities outward and to deflect potential negative attention from himself.

Some people did attempt to stop the open ridicule of isolates. Most of the successful attempts were made by girls who were starting to define such ridicule as rude and insensitive. As early as sixth grade, girls began to reprimand their peers, claiming that they were taking the right of free speech too far. In one incident, an overweight isolate had asked a sixth-grader if she could borrow some money.

> When I came back, Andrea was reprimanding Ilene. They explained that while I was away, Gloria had walked up to Andrea and had asked Andrea to loan her some money. Before Andrea could say anything, Ilene had said, "Well, she'll lend you some money, but not money that you're gonna eat more with!" This made Andrea angry that Ilene was so rude to Gloria, and caused a full-fledged fight between them. Andrea got more and more angry, to the point where she started yelling at Ilene, saying, "If you open your trap once more and say that kind of thing. . . . That was really rude. Everybody else has the right to live! Sure there's freedom of speech but you're taking it too far!" [Stephanie's notes]

Comments such as these seemed to be effective in reducing the amount of open ridicule among girls. By eighth grade, incidents of such ridicule still occurred among girls but were relatively rare. Boys seldom questioned the appropriateness of ridiculing isolates—once, two boys discussed how special education students should be left alone because "it wasn't their fault," and on another occasion, two boys debated whether it was appropriate to pretend to flatter a female isolate. Thus, there was little reduction in the amount of ridicule by boys over the three years of middle school.

In general, isolates had few ways to escape from their position of being the most unpopular students in the school, since so few people were willing to associate with them. Although certain verbal strategies minimized the degree of ridicule they faced, the main problem stemmed from other students' desire to find someone with lower status than themselves whom they could ridicule or mock. This suggests a high degree of insecurity among many youth in the school over their own social standing.

The Complex Nature of Social Rankings

It is evident that students at Woodview were strongly influenced by social ranking within the school and within the larger society. Had this school not provided opportunities for certain students to have more visibility than others through participation in elite activities, such as cheerleading, football, and basketball, clear popular groups might not have emerged. The lack of any distinct popular groups in the sixth grade, where these activities were not offered, supports this idea. At the same time, the overall stratification of high- and low-status students reflected a social class division as well as the division of popular versus nonpopular groups. This division was also not as strong in sixth grade.

The fact that Woodview inadvertently created a scarce resource by giving so few students a chance to become visible created a very competitive atmosphere, which may have contributed to the high degree of rejection and ridicule of isolates. Many of the students who attended this school were later interviewed as part of a study of high school peer cultures. They reported that the middle school cliques were so rigid and so restricted that only a few students could be in popular groups, while the rest perceived themselves to be "dweebs" and "nerds." In high school, they found that they had many more opportunities to get involved in extracurricular activities and to gain a sense of meaningful group acceptance, making them feel much more socially competent. Some high school students also reported being less intimidated by classmates in other groups, and high school students in general had more contact across cliques.

Most students in this middle school tried to avoid being isolates and sought greater recognition from their peers, but they expressed some ambivalence about the status processes going on around them. This was especially true for girls, who perceived the status system to be quite arbitrary. By referring to popular girls as snobs, they were in essence saying that these girls were unwilling to spend time with them because of the "snobby" girls' elitist attitudes rather than their own deficiencies. This reverse status ranking, attributing negative traits to those at the top of the ranking, is an initial stage in the process of resisting social rankings and their implied evaluations.

As students get older, reverse status ranking becomes stronger. By high school, students who were not members of the "preppy" or "trendy" cliques were even more vocal about their negative evaluations of these cliques, saying that students in them were too materialistic, or that they followed every trend without ever thinking for themselves. A British study also found that working-class boys grow increasingly disdainful of their middle-class peers, whom they perceive as being passive, boring, and less sexually competent.

It would be interesting to know what factors contribute to greater resistance toward social class and other social hierarchies as people get older. In this school, the boys' social hierarchy received little criticism, in part because male popularity was perceived to be based on merit. It may be that as individuals encounter more cases where ranking decisions appear arbitrary or even unfair, they begin to develop greater skepticism about the legitimacy of such decisions and the entire ranking system.

THINKING CRITICALLY

1. Why are the male athletes popular but not the female athletes? What explanation is given in this reading, and what explanation would you add?

2. Explain how popular girls could also be widely disliked and why the same does not apply to popular boys.

3. If cheerleaders are so widely disliked (although popular), why would so many girls want to be cheerleaders?

4. The authors note that status hierarchies are more rigid in middle school than in high school. Can you explain why in terms of identity formation processes?

The Complex World of Peer Crowds

In American society, group social life becomes increasingly complex during adolescence, as students in middle school and high school begin to think of others in terms of social categories, or "crowds." In this reading, the authors explore the functions of crowds: assisting adolescents in forming a social identity and locating others in a social framework, channeling adolescents' friendships and romantic relationships, and providing the context in which relationships take place. The reading is mostly theoretical and relies on previous ethnographic studies, but the authors also use new data of their own to illustrate their points.

Reading 8.2

Casting Crowds in a Relational Perspective: Caricature, Channel, and Context

B. B. Brown, M. S. Mory, and D. Kinney

For most individuals in our society, the transition from childhood to adolescence, often heralded by entry into middle school or junior high school, is accompanied by major transformations in peer relationships. One such transformation is the emergence of peer "crowds." Crowds refer to collections of adolescents identified by the interests, attitudes, abilities, and/or personal characteristics they have in common. They differ from other groupings of adolescents, such as friendship groups or "cliques," in that they are based on a person's reputation rather than interaction patterns (Brown, 1990). A crowd defines what a person is like more than who she or he "hangs around with." Of course, because "birds of a feather flock together," it is common for adolescents to interact with peers from the same crowd and avoid relationships with peers from other crowds with markedly different reputations. Yet such interaction patterns are not a prerequisite of crowd affiliation.

Our intent in this chapter is to provide a systematic analysis of how relational principles reveal the structure and function of adolescent crowds. We perceive three major ways in which crowds may be cast in relational perspective. First, adolescents construct an image, or *caricature*, of each crowd that reflects their perceptions of the typical or stereotypical traits of its members. These caricatures trace the symbolic relationships that exist among crowds: How crowds are different from one another and how well crowds get along with each other. This helps teenagers to understand the alternative "social identities" that are available, as well as to appreciate the norms governing relationships and peer interactions within their social milieu. Second, in a more concrete fashion, crowd affiliation serves to *channel* teenagers toward forming relationships with certain peers rather than others. Crowds are arranged in "social space" in such a way that relationships between teenagers in different crowds are facilitated in some cases and inhibited in others. Finally, crowds serve as *contexts* for peer relationships in which systematic variations in the quality of relationships can be observed as a function of the group's norms, orientations, and status position. Thus, whereas adolescents in one crowd may form lasting and caring friendships, adolescents in another crowd may display superficial and competitive relationships.

In the sections that follow, we will sketch out the relational issues that emerge when one approaches crowds as caricatures, channels, and contexts. Before embarking on this relational analysis, however, it seems wise to clarify our perspective on the nature of adolescent crowds.

The Nature of Adolescent Crowds

From ethnographic depictions one often gets the impression that adolescent crowds are very concrete entities (e.g., Cusick, 1973; Eckert, 1989; Eder, 1985). They have widely acknowledged labels and readily identifiable memberships. They lay claim to a particular hangout at school or in the neighborhoods, lunchroom table, or hallway or street corner. They have implicit control of certain school activities: The politicos preside over the student council, while the burnouts dominate the auto shop. To be sure, such depictions reflect a concrete and visible reality in most American high schools, namely, cliques that embody the attitudes, behaviors, and lifestyles that define a particular crowd.

Yet such depictions have perplexed other ethnographers, who witness blatant contradictions between the spoken norms of a crowd and crowd members' observable behavior. Varenne (1982), for example, was bemused that members of two crowds routinely depicted as archrivals could often be observed interact-ing with each other, or that a student widely regarded as a member of the popular crowd, known for its trendy style of dress, often came to school in blue jeans and a work shirt—the signature apparel of a very different crowd. Such contradictions led Varenne to propose that crowds seemed to exist much more "in teenagers' heads" than in reality.

How visible and distinctive are adolescent crowds? Certainly, individuals or cliques that are widely acknowledged representatives of a particular crowd can be easily located in most schools. They also can easily become the target of ethnographic or participant observer studies. But to a certain degree, adolescent crowds exist more profoundly at the cultural and symbolic level than at the level of definitive individual behaviors (Lesko, 1988). Crowds stipulate (in stereotypic ways) a set of alternative value systems, lifestyles, and behavioral repertoires that are readily recognizable within the adolescent social system. In other words, each crowd represents a different prescriptive identity or identity prototype. Thus teenagers may feel quite comfortable characterizing jocks as individuals who are "out for" sports teams, out for a good time on the weekend, into the latest styles, and only moderately concerned with academic achievement, even though they recognize that several peers associated with the jock crowd do not manifest all of these characteristics.

In fact, a teenager's actual attitudes and behaviors are unlikely to jibe perfectly with the normative image of any single crowd in his or her social milieu. If a teenager's characteristics are highly similar to the prototypic attitudes and behaviors of a specific crowd he or she is likely to be associated with that crowd by most peers. But for many, if not most, adolescents, the fit between personal attitudes and behaviors and the prototypic characteristics of a given crowd is an imperfect one. As a result, a certain teenager may be viewed as a member of crowd X by some peers, a member of crowd Y by other peers, and a member of *both* crowds by still other peers. In other words, although some adolescents fit neatly into a specific crowd, many others seem to have multiple or partial crowd affiliations, often of varying intensities.

Second, exclusive membership in a particular crowd is readily disavowed by adolescents. Few adults would deny their occupation or their neighborhood of residence. They might "waffle" a bit about their political party affiliation or their socioeconomic status. Rarely, however, do social scientists encounter the sort of reluctance or denial that we and others (Lesko, 1988; Varenne, 1982) have observed when asking adolescents, "What crowd do you belong to?" "I really don't belong to any crowd" or "I mix with several crowds" are common responses. There are several reasons for such responses. One is that students are reluctant to appear close-minded and exclusionary, as if they only interact with peers in one particular crowd. Another is that because they mix with several crowds during the school day (even if they tend to hang out with one specific group after school or on weekends), it is difficult for them to see themselves as belonging to just one crowd. What's more, because crowds are meant to depict one's global identity, or basic reputation with peers, rather than just one facet of self (as occupation or religious affiliation or political party membership do for adults), being "typecast" too rigidly into one crowd violates the American emphasis on individuality, autonomy, and personal uniqueness.

Finally, some crowds are legitimate, meaningful categories but are—almost by definition—unobservable. The "loners," for example, comprise a crowd of adolescents who are described as having no friends, no hangouts, no group activities; yet they possess (in the minds of adolescents) as clear a prototypic identity as any other group (Brown, Lohr, & Trujillo, 1990).

Such characteristics give teenage crowds a different dynamic than other groupings of adolescents or adults. They also affect the effort to examine and understand the relational characteristics of crowds. For one thing, they encourage analyses on a symbolic as well as a behavioral level. That is, researchers must attend to adolescents' social construction of peer crowds, to the way that teenagers employ crowd labels, and to crowd characterizations to explain and understand their social world. It is to this symbolic level that we now turn attention.

Crowds as Caricatures

Those who have studied teenage crowds have found most adolescents to be willing if not eager to characterize the crowds that dominate their social milieu. From our own interviews with teenagers come these portrayals of various crowds: "Oh, yeah; they all wear these tight-fitting jeans and sit around the commons in between classes like they own the place!" "You'd be crazy to walk down the B-wing by yourself because the headbangers, they, like, attack you." "They all wear glasses and 'kiss up' to teachers, and after school they all tromp uptown to the library, or they go over to somebody's house and play some stupid computer game until 9:00 at night—and then they go right to bed 'cause their mommies make 'em." Such depictions appear to be more elaborated and animated when elicited from dyads or groups of teenagers rather than from individuals.

What are teenagers attempting to accomplish with these pronouncements? Are these earnest attempts at accurate depictions of various crowds, or whimsically oriented exaggerations of reality? The answer depends in part on one's perspective on how individuals make sense of the world around them. Meaning emanates from the process of interactions between people, such that individuals construct reality (or come to an understanding of reality) through interactions with each other (Berger & Luckman, 1967; Blumer, 1969). At adolescence, this would include building an understanding of crowds. Thus one's image of a crowd is honed not simply through personal observation and interpretation of crowd members' attitudes and activities, but also through conversations about and evaluations of the crowd with friends. In short, through social interactions, teenagers construct *caricatures* of crowds, somewhat distorted but consensually validated images of groups that serve to structure social interactions and facilitate identity development.

How can teenagers maintain an image of crowds that is avowedly inaccurate? Why would a caricature of crowds (including their own group) serve their developmental agenda better than accurate portrayals of peer groups? To answer these questions we draw upon principles of social identity theory (Tajfel, 1981). This theory was crafted by European social psychologists to explain principles of group formation and intergroup or intragroup interaction. Among its major tenets are that once group membership has been established, individuals will tend to (a) accentuate differences between one's own group and other groups, (b) overstate the positive characteristics of one's own group, and (c) overstate the negative characteristics of other groups. The exaggerated images of the "in-group's" strengths and the "out-group's" shortcomings are worked out and reinforced through in-group interactions; that is, they are consensually validated. Their expression reaffirms group membership and builds the solidarity of the group as a whole.

Yet focusing narrowly on rather cohesive cliques of teenagers may oversimplify the nature of symbolic relationships among adolescent crowds, thus overstating the degree to which such crowds fit the group dynamics described by social identity theory. As stated earlier, many teenagers maintain multiple crowd affiliations or avoid being associated with any crowd at all. Thus, rather than being clearly differentiable clusters of individuals, crowds exist as identity prototypes whose memberships are nonexclusive and partially overlapping. With divided group loyalties, teenagers may not so readily manifest patterns of "in-group" favoritism and "out-group" denigration.

To be sure, there are several good reasons for adolescents to appraise crowds objectively and strive for consensus on each crowd's characteristics. Crowds stipulate the range of identities or identity prototypes that are readily recognized by peers. They indicate how one's attitudes and behaviors would have to change in order to shift from one social identity to another. And by providing a system for categorizing unknown peers into social types with predictable characteristics, they allow teenagers to anticipate the sort of relationship that would develop if one were to engage a particular unknown peer in social interaction. Yet these reasons for accurate appraisals of crowds are offset

by the need to cast one's own group (which is often tantamount to one's own provisional identity) in a positive light and the need to understand the relationships among crowds from the perspective of one's own group. In other words, adolescents' depictions of each crowd are filtered through the biases of their own personal and social identity. The result is a set of caricatures that sketch out the *symbolic relationships* that exist among crowds. They serve as an abstract "road map" of the interrelationships among crowds in the system, based on one's own place within the system.

In sum, we propose that adolescents' caricatures of crowds serve a variety of functions. They clarify the alternative identity prototypes that exist in the social system; they bolster the identity prototype that one has selected (at least tentatively) for oneself; they demarcate probable friends and foes, collaborators and competitors in social interactions; and they predict the relative ease or difficulty of switching identities or forming friendships across crowds. They encode a great deal of subjective information about the teenage social system. That is, they trace the symbolic relationships that exist among crowds. But these symbolic relationships, in turn, affect actual relationships an adolescent has with agemates. In large measure, they do so through their capacity to channel adolescents toward interacting with certain peers and not others, an issue to which we now turn our attention.

Crowds as Channels

Although caricatures sketch out symbolic rather than literal relationships between crowds, they are by no means divorced from reality. They may provide overgeneralizations that flatter one's own crowd and other groups with whom one bears some affinity, but they are basically accurate portrayals of relationships among individuals in the social milieu. For example, it may not always have been true, as students in one school we studied maintained, that populars would only date fellow populars, or maybe a jock (their neighbors in the social status hierarchy). Yet, generally speaking, if you weren't in the popular or jock crowds, you just weren't on a popular kid's date list. The general accuracy of caricatures is what makes them useful road maps to adolescent relationships. Crowds do indeed help structure social interactions for teenagers. One of the major means of doing so is to *channel* adolescents into relationships with certain peers and away from interactions with others.

The combined activities of recognizing and caricaturing crowds and then sorting peers into these groupings help adolescents predict whether a given peer will be open or hostile to interpersonal overtures and whether one's friends are likely to encourage or protest one's association with a particular peer. This is accomplished by encoding three key features into crowd caricatures: the degree to which persons from a particular crowd have much in common (attitudes, interests, activities) with members of one's own group, the degree to which that crowd is receptive to association with one's own crowd (or any other crowd), and the degree to which it would be socially desirable to be associated with that crowd or its members. In other words, crowd affiliations direct adolescents toward associations with peers whose crowds are *proximal, permeable,* and *desirable.* This section will explain and illustrate these three major principles by which crowd affiliations channel adolescents into or away from associations with particular peers.

Proximity: Mapping "Social Distance" Among Crowds

One of the key ingredients in the formation of friendships is physical proximity: Two people are more likely to become friends if they live near each other or work near each other—or, for adolescents, if they attend the same school or occupy the same classroom (Newcomb, 1961; Priest & Sawyer, 1967). We would argue that this principle can be extended to peer groups: Two teenagers are more likely to be friends if they are part of proximal crowds (or better yet, the *same* crowd). In this case, however, proximity is not measured in terms of physical distance but "social distance." That is,

crowds are arranged in what might be termed "symbolic social space." Adolescents who enter a social system complex enough to feature crowds must not only construct an image of each crowd (through the caricaturing described earlier) but also locate each crowd in social space. The closer two crowds are on this social map, the more compatible their memberships will be, and thus the more receptive members of one crowd should be to forging relationships with peers in the other crowd.

Just as physical proximity affects the likelihood that two individuals will initiate an interpersonal relationship, "reputational" proximity—the comparative similarity of two crowds—appears to channel adolescents into relationships with peers from certain crowds more so than others. Most adolescents are predisposed to select close friends from within their own crowd; when they venture beyond this group it is more often to peers in neighboring crowds than peers in crowds that bear little similarity to their own group. Yet social distance is not the only facet of crowds to affect friendship selection. Even among neighboring crowds, teenagers must be able to cross the boundaries between their groups in order to strike up a friendship.

Permeability: The Receptiveness of Crowds to Outsiders

One of the consequences of the "in-group favoritism" and "out-group denigration" that, according to social identity theory, characterizes relationships between groups is the tendency of group members to "close their doors" to outsiders. This raises the expectation that adolescent crowds would be equally impermeable. Forging relationships across crowds should be a formidable task. Yet as we have already mentioned, the ambiguous, dynamic, and nonexclusive nature of crowd affiliations forces some modifications in the principles of this theory. This raises questions about how rigidly boundaries are maintained across crowds. Perhaps adolescents tend not to befriend peers in proximal crowds, choosing instead peers in groups that, although more distant, are more receptive to intercrowd associations.

Interestingly, ethnographers disagree about the permeability of adolescent crowds, and their contrasting portrayals seem to be as much a function of their conceptual focus as the reality of intercrowd relationships. Those who have focused on two groups that engage in antagonistic relationships or display markedly different normative attitudes and behaviors emphasize impermeability. Cusick (1973) contrasted a male clique from the jock crowd with a more alienated crowd of underachievers; according to Cusick, the two crowds were hostile, exclusive, and impermeable. Schofield (1981) emphasized the barrier that European-American girls in the popular crowd constructed to cross-racial associations; African-American girls were systematically ignored by the popular crowd, contributing sharply to the de facto segregation that existed within this ostensibly integrated school. Eder (1985) regarded the construction of boundaries between the populars and the normals as a mechanism for popular girls to contend with the overload of friendship overtures and a mechanism for normals to respond to the rejection they encountered in attempting to befriend populars.

On the other hand, ethnographers who have considered a wider array of crowds provide a more complex portrait of permeability. Larkin (1979), for example, found a fair amount of intermingling among members of the three crowds that formed the social elite of the high school he observed, but he also noted that these groups were rather unreceptive to interactions with peers in crowds at the other end of the status hierarchy: the greasers and the blacks. In fact, when out of earshot of black students, elite crowd members frequently made remarks that revealed their racial prejudices.

Thus although it is possible to conceive of crowd permeability in absolute terms—all crowds are equally impermeable, or some crowds are open to outsiders while others remain rather impermeable—it is likely that permeability operates in a more relative fashion: A given crowd is open to interactions with members of certain crowds but not receptive to relationships with

members of other crowds. The most compelling evidence for this perspective comes from Kinney's (1993) recent efforts to trace the evolution of the peer group structure and the interrelationships among crowds in one Midwestern community. Based on conversations with and observations of adolescents in a variety of crowds in the community's high school, Kinney formulated a composite map of the crowd structure that effectively integrates the principles of proximity and permeability. He found that the structural arrangement of crowds evolved through three phases from students' middle school to late high school years (see Figure 8.2.1).

In middle school, the crowd system consisted simply of two crowds: The high-status and relatively small group of "trendies," and the balance of the student body, known as "dweebs." A clear and stringent boundary was drawn between these two crowds. The transition to high school, with its more elaborated social structure and broader range of extracurricular activities, gave dweebs an opportunity to gain admission to one of a variety of new crowds: "normals," "headbangers," "grits," and "punkers." Headbangers began to vie with trendies for top social status, while the grits and punkers drifted to the bottom of the status hierarchy. Each group remained rather impermeable although the boundaries between trendies, normals, and headbangers were not as strong as between these groups and the grits or punkers. By the end of high school, peer status played a less prominent role in differentiating crowds, leading Kinney to depict the crowd structure in a more "flattened" egg shape (compared to the tall pyramid of middle school). Headbangers were essentially equal in status to the trendies, and normals had made inroads to higher status as well. Although the normals remained effectively isolated from the headbanger crowd, the boundaries between each of these groups and the trendies became more permeable. The boundary between grits and headbangers effectively disappeared with the emergence of a hybrid group known as the "grit-headbangers." What is more, a number of individuals actually transferred crowd affiliations (as indicated by the arrows between crowds in Figure 8.2.1), which further served to break down

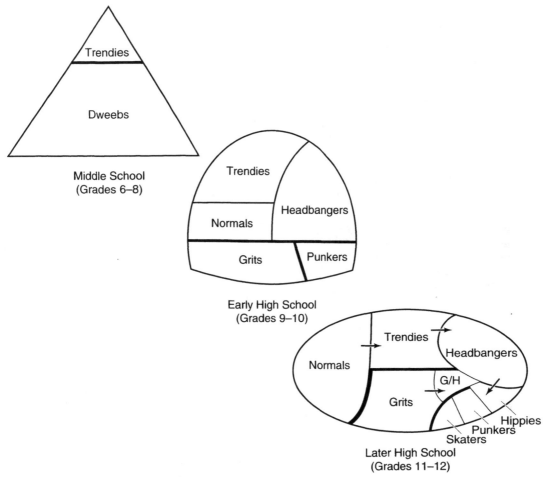

FIGURE 8.2.1 Developmental changes in crowd structure. This is a composite view, combining the perspectives of students from a variety of crowds. Line widths represent degree of impermeability between crowds. Vertical location indicates each crowd's position in the school's peer status hierarchy. "G/H" = Grit-Headbangers.

barriers between crowds. Yet such barriers did not disappear completely; boundaries between the grits and both the trendies and the punkers, for example, remained rather impenetrable.

The important lesson to be learned from this study is that only through the joint consideration of proximity and permeability among crowds can one account for the pattern of social relationships that is observed among teenagers in a given social context. Crowds must not only be similar to each other but also open to each other for adolescents from different crowds to easily negotiate a friendship or a romantic relationship.

Desirability

However powerful the principles of proximity and permeability are in channeling adolescents to relationships with peers in particular crowds, teenagers' befriending behavior still seems to frequently defy these principles. A boy will conscientiously court a girl from a crowd that is not only very dissimilar to his own but also unreceptive to associations with members of his crowd (a standard plot line in films about teenage romance; e.g., *Say Anything, Stand By Me, Grease*). A girl will studiously avoid associations with members of a crowd that is both proximal and permeable. How can one account for these apparently aberrant relational behaviors? A third principle, desirability, seems to be a key factor. Sometimes, affiliation with a certain crowd is so desirable that an adolescent is willing to ignore the great social distance between the crowd and his or her own group and risk rebuffs from the crowd's cliquish membership. Other times, membership is so undesirable that a teenager will pass up associations with a crowd that is open and close at hand.

To understand the role of desirability, it helps to bear in mind the tentativeness and uncertainty of crowd affiliation in adolescence and the power of social relationships to establish or validate one's location in the crowd system. Unlike other group memberships, crowd affiliation is not obvious, indisputable, and immutable. There is always the possibility that by changing one's attitudes, activities, or associates, one will be recognized as a member of a different crowd. Befriending, or being befriended by, members of another crowd is one of the primary mechanisms by which such shifts in crowd affiliation occur.

To be sure, desirability is related to status: The higher a crowd is on the status hierarchy, the more desirable it is (Coleman, 1961; Eckert, 1989; Eder, 1985). Yet we sense there is more to the principle of desirability than status strivings. An additional dimension is suggested by ethnographic observations of how adolescents avoid contact with a certain crowd because of its *undesirability*. Fordham and Ogbu (1986) found that students in one inner high school, attended primarily by economically disadvantaged African-American youth, conscientiously avoided behavior and friendship patterns that would tie them to the "brainiacs." This crowd was derided by peers as weak and effeminate, as

well as supercilious in their efforts to "act white." Their depiction of braniacs suggested it was a low-status group. Thus students' efforts to avoid association with its members could be interpreted as more evidence that desirability simply reflects peer status.

We, however, have noted a similar disinclination to be labeled a brain among European-American students (Brown, 1989c). In such populations the brain crowd is *not* a low-status group; in fact, it consistently occupies a middle position in the peer status hierarchy (Brown, 1989b). What is more, the brains are commonly caricatured with a mixture of positive and negative traits (Brown et al., 1990). According to our conversations with adolescents, the reluctance to associate with brains (or to be labeled a brain) stems not from reservations about the brain crowd per se but from its close proximity to another crowd that is at or near the bottom of the peer status hierarchy: the nerds. More specifically, students worry that by being associated with the brain crowd they will be misperceived as nerds. Their worries seem well founded. In both two-dimensional renditions of the symbolic social map of crowds, brains and nerds emerge as fairly close neighbors. In fact, in our pilot study with college students who were reflecting back on the crowd structure of their high school, the brains were rated as more similar to the nerds than any other crowd. The pair's similarity was surpassed only by perceived similarity among populars, jocks, and partyers, and between nerds and loners. As a result, brains may scrupulously avoid contact with nerds for fear of being misperceived as part of a less desirable, neighboring crowd. What is more, many students may avoid contact with brains because of their close proximity to the low-status nerd crowd. Thus in this instance, associations with a very proximal and permeable crowd (nerds) is avoided (by brains) because of the undesirability of that crowd.

The more complicated dynamics of desirability are also illustrated in data we gathered from middle and high school students in two Midwest communities. A group of students who had been classified by peers as members of major crowds in their school was given a questionnaire that asked them to rate how willing they would be (from 1 = "no way" to 5 = "definitely willing") to be members of each major crowd in their school. The desirability of major crowd types varied somewhat by sex (girls were more willing than boys to be normals and populars but less willing to be jocks) and grade level (from Grades 7 through 12 the desirability of nerds traced a U-shaped pattern, whereas the desirability of populars and jocks followed an inverted U-shaped pattern). Of greater interest to this discussion, however, are how ratings of the desirability of a given crowd differed among respondents associated with various crowds. Table 8.2.1 summarizes these results.

Desirability did not follow the peer status hierarchy. Normals had the highest and druggies the lowest desirability ratings, despite the fact that both groups occupied middle positions in the status hierarchy. Also, with one exception (outcasts), a given crowd's highest rating came from the crowd's own members. In some cases, the disaffection between crowds appears to be mutual: The brains were less willing to be druggies, and the druggies were less willing to be brains, than were members of any other crowd. In other cases, mutuality was lacking: The lowest desirability rating for populars came from druggies, but populars gave the

druggie crowd a higher rating than any group except druggies themselves.

The curious relationship between brains and nerds is also reflected in these data. Loners and nerds are generally regarded as very similar, proximal crowds. Here, however, brains gave loners a higher rating than any other crowd, but they gave nerds the lowest desirability rating of any group. The data in Table 8.2.1 are just a modest first step toward understanding how desirability of crowds affects adolescents' friendship choices, but they reaffirm that desirability does not operate in an absolute manner (e.g., according to a crowd's position on the peer status hierarchy). Instead, it varies according to an adolescent's own crowd affiliation.

Crowds as Contexts for Social Relationships

The relational feature of crowds that has attracted the most attention from researchers—primarily ethnographers—is the manner in which crowds provide a context for peer interactions. Ethnographers are fond of contrasting the quality and character of relationships that are displayed by members of different crowds. They have considered relationships with adults (particularly school personnel) as well as peers,

TABLE 8.2.1 Differences Among Students Associated With Various Crowds in the Mean Desirability Rating Given to Each Crowd Type

R's Crowd	MEAN DESIRABILITY RATING GIVEN TO:						
	Brains	Druggies	Jocks	Loners	Nerds	Normals	Populars
Total	3.01	1.44	3.22	1.91	1.52	3.46	3.45
Brains	3.80	1.09	3.27	2.13	1.15	3.41	3.50
Druggies	2.54	1.91	2.68	1.78	1.71	3.03	3.19
Jocks	3.21	1.26	4.23	1.77	1.51	3.55	3.59
Outcasts[a]	2.95	1.39	2.99	2.05	1.62	3.81	3.32
Populars	2.95	1.45	3.52	1.88	1.46	3.23	3.97
Others	2.80	1.41	3.02	1.88	1.49	3.52	3.30

Note: Ratings indicate how willing Rs would be to be a member of the crowd in question (1.00 = "no way!"; 5.00 = "very willing").
[a]Classifications of Rs into crowds are based on peer ratings. The outcasts includes Rs classified as loners or nerds.

and relationships with members outside one's crowd as well as with fellow crowd members.

Certainly, ethnographic studies provide fascinating accounts of the different patterns of peer and adult relationships that characterize adolescents from different crowds. But our understanding of crowds as contexts for interpersonal relationships is constrained by the restricted range of crowds and relationships that they have considered. For example, few investigators have ventured beyond the study of intracrowd friendships and what might be called intercrowd "acquaintanceships" (the treatment of outsiders); other types of relationships, most notably romantic relationships, have been virtually ignored. Because crowds have been proposed as the primary socializing agent of adolescent heterosexual relationships (Dunphy, 1963), this is a glaring deficiency for future research to address.

As a modest step in this direction, we offer findings from our own self-report survey of a sample of over 800 adolescents (Grades 7–12) in two Midwestern communities. The sample was drawn primarily from five of the most prominent crowds in these schools: brains, druggies, jocks, populars, and outcasts (a combination of loners and nerds); participants' crowd affiliations were ascertained by peer ratings (Brown, 1989a). The survey included several basic questions about best friends and romantic (boyfriend/girlfriend) relationships. It also contained scales to assess the importance that respondents attached to socializing with peers, the amount of peer pressure they felt to socialize with peers, and the degree to which they actually engaged in socializing behaviors (going out with friends, conversing with friends on the phone, attending school dances and sporting events, etc.). Respondents also indicated, on a 4-point Likert scale (1 = none; 4 = a great deal), how much time on weekends they spent with different categories of associates. Finally, they noted how often in the past month they had gone out with someone of the opposite sex, both in the company of other peers and just as a couple; scores on these items ranged from 1 (never) to 5 (almost every day).

Although ethnographers have highlighted the different relational styles of groups that in our schools were called populars and druggies, we found these crowds to be strikingly similar on the questions we asked. We found the most consistent differences between populars and druggies on the one hand and brains and outcasts on the other. Crowd members did not differ significantly in whether they had a best friend (80% to 90% of each crowd did) or how long this person had been their best friend (from 3 to 3.5 years), but there were significant differences in time spent with one's best friend. The average for druggies (13 hours per week) was over 50% higher than that for brains (8 hours); the other groups averaged between 9.5 and 11 hours per week.

The contrast was even sharper with regard to romantic relationships (see Table 8.2.2). Nearly two thirds of the druggies claimed to have a boyfriend or girlfriend at the time of the survey, compared to just over one quarter of the brains. Among those with a boyfriend or girlfriend, the relationship had lasted twice as long for druggies as for brains, and occupied considerably more of druggies' free time each week. The incidence of dating, whether with a group of peers or just as a couple, was considerably higher for druggies than brains. On all of these items, responses of brains and outcasts did not differ significantly, nor did the responses of druggies and populars.

These contrasts carried over to respondents' allocation of time among social network members on weekends. Brains and outcasts appeared to balance their time more evenly between family and peers (lovers and close friends), whereas druggies and populars tipped the balance more clearly in favor of peers. In the scale scores, although brains accorded comparatively low importance to peer interactions and reported a low incidence of socializing with peers, the pressure they felt from friends to spend time with peers was relatively high. On these scales, outcasts reflected their image as social isolates, reporting comparatively little pressure from friends to socialize with peers and a lower incidence of peer social activities than adolescents in other groups. It also appeared as if jocks were more oriented toward group relationships than other crowds. Unlike

TABLE 8.2.2 Crowd Differences in Self-Reported Characteristics of Romantic Relationships

CHARACTERISTIC	BRAINS	DRUGGIES	JOCKS	OUTCASTS	POPULARS	OTHERS
% who have had a boy/ girlfriend this year	58	94	84	60	88	73
% who currently have a boy/girlfriend	28	64	46	33	55	40
Duration of relationship (in months)	5	10	7	6	8	5
Hours per week spent with boy/girlfriend	8.85	13.64	9.23	11.03	13.58	10.78
Frequency of dating:						
with a group	1.86	2.97	2.57	1.97	2.90	2.44
just as a couple	1.63	2.89	2.36	1.91	2.49	2.17

other respondents with a boyfriend or girlfriend, jocks devoted almost as much time on weekends to their friendship group as their romantic relationship.

Of course, these data lack the depth of insight that is provided by ethnographic work. Yet they broaden the perspective of ethnographies to indicate that each crowd has a distinct profile of characteristics in peer relationships. These distinctions undoubtedly affect the ease with which adolescents can move among crowds. A teenager whose lack of interest in romantic relationships caused little concern among fellow brains would probably feel very uncomfortable amidst the more intense dating pressures of the druggies or populars. A loner, accustomed to focusing interaction on a few close friends, might find membership in the jock crowd, with its emphasis on group interactions, to be a major adjustment. If future studies can integrate the more qualitative relational focus of ethnography with the broader sampling of survey research, they can provide a more comprehensive portrait of the distinctive contexts for social relationships that exist in the peer group system within a particular community.

In sum, we have barely begun to explore the factors that shape the nature of social relationships in the diverse array of crowds that comprise adolescents' social system. It is clear, however, that crowd affiliation is a significant factor in the quality of adolescents' social relationships. It would be difficult to fully appreciate the nature of adolescents' relationships with peers and adults without taking their crowd affiliation into consideration.

REFERENCES

Berger, P., & Luckman, T. (1967). *The social construction of reality.* Garden City, NY: Doubleday.

Blumer, H. (1969). *Social interactionism: Perspective and method.* Englewood Cliffs, NJ: Prentice Hall.

Brown, B. B. (1989a). *Social type rating manual.* Madison, WI: University of Wisconsin–Madison, National Center on Effective Secondary Schools.

Brown, B. B. (1989b, March). Can nerds and druggies be friends? Mapping "social distance" between adolescent peer groups. In G. Ladd (Chair), *Peer relationships and school adjustment.* Symposium presented at the annual meetings of the American Educational Research Association, San Francisco.

Brown, B. B. (1989c, March). Skirting the "brain-nerd" connection: How high achievers save face among peers. In J. Braddock (Chair), *The ecology of student achievement in high schools: Noninstructional influences.* Symposium presented at the annual meeting of the American Educational Research Association, San Francisco.

Brown, B. B. (1990). Peer groups and peer cultures. In S. S. Feldman and G. R. Elliot (Eds.), *At the threshold: The developing adolescent* (pp. 171–196). Cambridge, MA: Harvard University Press.

Brown, B. B., Lohr, M. J., & Trujillo, C. M. (1990). Multiple crowds and multiple lifestyles: Adolescents' perceptions of peer group characteristics. In R. E. Muss (Ed.), *Adolescent behavior and society: A book of readings* (pp. 30–36). New York: Random House.

Coleman, J. S. (1961). *The adolescent society.* New York: The Free Press.

Cusick, P. A. (1973). *Inside high school.* New York: Holt, Rinehart and Winston.

Dunphy, D. (1963). The social structure of urban adolescent peer groups. *Sociometry, 26,* 230–246.

Eckert, P. (1989). *Jocks and burnouts: Social categories and identity in the high school.* New York: Teachers College Press.

Eder, D. (1985). The cycle of popularity: Interpersonal relations among female adolescents. *Sociology Education, 58,* 154–165.

Fordham, S., & Ogbu, J. U. (1986). Black students' school success: Coping with the burden of "acting white." *Urban Review, 18,* 176–206.

Kinney, D. A. (1993). From "nerds" to "normals": Adolescent identity recovery within a changing social system. *Sociology of Education, 66,* 21–40.

Larkin, R. W. (1979). *Suburban youth in cultural crisis.* New York: Oxford University Press.

Lesko, N. (1988). *Symbolizing society: Stories, rites, and structure in a Catholic high school.* Philadelphia: Falmer.

Newcomb, T. (1961). *The acquaintance process.* New York: Holt, Rinehart, and Winston.

Priest, R., & Sawyer, J. (1967). Proximity and peership: Bases of balance in interpersonal attraction. *American Journal of Sociology, 72,* 633–649.

Tajfel, H. (1981). *Human groups and social categories: Studies in social psychology.* Cambridge: Cambridge University Press.

Varenne, H. (1982). Jocks and freaks: The symbolic structure of the expression of social interaction among American senior high school student. In G. Spindler (Ed.), *Doing the ethnography of schooling* (pp. 213–235). New York: Holt, Rinehart and Winston.

THINKING CRITICALLY

1. Describe how perceptions of crowds are related to the developmental challenge of forming an identity in adolescence.

2. In what sense are crowds caricatures? Apply this idea to the following specific crowds: jocks, nerds, headbangers.

3. What do the authors mean by the "proximity" of crowds? How does "social distance" differ from physical distance?

4. How are desirability and status related? Is it possible for a crowd to be desirable to members of another crowd without being high-status?

PART

IX Dating, Love, and Sexuality

Learning the Ways of Romance

Early adolescence is often the time when romantic relationships first develop. Nevertheless, there have been surprisingly few studies on romantic relationships in adolescence. This reading provides useful basic information about adolescents' dating relationships, including the typical length of relationships, what qualities adolescents look for in their dating partners, and what adolescents see as the advantages and disadvantages of dating.

Reading 9.1

Concepts of Romance in 15-Year-Old Adolescents

C. Feiring

From *Journal of Research on Adolescence*, 6, pp. 181–200. Copyright © 1996 by Blackwell Publishers Ltd. Reprinted by permission.

Early romantic experiences are believed to play a central role in the development of the self and the ability to be intimate with significant others. Interaction and relationships with the other sex are believed to influence the course of subsequent romantic involvements and marriage in adulthood (Erikson, 1968; Sullivan, 1953). Although romantic relationships presumably involve more than sexual encounters, the adolescent literature emphasizes the sexual aspects of emerging heterosexual relationships and patterns of dating.

Dating is viewed as the social process through which adolescents practice and experiment with heterosexual relationships. In early adolescence, interest in other-sex friends increases and they become more likely partners for interaction and companionship (Blyth & Foster-Clark, 1987; Buhrmester & Furman, 1987; Epstein, 1986; Feiring & Lewis, 1991; Hallinan, 1978–79; Schofield, 1981). This process appears to follow a progression from being in situations in which other-sex peers are likely to be present, to participation in mixed-sex group activities, to group dating in which couples see each other in a group context, to individual dyads going out alone (Blyth & Padgham, 1987; Dunphy, 1963). By 15 years of age, most teenagers have had some experience dating (Blyth, Hill, & Thiel, 1982; Buhrmester & Furman, 1987; Csikszentmihalyi, Larson, & Prescott, 1977; Hansen, 1977; Wright, 1982). For many adolescents, sexual activity takes place as part of dating. By 15 years of age, most girls and boys from the White middle class report having had at least some sexual experience (Smith & Udry, 1985; Zelnik & Shah, 1983).

Theories of dating focus on the development of sexual identity rather than the attachment, friendship, or caregiving aspects of heterosexual relationships (Feinstein & Ardon, 1973; McCabe, 1984). The earliest stages of adolescent sexual identity development involve first directing attention to, but having minimal interaction with, other-sex peers. This is followed by numerous short-term relationships in which the practice of basic sexual relations and comfort with the other sex are achieved.

It is generally believed that social skills learned in maintaining and developing same-sex friendships, such as companionship and intimacy, are further developed in romantic relationships. Dating has been observed to serve diverse purposes, some of which overlap with friendship. These functions include recreation, autonomy seeking, status seeking, sexual experimentation, social skills practice, and courtship (Grinder, 1966; Hansen & Hicks, 1980; Husbands, 1970; McDaniel, 1969; Rice, 1975; Skipper & Nass, 1966; Smith, 1962).

The interpersonal nature of romantic relationships in early to middle adolescence has received limited attention (Furman & Wehner, 1994; Katchadourian, 1990; Savin-Williams & Berndt, 1990). The conceptualization of the qualitative, interpersonal nature of romance in this time period is problematic because most work on romantic relationships has been done in late adolescence or adulthood (e.g., Ainsworth, 1989; Hazan & Shaver, 1994; Lee, 1977, 1988; Sternberg, 1986).

The work of Sullivan (1953) and, more recently, Furman and Wehner (1994) suggests that peer relationships and the affiliative behavioral system are critical for the development of adolescent romance. Sullivan asserted that intimacy experiences with friends provide the adolescent with consensual validation of self-worth and create the opportunity for learning sensitivity and caregiving. During adolescence, the mature type of intimacy is increasingly sought in heterosexual relationships. Sullivan proposed that the need for security, intimacy, and lustful satisfaction must all be coordinated in order for the adolescent to achieve satisfactory relations with the other sex. Close friendships with same-sex friends and romantic relationships share common attributes in adulthood (Davis & Todd, 1982). Intimacy, understanding, and enjoyment of each other's company are common attributes; fascination and exclusiveness distinguish romantic relationships from friendships. Essential features of romantic relationships, such as collaboration, affiliation, and reciprocal intimacy, are developed in friendships with peers (Berndt & Hoyle, 1985; Furman & Wehner, 1994; Sharabany, Gershoni, & Hofman, 1981; Youniss & Smollar, 1985).

In the theory of adolescent romantic relationships offered by Furman and Wehner

(1994), close relationships involve the integration of affiliative, attachment, caregiving, and sexual reproductive behavioral systems. Mature attachments to romantic partners are seen as unlikely to emerge early on in romantic life when relationships are casual and short-lived. Rather, a number of short-term relationships may serve as the context for the development of affiliative and sexual behavioral systems in romantic encounters. It is not until the onset of more stable or committed relationships, usually in late adolescence or young adulthood, that the attachment and caregiving behavioral systems emerge as a central part of romantic relationships.

This study examines 15-year-olds' descriptions of their dating partners as well as romance in general. Of central concern is an understanding of these adolescents' conscious views of the benefits and costs of romantic relationships. Two major issues are addressed. The first issue involves the extent to which descriptions of dating partners and romance resemble characteristics of attachment and affiliative behavioral systems. Affiliative more than attachment qualities were expected to characterize descriptions of dating partners and romance. Contact with the other sex and dating appear to most often emerge within a group context of friends and peers (Blyth & Padgham, 1987; Dunphy, 1963; Feinstein & Ardon, 1973). Within this context, affiliative qualities and skills should be most important. In addition, as suggested by Furman and Wehner (1994), the attachment system should not become central until stable or committed relationships emerge. Because 15-year-old adolescents are more likely to be engaged in casual short-term relationships (Feinstein & Ardon, 1973), attachments to partners are less likely to develop.

The second issue of interest involves the nature of gender differences in descriptions of dating partners and romance. Society encourages women and men to have somewhat different attitudes toward the desire for intimacy, love, and sex. Women are socialized to be more relationship and caregiving oriented and expressive of love (Hatfield & Rapson, 1987b; Hazan & Shaver, 1994). Weak gender differences have been found in the frequency and intensity of adult passionate love, with women reporting higher scores than men (DeLamater, 1982; Hatfield & Rapson, 1987a; Peplau, 1983). Women also may be more anxious about being unloved and rejected (Bartholomew, 1991; Brennan, Shaver, & Tobey, 1991).

Research on the development of same-sex and other-sex friendships indicates that intimacy is more important and emerges earlier for girls than boys (Belle, 1989; Berndt, 1982; Bigelow & LaGaipa, 1975; Blyth & Foster-Clark, 1987; Buhrmester & Furman, 1987; Furman & Buhrmester, 1985; Rivenbark, 1971; Sharabany et al., 1981). Girls are more likely to base their friendships on mutual support and self-disclosure than are boys, who rely on joint activities and companionship. Work on older adolescents suggests that girls initially emphasize the interpersonal aspects of romantic relationships such as commitment and self-disclosure, whereas boys focus more on their partners' physical attractiveness and sexual relations (Maddock, 1973; McCabe, 1984). Consequently, girls were expected to emphasize intimacy more than boys. Boys were expected to emphasize physical attraction more than girls.

In summary, although romantic relationships are known to emerge in early to middle adolescence, little is known about the interpersonal nature of romantic involvements as they begin to develop. This study provides new information on the relationship qualities of romantic involvements as described by a sample of White, middle class 15-year-olds. . . .

Method

Study Participants

The sample consisted of 117 White, middle class 15-year-olds who have been participating in a longitudinal study from infancy. Sixty of the adolescents were girls and 57 were boys. Fifty-nine were from upper middle and 58 were from middle socioeconomic status families (Feiring & Lewis, 1981). The large majority of adolescents were from two-parent families (94%), and all were White, of European descent, and residing in suburban communities.

Procedure

The participants were interviewed in their homes by a same-sex young adult concerning dating and friendships. Interviewers were trained to provide nonevaluative feedback to make the adolescents feel comfortable and encourage them to talk. Following the adolescents' initial responses to the interview questions, the interviewer probed for additional information without pressuring the participant to talk. In regard to dating, the participants were administered a structured interview with specific questions that allowed for open-ended responses about these topics:

1. The duration of the relationship and frequency of contact (in person and on the phone) with their current or most recent girlfriend or boyfriend.
2. When going on dates, the type and frequency of activities they engaged in as part of a group and alone as a couple.
3. Their likes and dislikes about their current or most recent girlfriend or boyfriend.
4. The advantages and disadvantages of having a girlfriend or boyfriend.

The interviews were audiotaped, and the adolescents' comments transcribed for coding.

Coding, Reliability, and Limitations of Dating Data

For the interview questions concerning likes and dislikes and advantages and disadvantages of having a girlfriend or boyfriend, the transcripts were reviewed to determine what categories best described the data. The categories derived were as follows:

> *Likes about girlfriend or boyfriend:* (a) positive personality (e.g., funny, outgoing, nice), (b) intimacy (e.g., open about feelings, can talk to each other about problems), (c) support (helps me, cares about me, there for me), (d) companionship (enjoy each other's company, have fun together), (e) physical attraction (e.g.,

cute, pretty), and (f) common interest (e.g., like same activities, have same attitudes).

Dislikes about girl or boyfriend: (a) negative personality traits (e.g., stubborn, obnoxious, bossy), (b) negative interpersonal relations (e.g., fights, hassles, breaks dates, nags), (c) jealousy, and (d) nothing (could not think of anything negative).

Advantages of having a girl or boyfriend: (a) intimacy, (b) support, (c) companionship, (d) friendship (e.g., having a good, close friend), (e) social status (e.g., image), and (f) learn about the other sex (e.g., finding out how to be with girls or boys).

Disadvantages of having a girl or boyfriend: (a) too much commitment (e.g., cuts down on freedom, always tied down, too much time together), (b) negative interpersonal relations, (c) jealousy, (d) costs money, (e) worry about other's feelings, and (f) nothing (could not think of any disadvantages).

Using these categories, each participant's answers were coded according to whether they mentioned a given category in response to a particular question (e.g., likes about girlfriend or boyfriend). In order to establish interrater reliability on these categories, 20 transcripts (10 girls, 10 boys) were coded independently by two raters. Interrater reliability for each category was calculated using Cohen's Kappa. On all but three categories, agreement was perfect. The exceptions were companionship (for likes, $\kappa = .77$), negative personality traits (dislikes, $\kappa = .88$), and jealousy (dislikes, $\kappa = .77$).

The interview data used in this study are thus highly reliable and provide adolescents' own descriptions of romantic relationships rather than investigator-imposed ratings. Nevertheless, the data do not provide in-depth information about adolescents' feelings and thoughts about romantic relationships. The majority of adolescents did not answer each interview question with more than several sentences. The limited nature of adolescents' discussion is not unusual when they are interviewed by an unfamiliar friendly adult (W. Furman, personal communication, 1993; R. Kobak, personal communication, 1993). There also is the tendency to present socially desirable information and inhibit the discussion of negative or highly personal feelings or thoughts. This suggests that adolescents would be less likely to mention characteristics of relationships such as fights, jealousy, or sexual behavior.

Results

This section begins with a discussion of the structure of dating in this adolescent sample, followed by a report of the positive (likes about partner and advantages of having a girlfriend or boyfriend) and negative (dislikes about partner and disadvantages of having a girlfriend or boyfriend) aspects of romantic relationships.

Structure of Dating

Table 9.1.1 presents data on the occurrence of dating, duration and frequency of contact, context of dates, and type of dating activities. Although the majority of the sample reported having had a girlfriend or boyfriend in the past 3 years, most of the teenagers interviewed were not currently dating. Girls and boys did not differ on whether they had dated.

As expected, short-term relationships, averaging 4 months, characterized the majority of the sample. Only 8% of those adolescents with dating experience had a relationship for 1 year or longer. As a point of comparison, 97% of the

TABLE 9.1.1 The Structure of Dating

OCCURRENCE OF DATING	TOTAL		
Have dated	88%		
Currently dating	21%		
Never dated	12%		
DURATION AND FREQUENCY	M	SD	MEDIAN
Length of relationships (weeks)	16.7	18.8	12
Frequency of contact (days per week)			
In person	5.6	2.1	7
By phone	5.5	2.2	7
Context (number of times per week)			
Group			
Total	7.5	7.5	4
Boys	5.4	4.9	4
Girls	9.4	8.7	8
Alone			
Total	4.9	4.9	4
Boys	5.4	5.9	4
Girls	4.6	3.8	4
TYPE OF DATE	GROUP%	ALONE%	
Activities			
Movies	74	72	
Dinner	18	20	
Hang out	32	35	
Parties	30	6	
Home visits	0	30	

adolescents have known their current same-sex best friend for 1 year or more.

Although the length of dating relationships is relatively brief, contact is very frequent. The adolescents report seeing each other in person and talking on the phone almost daily. There were no gender differences in length or frequency of contact.

Eighty-eight percent of the sample answered the questions about dating partners because they had current or recent (past 3 years) experience dating. Of this sample, 53 were girls and 50 were boys; 49 were upper middle and 54 were of middle socioeconomic status.

Context. A repeated-measures analysis of variance was performed on the number of times per month that adolescents dated their partners in a group compared to a couples-alone context (between-subjects factor = sex; within-subject factor = context). Dating occurred more in a group than in a couples-alone context, context effect, $F(1, 103) = 7.9$, $p = .01$, and girls reported a greater number of dates in a group context than boys, Sex × Context interaction, $F(1, 103) = 7.6$, $p = .01$. There were no

gender differences in number of dates in a couples-alone context.

Activities. Adolescents were asked to describe what activities they engaged in with their dating partners and whether they had done this activity as part of a group or as a couple alone. Going out to movies, dinner, and hanging out at the mall or school are activities adolescents were equally as likely to report having done in a group or as a couple alone. Parties were more often reported as a group activity, whereas visiting each others' homes was only reported as a couples-alone activity.

Positive Aspects of Romantic Relationships

Likes About Dating Partner. Table 9.1.2 shows the types of qualities most often mentioned by the adolescents when asked to describe what they liked about their dating partners. Data are given for the total sample and by sex of adolescent. Chi-square analyses by sex of adolescent were performed to determine if there were gender differences in types of

TABLE 9.1.2 Positive Aspects of Romantic Relationships

QUALITIES	GIRLS %	BOYS %	TOTAL %
Likes about dating partner			
Positive personality traits	85	88	86
Physical attraction[a]	46	68	57
Intimacy[b]	42	26	34
Support[c]	44	14	29
Companionship	27	24	26
Common interests	6	10	8
Advantages of having a dating partner			
Companionship	71	60	66
Intimacy[d]	54	32	43
Support	36	23	30
Friendship	18	16	17
Social status[e]	18	7	12
Learn about opposite sex	9	16	12

[a]$\chi^2 = 4.11$, $p = .04$. [b]$\chi^2 = 3.01$, $p = .08$. [c]$\chi^2 = 9.51$, $p = .001$. [d]$\chi^2 = 4.73$, $p = .03$. [e]$\chi^2 = 3.05$, $p = .08$.

likes mentioned. Descriptions of positive personality traits (e.g., nice, funny) was the type of response most often given by the large majority of the sample. Physical attractiveness also was frequently mentioned, followed by intimacy, support, and companionship. Common interest was not mentioned very often. As expected, boys are more likely to mention physical attraction, whereas girls are more likely to mention support and intimacy when describing dating partners.

Advantages of Having a Dating Partner. Table 9.1.2 also shows the types of qualities mentioned by the adolescents when asked to describe advantages of having a dating partner. Companionship was the advantage most frequently mentioned by the sample. Intimacy and support also were mentioned fairly frequently, followed by friendship, social status, and learning about the opposite sex. Chisquare analyses by sex of adolescent revealed that girls mentioned intimacy and social status more than boys as advantages.

Negative Aspects of Romantic Relationships

Dislikes About Dating Partner. Table 9.1.3 shows the types of qualities mentioned by the adolescents when asked to describe dislikes about dating partners. These data are given for the total sample and by sex of adolescent. Negative personality traits (e.g., boring, stubborn) were mentioned most frequently as dislikes, followed by negative interpersonal relations (e.g., fights). Approximately one third of the sample had nothing negative to say about their dating partners. Jealousy was a dislike mentioned only by girls.

Disadvantages of Having a Dating Partner. Table 9.1.3 also shows the types of characteristics mentioned by the adolescents as disadvantages of having a dating partner. Too much commitment (the adolescents often used this phrase), especially in terms of time, was mentioned by the majority of the sample. Negative

interpersonal relations were mentioned fairly frequently, followed to a lesser extent by worried about other's feelings, jealousy, and costs money. A small percentage of the adolescents could not think of any disadvantages to having a dating partner. Only boys mentioned the disadvantage of having to spend money on dates.

Discussion

Structure and Context of Early Romantic Relationships

Consistent with other findings, most 15-year-old adolescents from this study have had some experience with dating (Hansen, 1977; Offer, 1969; Wehner, 1994; Wright, 1982). For all but a small minority, these adolescents are in what has been described as the casual stage of dating, in which the duration of relationships is brief, lasting on average only a few months (Feinstein & Ardon, 1973; Furman & Wehner, 1994; McCabe, 1984). This is in contrast to best same-sex friendships, which are relatively stable during this period, with most adolescents maintaining friendships for 1 year or more (Berndt, 1982; Crockett, Losoff, & Petersen, 1984). Although stability in same-sex friendships is evident by preadolescence (Berndt, 1982, 1989), it is not common in romantic relationships until late adolescence (Blyth & Padgham, 1987; Feinstein & Ardon, 1973; Wright, 1982). Stable, supportive, same-sex friendships in early to middle adolescence are related to good social adjustment, especially during times of transition or environmental change (Berndt, 1989; Berndt & Hawkins, 1987). In contrast, stable romantic relationships in this period have been associated with subsequent emotional and school problems (Neeman, Kojetin, & Hubbard, 1992). Premature stability in romantic relationships may preclude healthy development of self-identity (Erikson, 1968).

The short-term nature of these adolescents' romantic relationships may merit the label *casual,* but this term does not capture the daily involvement with boyfriends and girlfriends. When dating, these 15-year-olds report seeing and talking to their partners on the

TABLE 9.1.3 Negative Aspects of Romantic Relationships

QUALITIES	GIRLS %	BOYS %	TOTAL %
Dislikes about dating partner			
Negative personality	43	40	42
Negative interpersonal relations	25	26	25
Nothing	30	44	37
Jealousy[a]	19	0	10
Disadvantages of having a dating partner			
Too much commitment	79	65	72
Negative interpersonal relations	34	21	17
Worried about other's feelings and well being	9	11	10
Jealousy	7	5	6
Costs money[b]	0	9	4
Nothing	9	11	10

[a]$\chi^2 = 8.41$, $p = .01$. [b]$\chi^2 = 5.14$, $p = .02$.

phone almost daily. The average length of a phone conversation is reported to be 60 minutes! The quality of *fascination* has been used to differentiate romantic from friendship relationships in adolescents and adults (Davis & Todd, 1982; Hatfield & Rapson, 1987b). One adolescent used the expression "like a candle in the wind" to describe his current dating experiences. This statement captures the brief but intense nature of adolescent romance in this sample. Given the amount of attention focused on the dating partner, *short-term fascination* might best describe the initial stage of romance in adolescence.

Consistent with the work of Dunphy (1963) and Sullivan (1953), this study finds that adolescent romance emerges in a peer-group context. Group activities are much more frequent than activities engaged in alone as a couple. Both group and couple-alone activities are more likely to occur in public than in private settings. These findings indicate that it is the peer group that sets the stage to facilitate the transition to interactions and relationships with the other sex. It is not until late adolescence to young adulthood that dyadic dating is the norm (Dunphy, 1963, 1969; Padgham & Blyth, 1991). Dating in a group context appears to be more characteristic of girls than boys. For girls beginning to date, a group context may

have the advantage of providing constraints on sexual activity with one's dating partner.

Characteristics of Romance in 15-Year-Olds

Models of dating and mate selection in late adolescence and early adulthood propose that partners are initially selected on the basis of stimulus characteristics (e.g., desirable personality and physical attractiveness). If the relationship continues, common interests and values and then interpersonal compatibility become important (Kerckhoff & Davis, 1962; Murstein, 1976). These results indicate that stimulus characteristics of the partner are particularly important for adolescents' newly formed relationships with the other sex. Positive personality traits and physical attractiveness are the most frequently reported likes about the dating partner. Physical attraction is obviously a distinctive characteristic of romantic relationships (Hatfield & Rapson, 1987b; Steinberg, 1988). In the adolescents' reports, it is most often described in general terms, such as cute, pretty, or handsome, rather than in terms of sexuality (e.g., a good kisser).

The failure to explicitly discuss sexual attraction was more than likely due to the adolescents' discomfort in talking about such personal feelings and behavior in a face-to-face interview with an unfamiliar adult. Because adolescents were not asked directly about the importance of sexuality, failure to mention it does not mean it was not important for romantic relationships. Research suggests that most of this sample would be expected to have experience with some type of sexual behavior (Katchadourian, 1990; Smith & Udry, 1985).

Interpersonal qualities of the relationship also play a central role in adolescents' conscious views of romance. Given the casual nature and group context of romance in early to middle adolescence, affiliative qualities were expected to characterize descriptions more than attachment qualities. Consistent with this prediction and the work of Furman and Wehner (1994), the affiliative qualities of companionship, intimacy, and support were frequently mentioned as positive aspects of romantic relationships, whereas love and security were not. Companionship, a fundamental characteristic of friendship, is reported most frequently as an advantage of having a dating partner. Close same-sex friendships in adolescence also are characterized by intimacy, support, and extensive companionship (Youniss & Smollar, 1985). Developmentally, the emphasis on these characteristics in same-sex friendships emerges in early adolescence (Berndt, 1982; Bigelow & LaGaipa, 1975; Buhrmester & Furman, 1987). The results here indicate that these qualities—important for same-sex friendships—appear to provide the foundation for romantic relationships as well.

In general, adolescents were less likely to mention negative aspects compared to positive aspects of romantic relationships. Typical negative characteristics of close relationships, such as jealousy and fights, were not frequently mentioned. This may have been due to the adolescents' desire to make a positive impression during the interview or a tendency to conceptualize romantic relationships as being more of a positive than negative experience. The most frequently mentioned disadvantage of romantic relationships was too much commitment. The view of commitment as a negative characteristic rather than positive one by the majority

of the sample suggests that the attachment system does not predominate for these adolescents engaged in casual relationships with the other sex. This finding is in direct contrast to research showing the central importance of loyalty and commitment in adolescents' same-sex friendships (Berndt, 1981; Bigelow & LaGaipa, 1975, 1980; Douvan & Adelson, 1966; Hartup & Overhauser, 1991; Youniss & Smollar, 1985).

Gender Differences

Girls' development of intimacy skills in same-sex friendships appears to accelerate in adolescence. Girls are more likely than boys to report sharing feelings, acceptance, and understanding of each other as the basis for same-sex friendships (Berndt, 1982; Bigelow & LaGaipa, 1975; Blyth & Foster-Clark, 1987; Buhrmester & Furman, 1987; Hill, Thiel, & Blyth, 1981). Girls have been found to value intimate conversations and intimate knowledge of friends as part of friendship more than boys (Berndt, 1982). This study finds that girls are more likely than boys to mention intimacy and support when describing romantic relationships. This suggests some degree of continuity in girls' perceptions of the importance of intimacy and support for close relationships with the same and other sex.

During adolescence, boys do not show strong developmental increases in intimacy with same-sex friends and they do not report reaching as high a level of disclosure as girls (Blyth & Foster-Clark, 1987; Buhrmester & Furman, 1987). It may be that shared activities, more so than interpersonal disclosure, are the means by which boys achieve intimacy in same-sex friendships (Buhrmester & Furman, 1987). This may be the case for newly emerging romantic relationships as well. However, research on adults indicates that men are more likely to use other-sex rather than same-sex friends or lovers as primary confidants (Antonucci & Akiyama, 1987; Wheeler, Reis, & Nezlek, 1983). Thus, intimacy as self-disclosure is probably more important to men's views of romance in late adolescence or early adulthood (Feiring, 1993; Sharabany et al., 1981). Fifteen-year-old boys also may be more reluctant to mention intimacy and support because traditional masculine stereotypes do not stress expressiveness and disclosure. On the other hand, they do mention physical attraction more than girls, which is consistent with masculine stereotypes and research on how men decide whom to date (Hinde, 1984; Huston & Ashmore, 1986; McCabe, 1984). However, it is important to realize that the differences reported are relative ones, with considerable agreement between girls and boys in their views of romantic relationships.

In conclusion, this study represents an initial step in understanding adolescents' conscious views of romance as they begin to date. Although theory and research on adult love provide a point of departure, they do not suffi-

ciently address issues of importance during the adolescent period. Most notable is the importance of friendship and affiliative qualities in these adolescents' conceptions of romance. The challenge of adolescence is to integrate the sexual and social aspects of romantic relationships (Damon, 1983; Erikson, 1968; Sullivan, 1953). The sexual aspects of romantic relationships are, for the most part, first experienced in interactions with dating partners. Social aspects of romantic relationships have a basis in relationships with parents and close friends. How skills and expectations learned in close relationships with family and friends influence the nature of romance in adolescence is an important topic for future investigation.

REFERENCES

Ainsworth, M. D. S. (1989). Attachments beyond infancy. *American Psychologist, 44,* 709–716.

Antonucci, T. C., & Akiyama, H. (1987). An examination of sex differences in social support among older men and women. *Sex Roles: A Journal of Research, 17*(11/12), 737–749.

Bartholomew, K. (1991). Attachment styles among young adults: A test of a four-category model. *Journal of Personality and Social Psychology, 61,* 226–244.

Belle, D. (1989). Gender differences in children's social networks and supports. In D. Belle (Ed.), *Children's social networks and social supports* (pp. 173–188). New York: Wiley.

Berndt, T. J. (1981). Age changes and changes over time in prosocial intentions and behavior between friends. *Developmental Psychology, 17,* 408–416.

Berndt, T. J. (1982). The features and effects of friendship in early adolescence. *Child Development, 53,* 1447–1460.

Berndt, T. J. (1989). Obtaining support from friends during childhood and adolescence. In D. Belle (Ed.), *Children's social networks and social supports* (pp. 308–331). New York: Wiley.

Berndt, T. J., & Hawkins, J. A. (1987). *The contribution of supportive friendships to adjustment after the transition to junior high school.* Unpublished manuscript, Perdue University.

Berndt, T. J., & Hoyle, S. G. (1985). Stability and change in childhood and adolescent friendships. *Development Psychology, 21,* 1007–1015.

Bigelow, B. J., & LaGaipa, J. J. (1975). Children's written descriptions of friendship: A multidimensional analysis. *Development Psychology, 11,* 857–858.

Bigelow, B. J., & LaGaipa, J. J. (1980). The development of friendship values and choice. In H. G. Foot, A. J. Chapman, & J. R. Smith (Eds.), *Friendship and social relations in children* (pp. 15–44). New York: Wiley.

Blyth, D. A., & Foster-Clark, F. S. (1987). Gender differences in perceived intimacy with different members of ado-

lescents' social networks. *Sex Roles: A Journal of Research, 17* (11/12), 689–718.

Blyth, D. A., Hill, J. P., & Thiel, K. S. (1982). Early adolescents' significant others: Grade and gender differences with familial and non-familial adults and young people. *Journal of Youth and Adolescence, 11,* 425–450.

Blyth, D. A., & Padgham, J. J. (1987, August). *Stages of adolescent same- and other-sex peer relations.* Poster session presented at the meeting of the American Psychological Association, New York.

Brennan, K. A., Shaver, P. R., & Tobey, A. E. (1991). Attachment styles, gender, and parental problem drinking. *Journal of Social & Personal Relationships, 8,* 451–466.

Buhrmester, D., & Furman, W. (1987). The development of companionship and intimacy. *Child Development, 58,* 1101–1113.

Crockett, L., Losoff, M., & Petersen, A. C. (1984). Perceptions of the peer group and friendship in early adolescence. *Journal of Early Adolescence, 4,* 155–181.

Csikszentmihalyi, M., Larson, R., & Prescott, S. (1977). The ecology of adolescent activity and experience. *Journal of Youth and Adolescence, 6,* 181–194.

Damon, W. (1983). *Social and personality development.* New York: Norton.

Davis, K. E., & Todd, M. J. (1982). Friendship and love relations. In K. E. Davis & M. J. Todd (Eds.), *Advances in descriptive psychology, Vol. 2* (pp. 79–122). Greenwich, CT: JAI.

DeLamater, J. (1982, March). *Gender differences in sexual scenarios.* Paper presented at the meeting of the American Sociological Association. San Francisco, CA.

Douvan, E., & Adelson, J. (1996). *The adolescent experience.* New York: Wiley.

Dunphy, D. C. (1963). The social structure of urban adolescent peer groups. *Sociometry, 26,* 230–246.

Dunphy, D. C. (1969). *Cliques, crowds, and gangs.* Melbourne, Australia: Chesire.

Epstein, J. L. (1986). Friendship selection: Developmental and environmental influences. In R. C. Mueller & C. R. Cooper (Eds.), *Process and outcome in peer relationships* (pp. 129–160). New York: Academic.

Erikson, E. H. (1968). *Identity: Youth and crisis.* New York: Norton.

Feinstein, S. C., & Ardon, M. S. (1973). Trends in dating patterns and adolescent development. *Journal of Youth and Adolescence, 2* (2), 157–166.

Feiring, C. (1993, March). Developing concepts of romance from 15 to 18 years. In W. Furman (Chair), *Adolescent romantic relationships: A new look.* Symposium conducted at Society for Research in Child Development, New Orleans.

Feiring, C., & Lewis, M. (1981). Middle class differences in mother-child interaction and the child's cognitive development. In T. Field (Ed.), *Culture and early interactions* (pp. 63–94). Hillsdale, NJ: Lawrence Erlbaum Associates, Inc.

Feiring, C., & Lewis, M. (1991). The transition from middle childhood to early adolescence: Sex differences in the social network and perceived self-competence. *Sex Roles, 24*(7/8), 489–509.

Furman, W., & Buhrmester, D. (1985). Children's perceptions of the personal relationships in their social networks. *Developmental Psychology, 21,* 1014–1024.

Furman, W., & Wehner, E. A. (1994). Romantic views: Toward a theory of adolescent romantic relationships. In R. Montemayor, G. R. Adams, & T. P. Gullotta (Eds.), *Advances in adolescent development, Vol. 3: Relationships in adolescence* (pp. 168–195). Beverly Hills, CA: Sage.

Grinder, R. E. (1966). Relations of social dating attractions to academic orientation and peer relations. *Journal of Educational Psychology, 57,* 27–34.

Hallinan, M. T. (1978–79). The process of friendship formation. *Social Networks, 1,* 193–210.

Hansen, S. L. (1977). Dating choices of high school students. *The Family Coordinator, 26,* 133–138.

Hansen, S. L., & Hicks, M. W. (1980). Sex role attitudes and perceived dating-mating choices of youth. *Adolescence, 15,* 83–90.

Hartup, W. W., & Overhauser, S. (1991). Friendships. In R. M. Lerner, A. C. Petersen, & J. Brooks-Gunn (Eds.), *Encyclopedia of adolescence* (pp. 378–384). New York: Garland.

Hatfield, E., & Rapson, R. L. (1987a). Gender differences in love and intimacy: The fantasy vs. reality. In H. Gochros & W. Ricketts (Eds.), *Social work and love.* New York: Hayworth.

Hatfield, E., & Rapson, R. L. (1987b). Passionate love: New directions in research. In W. H. Jones & D. Pearlman (Eds.), *Advances in personal relationships, Vol. 1* (pp. 109–139). Greenwich, CT: JAI.

Hazan, C., & Shaver, P. (1994). Attachment as an organizational framework for research in close relationships. *Psychological Inquiry, 5,* 1–22.

Hill, J. P., Thiel, K. S., & Blyth, D. A. (1981). *Grade and gender differences in perceived intimacy with peers among seventh to tenth grade boys and girls.* Unpublished manuscript, Boys Town Center for the Study of Youth Development, Omaha, NE.

Hinde, R. A. (1984). Why do the sexes behave differently in close relationships? *Journal of Social and Personal Relationships, 1,* 471–501.

Husbands, C. T. (1970). Some social and psychological consequences of the American dating system. *Adolescence, 5,* 451–462.

Huston, T. L., & Ashmore, R. D. (1986). Women and men in personal relationships. In R. D. Asmore & F. K. Del Boca (Eds.), *The social psychology of female-male relations* (pp. 167–210). Orlando, FL: Academic.

Katchadourian, H. (1990). Sexuality. In S. S. Feldman & G. R. Elliott (Eds.), *At the threshold: The developing adolescent* (pp. 330–351). Cambridge, MA: Harvard University Press.

Kerckhoff, A. C., & Davis, K. E. (1962). Value consensus and need complementarity in mate selection. *American Sociological Review, 27,* 295–303.

Lee, J. A. (1977). A typology of styles of loving. *Personality and Social Psychology Bulletin, 3,* 172–182.

Lee, J. A. (1988). Love styles. In R. J. Sternberg & M. Barnes (Eds.), *The psychology of love* (pp. 38–67). New Haven, CT: Yale University Press.

Maddock, J. W. (1973). Sex in adolescence: Its meaning and its future. *Adolescence, 8*(31), 325–342.

McCabe, M. P. (1984). Toward a theory of adolescent dating. *Adolescence, 19*(73), 159–170.

McDaniel, C. O. (1969). Dating roles and reasons for dating. *Journal of Marriage and the Family, 31,* 97–107.

Murstein, B. I. (1976). *Who will marry whom? Theories and research in marital choice.* New York: Springer.

Neeman, J., Kojetin, B., & Hubbard, J. (1992, March). Looking for love in all the wrong places: A longitudinal study of adjustment and adolescent romantic relationships. In W. Furman (Chair), *Adolescent romantic relationships: Conceptualizations, characterizations, and functions.* Symposium conducted at the meeting of the Society for Research on Adolescence, Washington, DC.

Offer, D. (1969). *The psychological world of the teenager.* New York: Basic.

Padgham, J. J., & Blyth, D. A. (1991). Dating during adolescence. In R. M. Lerner, A. C. Petersen, & J. Brooks-Gunn (Eds.), *Encyclopedia of adolescence* (pp. 196–198). New York: Garland.

Peplau, L. A. (1983). Roles and gender. In H. H. Kelley, E. Berschied, A. Christensen, J. H. Harvey, T. L. Huston, G. Levinger, E. McClintock, L. A. Peplau, & D. R. Peterson (Eds.), *Close relationships* (pp. 220–264). New York: Freeman.

Rice, F. P. (1975). *The adolescent: Development, relationships and culture.* Boston: Allyn and Bacon.

Rivenbark, W. H. (1971). Self-disclosure patterns among adolescents. *Psychological Reports, 28,* 35–42.

Savin-Williams, R. C., & Berndt, T. J. (1990). Friendship and peer relations. In S. S. Feldman & G. R. Elliott (Eds.), *At the threshold: The developing adolescent* (pp. 277–307). Cambridge, MA: Harvard University Press.

Schofield, J. W. (1981). Complementary and conflicting identities: Images of interaction in an interracial school. In S. A. Asher & J. M. Gottman (Eds.), *The development of children's friendships* (pp. 53–90). New York: Cambridge University Press.

Sharabany, R., Gershoni, R., & Hofman, J. E. (1981). Girl-friend, boyfriend: Age and sex differences in intimate friendship. *Developmental Psychology, 17,* 800–808.

Skipper, J. K., & Nass, G. (1966). Dating behavior: A framework for analysis and an illustration. *Journal of Marriage and the Family, 28,* 412–420.

Smith, E. A. (1962). *American youth culture: Group life in teenage society.* New York: The Free Press of Glencoe.

Smith, E. A., & Udry, J. R. (1985). Coital and non-coital sexual behaviors of White and Black adolescents. *American Journal of Public Health, 75,* 1200–1203.

Steinberg, L. (1981). Transformations in family relationships at puberty. *Developmental Psychology, 17,* 833–840.

Sternberg, R. J. (1986). A triangular theory of love. *Psychological Review, 93*(2), 119–135.

Sullivan, H. S. (1953). *The interpersonal theory of psychiatry.* New York: Norton.

Wehner, E. A. (1992, March). Characteristics of adolescent romantic relationships and Links with parent-adolescent relationships and friendships. In W. Furman (Chair), *Adolescent romantic relationships: Conceptualizations, characterizations, and functions.* Symposium conducted at the meeting of the Society for Research on Adolescence, Washington, DC.

Wheeler, L., Reis, H., & Nezlek, J. (1983). Loneliness, social interaction, and sex roles. *Journal of Personality and Social Psychology, 45,* 945–953.

Wright, L. S. (1982). Parental permission to date and its relationship to drug use and suicidal thought among adolescents. *Adolescence, 17,* 409–418.

Youniss, J., & Smollar, J. (1985). *Adolescent relations with mothers, fathers, and friends.* Chicago: University of Chicago Press.

Zelnik, M., & Shah, F. K. (1983). First intercourse among young Americans. *Family planning perspectives, 15,* 64–70.

THINKING CRITICALLY

1. Consider the qualities mentioned as reasons for liking a romantic partner, listed in Table 9.1.2. If the participants in the study were five years older—emerging adults rather than adolescents—how do you think this list of qualities would be similar or different?

2. The authors note that long-term relationships in early adolescence tend to be associated with problems. Why do you think that would be so?

3. The participants in the study appeared be reluctant to talk openly about some aspects of their relationships, such as sexuality, perhaps because of the face-to-face interviewing method used. What method would you suggest to encourage greater openness by adolescents in a study such as this one?

4. The most frequently mentioned disadvantage of romantic relationships in this study was too much commitment. Explain how this finding might be related to the typical marriage age in the United States (age 25 for men, age 27 for women).

When Love Is Betrayed

Although most young people fall in love more than once in the course of adolescence and emerging adulthood, the commitments that young lovers have to one another are often tentative. Young people are pulled in opposite ways by their desire for intimacy, which leads them into love relationships that are intense emotionally and sexually, and their desire to pursue identity explorations, which leads them to seek relationships with various people. When these two desires collide, sexual betrayal sometimes results. As this reading describes, sexual betrayal among college students is common, and for those who are betrayed, it cuts deeply.

Reading 9.2

Sexual Betrayal Among Late Adolescents: Perspectives of the Perpetrator and the Aggrieved

S. S. Feldman and E. Cauffman

Although romantic relationships are common during the adolescent years, their dynamics are poorly understood. In particular, the causes and consequences of sexual infidelity during adolescence and young adulthood remain virtually unexplored, despite the fact that such betrayals may have significant emotional and interpersonal consequences. Sexual betrayal, in the context of the present discussion, refers to the unilateral breaking of a commitment to be sexually monogamous, without the awareness or sanction of one's romantic partner (Lieberman, 1988).

Although young people have become more sexually permissive over the past few decades, and although they engage in sexual intercourse at younger ages and have experience with a variety of different partners over time (Katchadourian, 1990), adolescents do not endorse sexual promiscuity. In fact, most sexual activity among teens occurs in the context of a relationship of some importance to them (Moore and Rosenthal, 1993). Furthermore, youths typically pursue only one relationship at a time in a practice known as *serial monogamy*. Sexual infidelity, in dating as well as in marriage, is seen as a major rule violation that is strongly disapproved of by people of all ages (Greeley, 1991; Hansen, 1987; Lieberman, 1988; Sheppard, Nelson, & Andreoli-Mathie, 1995; Thompson, 1984; Weis & Slosnerick, 1981).

Yet, despite strong societal sanction against betrayal or sexual infidelity, such occurrences are relatively common. Available data, though quite sparse and of questionable generalizability, suggest that approximately 50% of adult men and 40% of adult women engage in extramarital relations (Lawson & Samson, 1988; Thompson, 1984). Among adolescents, the data are even less substantial, but current estimates of betrayal range from 20% to 64%, depending on the definition of betrayal (Hansen, 1987; Roscoe, Cavanaugh, & Kennedy, 1988; Sheppard et al., 1995).

The developmental need to establish intimate relationships as well as to develop a coherent sense of self may place conflicting demands on the adolescent. These demands may place adolescents in the difficult position of choosing between the exploration of self and developing an intimate connection with others. Acts of betrayal may have serious consequences for the development of intimacy, yet adolescents also may need to experiment with different romantic partners in order to develop a clear sense of identity. This paradox may explain why incidents of betrayal are common, despite being viewed as morally wrong.

The Experience of Sexual Betrayal

We know relatively little about the effects of sexual betrayal on unmarried adolescents and young adults, because little research is available on the subject. The extant research typically focuses on *hypothetical* betrayal. Subjects are asked about possible reasons for betrayal and what they might do if they learned their partner was unfaithful (Roscoe et al., 1988), or they are asked to respond to vignettes (Mongeau, Hale, & Alles, 1994) or to complete stories involving sexual betrayal (Kitzinger & Powell, 1995).

The picture that emerges from such research is fragmentary. The most common motives generated by college students for betrayal include dissatisfaction or boredom with the relationship, seeking revenge on the partner, uncertainty about the relationship, and need for variety or experimentation. Emotions experienced in response to marital infidelity (measured using a story completion test) depend in part on the age and gender of the subject and the gender of the aggrieved, but generally include anger, emotional pain, indifference, and desire for revenge. Anticipated consequences of the betrayal to the relationship, as described

by "victims" of imagined betrayal, include terminating the relationship, seeking the reason for the betrayal, discussing the issue with the partner, and doing nothing. Whether these responses to hypothetical betrayal reflect the likelihood of responses to actual incidents is, as yet, unknown. Also, the viewpoint of the perpetrator—the person committing sexual betrayal—is under represented in the available research.

Overall, our knowledge of the experience of betrayal is quite limited. The goal of our study is to obtain a detailed picture of betrayal experiences among adolescents and young adults, and to examine the viewpoint of the perpetrator as well as the aggrieved.

Goals of the Present Study

Here our goal is to describe more fully the occurrence and experience of sexual betrayal in adolescents and young adults. To this end, we explore 4 specific issues:

1. the incidence of sexual betrayal in youths who have been in a romantic relationship, as reported by the perpetrator as well as the aggrieved;
2. the subjective experience surrounding betrayal of both the aggrieved and the perpetrator, including such descriptive information as:
   * who is the betrayal partner,
   * how did the aggrieved learn about the betrayal,
   * what were the motives for the betrayal,
   * what was the emotional response to the betrayal, and
   * what was the effect on the relationship;
3. differences in the experience of betrayal as described from the viewpoint of the aggrieved and the viewpoint of the perpetrator;
4. gender differences in both incidence of and response to betrayal.

Method

Sample

We recruited 302 college-age subjects from the lawns, cafeterias, and libraries of community colleges (37%), city colleges (21%), a large state university (18%), and a private university (24%) in the San Francisco Bay area. We screened subjects for age (18–24 years) and for language of education (at least 3 years of high school education must have been in English). Of the subjects eligible to participate, 10% of the males and 13% of the females refused to participate, usually because they did not have the time required to complete the 20-minute questionnaire. From the 302 questionnaires obtained, we dropped from the study those who were not heterosexual in orientation ($n = 10$), who were married ($n = 9$), and those who had never been in a romantic relationship (n = 67).

The resulting sample of 216 subjects was approximately equally divided between females (52%) and males (48%). Subjects were between 18 and 24 years old, with a mean age of 20.6 years. A majority (81%) were born in the United States. Fifty-nine percent came from nondivorced families; 41% had divorced parents. The ethnicity of the sample was as follows: non-Hispanic White (hereafter referred to as White) 55%, Latino 10%, African American 7%, Asian American 15%, Other 13%.

Procedures and Measures

Questionnaires focused on demographic information, history of dating, and sexual activity, including questions on betrayal and partner betrayal, as well as motives for and reactions to betrayal.

Betrayal behavior focused on both own betrayal behavior (perpetrator behavior) and on partner's betrayal behavior. To ensure that responses were not generalized, and to help subjects focus on specific incidents in their pasts, we asked subjects to list the initials of up to 4 romantic partners, and then to answer a series of questions about each relationship. Subjects responded to yes/no questions that asked, for each relationship, whether the subject had cheated on that partner, and whether that partner had ever cheated on the subject. For these questions, we left the term "cheated" undefined. In a separate question, in a different part of the questionnaire, we asked subjects to rate

on a 5-point scale how often they had ever petted or had sexual intercourse with another person while in a monogamous relationship. Similar questions were asked concerning the behavior of their partners while in an ongoing relationship with them. *Subject betrayal* was defined as having occurred if subjects reported having cheated on a partner or having petted or had sexual intercourse with another while in an ongoing relationship. *Partner betrayal* was defined analogously.

Response of the Perpetrator

Perpetrator motives were assessed by asking subjects to identify the reasons they became involved with another person while in a monogamous relationship. Subjects were presented with 19 possible motives, such as boredom and dissatisfaction with the existing relationship, the absence/unavailability of the regular partner, anger toward the regular partner, being under the influence of alcohol of drugs, and a desire to end the existing relationship. Subjects then were asked to check all motives that played a role in their betrayal.

Five composite motive scores were created on the basis of previous work with a related instrument (Feldman & Cauffman, 1999). This instrument, Acceptance of Betrayal, listed motives for betrayal on which youths rated their level of acceptability. A principal component analysis with varimax rotation resulted in 5 composites with highly satisfactory alpha coefficients. These composites are used to identify motive categories in the present work, although a factor analysis cannot be performed on these data because subjects were not asked to rate each item. *Bad Relations* consisted of such factors as "was not being treated well by the regular partner," and "wasn't sexually satisfied by the regular partner." *Escape Detection* included such motives as "the regular partner was out of town or unavailable," or "was certain that the regular partner would never know." *Unsure of the Relationship* included "was unsure or insecure about the existing relationship," and "wanted to test the strength of the ongoing relationship." *Magnetic Attraction* included such items as "was sexually attracted to the other person," and "was carried away and could not resist." *Vindictive* included "was angry and wanted to hurt the regular partner," and "wanted to make the regular partner jealous." Two items were not used in any of the composites. These involved being "under the influence of alcohol or drugs" and feeling "obligated to the new partner." . . .

Perpetrator's Betrayal Partner. The perpetrator's betrayal partner was assessed by having subjects choose, from 5 listed options, all the persons with whom they committed the act of betrayal. Categories included stranger, acquaintance, casual friend, ex-boyfriend or ex-girlfriend, and other.

Discovery of Perpetrator's Betrayal. Subjects were asked to describe how their regular partner found out about the betrayal. Subjects were asked to choose from 1 of the following 4 possibilities: I told my partner, someone else told my partner, my partner figured it out, and my partner never found out.

Perpetrator's Affective Reactions. Subjects rated themselves on 17 emotions, using a 4-point scale (0 = not at all, to 4 = very characteristic of how I felt). These items were subject to a principal component analysis that yielded 3 factors: Negative Emotional Reaction (5 items, α = .72) included angry, ashamed, ill, sad/depressed, and frustrated. Positive Emotions (4 items, α = .77) included proud, happy, excited, and relieved. Cognitive-Affective Reaction (8 items, α = .80) included the items guilty, immoral, confused, disappointed, insecure, mistrustful, disillusioned, and inadequate. Composites were created by averaging the scores of the appropriate items.

Perpetrator's View of the Aggrieved's Reaction to the Betrayal. Perpetrators responded to 8 items describing reactions of their regular partners upon learning of a betrayal, checking all items that applied. These items included: refused to talk about the betrayal; calmly discussed the betrayal; got upset; said mean/ spiteful things, swore, insulted, or yelled at perpetrator; withdrew, sulked, or refused to talk to perpetrator; reacted violently (smashing, hitting or breaking an object, threatening perpetrator verbally, pushing perpetrator around, slapping, hitting, grabbing, or shoving perpetrator).

Effect of Perpetrator's Betrayal on the Relationship. Subjects were asked to choose 1 of the following 6 items to describe the effect of betrayal on the relationship: the aggrieved partner never found out; the relationship was already over before the aggrieved partner discovered the betrayal; the perpetrator terminated the relationship; the aggrieved partner terminated the relationship; the relationship continued with renewed commitments to monogamy; or the relationship was renegotiated to include dating others or to define acceptable behaviors with others.

Response of the Aggrieved

Discovery of Betrayal. Subjects were asked how they found out about their partner's betrayal. Subjects chose 1 of the following 3 alternatives: partner told me, someone else told me; or I figured it out.

Aggrieved's Affective Reactions. Subjects rated 13 emotions on 4-point scales (0 = not at all, to 4 = very characteristic of how I felt). The responses were subjected to a principal component analysis that yielded 2 primary factors. Negative Emotional Reaction (5 items, α = .71) included the adjectives angry, ashamed, ill, sad/depressed, and frustrated; and Cognitive-Affective Reaction (8 items, α = .79) included the adjectives guilty, immoral, confused, disappointed, insecure, mistrustful, disillusioned, and inadequate.

Aggrieved's Behavioral Reactions. Subjects were presented with a list of possible responses and were asked to check all that applied to the aggrieved's reaction to the betrayal. Items included: never talked about the betrayal; discussed the betrayal calmly; got upset, cried, and then made up; said mean/spiteful things, swore, insulted, or yelled at partner; withdrew, sulked, refused to talk to partner; reacted violently.

Effect of the Betrayal on the Aggrieved's Relationship. Aggrieved subjects chose one of the following alternatives to describe the effect of betrayal on the relationship: the subject terminated the relationship, the betraying partner terminated the relationship, the relationship continued with renewed commitments to monogamy, the relationship was renegotiated to include dating with others or to define acceptable behaviors with others.

Results

The results are presented in 4 sections. First, we briefly describe the incidence of sexual betrayal. We then present the perpetrators' view of betrayal—the partners chosen, the motives involved, the emotions experienced, and the effect on the relationship. Next, we change perspectives and consider the viewpoint of the aggrieved. We describe their emotional and behavioral reactions and compare them with those reported by perpetrators. Finally, we examine gender differences in the experience of betrayal.

Incidence of Betrayal

Students reported significant experience with betrayal in romantic relationships. As shown in Table 9.2.1, 40% reported having been the perpetrator and more than half reported having been the aggrieved. More than 25% reported having experienced both sides of betrayal (i.e., as both perpetrator and aggrieved), and two-thirds had been in a relationship that involved betrayal (where they were either the perpetrator or the aggrieved). Thus, experience with sexual betrayal in some form was normative for this sample. Among those subjects who betrayed their partner, 62% reported that the betrayal involved sexual intercourse, whereas the remainder engaged in petting only. Among aggrieved subjects, 71% reported that their partner engaged in sex with another person, whereas the remaining 29% reported that their partner engaged in petting without intercourse.

Betrayal: Viewpoint of the Perpetrator. In this section, analyses are confined to the 40% of the sample ($n = 86$) who reported that they had betrayed one or more partners. The number of such subjects varied from 77 to 86 in the analyses presented here because of small amounts of missing data. Key findings are summarized in Table 9.2.2.

For the majority of perpetrators (65%), the new partner was well known to them prior to the betrayal. The most common betrayal partners included acquaintances, casual friends, and ex-lovers, as shown in Table 9.2.2. Relatively fewer youths betrayed their partner with a stranger.

Perpetrators reported a variety of motives for betrayal, with magnetic attraction toward the new partner the most frequent category and vindictiveness (e.g., trying to hurt partner or make

TABLE 9.2.1 Gender Differences in Incidence of Betrayal (%)

INCIDENCE OF BETRAYAL	TOTAL SAMPLE ($N \approx 216$)	MALE ($n \approx 104$)	FEMALE ($n \approx 112$)	GENDER DIFFERENCES (χ^2)
Perpetrator of betrayal	40	40	39	ns
Victim of betrayal	56	55	57	ns
Experienced betrayal as either perpetrator or victim	66	66	66	ns
Was both perpetrator and victim	28	28	27	ns

TABLE 9.2.2 Perpetrator's Report of Betrayal (%)

	TOTAL SAMPLE ($N \approx 86$)	MALE ($n \approx 41$)	FEMALE ($n \approx 45$)	GENDER DIFFERENCES (χ^2)
New partner				
Stranger	21	35	17	ns
Acquaintance	27	38	31	ns
Casual friend	38	21	36	ns
Perpetrator's motives				
Magnetic attraction	69	63	74	ns
Unsure of relationship	52	51	52	ns
Bad relationship	51	49	52	ns
Avoid detection	53	46	60	ns
Vindictiveness	16	20	12	ns
Partner learned of betrayal	56	58	55	ns
How betrayal was discovered[a]				
Perpetrator confessed	83	78	89	
Third party told	8	11	6	
Aggrieved figured it out	8	11	6	
Perpetrator's emotions				
Negative	50	56	46	ns
Positive	43	36	47	ns
Cognitive-affective	74	68	79	ns
Confrontation with partner				
Topic ignored	8	9	6	ns
Calm discussion	16	20	12	ns
Upset	36	40	33	ns
Mad	15	20	11	ns
Withdrew/sulked	13	11	14	ns
Violence	11	11	10	ns
Effect on relationship[a]				16.3[b]
Terminated by aggrieved	28	40	15	
Terminated by perpetrator	32	13	50	
Agreed to be monogamous	26	33	20	
Renegotiations	14	13	15	

[a]Because the subject could fall into only one of the following categories, only one chi-square analysis was conducted for this set of data.
[b]$p < .05$.

partner jealous) the least frequent. Motives falling into 3 other clusters were each mentioned by about half of the perpetrators. These clusters include bad relations with the regular partner, confidence that they could avoid detection, and being unsure of the existing relationship. Table 9.2.3 gives the frequencies for specific motives in each of these categories. The most frequently mentioned motives (noted by 40% or more of the sample) were sexual attraction to the new partner, inability to resist temptation, (regular) partner out of town or otherwise unavailable, and

being under the influence of alcohol or drugs at the time of the betrayal.

Perpetrators experienced a wide range of emotional responses to their own acts of betrayal. Almost as many subjects reported one or more positive emotions (43%) as reported negative emotions (50%). An examination of the incidence of the specific emotions, shown in Table 9.2.4, reveals that guilt was the most prevalent emotion (endorsed by 63%). Feeling ashamed, confused, and immoral were each characteristic of more than a third of the sample.

TABLE 9.2.3 Perpetrator's Report of Motives for Betrayal (%)

MOTIVES	TOTAL SAMPLE ($n \approx 86$)	MALES ($n \approx 41$)	FEMALES ($n \approx 45$)	GENDER DIFFERENCES (χ^2)
Magnetic attraction				
Sexual attraction	53	54	52	ns
In love	16	14	17	ns
Could not resist	45	46	45	ns
Unsure of relationship				
Insecure	33	26	38	ns
Wanted variety	25	31	19	ns
Wanted challenge	13	14	12	ns
Test the relationship	3	0	5	ns
Check attractiveness to others	14	17	12	ns
Bad relationship				
Bored	33	26	38	ns
Sexually dissatisfied	30	31	29	ns
Bad treatment	18	14	21	ns
Wanted to break up	23	20	26	ns
Avoid detection				
Could get away with it	10	14	17	ns
Partner would not know	18	20	17	ns
Partner away	48	43	52	ns
Vindictiveness				
To hurt partner	14	17	12	ns
To make partner jealous	7	9	5	ns
Other				
Under influence of alcohol/drugs	40	46	36	ns
Felt obligated	12	14	10	ns

According to the perpetrators, their acts of betrayal typically were revealed to the aggrieved partner. Forty-two percent of their partners never found out (and an additional 2% did not find out until after the relationship had been terminated). In cases in which the partner did find out ($n = 36$), 83% of the perpetrators claim to have confessed, 8% reported that the existing partner just "figured it out," and another 8% reported that the partner learned about the betrayal from a third party.

The reactions of aggrieved partners to the news of the betrayal (as described by the perpetrator) were quite variable. As shown in Table 9.2.2, a small minority of the aggrieved partners refused to talk about the betrayal, and a similar small percentage became violent, either smashing an object, threatening, or actually hitting the perpetrator. Other aggrieved partners purportedly discussed the issue calmly. The majority (64%), however, expressed considerable upset, either sulking or withdrawing, insulting or yelling at the perpetrator (getting mad), or being upset in unspecified ways. Clearly, the perpetrators paint a picture of a strong and negative reaction by the aggrieved partner.

After the aggrieved found out about the betrayal (as was the case for 56% of the perpe-

TABLE 9.2.4 Aggrieved's Reports of Betrayal (%)

	TOTAL SAMPLE ($n \approx 121$)	MALE ($n \approx 57$)	FEMALE ($n \approx 64$)	GENDER DIFFERENCES (χ^2)
How betrayal was discovered[a]				ns
Perpetrator confessed	50	54	44	
Third party told	30	26	41	
Aggrieved "figured it out"	20	21	15	
Aggrieved's emotions				
Negative	91	87	94	ns
Angry	62	54	68	ns
Sad	60	58	62	ns
Frustrated	53	50	55	ns
Ashamed	24	23	24	ns
Ill	18	10	23	ns
Cognitive-affective	91	85	96	ns
Confused	45	42	48	ns
Disappointed	61	60	62	ns
Guilty	7	10	3	ns
Mistrustful	59	41	63	5.9[b]
Disillusioned	38	31	43	ns
Insecure	40	38	42	ns
Inadequate	18	17	18	ns
Confrontation with partner				
Topic ignored	10	7	11	ns
Calm discussion	19	19	18	ns
Upset/cried & then "made up"	16	9	22	7.6[b]
Mad	15	15	15	ns
Withdrew/sulked	15	21	10	5.4[b]
Violence	9	13	4	3.1[b]
Effect on relationship[a]				ns
Terminated by aggrieved	48	56	41	
Terminated by perpetrator	15	18	13	
Agreed to be monogamous	8	5	11	
Renegotiations	8	5	11	

[a]Because the subject could only fall into one of the following categories, only one chi-square analysis was conducted for this set of data.
[b]$p < .05$.

trator sample), the relationship generally underwent some changes, as shown in Table 9.2.2. According to the perpetrator, the relationship was terminated in 60% of the cases, somewhat more often by the perpetrator than by the aggrieved. The relationship continued for the remaining 40%, with more than half of these couples agreeing to be monogamous and the remainder agreeing to date others or to define more clearly permissible behaviors with others.

In summary, the perpetrators' accounts reveal betrayal to be a common but nonetheless emotionally charged event. Close to half of those in a long-term relationship reported that they had betrayed at least one of their partners, usually with a person already known to them, and most often motivated by magnetic attraction to a new partner. The perpetrators seemed aware that they had violated moral standards, as indicated by the high prevalence of guilt. Although a significant minority reported "getting away" with their infidelity, the great majority of those whose partners found out claimed they confessed. In a majority of cases, the betrayal led to the dissolution of the relationship. Notably, however, there was considerable variation in responses to all the questions.

Betrayal: Viewpoint of the Aggrieved. In this section, analyses are confined to the 56% (n = 121) of the sample who reported that they had been betrayed by a romantic partner with whom they had an agreement to be monogamous. A summary of the main findings appear in Table 9.2.3.

The aggrieved reported discovering their partner's betrayal in a number of different ways. The information was obtained from the erring partner in 50% of the cases, from a third party in 30% of the cases, and by just figuring it out themselves in 20% of the cases. It is noteworthy that their descriptions, although matching the pattern of responses provided by the perpetrators, differ in important details. The aggrieved were less likely to state that the perpetrator confessed (50% vs. 83%, z-test of proportions, $z = 3.5$, $p < .001$), and more likely to claim that the aggrieved had figured it out (30% vs. 8%, $z = 2.7$, $p < .01$) or that a third party had relayed the information (20% vs. 8%, $z = 2.5$, $p < .01$).

Although betrayal by a romantic partner was normative in this sample of college students, it was nevertheless an emotionally laden event for the aggrieved. A majority of the aggrieved expressed negative emotions as being mostly or very characteristic of their reactions, with anger, sadness/depression, and frustration reported by 50% or more of the sample. Cognitive-affective emotions such as disappointment and mistrust also were reported by more than half the sample of the aggrieved.

The immediate reactions by the aggrieved to news of the betrayal are shown in Table 9.2.3, and ranged from ignoring the issue (10%), to calm discussion (19%), to being clearly upset (55% including such behaviors as being upset/crying, withdrawing/sulking, yelling/insulting, and violence). The aggrieved and perpetrator gave similar accounts of the aggrieved's reaction to the betrayal as revealed by chi-square tests.

Upon discovery of the betrayal, the majority of the aggrieved reported that the relationship was terminated—usually by the aggrieved, but in approximately one-third of the cases by the perpetrator. About a quarter of the aggrieved report that the relationship was renegotiated, either to affirm monogamy or to permit dating with others and more clearly define acceptable behavior with others. When we compared the accounts of the aggrieved and the perpetrators concerning the effects of betrayal on the relationship, similarities and differences are observed. The perpetrator and the aggrieved agreed that a majority of the relationships were terminated. However, the aggrieved were less likely than the perpetrators to claim that the perpetrators broke up the relationship (18% vs. 34%, respectively; $z = 1.95$, $p < .06$) and they were more likely to claim that the aggrieved broke off the relationship (54% vs. 26%, respectively; $z = 2.8$, $p < .01$). Thus, there appears to be a self-serving action bias on the part of the informant, indicating that the informant exercised some control over events following the betrayal.

In summary, the aggrieved typically discovered their partner's betrayal because the partner confessed. The predominant emotional reactions included anger, sadness, disappointment, and mistrust. In dealing with their partners, the aggrieved exhibited marked distress and often terminated the relationship. Overall, there was a general correspondence between reports by the aggrieved and by the perpetrators regarding how the aggrieved learned about and dealt with the betrayal, as well as what happened to the relationship. However, the aggrieved and the perpetrators alike tended to attribute responsibility for events in the aftermath of the betrayal to themselves more often than to the other party.

Gender Differences

Gender differences in the incidence of betrayal (see Table 9.2.1) were not observed. Males and females were equally likely to be perpetrators and equally likely to be the aggrieved as well. Gender differences were generally absent in the perpetrators' reports of betrayal (see Table 9.2.2). Gender differences also were generally absent in reports by the aggrieved, as shown in Table 9.2.3. There were, however, some gender differences in descriptions of the aggrieved's confrontation with the partner. Aggrieved females were more likely than aggrieved males to make up after crying and being upset, and were less likely to either withdraw/sulk or be violent.

Discussion

This study is the first investigation of the subjective experiences and emotional reactions of college students to sexual betrayal in their own relationships. Our study investigates the viewpoint of the perpetrator as well as the aggrieved in the betrayal relationship, and includes a diverse sample of youth, including youth from 2-year community and city colleges as well as 4-year colleges. Our findings indicate that most youth in supposedly monogamous relationships are familiar with betrayal and find it both emotionally charged and painful.

In this discussion, we supplement the findings of our study by presenting verbatim reports from youths who described their experiences with betrayal in interviews concerning their experiences with sexuality. Using a similar sampling procedure (30 females, 23 males), we interviewed 53 college youth ages 18–24, drawn from the same colleges used for the present study. In the interviews, which lasted approximately 90 minutes, we asked about sexual attitudes and practices and included questions on betrayal and faithfulness.

Incidence of Betrayal

Approximately two-thirds of the sample had experienced betrayal, either as the perpetrator or as the aggrieved. Although this prevalence of acts of betrayal is high, involving a majority of youth who had ever been in a romantic relationship, this figure is probably a significant underestimate of the actual incidence of betrayal because not all aggrieved discovered the betrayal of their partner. In fact, perpetrators in our study claim that more than 40% of their partners never learned of the betrayal.

The incidence of betrayal among our subjects can be compared to other reports of betrayal. Despite significant variability across studies in measures, definitions of betrayal, and samples, all studies concur that betrayal is a frequent event in the relationships of youth. In our data, 40% of the sample described themselves as perpetrators of sexual betrayal in at least one relationship, a figure that falls between the 38% incidence of general betrayal in the most important relationship reported by Sheppard et al. (1995) and the 51% reported by Roscoe et al. (1988). Similarly, 66% of our sample reported having been either the perpetrator or aggrieved in sexual betrayal, similar to the 63% reported by Hansen (1987).

There are several possible explanations for the fact that acts of betrayal appear so commonplace among teens and young adults. First, adolescents may experience significant difficulty communicating clearly with their partners about sexuality, commitments, and expectations for limiting sexual activities with others, a problem also found in adults (Blumstein & Schwartz, 1983; Sprecher & McKinney, 1993). Accordingly, misunderstandings are likely to occur. Second, betrayal in this age group may result from the complexities of balancing growing levels of intimacy (with its need for commitment and fidelity) with the establishment of a strong sense of identity (with its need for experimentation and exploration of alternatives). The emotions experienced by youth subsequent to betrayal give some support to this interpretation. For example, although 63% of perpetrators felt guilty, 43% reported feeling happy, proud, or excited. The fact that betraying one's partner can elicit positive emotions as well as negative ones suggests that the underlying motives of this act may be deeply rooted. Because adolescents are still exploring their own identities, experiences such as betrayal can elicit positive reactions in addition to feelings of guilt.

Motives for Betrayal

A significant strength of our study is its focus on actual incidents of betrayal, rather than responses to hypothetical situations. In other studies, when youth were asked to speculate about motives that might explain betrayal, they were more likely than those in our study to underestimate the role of sexuality (Roscoe et al., 1988). Compared to our subjects, youth explaining the motives in a hypothetical case of betrayal underestimated both sexual attraction toward a new partner (12% in Roscoe's study vs. 53% in our study) and the influence of sexual dissatisfaction with the ongoing relationship (10% vs. 30%). Youth who generated motives to explain hypothetical betrayal also underestimated, relative to our sample, the importance of situational considerations such as temporary absence of the partner (8% vs. 40%) and the effects of drugs and alcohol (0% in Roscoe's study vs. 40% in our study).

The prevalence of situational contributors to betrayal is notable. The absence of a partner and being under the influence of either drugs or alcohol were each given as motives by more than 40% of those who had betrayed a partner. Furthermore, these environmental situations are extremely common among college students. For example, separation of romantic partners may result from such common situations as partners attending different colleges or attending the same college but returning home to different parts of the country for vacations. Separations also result from work demands and opportunities, and recreational plans with same-sex friends. Similarly, alcohol and drug use by youth is normative. It is estimated that in 1992, 41% of youth in a national study consumed 5 or more alcoholic drinks in a row on at least one occasion in the 2 weeks prior to the study (Johnston, O'Malley, & Bachman, 1993). Thus, the environmental contexts of many youths put them at significant risk of betrayal.

In our interviews, youth often gave elaborate answers to explain how they came to betray their partners, often alluding to more than one motive. For example, a 21-year-old female who went away to summer school while in an ongoing monogamous relationship explains:

I was starting to have pretty severe doubts. I'd never dated anybody else and I was starting to wonder, "Why am I tied down?". . . I went into my friend's room one day and said, "That's it. I'm not in love with my boyfriend anymore. When I go home, I am going to break up with him." And within a couple of days I hooked up with someone to whom I was really attracted . . . and we had sex a short while later. . . . Technically, I cheated on him [my old boyfriend].

Similarly, a 23-year-old male, who had betrayed his partner only once, described how his girlfriend's absence was the primary motive:

The girl I was dating left to study in Mexico for a while and before she left we agreed, even though our relationship was not on the best of terms, that we would still be expecting to keep seeing each other when she got back. I don't know if I believed that or . . . I didn't want her to be unhappy there. . . . When she was gone I started messing around with another girl and it turned into a big mess.

Comparing the Viewpoints of the Aggrieved and the Perpetrator

The present study examines the perspective of the perpetrator as well as the aggrieved. There were few surprises regarding the aggrieved's emotions. We expected and found that the aggrieved experience high rates of negative emotions (anger, frustration, and sadness) and high rates of cognitive-affective emotions (disappointment, mistrust, confusion, and insecurity). These findings agree with those reported by others studying adolescents (Kitzinger and Powell, 1995) and adults (Buunk, 1995). Of greater interest are some relatively low-incidence responses indicating that some youth assume responsibility for bad things that happen to them. A small percentage of aggrieved youth felt inadequate (18%) and guilty (7%) in response to their partner's betrayal.

Perpetrators' emotions were significantly more variable than those of the aggrieved. Only one response—guilt—was experienced by more than half of the sample (63%), whereas 3 emotions—feeling ashamed, immoral, or confused—were reported by approximately one-third of the sample. Thus, the most frequently experienced emotions had a strongly self-evaluative component, giving evidence that youth were aware that they were breaking community or personal standards. A 19-year-old female who betrayed her partner describes her reaction:

> I broke out in spots all over my body. It was from stress. . . . That's what the doctor told me. I felt so incredibly guilty and I knew if I told [my partner] that I might not be able to have the same relationship, and I didn't want to jeopardize it, 'cause once the betrayal happened, . . . it really made me realize how special he was to me; I just felt incredibly guilty and I wanted to tell him, but I couldn't, I guess.

More surprising than the reports of guilt and other cognitive-affective responses was that 40% of the perpetrators reported one or more positive emotions. One of our interview respondents, a male 22-year-old, illustrates this as he describes the first time he betrayed a partner:

> At the time, it was a new experience for me, and I was just kind of experimenting . . . and I didn't really feel bad about doing that for some reason. . . . I thought "this is kind of neat, people do this all the time, I'm just seeing what it's like."

We suggest that the positive emotional responses reported by many youth indicate not that they are happy that they betrayed a partner, but that they were celebrating their ability to attract a new partner and the success of their experimentation. Thus, through betrayal, they proved to themselves that they were attractive to others and that they had options.

In describing the betrayal experience, the perpetrators and the aggrieved generally agree on some key dimensions. For example, they agree that confession by the perpetrator is the most common way in which the aggrieved discover betrayal, that upset is the most common reaction by the aggrieved, and that the re-

lationship is terminated in a majority of cases. Clearly, as evidenced by the emotional reactions reported, and by the number of couples who chose to terminate the relationship, infidelity is a major distressing event in the lives of youth. This finding stands in contrast to that reported by Roscoe et al. (1988), who asked youth about responses to hypothetical betrayal. He found a more rational approach. More youth in his sample expected that they would be calm and reasonable in discussing betrayal, with a focus on finding out the reason for the betrayal, working toward improving the relationship, and forgiveness. In contrast, in our study, the reports of both the perpetrators and the aggrieved describe considerably more pain and emotion in confronting an actual betrayal.

The development of intimacy and trust during adolescence is a challenging task. Balancing these tasks with the exploration of one's identity places further strains on adolescents. The data presented here paint a picture in which males and females alike often betray their romantic partners, leading to guilt because they do not condone such behavior, but also, for many, leading to feelings of happiness and excitement as their interpersonal horizons and their insight regarding their own identity expand. Meanwhile, many youth experience betrayal by a partner and suffer negative emotions, which forces them to reevaluate the relationship.

The relations between betrayal behavior and the conflicting challenges of intimacy and identity development remain speculative because the present study does not examine intimacy or identity directly. Nevertheless, this study provides a valuable first look at the complex implications of sexual betrayal during adolescence and suggests a number of areas that warrant further investigation. Future studies might examine the empirical relations between intimacy, identity, and betrayal. Also, additional research might examine ways in which responses to incidents of betrayal evolve with age or with experience. Finally, a study placing greater emphasis on the nature and quality of relationships would help to distinguish between those transgressions that occur in otherwise committed relationships and those that occur in relationships that are less serious or are already faltering. Our hope is that by performing a preliminary investigation of adolescent sexual betrayal, from the perspectives of the perpetrator as well as the aggrieved, we have illuminated the basic features of this topic's landscape sufficiently to provide a starting point for more detailed explorations of this ubiquitous, emotionally charged phenomenon. . . .

REFERENCES

Blumstein, P., & Schwartz, P. (1983). *American couples.* New York: Morrow.

Buunk, B. (1995). Sex, self-esteem, dependency, and extradyadic sexual experience as related to jealousy response. *Journal of Social and Personal Relationships, 12,* 147–153.

Feldman, S. S., & Cauffman, E. (1999). Your cheatin' heart: Sexual betrayal attitudes and behaviors and their correlates. *Journal of Research on Adolescence, 9.*

Greely, A. M. (1991). *Faithful attraction: Discovering intimacy, love, and fidelity in American marriage.* New York: Doherty.

Hansen, G. L. (1987). Extra dyadic reactions during courtship. *Journal of Sex Research, 29,* 361–387.

Johnston, L. D., O'Malley, P. M., & Bachman, J. G. (1993). *National survey results on drug use from monitoring the future study, 1975–1992. Vol. 1. Secondary school students.* U.S. Department of Health and Human Services (National Institute on Drug Abuse Publication No. 93–3597). U.S. Government Printing Office, Washington, DC.

Katchadourian, H. (1990). Sexuality. In S. S. Feldman and G. R. Elliott (Eds.), *At the threshold: The developing adolescent* (pp. 330–351). Cambridge, MA: Harvard University Press.

Kitzinger, C., & Powell, D. (1995). Engendering fidelity: Existentialist and social constructionist readings of a story completion task. *Feminist Psychology, 5,* 345–372.

Lawson, A., & Samson, C. (1988). Age, gender and adultery. *British Journal of Sociology, 39,* 409–440.

Lieberman, B. (1988). Extrapremarital intercourse: Attitudes toward neglected sexual behavior. *Journal of Sex Research, 24,* 296–298.

Mongeau, P., Hale, J., & Alles, M. (1994). An experimental investigation of accounts and attributions following sexual infidelity. *Community Monographs, 61,* 326–344.

Moore, S., & Rosenthal, D. A. (1993). *Sexuality in adolescence.* New York: Routledge.

Roscoe, B., Cavanaugh, L., & Kennedy, D. (1988). Dating infidelity: Behaviors, reasons, and consequences. *Adolescence, 23,* 35–43.

Sheppard, V., Nelson, E., & Andreoli-Mathie, V. (1995). Dating relationships and infidelity: Attitudes and behavior. *Journal of Sex and Marital Therapy, 21,* 202–212.

Sprecher, S., & McKinney, K. (1993). *Sexuality.* Newbury Park, CA: Sage.

Thompson, A. P. (1984). Emotional and sexual components of extramarital relations. *Journal of Marriage and Family, 46,* 35–42.

Weis, D. L., & Slosnerick, M. (1981). Attitudes toward sexual and nonsexual extramarital involvement among a sample of college students. *Journal of Marriage and the Family, 43,* 349–358.

THINKING CRITICALLY

1. All the participants in the study were college students. Do you think rates of sexual betrayal would be higher or lower for noncollege persons in the same age group? How does the college setting lend itself to possibilities for sexual betrayal?

2. Among the "perpetrators," almost as many persons reported one or more positive emotions (43%) as reported negative emotions (50%). How do the authors explain that? How would you explain it?

3. Explain why about half of perpetrators confessed their betrayal to their partners. Base your explanation at least in part on results given in this reading.

4. The authors suggest that future studies should take into account the degree of commitment that existed in the (betrayed) relationship. How would you measure commitment in such as study?

PART X School

Ethnic Differences in School Performance

The United States has long been ethnically diverse, but it has become even more diverse in recent years with a large influx of immigrants from Latin America and Asia. Research on adolescents in immigrant families has consistently found that they do very well in school, better, on average, than adolescents born in the United States. This article explores the reason for the high academic achievements of immigrant adolescents and locates their motivation in the strong sense of duty and obligation they have to their families.

Reading 10.1

Family Obligation and the Academic Motivation of Adolescents From Immigrant and American-Born Families

A. J. Fuligni and V. Tseng

Reprinted from A. J. Fuligni and V. Tseng, "Family obligation and the academic motivation of adolescents from immigrant and American-born families." From *Advances in Motivation and Achievement, 11*, pp. 159–183, with permission from Elsevier Science.

To the surprise of many observers, the largest and most culturally-diverse group of children from immigrant families in history is doing remarkably well in American schools. Children of foreign-born parents tend to receive equal or even higher grades than students whose parents were born in the United States. These students demonstrate surprising success despite facing many challenges such as being newcomers to a new society, less exposure to the English language, and having parents who often know little about the workings of American schools. Numerous studies, ranging from quantitative analyses of national samples to ethnographic examinations of small communities, have noted the achievements of this unique group of students (Caplan, Choy, & Whitmore, 1991; Fuligni, 1997; Gibson & Bhachu, 1991; Kao & Tienda, 1995; Matute-Bianchi, 1991; Rosenthal & Feldman, 1991; Rumbaut, 1994; Steinberg, 1996; Suarez-Orozco, 1991; Suarez-Orozco & Suarez-Orozco, 1995).

Important differences do exist among immigrant families themselves, with children from Asia exhibiting higher performance than students from Europe, who in turn do better than those from Latin America. Variations are also evident among those from different countries in Asia and Latin America. Nevertheless, when compared to students from the same cultural and ethnic background, students from immigrant families do just as well or even better than those from native-born families. The only departure from this trend is that immigrant Latin American students are slightly less likely to graduate from American high schools than second and third generation Latin American children (McMillen, 1997).

Socioeconomic factors do not appear to explain the academic successes of students from immigrant families as compared to their peers from native-born families. Generational differences in academic achievement remain after controlling for the educational and occupational statuses of children's parents (Fuligni, 1997; Kao & Tienda, 1995). In fact, the relative success of students from immigrant families often becomes greater after such controls, reflecting the fact that many of them do better in

school than would be expected from their socioeconomic backgrounds (Kao, 1999). Even some refugees from war and economic deprivation have been found to attain high levels of educational achievement (Caplan et al., 1991).

Socioeconomic factors are important, however, for understanding the large variation in educational adjustment within the population of children from immigrant families. As a group, immigrants from Asia tend to be more highly educated and are more likely to work in professional occupations than those from Latin America (U.S. Bureau of Census, 1993). Diversity also exists within these large groupings, with immigrants from countries such as Taiwan, India, and Cuba having higher socioeconomic profiles than individuals from other Asian and Latin American nations. . . . Yet even children from the lower socioeconomic immigrant groups tend to do just as well or even better than their native-born peers of similar backgrounds. Factors such as parental education and income simply do not explain why the children from immigrant families do so well in American schools.

Recent studies have begun to suggest other features of the contexts in which these children develop that could help to explain the achievements of students from immigrant families. Specifically, the values and beliefs that are associated with the families' cultural backgrounds seem to play an important role in their academic endeavors. In particular, it has been suggested that an emphasis upon supporting and assisting the family—in conjunction with a value of education—may lead the students from immigrant families to excel in school. In this chapter, we examine the complex role played by the value of family obligation in the academic motivation and achievement of adolescents from different social and cultural backgrounds. The success of students from immigrant families provides a jumping-off point for this exploration, but we hope that our analysis will provide a more general understanding of the role that family obligation may play in the motivation of all adolescents.

We first describe the nature and sources of family obligations within families' cultural backgrounds and experiences as immigrants in a new society. Next, we review research that suggests that these family obligations may be implicated in the achievement motivation and behaviors of children from immigrant families during adolescence. Finally, we present results from our own study of adolescents from immigrant and native-born families in which we directly examine the links between adolescents' family obligations and their academic motivation.

The Sources and Nature of Family Obligations

The importance of assisting and supporting the family can be found in the cultural backgrounds of many immigrant families. Asian and Latin American societies, in particular, have often been described as possessing a collectivistic orientation that emphasizes the goals and interests of the group over those of individual members (Triandis, 1995). The activities and decisions of individuals within cultures with such an orientation are expected to reflect the imperatives and needs of the larger group (Markus & Kitayatna, 1991). Collectivistic traditions are often contrasted with more individualistic orientations in which individuals tend to make decisions and behave in ways that emphasize self-actualization and the distinctiveness of the individual. Although both collectivistic and individualistic orientations can be found within the same cultures and even the same individual, Western societies such as the United States are often characterized as placing greater importance on individualism.

Collectivistic traditions do not necessarily mean indiscriminate consideration of the needs of others. Distinctions are often made between members of the in-group versus the out-group, and a critical aspect of a collectivistic ideology is a strong concern for the fate and well-being of one's own family (Huang, 1994; Rhee, Uleman, & Lee, 1996). This emphasis on family support and assistance takes on an immediate and practical importance for Asian and Latin American families when they immigrate to a new country such as the United States. Parents and other adult family members often know very little about the workings of their new societies. Attending American schools, children tend to assimilate to American society more quickly than their parents. As a result, children often help their families with negotiating the official tasks and more informal demands of the new country (Zhou, 1997).

Yet immigration does more than simply create an immediate need for family support and assistance. The motivation behind a family's move to the United States also engenders in children a belief that their duty is to succeed in the new country. Many immigrants leave their native countries with the intention of providing better lives for their children. Parents often sacrifice their existing jobs and extended family networks in order to give their children better educational and occupational opportunities. As a result, the children from immigrant families often believe that one of their primary obligations to the family is to succeed in school and eventually secure gainful employment (Caplan et al., 1991; Suarez-Orozco & Suarez-Orozco, 1995). The desire to help the family fulfill their dreams may lead students with foreign-born parents to place more importance on education, to spend more time studying and less time engaging in risky behavior, and to aspire to more post-secondary schooling than their peers from native-born families.

Family Obligations and Academic Motivation

In recent years, an increasing number of studies have been conducted on the adjustment of youths from immigrant families. Using a mix of qualitative, projective, and quantitative techniques, these studies have highlighted the great sense of duty and obligation that is socialized by foreign-born parents and internalized by their children. Regardless of the families' specific countries of origin, adolescents with immigrant parents believe in the importance of supporting and assisting their families both in the present and in the future. This obligation, in turn, appears to have implications for the students' academic motivation and achievement. In many cases, these students demonstrate a remarkable degree of success at school. For other children, however, the need to assist the family at times seems to interfere with their educational endeavors because of immediate economic need or the pressure of traditional gender roles.

The educational significance of family obligations was demonstrated in Gibson's ethnographic work with a Sikh community in the Central Valley of California (Gibson, 1995; Gibson & Bhachu, 1991). The Sikh families Gibson studied had little formal education and generally earned minor incomes by working in the agricultural industry. In addition to their low socioeconomic status, the Sikh parents possessed a limited knowledge of English. Given the uniqueness of their dress and appearance in the Central Valley, the adolescents from Sikh families contended with verbal and physical abuse from the majority students in the schools. Despite these challenges, the Sikh adolescents received high grades and tended to take the toughest classes that were offered. The students overcame the numerous barriers to their educational progress and ranked among the best students in the school.

To explain the academic success of the Sikh students, Gibson pointed to a collection of values that included the belief that doing well in school brought honor to the family and community. Poor academic performance, in contrast, resulted in shame. The power of shame can be especially strong within a close immigrant community, where gossip spreads quickly and the community holds rigid standards for members' behavior (Gibson & Bhachu, 1991). Families within the Sikh community also emphasized the students' obligation to do well in school so that the youths may obtain better jobs than the parents. Virtually all parents were involved in farming, and they reminded their children that "the fields are waiting" when children fell behind in their studies (Gibson, 1995).

The Central American and Mexican families studied by Suarez-Orozco (Suarez-Orozco, 1991; Suarez-Orozco & Suarez-Orozco, 1995) emphasized similar themes of familial duty and obligation in regards to their adolescents' school performance. The academic motivation of these students was strong and often re-

marked upon by the teachers of the school. These youths were often seen by the school staff as eager to learn and as more desirable students than those born in the United States. Students from Latin America generally do not do as well in school as their Asian counterparts (Kao & Tienda, 1995), but their desire to achieve tends to remain high. Through the use of interviews and projective tests, Suarez-Orozco concluded that one source of this persistent motivation is a desire to assist and support the family.

Many of the Central American parents Suarez-Orozco spoke to emphasized the fact that their primary reason for immigrating was to provide better lives and opportunities for their children:

> We came here for them so that they may become somebody tomorrow. . . . I am too old. At my age, it is too late for me. (1991, p. 45)

The families' motivations for immigration were quite clear to the adolescents from Central America and Mexico. They knew about the sacrifices their parents made to get to the United States, and many of the students were determined not to let their parents down. As one Salvadoran boy in the study stated, "I believe the most important thing I can do for my parents is to become a doctor; that would make them happy" (p. 51).

Themes of family responsibility and obligation run through most studies of immigrant families, regardless of the families' cultural backgrounds. For example, studies of Vietnamese immigrants in both Southern California and New Orleans have highlighted the same topics of respect, honor, and duty (Caplan et al., 1991; Zhou & Bankston, 1998). In addition to interviews and ethnographic observations, these two studies employed more quantitative approaches in which they asked parents and children to rate the importance of particular values. When asked to rank the importance of a large set of values, the Vietnamese children in the Caplan et al. (1991) study listed "respect for family members," "education and achievement," "freedom," "family loyalty," and "hard work" as the top five values. Similarly, the youths studied by Zhou and Bankston (1998) reported that "obedience" and "working hard" were the most important values in their families.

Despite the association between family obligations and academic motivation, the actual obligations themselves can carry additional demands and expectations that may ironically interfere with the educational progress of some youths. For example, the more immediate needs of the family can prevent some adolescents from fully realizing their dreams of academic success, especially for girls. Adolescents' obligation to succeed in school can eventually conflict with traditional gender roles within some immigrant families. Families from cultures in which women do not pursue education may question the propriety for their girls to attend school beyond the twelfth grade (Gibson & Bhachu, 1991). As a result, adolescent girls from immigrant families may be faced with the need to negotiate the competing obligations of academic success and assisting the family at home. For the Sikh girls studied by Gibson, this meant that the girls would take secretarial courses in high school despite the fact that they were doing well in their more academically-oriented classes.

Together, these studies of immigrant families offer support for the idea that the strong academic motivation of children and adolescents from immigrant families stems in part from a desire to support and assist the family. The youths in immigrant families recognize the sacrifices that their parents have made to come to the United States, and adolescents believe that they owe it to their families to do well in school. This motivation, in turn, leads many students from immigrant families to achieve a high level of academic achievement. The actual connection between motivation and educational success, however, may depend upon whether pressing economic needs of the family and traditional gender roles impede the academic progress of the youths from immigrant families.

Despite the compelling evidence from prior research, however, it remains unclear whether family obligation is a value that is truly unique to adolescents from immigrant families. All of the studies described above included only adolescents with foreign-born parents.

Suarez-Orozco and Suarez-Orozco (1995) compared foreign-born and American-born Mexican adolescents, but all of the youths came from immigrant families. The ethnographic evidence provides a very convincing case for a profound sense of sense of duty on the part of those from immigrant families, and that this sense of duty is often coupled with a desire to "repay" parents for making sacrifices in order to be in the United States. But, as suggested by Suarez-Orozco and Suarez-Orozco (1995), the emphasis on family obligation may be a value more strongly associated with the adolescents' cultural background than with their membership in immigrant families. If so, do Latin American and Asian adolescents from American-born families also believe in the importance of supporting, assisting, and respecting their families? What implications do generational similarities or differences in family obligation have for understanding the academic motivation and achievement of the adolescents from immigrant and American-born families? In the following section, we describe a study in which we attempt to address these questions by complimenting the existing research with a direct assessment of the links between family obligation and academic motivation among youths from both immigrant and American-born families.

A Study of Adolescents From Asian, Latin American, and European Backgrounds

For the past several years, we have been conducting a study of adolescents from immigrant and native-born families with Asian, Latin American, and European backgrounds. Our goal has been to examine the role of adolescents' cultural beliefs about authority, autonomy, and education in their actual family relationships and academic achievement. We have already presented results regarding the academic achievement, motivation, and family obligations of these youths in two previous papers (Fuligni, 1997; Fuligni, Tseng, & Lam, 1999). We first describe the findings from these two papers and then present some original analyses in which we more systematically examine the links between family obligations and academic motivation.

Previous Analyses

The youths in our study attended school in an ethnically diverse district in the San Francisco Bay area that included a large number of immigrant families. Over 85 percent of the students in our study came from Latin American (Mexican, Central/South American), East Asian (predominantly Chinese), Filipino, and European backgrounds. Overall, approximately two-thirds of the students had at least one foreign-born parent while the remainder came from families in which both parents were born in the United States. The distribution of immigrant and American-born families varied across ethnic backgrounds, such that the majority of all but those from European backgrounds had foreign-born parents. The adolescents also varied in terms of their socioeconomic background. Students from East Asian and Filipino families had parents with the highest educational and occupational levels, whereas those from Latin American families had parents with the lowest levels of education and occupation. As part of the study adolescents completed questionnaires that tapped their beliefs and values regarding the family and education. The students' year-end grades in their courses also were obtained from official school records.

Academic Motivation and Achievement. In an initial paper, the academic achievement and motivation of 1,100 students from the sixth, eighth, and tenth grades were examined (Fuligni, 1997). Results indicated that the adolescents from immigrant families reported a consistently higher level of academic motivation than those from native-born families. Students with foreign-born parents placed more importance upon learning mathematics and English, aspired to higher levels of educational attainment, valued academic success more, and spent more time studying and doing homework than those with American-born parents. These differences generally held up even when ado-

lescents within the same ethnic group were compared to one another (e.g., immigrant Latin American families versus American-born Latin American families). The greater motivation of the students from immigrant families, in turn, accounted for their tendency to receive equal or even higher grades in mathematics and English than their peers from American-born families—even after controlling for differences in socioeconomic background and language use. The only departure from this trend was that foreign-born Latin American students had more difficulty in mathematics than American-born Latin American students (regardless of the parents' place of birth). This finding was attributable to the fact that foreign-born Latin American students came from extremely low socioeconomic backgrounds.

Family Obligations. More recently, we examined the adolescents' attitudes toward their family obligations in a second paper that involved approximately 800 tenth and twelfth grade students from Chinese, Filipino, Mexican, Central and South American, and European families (Fuligni at al., 1999). We measured the youths' attitudes toward three types of family obligations. The first, which we called current assistance, referred to degree to which adolescents believed that they should assist with household tasks and spend time with the family. Youths indicated how they often they felt they should engage in activities such as run errands for the family, help out around the house, take care of brothers and sisters, and spend time with other family members. The second type of obligation was called family respect and students were asked to evaluate the importance of respecting parents and older family members, doing well for the sake of the family, and making sacrifices for the family. The final aspect of family obligations that we assessed involved the value the students placed upon supporting the family in the future. Youths indicated how important they believed it was to help their parents financially in the future, live or go to college near their parents, and help take care of their parents and other family members in the future. All three scales were highly reliable, with alpha coefficients well above .70 for the various ethnic groups.

Adolescents from the four non-European groups endorsed all three aspects of family obligations more strongly than those with European backgrounds. Chinese, Filipino, Mexican, and Central/South American youths believed that they should assist and spend time with their family, respect their parent's wishes and make sacrifices for the family, and support their family in the future more than did their European-American peers. Surprisingly, however, adolescents from immigrant families possessed a stronger sense of obligation to the family than their peers from native-born families only as it applied to their support of the family in the future. Among all youths except those from Central/South American families, those with foreign-born parents placed the greatest importance upon caring for and supporting their parents and other family members when the youths become adults. In contrast, adolescents from native-born families held attitudes toward their current assistance and respect for the family that were just as strong as those of adolescents from immigrant families.

There was no association between the adolescents' socioeconomic background and their attitudes toward their obligations. Adolescents' gender was also unrelated to their views regarding family obligation.

Conclusions From Previous Analyses. These findings suggest an emphasis on family obligation is not necessarily a uniquely immigrant value, and that the value of supporting and assisting the family is also shared by adolescents from American-born families with Latin American and Asian backgrounds. Conclusions about generational similarity should be tempered, however, until adolescents from immigrant and American-born families are compared on other dimensions of family obligation. Despite our attempts to measure adolescents' views regarding their duty to the family in a comprehensive manner, we may have missed more subtle aspects of family obligation that are unique to immigrant families. In the next section, we report analyses in which we address a variety of new questions.

Additional Analyses

For this paper, we conducted additional analyses in which we examined four measures of the students' academic motivation. The first measure was of the students' value of mathematics, and it included items such as "In general, I find working on math assignments interesting" and "In the future, how useful do you think math will be in your everyday life?" The second was of the students' value of English and it included the same questions as those for mathematics, only specified for English. For the third measure, tapping the value of academic success, adolescents were asked to rate the importance of outcomes such as "Doing well in school" and "Going to college after high school." The final measure tapped students' perceptions of the future utility of education. Students responded to statements such as "Going to college is necessary for what I want to do in the future" and "Doing well in school is the best way for me to succeed as an adult." All of the scales were highly reliable with internal consistencies well above .70 and .80.

We first estimated the bivariate correlations between adolescents' beliefs about their family obligations and the four aspects of their academic motivation (see Table 10.1.1). These correlations demonstrate a notable and consistent link between an emphasis upon assistance to the family and a general value of academic achievement. Adolescents who believed that they should assist, support, and respect their family placed a stronger value upon learning mathematics and English and achieving a measure of academic success. These youths also had a stronger belief in the utility and importance of schooling for their future occupational successes as adults.

Individual Differences in Motivation. We conducted additional analyses to further explore the nature of the individual-level associations between family obligations and academic motivation. The ethnographies discussed earlier suggested that family obligation may be connected to a specific belief in the usefulness of education for the adolescent's and family's

TABLE 10.1.1 Correlations Between Attitudes Toward Family Obligations and Educational Values

	CURRENT ASSISTANCE	RESPECT	FUTURE SUPPORT
Value of mathematics	.25*	.33*	.23*
Value of English	.20*	.13*	.10*
Academic success	.33*	.40*	.28*
Future utility of education	.26*	.33*	.22*

Note: Ns = 774–803.
*p < .001.

future (e.g., Suarez-Orozco & Suarez-Orozco, 1995). To examine this possibility, we broke down the measures of students' values of mathematics and English into their original subcomponents as designed by Eccles (1983). The first component, the *intrinsic value* of the subjects, included the items "In general, I find working on math [English] assignments interesting" and "How much do you like math [English]?" The second component tapped more of a *utility value* of the subjects and included questions such as "In the future, how useful do you think math [English] will be in your everyday life?" and "How useful do you think math [English] will be for what you want to be after you graduate from school and go to work?" If family obligation is indeed more salient for a belief in the usefulness of education, it should be more highly correlated with youths' utility values of their subjects rather than their intrinsic values.

As shown in Table 10.1.2, adolescents' sense of obligation to the family was more strongly related to the youths' belief in the usefulness of math and English than it was to how

much they liked the subjects. These differential relations were especially true for the students' values of mathematics, where the associations between obligation attitudes and the utility value were as much as twice as large as the same relations with the intrinsic value. In addition, the links between youths' family obligations and their belief in the usefulness of mathematics tended to be greater than the relations with the students' belief in the usefulness of English. Though perhaps surprising, given the importance of learning English for the adjustment of immigrants, this differential association is consistent with the suggestion that students from some immigrant and minority groups tend to focus on technical subjects and skills because they are believed to be more useful for obtaining stable and secure occupations (Sue & Okazaki, 1990).

These results indicate that the link between adolescents' sense of family obligation and their educational attitudes is strongest for youths' belief in the utility of education. The patterns of correlations suggest that education is seen as a means by which youths may fulfill duties and obligations to their families.

TABLE 10.1.2 Correlations Between Attitudes Toward Family Obligations and Utility and Intrinsic Values of Mathematics and English

	CURRENT ASSISTANCE	RESPECT	FUTURE SUPPORT
Utility value of mathematics	.25*	.34*	.25*
Intrinsic value of mathematics	.16*	.20*	.12*
Utility value of English	.20*	.17*	.14*
Intrinsic value of English	.19*	.14*	.07

Note: Ns = 774–802.
*p < .001.

Individual Differences in Academic Achievement.   Given the link between obligations and the value of education, the question remains how these attitudes may be related to students' actual achievement at school. On the one hand, the strong value on education of those with a sense of duty to support their families may lead them to do particularly well in school. On the other hand, there may become a point at which such a strong emphasis on helping and assisting the family may interfere with students' academic efforts. As we reported in one of our earlier papers, we have found evidence for both of these patterns in our study (Fuligni et al., 1999). Significant curvilinear associations between youths' attitudes towards their obligations and their school grades were observed such that adolescents who reported either the weakest or the strongest endorsement of their obligations possessed the lowest grade-point averages (see Figure 10.1.1). In contrast, youths with a moderate sense of obligation tended to receive the highest grades. These associations remained even after controlling for students' ethnic and socioeconomic backgrounds.

Individual Differences in Post-Secondary Aspirations and Plans.   The connections between adolescents' attitudes toward family obligations and their educational motivation are also apparent in their aspirations and plans for the future. Students were asked how far they would like to go in school, and they responded to a set of options that ranged from dropping out of high school to attending graduate or professional school. The actual associations between adolescents' beliefs about family obligations and their educational aspirations are presented in Table 10.1.3. Consistent with their emphasis on academic success during high school, adolescents with a stronger sense of obligation to the family hoped to continue their education beyond secondary school. Adolescents who aspired to attend four-year colleges and graduate or professional school placed greater importance on their obligations to assist their families in daily household chores, respect family members, and support the family in the future than did those who aspired to attend two-year colleges, $F(3, 723) = 3.30$ to $F(3, 725) = 6.09$, $ps < .05–.001$.

Conclusions and Future Research

Findings from both qualitative and quantitative research indicate that adolescents from immigrant families emphasize the importance of education and school success, and that this strong academic motivation has much to do

FIGURE 10.1.1 Curvilinear associations between family obligations and academic achievement. Sample is broken into low, medium, and high tertiles for each aspect of family obligation.

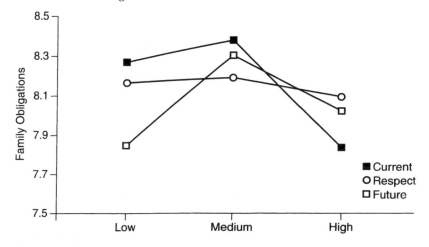

TABLE 10.1.3 Family Obligations Across Students' Levels of Educational Aspiration

Family Obligation	EDUCATIONAL ASPIRATIONS			
	High School M (SD)	2-Year College M (SD)	4-Year College M (SD)	Graduate School M (SD)
Current assistance	2.68 (0.88)	2.57 (0.73)	2.96 (0.74)	3.10 (0.79)
Respect	3.28 (0.86)	3.21 (0.91)	3.53 (0.86)	3.67 (0.79)
Future support	2.88 (1.07)	2.64 (0.96)	2.97 (0.91)	3.04 (0.92)

Note: Ns = 720–729.

with the youths' unexpected level of performance in American schools. It remains unclear, however, the degree to which the generational differences in motivation can be attributable to a greater sense of family obligation among these students. Youths from immigrant families clearly place a strong value upon the importance of assisting, supporting, and respecting their families. But the dimensions of this familial duty that are unique to immigrant families, as opposed to American-born families, remain to be elucidated. The studies of Gibson and Suarez-Orozco (Gibson & Bhachu, 1991; Suarez-Orozco, 1991) suggest that feelings of debt and guilt may give the family obligations among adolescents from immigrant families an additional motivational quality that pushes these students beyond their peers. We did not tap these dimensions in our study, and given that Gibson and Suarez-Orozco only studied immigrant families, additional research should directly compare adolescents from immigrant and American-born families in terms of these and other emotional elements of family obligation.

Given that adolescents from immigrant and American-born families only differed in terms of their future obligations, the extent to which family obligations explains generational differences in academic motivation and performance may be most evident in the years after high school. In contrast to the recent surge of research on the secondary school performance of children from immigrant families, virtually nothing is known about the experiences of these youths during young adulthood. The results of studies of adolescents suggest that these students may very well continue their surprising educational performance into young adulthood. These youths possess a consistently strong academic motivation that includes a belief in the utility of education for their future lives. Given the great economic variation among immigrant families, the need to assist the family immediately will likely cause some youths to delay or even forgo their postsecondary education. Nevertheless, we still expect these youths to pursue more training and education than their peers in similar economic circumstances. As we continue to follow the youths in our study as they make their transition into adulthood, we expect to observe a rich variety of strategies by which youths with a sense of familial duty and obligation balance the immediate needs of their families with their attempts to receive enough schooling in order to ensure their families' long-term economic stability.

REFERENCES

Caplan, N., Choy, M. H., & Whitmore, J. K. (1991). *Children of boat people: A study of educational success.* Ann Arbor: University of Michigan Press.

Fuligini, A. J. (1997). The academic achievement of adolescents from immigrant families: The roles of family background, attitudes, and behavior. *Child Development, 68,* 261–273.

Fuligini, A. J., Tseng, V., & Lam, M. (1999). Attitudes toward family obligations among American adolescents from Asian, Latin American, and European backgrounds. *Child Development, 70,* 1030–1044.

Gibson, M. A. (1995). Additive acculturation as a strategy for school improvement. In R. G. Rumbaut & W. A. Cornelius (Eds.), *California's immigrant children: Theory, research, and implications for educational policy* (pp. 77–106). San Diego, CA: The center for U.S.-Mexican Studies, University of California, San Diego.

Gibson, M. A., & Bhachu, P. K. (1991). The dynamics of educational decisionmaking: A comparative study of Silhs in Britain and the United States. In M. A. Gibson & J. U. Ogbu (Eds.), *Minority status and schooling: A comparative study of immigrant and involuntary minorities* (pp. 63–96). New York: Garland.

Huang, L. N. (1994). An integrative approach to clinical assessment and intervention with Asian-American adolescents. *Journal of Clinical Child Psychology, 23*(1), 21–31.

Kao, G. (1999). Psychological well-being and educational achievement among immigrant youth. In D. J. Hernandez (Ed.), *Children of immigrants: Health, adjustment, and public assistance* (pp. 410–477). Washington, DC: National Academy Press.

Kao, G., & Tienda, M. (1995). Optimism and achievement: The educational performance of immigrant youth. *Social Science Quarterly, 76,* 1–19.

Markus, H. R., & Kitayama, S. (1991). Culture and self: Implications for cognition, emotion, and motivation. *Psychological Review, 98,* 224–253.

Matute-Bianchi, M. E. (1991). Situational ethnicity and patterns of school performance among immigrant and non-immigrant Mexican-descent students. In M. A. Gibson & J. U. Ogbu (Eds.), *Minority status and schooling: A comparative study of immigrant and involuntary minorities* (pp. 205–248). New York: Garland.

McMillen, M. (1997). *Dropout rates in the United States: 1995.* Washington, DC: U.S. Government Printing Office.

Rhee, E., Uleman, J. S., & Lee, H. K. (1996). Variations in collectivism and individualism by in-group and culture: Confirmatory factor analyses. *Journal of Personality and Social Psychology, 71.*

Rosenthal, D. A., & Feldman, S. S. (1991). The influence of perceived family and personal factors on self-reported school performance of Chinese and Western high school student. *Journal of Research on Adolescence, 1,* 135–154.

Rumbaut, R. G. (1994). The crucible within: Ethnic identity, self-esteem and segmented assimilation among children of immigrants. *International Migration Review, 28,* 748–794.

Steinberg, L. (1996). *Beyond the classroom: Why school reform has failed and what parents need to do.* New York: Simon and Schuster.

Suarez-Orozco, C., & Suarez-Orozco, M. M. (1995). *Transformations: Immigration, family life, and achievement motivation among Latino adolescents.* Stanford, CA: Stanford University Press.

Suarez-Orozco, M. M. (1991). Immigrant adaptation to schooling: A Hispanic case. In M. A. Gibson & J. U. Ogbu (Eds.), *Minority status and schooling: A comparative study of immigrant and involuntary minorities* (pp. 37–62). New York: Garland.

Sue, S., & Okazaki, S. (1990). Asian-America educational achievements: A phenomenon in search of an explanation. *American Psychologist, 45,* 913–920.

Triandis, H. C. (1995). *Individualism and collectivism.* New York: Simon and Schuster.

U.S. Bureau of Census (1993). *We the American: Foreign born.* Washington, DC: U.S. Government Printing Office.

Zhou, M. (1997). Growing up American: The challenge confronting immigrant children and children of immigrants. *Annual Review of Sociology, 23,* 63–95.

Zhou, M., & Bankston, C. L. (1998). *Growing up American: How Vietnamese children adapt to life in the United States.* New York: Russell Sage Foundation.

THINKING CRITICALLY

1. Explain what Sikh parents mean by telling their children that "the fields are waiting" when the children fall behind in their studies.

2. What were the goals of the study described here, and how did the authors expect it to add to what is already known?

3. What do you think it is about American society that leads most adolescents who are born in the United States to take a rather relaxed attitude toward academic success?

4. The authors focus on differences between immigrant adolescents and American-born adolescents. Do you think there might be differences among American-born adolescents depending on how many generations their families had been in the United States? Why or why not?

How College Affects Students

With nearly two-thirds of emerging adults in the United States now obtaining at least some college education, the question of how college influences them is of considerable interest. Ernest Pascarella and Patrick Terenzini are scholars who have been studying this topic for nearly three decades. In the book from which this reading is drawn, they present a grand synthesis of all the research that has been done on how college affects students. Here, they summarize their findings, focusing on learning and cognitive change, psychosocial changes, attitudes and values, and moral development.

Reading **10.2**

How College Makes a Difference: A Summary

E. T. Pascarella and P. T. Terenzini

In the preceding chapters we have reviewed the evidence on a wide range of specific college outcomes. This chapter is our summary. It attempts a comprehensive synthesis of what we know about the impact of college on students; in short, it seeks to provide a general answer to this question: In what areas and through what kinds of conditions, activities, and experiences does college affect students?

Consistent with the composite findings of Feldman and Newcomb (1969) and Bowen (1977), our synthesis of the evidence indicates that the college years are a time of student change on a broad front. A number of the shifts we observed appear to be fairly substantial in magnitude. It is the breadth of change and development, however, that is perhaps the most striking characteristic of the evidence. Students not only make statistically significant

gains in factual knowledge and in a range of general cognitive and intellectual skills; they also change on a broad array of value, attitudinal, psychosocial, and moral dimensions. There is some modest tendency for changes in intellectual skills to be larger in magnitude than changes in other areas, but the evidence is quite consistent in indicating that the changes coincident with the college years extend substantially beyond cognitive growth. Thus, the change that occurs during the college years does not appear to be concentrated in a few isolated areas. Rather, the research portrays the college student as changing in an integrated way, with change in any one area appearing to be part of a mutually reinforcing network or pattern of change in other areas.

There are some very clear directions to this overall pattern of change in college. The nature of the changes that occur and our best estimates of their average magnitude are shown in Tables 10.2.1 through 10.2.4. We turn now to a brief summary of those changes.

Learning and Cognitive Change

As shown in Table 10.2.1, students make gains from freshman to senior year on a variety of different dimensions of learning and cognition. Modest advances are evident in general verbal and quantitative skills, and fairly substantial advances are demonstrated in knowledge of the specific subject matter related to one's major field of study. These conclusions, particularly the latter, are not very surprising. Indeed, more surprising would be the discovery that such changes did not occur during college. Less intuitively obvious, perhaps, are the gains that students make on a range of general intellectual competencies and skills that may be less directly or explicitly tied to a college's formal academic program. Compared to freshmen, seniors are not only more effective speakers and writers, they are also more intellectually advanced. This intellectual change includes an

improved ability to reason abstractly or symbolically and to solve problems or puzzles within a scientific paradigm, an enhanced skill in using reason and evidence to address issues and problems for which there are no veritably correct answers, an increased intellectual flexibility that permits one to see both the strengths and weaknesses in different sides of a complex issue, and an increased capacity for cognitively organizing and manipulating conceptual complexity.

It is likely that gains in college on such dimensions as abstract reasoning, critical thinking, reflective judgment, and intellectual and conceptual complexity also make the student more functionally adaptive. That is, other things being equal, this enhanced repertoire of intellectual resources permits the individual to adapt more rapidly and efficiently to changing cognitive and noncognitive environments. Put another way, the individual becomes a better learner. It is in this area, we believe, that the intellectual development coincident with college has its most important and enduring implications for the student's postcollege life.

TABLE 10.2.1 Summary of Estimated Freshman-to-Senior *Changes:*
Learning and Cognitive Development

OUTCOME	ESTIMATED MAGNITUDE OF CHANGE	
	Effect Size[a]	Percentile Point Difference[b]
General verbal skills	.56	21
General quantitative skills	.24	10
Specific subject matter knowledge	.84	31
Oral communication skills	.60	22
Written communication skills	.50	19
Piagetian (formal) reasoning	.33	13
Critical thinking	1.00	34
Use of reason and evidence to address ill-structured problems (reflective judgment, informal reasoning)	1.00	34
Ability to deal with conceptual complexity	1.20	38

[a]Effect size = (senior mean minus freshman mean) divided by freshman standard deviation.
[b]Effect size converted to the equivalent percentile point under the normal curve. This is the percentile point difference between the freshman- and senior-year means when the freshman mean is set at the 50th percentile.

TABLE 10.2.2 Summary of Estimated Freshman-to-Senior *Changes: Attitudes and Values*

OUTCOME	ESTIMATED MAGNITUDE OF CHANGE		
	Effect Size[a]	Percentile Point Difference[b]	Percentage Point Difference Between Freshmen & Seniors[c]
Aesthetic, cultural, and intellectual values	.25–.40	10–15	
Value placed on liberal education			+20 to +30%
Value placed on education as vocational preparation			−10 to −30%
Value placed on intrinsic occupational rewards			+12%
Value placed on extrinsic occupational rewards			−10 to −15%
Altruism, social and civic conscience, humanitarianism	.10–.50	4–19	+2 to + 8%
Political and social liberalism	.20	8	+15 to +25%
Civil rights and liberties			+5 to +25%
Religiosity, religious affiliation	−.49	19 (in religiosity)	Up to −11% in conventional religious preferences
Traditional views of gender roles			−10 to −25%

[a]Effect size = (senior mean minus freshman mean) divided by freshman standard deviation.
[b]Effect size converted to the equivalent percentile point under the normal curve. This is the percentile point difference between the freshman- and senior-year means when the freshman mean is set at the 50th percentile.
[c]Percentage point increase or decrease of seniors (versus freshmen) holding a particular view or position.

Attitudes and Values

Table 10.2.2 shows our estimates of the typical freshman-to-senior changes during college in the general area of values and attitudes. A number of these changes are quite consistent with the changes noted in the area of learning and cognitive development. Students not only become more cognitively advanced and resourceful, but they also make gains in their aesthetic, cultural, and intellectual sophistication, gains that are complemented by increased interests and activities in such areas as art, classical music, reading, and creative writing; discussion of philosophical and historical issues; and the humanities and performing arts. Similarly, there are clear gains in the importance students attach to liberal education and exposure to new ideas. In short, the enhancement of cog-

nitive skills during college appears to be concurrent with an increased valuing of and interest in art, culture, and ideas.

If one theme underlying changes in values and attitudes during college is that they tend to be supportive of or at least consistent with observed changes in cognitive growth, a second theme is that the changes also coalesce around a general trend toward liberalization. Considering consistent changes in the areas of sociopolitical, religious, and gender role attitudes and values, it would appear that there are unmistakable and sometimes substantial freshman-to-senior shifts toward openness and a tolerance for diversity, a stronger "other-person orientation," and concern for individual rights and human welfare. These shifts are combined with an increase in liberal political and social values and a decline in both doctrinaire religious beliefs and traditional

TABLE 10.2.3 Summary of Estimated Freshman-to-Senior *Changes: Self and Relational Systems in Psychosocial Development*

OUTCOME	ESTIMATED MAGNITUDE OF CHANGE		
	Effect Size[a]	Percentile Point Difference[b]	Percentage Point Difference Between Freshmen & Seniors[c]
Self Systems			
Identity status			+15 to +25% (in reaching identity achievement status)
Ego development	.50	19	
Self-concept			
Academic			+4 to +14% (rating self "above avg.")
Social			+7% (rating self "above avg.")
Self-esteem	.60	23	
Relational Systems			
Autonomy, independence, and locus of control	.36	14	
Authoritarianism	−.81	29	
Ethnocentrism	−.45	17	
Intellectual orientation	.30	12	
Interpersonal relations	.16	6	
Personal adjustment and psychological well-being	.40	16	
Maturity and general personal development	Not available		

[a]Effect size = (senior mean minus freshman mean) divided by freshman standard deviation.
[b]Effect size converted to the equivalent percentile point under the normal curve. This is the percentile point difference between the freshman- and senior-year means when the freshman mean is set at the 50th percentile.
[c]Percentage point increase or decrease of seniors (versus freshmen) holding a particular view or position.

TABLE 10.2.4 Summary of Estimated Freshman-to-Senior *Changes: Moral Development*

OUTCOME	ESTIMATED MAGNITUDE OF CHANGE		
	Effect Size[a]	Percentile Point Difference[b]	Percentage Point Difference Between Freshmen & Seniors[c]
Use of principled reasoning in judging moral issues	Difficult to estimate magnitude of effect, but major change during college is from the use of "conventional" to "postconventional" or "principled" reasoning		

[a]Effect size = (senior mean minus freshman mean) divided by freshman standard deviation.
[b]Effect size converted to the equivalent percentile point under the normal curve. This is the percentile point difference between the freshman- and senior-year means when the freshman mean is set at the 50th percentile.
[c]Percentage point increase or decrease of seniors (versus freshmen) holding a particular view or position.

attitudes about gender roles. The clear movement in this liberalization of attitudes and values is away from a personal perspective characterized by constraint, narrowness, exclusiveness, simplicity, and intolerance and toward a perspective with an emphasis on greater individual freedom, inclusiveness, complexity, and tolerance.

A third unifying thread that characterizes attitude and values change during college is a shift away from the instrumental or extrinsic values of education and occupation toward a higher valuing of intrinsic rewards. Compared to freshmen, seniors attach greater importance to the value of a liberal education and less importance to the value of a college education as vocational preparation. Consistently, seniors (as compared to freshmen) also place greater value on the intrinsic characteristics of a job (intellectual challenge, autonomy, and so forth) and less value on extrinsic rewards (salary, job security, and the like).

At first glance such changes may seem inconsistent with what was clearly an increasing trend between 1970 and 1985 toward vocationalism or materialism in the reasons underlying an individual's decision to attend college (Astin, Green, & Korn, 1987). The motivation for attending college and the changes that occur during college, however, may be largely independent of each other. Thus, even if succeeding cohorts of recent freshmen have increasingly chosen to attend college for its instrumental or extrinsic returns, it would still appear that the freshman-to-senior changes that occur during college lead to an increased value being placed on the nonvocational aspects of one's educational experience and the intrinsic rewards of one's prospective work.

Psychosocial Changes

The motif noted earlier of the interrelatedness of student change during the college years is apparent in the several areas of student psychosocial change summarized in Table 10.2.3. While the changes in these areas are, on the whole, more modest than those relating to learning and cognitive development, they are approximately the same size as the shifts in attitudes and values. Moreover, their general character and direction are clearly consistent with those of the other two areas. Gains in various kinds of substantive knowledge and in cognitive competence may provide both a basis and the intellectual tools for students to examine their own identities, self-concepts, and the nature of their interactions with their external world.

Thus, perhaps as a partial consequence of their cognitive gains, students appear to move toward greater self-understanding, self-definition, and personal commitment, as well as toward more refined ego functioning. Similarly, students' academic and social self-images, as well as their self-esteem, while perhaps somewhat bruised initially, not only recover but become more positive over the college years.

The psychosocial changes experienced during the college years extend beyond the inner world of the self to include the relational aspects of students' lives: the manner in which they engage and respond to other people and to other aspects of their external world. As students become better learners, they also appear to become increasingly independent of parents (but not necessarily of peers), gain in their sense that they are in control of their world and what happens to them, and become somewhat more mature in their interpersonal relations, both in general and in their intimate relations with others, whether of the same or opposite sex. They also show modest gains in their general personal adjustment, sense of psychological well-being, and general personal development and maturity. Moreover, consistent with the observed shifts toward greater openness in attitudes and values, the evidence quite consistently indicates that students gain in their general intellectual disposition or orientation toward their world, their willingness to challenge authority, their tolerance of other people and their views, their openness to new ideas, and their ability to think in nonstereotypic ways about others who are socially, culturally, racially, or ethnically different from them.

Moral Development

As suggested in Table 10.2.4, there is clear and consistent evidence that students make statistically significant gains during college in the use of principled reasoning to judge moral issues. This finding holds across different measurement instruments and even different cultures. The absence of descriptive statistics in much of the evidence, however, makes it difficult if not impossible to estimate with confidence the magnitude of the freshman-to-senior change in the same way that we have done for other outcomes. The magnitude of the freshman-to-senior gain may not be as important as the fact that the major shift during college is from conventional to postconventional or principled judgment. (The former is based strongly on morality as obedience to rules and meeting the expectations of those in authority, while the latter is based strongly on a view of morality as a set of universal principles of social justice existing independently of societal codification.) This shift in and of itself represents a major event in moral development.

The freshman-to-senior changes in moral judgment noted in our synthesis are another example of how change during college on one dimension is typically consistent with change in other areas. Measures of moral reasoning are themselves positively correlated not only with areas of general cognitive development that increase during college (such as abstract reasoning, critical thinking, and reflective judgment) but also with the general liberalization of personality and value structures coinciding with college attendance (for example, decreases in authoritarianism or dogmatism; increases in autonomy, tolerance, and interpersonal sensitivity; increased concern for the rights and welfare of others). Thus, the enhancement of principled moral judgment during college is embedded within an interconnected and perhaps mutually reinforcing network of cognitive, value, and psychosocial changes that occur at approximately the same time.

Some Final Thoughts on Change During College

Our conclusions about the changes that occur during college differ in only minor ways from those of Feldman and Newcomb (1969) and Bowen (1977). Indeed, taken as a total body of evidence, all three syntheses suggest that a reasonably consistent set of cognitive, attitudinal,

value, and psychosocial changes have occurred among college students over the last four or five decades. Students learn to think in more abstract, critical, complex, and reflective ways; there is a general liberalization of values and attitudes combined with an increase in cultural and artistic interests and activities; progress is made toward the development of personal identities and more positive self-concepts; and there is an expansion and extension of interpersonal horizons, intellectual interests, individual autonomy, and general psychological maturity and well-being. Thus, it can be said that the nature and direction of freshman-to-senior changes appear to be reasonably stable and to some extent predictable.

It may be that the absolute magnitude of freshman-to-senior changes is not as educationally important as either the qualitative nature or the breadth and scope of the changes. One danger in focusing on quantitative estimates of change such as effect size is that one tends to consider change as happening on a continuum where all change is smoothly continuous and equally important. Many developmental theorists would argue that development does not always happen in such even and equivalent fashion. Moreover, not all changes are equivalent in size or importance: Some shifts are particularly critical to development irrespective of whether or not they are reflected in a large quantitative change on some continuous scale. For example, the qualitative shift during college from a style of reasoning based on beliefs to one relying on evidence in making judgments represents a key prerequisite to rational problem solving. Similarly, the shift from conventional to principled reasoning during college represents a major qualitative advance in moral development. On both of these dimensions of development, the qualitative nature of the change is likely to be of greater consequence than the magnitude of the change.

We would also suggest that the magnitude of change on any particular dimension or set of dimensions during college may not be as significant as the pronounced breadth of interconnected changes we noted in our synthesis. As posited by major models of student development, the evidence indicates not only that individuals change on a broad developmental front during college but also that the changes are of a mutually consistent and supporting nature. Although there may be insufficient empirical grounds to speak of changes in one area causing or permitting changes in other areas, it is clear from the body of evidence we reviewed that the changes coincident with college attendance involve the whole person and proceed in a largely integrated manner. Certainly the notion of broad-based integrative change during college is not a new finding, but the evidence we reviewed was sufficiently compelling to warrant its reaffirmation.

There are, of course, at least three nontrivial problems endemic to the study of freshman-to-senior change. The first stems from the fact that the evidence is based largely on studies measuring typical or average change in some sample (longitudinal studies) or typical or average differences between samples (cross-sectional studies). By focusing on average group shifts or differences, the findings of such studies tend to mask individual differences in patterns of change. Some students may change substantially during college, some may change little or not at all, and some may actually shift in a direction counter to the typical movement of the group. Moreover, some students may change in one way on certain variables and in opposite ways on other variables. Thus, although the average change may be our best estimate of the dominant shift or development occurring in a group, it is not without limitations.

A second problem is that freshman-to-senior change during college does not necessarily reflect the impact of college. Many of the dimensions on which change occurs during college may have a developmental base. If so, this means that individuals tend to exhibit more sophisticated levels of development through the process of maturation or simply growing older.

Consequently, similar individuals not attending college might well change in essentially the same ways as college students over the same time period. In the absence of a control group of noncollege attendees (a typical weakness in most studies of change during college), it is essentially impossible to separate the changes due to college attendance from those attributable to natural maturation.

The focus on change during college as an indication of college impact can also be misleading in another way. Just as the presence of change does not necessarily indicate the impact of college, so too the absence of change does not necessarily indicate the absence of college impact. One important consequence of college attendance may be to fix development at a certain level and prevent reversion or regression (Feldman & Newcomb, 1969). If such were the case on a specific trait, little or no freshman-to-senior change would be noted. Those not attending college, however, might well regress or change in a negative direction.

Finally, it is important to differentiate change from development. Whereas change simply means that some fact or condition at Time 2 is different from what it was at Time 1, development implies ordered, predictable, even hierarchical shifts or evolution have taken place in fundamental structures or processes. In many areas of observed change during college, it is tempting simply to conclude that observed change reflects some form of internal growth or development in the individual, that an inner restructuring has taken place, and that the senior is functioning with an advanced set of inner rules or perspectives not present in the typical freshman. It behooves us to bear in mind that change during the college years is produced by multiple influences, some internal (and perhaps ontogenetic) and others external to the individual.

REFERENCES

Feldman, K., & Newcomb, T. (1969). *The impact of college on students*. San Francisco: Jossey-Bass.

Bowen, H. (1977). *Investment in learning: The individual and social value of American higher education*. San Francisco: Jossey-Bass.

Astin, A., Green, K., & Korn, W. (1987). *The American freshman: Twenty-year trends, 1966–1985*. Los Angeles: University of California, Graduate School of Education, Higher Education Research Institute.

THINKING CRITICALLY

1. What do the authors of this reading mean when they state that attending college makes a person "a better learner"? Can you think of an example from your own college experience of how that statement may apply?

2. How are the changes in attitudes and values discussed in this reading similar to the psychosocial changes?

3. Why do the authors state that "freshman-to-senior change during college does not necessarily reflect the impact of college?" What kind of research would address this problem?

4. What do you think explains the shift during college to more liberal political and religious views?

PART

XI Work

The Costs and Benefits
of Employment in Adolescence

Holding a part-time job at some point during high school has become a typical experience for American adolescents, although it remains relatively rare in other industrialized countries. The effects of part-time work on adolescent development has been a topic of considerable research since the early 1980s, and a topic of considerable debate as well, with some scholars arguing that the effects of part-time work are largely negative and others stressing the potential benefits of part-time work. The authors of this reading generally emphasize the potential benefits, but they present a balanced summary of the research on both sides of the issue. They discuss the complex issues involved in understanding the effects of part-time employment on adolescent development.

Reading 11.1

How Do Prior Experiences in the Workplace
Set the Stage for Transitions to Adulthood?

J. T. Mortimer, C. Harley, and P. J. Aronson

Transitions to Adulthood in a Changing Economy: No Work, No Family, No Future? edited by A. Booth, A. C. Crouter, and M. J. Shanahan. Copyright © 1999 by Praeger Publishers. Reproduced by permission of Greenwood Publishing Group, Inc., Westport, CT.

Despite the fact that almost all adolescents in the United States are employed at some time while they are attending high school, social scientists have directed relatively little attention to work as a context for late adolescent development or as an experience influencing the transition to adulthood. There are good reasons to expect that early employment experiences would have positive consequences, especially for movement into a full-time work role, which is a critically important component of the adult transition. Working during adolescence would appear to have obvious relevance for vocational development, as well as for the accumulation of both human and social capital. Still, some have cautioned that employed youth are characterized by "precocious maturity" which precipitates problem behaviors during adolescence and premature entry to adultlike roles. Others warn of "premature affluence" evoking unrealistic attitudes about money and profligate spending patterns, which render transitions to economic and residential independence problematic.

In view of this controversy, what case can be made for adolescent work? It should be recognized, first of all, that the adult work role is a key dimension of the adolescent "possible self" (Markus, Cross, & Wurf, 1990). Almost all adolescents in the United States today, including both boys and girls, expect to be employed in adulthood (Johnson & Mortimer, in press) and may understand, to a greater or lesser extent, the great social and psychological importance of the work role. It is the basis for economic independence from parents, a major determinant of purchasing power and consequent life style, and a key component of adult identity. Parents, teachers, and other "significant others" may impress upon the adolescent that this phase of life is a time of preparation and acquisition of credentials for subsequent educational and vocational roles.

Taking on a part-time job in adolescence may therefore assume special social meaning, signifying progress in moving toward the adult work role. Being employed alongside adults, or having substantial responsibility in the absence of adult supervision, could encourage a sense of being "grown up," social contribution, and

independence. The adolescent may acquire skills that are transferable to other jobs, such as how to use a cash register or computer keyboard. But probably most important, the experience of employment could encourage the kind of thinking that is essential to vocational development and "planful competence" (Clausen, 1991). That is, the adolescent may have occasion to do different kinds of work, and get a sense of what he or she may be "good at." Even a so-called "menial" job may encourage the young person to reflect on what is liked and disliked about the current job. If the job does not correspond to what is thought of as a desirable work role, this might evoke thinking about the kinds of experience, skills, and credentials that may be needed to obtain a more satisfying job or career. Thus, adolescent work experiences, both good and bad, could help clarify work values and job preferences.

Furthermore, obtaining and keeping a job requires certain behaviors and social skills which may be difficult to acquire in other contexts. In attempting to obtain a job, the young person learns job-seeking skills, where to look for employment, how to activate one's "social capital" to identify job openings, and how to expand thinking about job possibilities. The novice job applicant learns how to conduct himself or herself at an interview, fill out employment applications, meet the expectations of supervisors, accept responsibility, and get along with customers and clients who may come from unfamiliar social backgrounds.

Job schedules for young people frequently change in response to employer needs as well as the shifting circumstances in other realms of young people's lives. The newly employed adolescent will need to develop time management skills, given the need to juggle the work schedule with the demands of other important roles—as student, family member, friend. Young people see their parents performing similar juggling acts; they may come to realize that conflicting time demands are endemic in adult life. The growing capacity to handle such conflicts could promote a general sense of competence and efficacy.

Prevalent social norms prescribe independence for teens in the use of earnings

(Phillips & Sandstrom, 1990), while also encouraging responsibility for expenses that previously were assumed by parents. The young jobholder will come to learn money management skills—what things cost, how to make earnings go farther, and the importance of saving. Some young people will decide to set aside a portion of their earnings for long-term goals, such as college or a car. Others may use all their earnings for immediate consumption. In either case, these uses of earnings—the most tangible product of the adolescent's labors—will affect the social and psychological meanings of employment and thereby may condition its consequences for development and the transition to adulthood.

All of these potential benefits of early employment are fully understandable within the context of prevailing cultural emphases—the work ethic, individualism, and economic independence. It is therefore not surprising that a series of special task forces and commissions in the 1970s, directed to evaluate the place of work in young people's lives, advocated greater opportunity for adolescents to combine working and schooling (Carnegie Council on Policy Studies, 1980; National Commission on Youth, 1980; President's Science Advisory Committee, 1974). Moreover, most parents highly approve of their children's jobs (Phillips & Sandstrom, 1990).

Still, a strong case against adolescent employment has arisen, prompted largely by Ellen Greenberger and Laurence Steinberg, developmental psychologists whose writings about teenage employment began to appear in the early 1980s and culminated in the publication of *When Teenagers Work: The Psychological and Social Costs of Teenage Employment* in 1986. Rather quickly, the general consensus that adolescent work is beneficial was replaced by the opposite view: that working places adolescents at risk and jeopardizes their transition to adulthood. Greenberger and Steinberg allege that working has all-too-large "opportunity costs." This is, adolescents should be engaging in activities that are appropriate to this "moratorium period," when their time should be free to explore alternative identities and interests and to develop close human relationships. Instead, after school they rush to the workplace where

they perform menial tasks having little developmental benefit.

Furthermore, according to their argument, working leads to withdrawal from school (psychologically as well as physically), promotes behaviors that interfere with learning, and reduces investment in homework and academic achievement. The young person comes to think of him or herself as an adult: this "precocious maturity" may encourage the acquisition of adult-like ways of spending leisure time—drinking alcohol, smoking, and taking drugs—which pose risks to health. Indeed, the very stresses that result from juggling school, work, and other responsibilities can produce role overload and distress which the young person may alleviate through use of these mood-altering substances.

Bachman (1983), in a similar vein, warns of "premature affluence." The adolescent who is employed about 20 hours a week, common among high school seniors, is in a rather unusual economic situation. With parents bearing most daily living expenses, the youth may have an unusual amount of discretionary income which can be used for special purchases that will likely be out of their reach when they themselves have to pay for their housing, food, utilities, and so forth. Buying designer jeans and sneakers, expensive rock concert tickets, and other entertainments may be of no benefit to money-management skills. Moreover, if young people come to think of themselves as adults too soon, they may also move too quickly into adult family-like roles, e.g., through early sexual behavior, cohabitation, marriage, and parenting.

This lively debate, pro and con, has stimulated a good deal of research by sociologists, economists, and psychologists, much of which utilizes longitudinal data to assess both the contemporaneous impacts of working while in high school on the development of psychological competencies and traits which would likely mediate the effects of early employment on the transition to adulthood.

This chapter will review the evidence, featuring findings from the Youth Development Study (YDS), one of the few longitudinal studies designed explicitly to examine the impacts of teenage employment on mental health, adjustment, and the transition to adulthood. The study was initiated in the fall of 1987, when a sample of 1,000 ninth graders was randomly selected from a list of those enrolled in the St. Paul Public School District. The ninth graders and their parents were initially surveyed in the spring of 1988, the adolescents in their school classrooms, their parents by mailed questionnaire. The parents were again surveyed when most of the children were in their senior year of high school; the children were surveyed each year of high school, and then followed, by mail survey, through the four years thereafter. We were successful in obtaining "coverage" of 96 percent of the children by at least one responding parent in the first wave, and of 79 percent of the children in Wave 4. Retention in the panel of adolescents has been excellent: 93 percent through the four years of high school, and 78 percent over eight years. At the end of this period, most of the young people were 21 or 22 years of age.

In this chapter, we would first like to address this set of issues from the perspectives of working teens themselves. Second, we will examine what is known about the effects of working during high school from studies that compare contemporary youth who have had different levels of investment in work. Researchers have examined the intensity (hours) and patterning of adolescent work in relation to contemporaneous and early adult outcomes. Finally, we will consider the quality of adolescent work. The different kinds of experiences young people have in the workplace, as phenomena influencing the course of their development and attainment, have been given very little attention. What features or dimensions of youth jobs may be considered "good" or "bad," and what are their consequences?'

Adolescents' Perceptions of Costs and Benefits

When considering the effects of teenage employment, it is important to acknowledge that the kinds of jobs available to prior generations

of youth and contemporary young people are different. This historical change, in fact, is one of the major grounds of the critique of contemporary adolescent work. Greenberger and Steinberg (1986) argue that contemporary working youth are less likely to be able to acquire employment that involves the acquisition of skills that would prepare them for their future occupations. They believe that within the past 25 years adolescent work has declined in educational value and economic significance, and provides less meaningful exposure to intergenerational contact and guidance. According to their analysis, contemporary young workers are less likely to have adult employers or co-workers who have any stake in the young workers' futures. Thus, there is no adult who can lead, take an active interest in, or guide the young person through the transition to adulthood.

Young people of prior generations were more likely to be employed within the more communal, rural contexts of farms or in small businesses owned by family members or other small town residents. Even if not working within the context of the immediate or extended family, the adolescents' employers and co-workers would likely be acquainted with their parents or other family members. Because fewer young people went on to post-secondary education, those who were employed during high school were more frequently placed at entry levels in organizations, and in jobs they would continue after finishing high school. This created apprentice-type relations with employers and co-workers, facilitating the transition to the full-time work role.

In contrast, typical teenage workers today are employed in the commercial, service, or retail sectors, in restaurants, grocery stores, movie theaters, and similar locales. Their employers and co-workers are unlikely to be known by their parents. Indeed, Greenberger (1988) emphasizes that many youth workplaces today are highly age-segregated, with young people being supervised by others who may be the same age or only a year or two older.

Elsewhere, using decennial census data from 1940 to 1980, we have documented such trends in employment among youth aged 16–17 (Aronson, Mortimer, Fierman, & Hacker, 1996:34–36). For example, retail trade, including eating and drinking establishments, has greatly increased its share of youth employment from only 15 percent of adolescents in 1940 to 54 percent of males and 59 percent of females in 1980; farming and manufacturing jobs, in contrast, have employed declining proportions of youth workers during the past several decades.

In our study, adolescents were asked Likert-style forced-choice questions. To illustrate their aggregate endorsement of the various "benefits" and "costs" of employment, for each item the two highest response categories were combined (for example, agree or strongly agree).

Gaining responsibility was the most frequently reported benefit of employment (see Table 11.1.1). Ninety percent of the girls and 80 percent of the boys responded that their job had helped them to learn to take responsibility for their work. Money management was likewise an important benefit, with two-thirds of the girls and over half the boys agreeing that their job helped them to learn how to manage money.

Another widely perceived gain was the acquisition of social skills. Most adolescents thought that their jobs helped them to follow directions; and for a substantial minority, the jobs provided opportunity to learn new things. About three-quarters of boys and girls thought that their jobs had increased their propensity to be on time. Over a fourth of the youth felt that their jobs had influenced their career decisions. Greater independence from the family, as a consequence of work, was a widely acknowledged outcome.

Adolescents perceived difficulties in employment less frequently than benefits. Still, almost half reported less time to spend with friends because of their jobs. Fatigue was another problem—feeling drained of energy after work. Nearly half felt they had less time to do homework because of their jobs; one out of four thought that their grades had suffered as a result of working. There were no significant differences among the adolescents in perceived benefits and costs of employment, depending on the broad category of job that was held.

It may be concluded that adolescents overwhelmingly believe their early jobs are more beneficial than problematic. They em-

TABLE 11.1.1 Percentages of Adolescent Children Indicating Benefits and Costs of Employment in Wave 3

	GIRLS	BOYS
Benefits		
Responsibility	90.2	80.3
Money management	65.7	57.4
Learned social skills	87.7	78.3
Work experience/skill development	43.4	42.1
Work ethics	73.3	68.1
Independence	75.0	77.7
Time management	78.6	74.5
Learned about life/shaped future	26.2	29.0
Problems		
Less leisure time	49.4	49.0
Lower grades	28.1	24.6
Less time for homework	47.9	48.8
Think about work during class	7.7	11.4
Fatigue	51.2	45.1

Source: Aronson et al. (1996), Table 2.10.

phasized gaining responsibility, money and time management, social skills, work skills, good work habits, and independence. Among the adolescents who perceived costs, the main concerns were fatigue, interference with schooling, and the scarcity of leisure time. Overall, however, the responses of the adolescents show extremely positive assessments of their work experiences.

Adolescent Employment, the Development of Competencies, and the Transition to Adulthood

The evidence brought to bear thus far on the effects of teen work is quite subjective. Given the general public approval of working, and the rather discretionary character of adolescent employment (which is generally much more mandatory in adulthood), it may seem hardly surprising that adolescents would attach positive meanings to their early work experiences, seeing them as providing learning experiences and promoting adaptation to adult roles. We now turn to more objective evidence—to an array of indicators that can be examined in relation to the intensity of adolescent work at particular times of observation during high school, or to the character of youth work histories over a longer duration. In this section, I summarize the extant evidence, drawn from the YDS and other studies. Because the analyses upon which these findings and conclusions are based have been published elsewhere, they are only summarized here (see Mortimer, Finch, Ryu, Shanahan, & Call, 1997; Mortimer & Johnson, 1997; Mortimer, Steinberg, & Hamilton, in press).

Problem Behavior

It is in the domain of "problem behavior" that the case against adolescent employment is the most clear, with evidence drawn from cross-sectional studies, longitudinal studies, and analyses incorporating a wide variety of pertinent controls. Some of the behaviors found to be associated with adolescent employment are considered to be legitimately engaged in by adults (if not excessively) but pose problems when

they are taken up by youth. It is with respect to these behaviors that we find evidence for "precocious maturity." Here is a domain where subjective judgment and objective evidence depart from one another. When asked about costs or problems associated with working, adolescents did not mention problem behaviors, deviant acts, or association with peers (or older coworkers) who may have led them "astray."

Substance use is more prevalent among youth who work long hours (Greenberger & Steinberg, 1986; Mortimer et al., 1996), including cigarettes, alcohol, and illegal (marijuana, cocaine) drug use (Bachman & Schulenberg, 1993; Mihalic and Elliot, 1995; Schulenberg & Bachman, 1993; Steinberg & Dornbusch, 1991). In the YDS, students who worked longer hours more frequently used alcohol each year, with background and ninth grade alcohol use controlled (Mortimer et al., 1996).

It becomes crucial in evaluating the implications of these findings for adult adjustment to know whether early onset of, say, drinking behavior signifies continued high use. However, findings across studies are mixed. Four years following high school, YDS panel members who worked more intensively during high school were no longer more frequent drinkers than those who had less high school labor force participation. During the post–high school period, the other students "caught up," thereby erasing earlier differences between work pattern groups (Mortimer & Johnson, 1997). However, data from the National Youth Survey show that the duration of adolescent work had a positive effect on alcohol and marijuana use (males only) at the age of 27 and 28 (Mihalic & Elliot, 1995).

These findings would appear to support notions of "precocious development" (Greenberger & Steinberg, 1986) or "pseudomaturity" (Bachman & Schulenberg, 1993), as does the relation between employment and earlier (Mihalic & Elliot, 1995) and more frequent (Bachman and Schulenberg, 1993) dating. Youth employment does appear to foster behaviors which would validate a premature claim to adult status (Jessor, Donovan, & Costa, 1991). With respect to other indicators of "precociousness," however, such as early cohabitation, marriage, and parenthood, the YDS has failed to find any linkage between investment in work during high school and these indicators of the timing of transition to adult family roles.

In comparison to students who do not work, employed students also engage in more deviance and school misconduct (Greenberger & Steinberg, 1986; Steinberg & Dornbusch, 1991; Tanner & Krahn, 1991). Occupational deviance has been linked to the peer culture; giving away goods in retail stores or working while "high" may impress friends (Greenberger, 1988). Long hours of work have also been related to theft, trouble with the police (for males), and, especially if working more than 30 hours, aggressive behavior (Bachman & Schulenberg, 1993). National Youth Survey data showed that minor delinquency was greater for adolescents working full-time than part-time and greater for those part-time workers than for the nonworkers (Wofford, 1988). However, adolescents who did not work were more likely to commit serious offenses.

School Performance

Clearly, school is the central "business" of the child's and adolescent's life. To the extent that working undermines human capital investment through school-based learning, it is indeed cause for concern. Because of this, the effect of adolescent employment on academic performance has been given considerable attention. Some studies have yielded negative associations between employment, or hours spent working, and grades (Greenberger & Steinberg, 1986; Lewin-Epstein, 1981; McNeil, 1984; Ruscoe, Morgan, & Peebles, 1996: Steinberg & Dornbusch, 1991). But given that academic motivation and performance is an important source of selection to work, it is necessary to take prior differences into account. Longitudinal studies, incorporating relevant controls, have yielded mixed findings. Some report negative effects of work hours on grades (Mortimer & Finch, 1986, based on the Youth in Transition study; Marsh, 1991, based on High School and Beyond). Others report no significant effect on student grades, either for employment (Mihalic & Elliot, 1995, based on the National Youth

Survey), or hours spent working (Mortimer et al., 1996, based on the Youth Development Study; Schoenhals, Tienda, & Schneider, 1997, and Warren, LePore, & Mare, 1997, based on the National Education Longitudinal Survey, or NELS data set). In the YDS, student grades were also unrelated to the pattern of investment in work, whether of greater or lesser intensity over a three-year period during high school (Mortimer & Johnson, in press). In the YDS, the only statistically significant association between working hours and grades, which held with prior academic performance controlled, occurred during the senior year of high school. High school seniors who worked at lower intensity (20 hours per week or less) had higher grades than students who worked more intensively and those who did not work at all (Schill, McCartin, & Meyer, 1985, and Lillydahl, 1990, report similar curvilinear patterns).

It is self-evident that any time that is spent working cannot be spent studying (except in unusual situations—for example, a babysitter might study while children are sleeping). Why, then, is there not a consistent negative effect of investment in employment on grades? An answer to this perplexing question is suggested by studies of adolescent time use. Using the NELS data, Schoenhals et al. (1997) report that time at work had no significant effect on time spent doing homework or on discretionary reading (not required by school). Others have also reported null findings with respect to the relation between working and homework (Mortimer et al., 1996; Mortimer & Johnson, in press). However, in the NELS study, hours worked per week had a strong negative relation to time spent watching television in tenth grade. If this is what is sacrificed as work hours increase, it is no wonder that grades do not consistently suffer. Moreover, students in the National Youth Survey who worked more than 20 hours per week had the greatest involvement in school activities (Mihalic & Elliott, 1995).

Furthermore, Steinberg and Cauffman (1995) suggest that because the national average for time spent on homework is so low (less than 4 hours per week), it is unlikely that employment will diminish students' already very modest involvement in this activity. However, teachers may diminish homework demands given knowledge of the students' demanding work schedules. Moreover, employed students could select less demanding courses so as to maintain acceptable grades despite their jobs.

Educational Attainment

Educational attainment is a prime indicator of human capital investment with major consequences for the transition to the adult work role. If employment in youth were to detract from years of schooling or the attainment of particular degrees, this would diminish occupational prestige and earnings and, therefore, the economic wherewithal for family formation and parenthood. There is, in fact, evidence that excessive employment, in terms of hours of work, does limit educational attainment. On the other hand, there is also evidence that learning to maintain an appropriate balance between school and work by limiting work hours so that work does not unduly interfere with educational pursuits fosters continuance in school. If the student limits working hours, the monetary and other benefits of employment can be sustained without disrupting the student role. Furthermore, since most young people who go to college (or pursue other post-secondary education) at least partially support themselves economically while they are going to school, learning to balance school and work earlier, while still in high school, could even be beneficial with respect to post-secondary educational attainment.

Supporting this line of reasoning, Tienda and Ahituv (1996), using National Longitudinal Survey of Youth (NLSY) data, report that those who work the previous year are *less* likely to quit school at ages 17–19 than those who do not work at all. However, persistence in school decreased as average weekly work hours increased. Consistently, D'Amico's (1984) analysis of NLSY data showed that employment at low intensity (less than 20 hours per week) lessened school drop-out rates among eleventh graders. Using data from High School and Beyond, working more than 14 hours per week in

the sophomore year had a negative effect on school enrollment two and four years later (Chaplin & Hannaway, 1996).

Taking a longer purview, Carr et al. (1996) found that among NLSY participants age 16–19 in 1979, more hours of work per week during high school predicted a small but significant decrement in the level of educational attainment achieved for both males and females by the age of 28–31 in 1991. (Weeks worked in high school decreased males' educational attainment.) Among males in the YDS, one pattern of high school work investment proved to be especially beneficial: near-continuous employment limited on the average to 20 hours a week or less. Males who pursued this pattern were found to have the most months of post-secondary schooling (Mortimer & Johnson, 1997, in press) during the years following high school. Males who worked at higher levels of intensity (more than 20 hours per week on the average) as well as those who had more limited work experience (not working at all during high school or working only a short duration) had less post-secondary educational attainment. Thus, no advantage was found for those who refrained from paid employment throughout the high school years. These differences were not explained by selection on the basis of family background characteristics or prior academic interest or achievement in school.

On the basis of these studies, it may be concluded that highly intensive work in adolescence may detract from educational persistence. However, those students who limit their hours of employment may achieve higher levels of educational attainment, which would foster their transition to the full-time work role and economic independence.

Early Adult Work-Related Attainments (Employment, Unemployment, Earnings)

In presenting the case for adolescent work, we referred earlier to manifold potential consequences for vocational socialization, career decision making, and "planful competence." Consistent with these expectations, paid employment during high school is repeatedly found to have positive work-related sequelae, including obtaining a job after leaving high school, the duration of employment and/or unemployment, and income attainment (Freeman & Wise, 1979; Lowe & Krahn, 1992; Marsh, 1991; Meyer & Wise, 1982; Mihalic & Elliot, 1997; Mortimer & Finch, 1986; Steel, 1991; Stern & Nakata, 1989).

Moreover, the relation between hours of work during high school and attainment outcomes is uniformly positive. Marsh (1991) reports that hours worked while attending high school reduces the risk of unemployment two years following. Steel's (1991) analysis of NLSY data showed that for whites, hours of high school employment had a positive effect on weeks of employment two years thereafter. Carr, Wright, and Brady (1996) report that the gains of youth who were employed during high school persist up to a decade following. With educational attainment controlled, employment in high school (their measure took into account both the intensity and duration of work) had positive effects on employment and wages ten years later for young people who participated in the NLSY.

In the YDS (Mortimer & Johnson. 1997), a long duration of work during high school (measured in months) was linked to more part-time work thereafter, which was found to be linked to and supportive of post-secondary education. More intensive high school employment (averaging more than 20 hours per week) preceded earlier entry to the full-time labor market. For males, near-continuous high intensity employment predicted higher earnings four years after high school.

Links Among Adolescent Quality of Work, Developmental Outcomes, and the Transition to Adulthood

Much evidence points to the conclusion that it is the quality not the quantity of work that is the most consequential for developmental outcomes that may augur either a smooth or a more problematic transition to adulthood. Senior participants in the Monitoring the Future

study whose jobs offered opportunities to use their skills, and learn new skills, reported higher life satisfaction and hope for the future (Schulenberg & Bachman, 1993). In the YDS, opportunities for advancement and the compatibility of school and work, for boys, and good pay, for girls, promoted a sense of self-efficacy over time (Finch, Shanahan, Mortimer, & Ryu, 1991). Boys' sense of efficacy increased when their supervisors included them in discussions about work tasks and did not subject them to close supervision; girls' efficacy rose when provided with early opportunities at work to be helpful to others (Call, 1996; Call, Mortimer, & Shanahan, 1995). Job stressors (e.g., time pressure, overload) and the early need to make autonomous decisions on the job heightened males' depressive affect, while the acquisition of useful skills on the job diminished males' distress (Shanahan, Finch, Mortimer, & Ryu, 1991; Shanahan, 1992). Among females, work stress and responsibility for things that are outside one's control were related to an increase in depressed mood (Shanahan et al., 1991) and a decline in self-efficacy (Finch et al., 1991).

The quality of work experience may, in fact, condition the effects of work hours on development. In a cross-sectional study of tenth through twelfth grade urban white Canadians, hours worked was positively associated with self-esteem when autonomy and role clarity were high (Barling, Rogers, & Kelloway, 1995). Shanahan (1992) reports that work stress and self-direction increased depressed mood only among boys working more than the median number of hours in the tenth and twelfth grades. Data from the Monitoring the Future studies showed that skill utilization at work was associated with a decrease in cigarette, alcohol, and marijuana use. Moreover, adolescents who describe their jobs as not using their skills, unconnected to the future, and "the kind of work that people do just for the money" used cigarettes more frequently as work intensity increased (Schulenberg & Bachman, 1993). Work intensity was found to be less consequential for youth who described their jobs as relevant to their futures.

Though little research has addressed this issue, the quality of adolescent work has been found to be associated with subsequent occupational outcomes. For example, skill utilization in adolescent work predicts success in the job market during the first three years after high school (Stern & Nakata, 1989).

Thus, a variety of studies point to work quality and especially skill utilization as the dimension of work that lessens distress and problem behaviors and promotes competence, work values, and occupational outcomes.

Summary and Conclusion

We see from this review of the research that answering the question, "How do prior experiences in the workplace set the stage for transitions to adulthood?" is no simple matter. We have shown that adolescents described their jobs in quite favorable terms, with most agreeing that working has helped them to develop a sense of responsibility, time and money management capacities, and social skills. Such evaluations provide useful information, but are, of course, entirely subjective. But even with more objective information—for instance, about the intensity of work and individual outcomes—addressing this question is still rather difficult, for there are many types, patterns, and facets of employment to consider.

On the basis of the extant evidence, drawn from the St. Paul Youth Development Study, as well as nationally representative panel studies, the following conclusions can be made. First, there is no solid evidence that working or hours of work influence general psychological competencies or resources for the transition to adulthood (e.g., self-efficacy or self-esteem). Second, adolescent employment appears to induce earlier substance use and is associated with a range of problem behaviors. It is not known whether these problem behaviors remain at higher levels among young people who previously were employed more intensively as they move into adulthood. Third, evidence that employment, or the intensity of work, influences students' academic performance is mixed. Several studies of representative panels

of youth, incorporating stringent controls, have yielded no evidence that students' grades suffer as a result of working.

With respect to educational attainment, a prime determinant of subsequent occupational and economic achievement, investment in work (as indicated by the accumulation of work hours) predicts a significant decrement in eventual years of schooling. However, a long-term, continuing balance of school and work, limited to 20 hours per week or less, has been found to predict *more* months of post-secondary schooling. Students who learn how to combine schooling and working while they are still in high school apparently continue to pursue this pattern in the interest of further post-secondary attainment.

The clearest case for adolescent employment derives from its demonstrated effects on vocational outcomes. Those who work more during high school appear to make a smoother transition to the adult work role, consistently achieving more months of employment, less unemployment, and higher earnings in the early career.

Though relatively little attention has been directed to the quality of work experience, there is mounting evidence—contrary to the view that all teenage work is the same—that there are meaningful variations along several work dimensions that affect psychosocial functioning. For teens, there are developmental benefits to working in jobs that provide opportunities for skill acquisition and utilization, helping others, and sharing decision making with supervisors. Under these circumstances, the teen's sense of efficacy increases. Use of skills on the job is also linked to vocational value development. On the other hand, when the teen is exposed to stressful work, negative outcomes are apparent. Given the importance of what the youth does on the job, it is reassuring to know that youth generally describe their jobs in a manner that would predict the more salutary outcomes.

So how might I characterize this rather unwieldy set of findings? We might think of adolescent work as a kind of transitional activity or gateway to one of the most important of the adult roles. As such, it may signify to the young person and significant others alike a change in status. But just as there are many markers of adulthood, each with its own set of meanings and valence, so, too, early work as an important entry point may hasten acquisition of them all. So as long as there are "good" and "bad" elements of adult roles, or as long as we demarcate adolescence as a time when certain behaviors legitimately enacted by adults are proscribed, it

may well be the case that employment, which calls upon the adolescent to enact "adult-like" behaviors—independence, responsibility, being on time, etc.—will also lead the young person to reject what are perceived to be more child-like feelings and behavior, to feel more like an adult, to take on elements of an "adult" identity, and to act like an adult in diverse respects, desirable and not.

REFERENCES

Aronson, P. J., Mortimer, J. T., Zierman, C., & Hacker, M. (1996). Generational differences in early work experiences and evaluations. In J. T. Mortimer & M. D. Finch (Eds.), *Adolescents, work, and family: An intergenerational developmental analysis* (pp. 25–62). Newbury Park, CA: Sage.

Bachman, J. G. (1983). Premature affluence: Do high school students earn too much? *Economic Outlook USA, 10,* 64–67.

Bachman, J. G., & Schulenberg, J. (1993). How part-time work intensity relates to drug use, problem behavior, time use, and satisfaction among high school seniors: Are these consequences or merely correlates? *Developmental Psychology, 29,* 220–235.

Barling, J., Rogers, K. A., & Kelloway, E. K. (1995). Some effects of teenagers' part-time employment: The quantity and quality of work makes the difference. *Journal of Organizational Behavior, 16,* 143–154.

Call, K. T. (1996). The implications of helpfulness for possible selves. In J. T. Mortimer & M. D. Finch (Eds.), *Adolescents, work, and family: An intergenerational developmental analysis* (pp. 63–96). Newbury Park, CA: Sage.

Call, K. T., Mortimer, J. T., & Shanahan, M. (1995). Helpfulness and the development of competence in adolescence. *Child Development, 66,* 129–138.

Carnegie Council on Policy Studies in Higher Education. (1980). *Giving youth a better chance.* San Francisco: Jossey-Bass.

Carr, R. V., Wright, J. D., & Brody, C. J. (1996). Effects of high school work experience a decade later: Evidence from the National Longitudinal Survey. *Sociology of Education, 69,* 66–81.

Chaplin, D., & Hannaway, J. (1996). *High school enrollment: Meaningful connections for at-risk youth.* Paper presented at the annual meeting of the American Educational Research Association, New York.

Clausen, J. S. (1991). Adolescent competence and the shaping of the life course. *American Journal of Sociology, 96,* 805–842.

D'Amico, R. J. (1984). Does employment during high school impair academic progress? *Sociology of Education, 57,* 152–164.

Finch, M. D., Mortimer, J. T., & Ryu, S. (1997). Transition into part-time work: Health risks and opportunities. In J. Schulenberg, J. L. Maggs, & K. Hurrelmann (Eds.), *Health risks and developmental transitions during adolescence* (pp. 321–344). New York: Cambridge University Press.

Finch, M. D., Shanahan, M. J., Mortimer, J. T., & Ryu, S. (1991). Work experience and control orientation in adolescence. *American Sociological Review, 56,* 597–611.

Freeman, R. B., & Wise, D. A. (1979). *Youth unemployment.* Cambridge, MA: National Bureau of Economic Research.

Greenberger, E. (1988). Working in teenage America. In J. T. Mortimer & K. M. Borman (Eds.), *Work experience and psychological development* (pp. 21–50). Boulder, CO: Westview.

Greenberger, E., & Steinberg, L. D. (1986). *When teenagers work: The psychological and social costs of teenage employment.* New York: Basic Books.

Jessor, R., Donovan, J. E., & Costa, F. M. (1991). *Beyond adolescence: Problem behavior and young adult development.* New York: Cambridge University Press.

Johnson, M. K., & Mortimer, J. T. (in press). Work-family orientations and attainments in the early life course. In T. L. Parcel & D. B. Cornfield (Eds.), *Work and family: Research informing policy.* Newbury Park, CA: Sage.

Lewin-Epstein, N. (1981). *Youth employment during high school.* Washington, DC: National Center for Education Statistics.

Lillydahl, J. H. (1990). Academic achievement and part-time employment of high school students. *Journal of Economic Education, 21,* 307–316.

Lowe, G. S., & Krahn, H. (1992). Do part-time jobs improve the labor market chances of high school graduates? In B. D. Warne (Ed.), *Working part-time: Risks and opportunities* (pp. 131–141). New York: Praeger.

Markus, H., Cross, S., & Wurf, E. (1990). The role of the self-system in competence. In R. J. Sternberg

& J. Kolligan, Jr. (Eds.), *Competence considered.* New Haven, CT: Yale University Press.

Marsh, H. W. (1991). Employment during high school: Character building or subversion of academic goals? *Sociology of Education, 64,* 172–189.

McNeil, L. (1984). *Lowering expectation: The impact of student employment on classroom knowledge.* Madison: Wisconsin Center for Educational Research.

Meyer, R. M., & Wise, D. A. (1982). High school preparation and early labor force experience. In R. B. Freeman & D. A. Wise (Eds.), *The youth labor problem: Its nature, causes, and consequences* (pp. 277–347). Chicago: University of Chicago Press.

Mihalic, S. W., & Elliot, D. (1997). Short and long-term consequences of adolescent work. *Youth and Society, 28*(4), 464–498.

Mortimer, J. T., & Finch, M. D. (1986). The effects of part-time work on self-concept and achievement. In K. Borman & J. Reisman (Eds.), *Becoming a worker* (pp. 68–89). Norwood, NJ: Ablex.

Mortimer, J. T., Finch, M. D., Ryu, S., Shanahan, M. J., & Call, K. (1996). The effects of work intensity on adolescent mental health, achievement, and behavioral adjustment: New evidence from a prospective study. *Child Development, 67,* 1243–1261.

Mortimer, J. T., & Johnson, M. K. (1997). New perspectives on adolescent work and the transition to adulthood. In R. Jessor (Ed.), *New perspectives on adolescent risk behavior.* New York: Cambridge University Press.

Mortimer, J. T., & Johnson, M. K. (in press). Adolescent part-time work and educational achievement. In K. Borman & B. Schneider (Eds.), *Youth experiences and development: Social influences and educational challenges.* Chicago: National Society for the Study of Education Yearbook.

Mortimer, J. T., Steinberg, L. D., & Hamilton, S. (in press). Child and adolescent functioning. Chapter for the Child Labor Panel Report, National Academy of Sciences, Washington, DC.

National Commission of Youth. (1980). *The transition to adulthood: A bridge too long.* Boulder, CO: Westview Press.

Phillips, S., & Sandstrom, K. L. (1990). Parental attitudes toward youth work. *Youth and Society, 22,* 160–183.

President's Science Advisory Committee. (1974). *Youth: Transition to adulthood.* Chicago: University of Chicago Press.

Ruscoe, G., Morgan, J. C., & Peebles, C. (1996). Students who work. *Adolescence, 31,* 625–632.

Schill, W. J., McCartin, R. M., & Meyer, K. (1985). Youth employment: Its relationship to academic and family variables. *Journal of Vocational Behavior, 26,* 155–163.

Schoenhals, M., Tienda, M., & Schneider, B. (1997). The educational and personal consequences of adolescent employment. Unpublished manuscript.

Schulenberg, J., & Bachman, J. G. (1993). *Long hours on the job? Not so bad for some types of jobs: The quality of work and substances use, affect, and stress.* Paper presented at the biennial meeting of the Society for Research on Child Development, New Orleans, LA.

Shanahan, M. J. (1992). *High school work experiences and depressed moods.* Paper presented at the American Sociological Association, Pittsburgh, PA.

Shanahan, M. J., Finch, M. D., Mortimer, J. T., & Ryu, S. (1991). Adolescent work experiences and depressive affect. *Social psychology Quarterly, 54,* 299–317.

Steel, L. (1991). Early work experience among white and non-white youths: Implications for subsequent enrollment and employment. *Youth and Society, 22,* 419–447.

Steinburg, L. D., & Cauffman, E. (1995). The impact of employment on adolescent development. *Annals of Child Development, 11,* 131–166.

Steinburg, L. D., & Dornbusch, S. M. (1991). Negative correlates of part-time employment during adolescence: Replication and elaboration. *Developmental Psychology, 27,* 304–313.

Stern, D., & Nakata, Y. F. (1989). Characteristics of high school students' paid jobs, and employment after graduation. In D. Stern & D. Eichorn (Eds.), *Adolescence and work: Influences of social structure, labor markets, and culture* (pp. 189–234). Hillsdale, NJ: Lawrence Erlbaum.

Tanner, J., & Krahn, H. (1991). Part-time work and deviance among high school seniors. *Canadian Journal of Sociology, 16*(3), 281–302.

Tienda, M., & Ahituv, A. (1996). Ethnic differences in school departure: Does youth employment promote or undermine educational attainment? In G. Magnum & S. Magnum (Eds.), *Of heart and mind: Social policy essays in honor of Sar A. Levitan* (pp. 93–110). Kalamazoo, MI: W. E. Upjohn Institute for Employment Research.

Warren, J. R., LePore, P. C., & Mare, R. D. (1997). *Employment during high school: Consequences for students' grades in reading and mathematics.* Paper presented at the annual meetings of the Population Association of America, Washington, DC.

Wofford, S. (1988). *A preliminary analysis of the relationship between employment and delinquency/crime for adolescents and youth adults.* National Youth Survey No. 50. Boulder, CO: Institute of Behavioral Science, University of Colorado.

THINKING CRITICALLY

1. What is meant by "precocious maturity"? Do you agree with the authors that precocious maturity explains why adolescents who work also have higher rates of substance use?

2. Compare Bachman's (1983) findings regarding "premature affluence" with the findings here that adolescents state that money management is one of the benefits of working. How would you reconcile the two findings?

3. Summarize the complex relationship between work and grades in adolescence. Why are the two generally unrelated?

4. The authors state that high-quality work is generally related to benefits for adolescence. Yet the kind of jobs adolescents typically hold—restaurant work, retail, and so forth—is rarely of high quality. Is it possible to change these jobs to make them higher quality, or is the low quality inevitable given the limitations on adolescents' skills and on what employers are willing to pay them?

Cross-National Variation in the Post–High School Transition to Work

In all industrialized societies, young people must make the transition at some point from school to work. The form and structure of this transition, however, varies widely across societies. In this reading, an expert on the school-to-work transition analyzes national differences in how the transition takes place and the options young people are offered in Japan, Germany, Austria, Switzerland, Denmark, Sweden, and the United States. He discusses both the strengths and limitations of each type of system.

Reading 11.2

Employment Prospects as Motivation for School Achievement: Links and Gaps Between School and Work in Seven Countries

S. F. Hamilton

Young people are motivated to work hard in secondary school by their expectations regarding the "payoff" for school achievement in the labor market. Those expectations, in turn, are shaped by institutional links between education and employment. This two-step hypothesis frames a comparison among school/work connections in seven countries: the United States, Japan, Germany, Austria, Switzerland, Denmark, and Sweden.

Transparency and Permeability

Two characteristics of the nexus between labor market and educational system deserve special attention. I shall label them transparency and permeability. *Transparency* refers to *how well youth can see though the educational system and labor market and plot a course from where they are in the present to a distant future goal.* In a transparent system, young people are knowledgeable about education and training requirements of various occupations and how to meet them. They can readily explain how a person enters a particular career. *Permeability* refers to the *ease of movement from one point in the education-labor system to another.* In a permeable system, it is relatively easy to move from one part of the educational system or labor market to another, and to change career directions.

Formal credentials or qualifications are central to both transparency and permeability. However, they have an adverse relation to each other. While the existence of specific educational qualifications for employment makes connections between education and the labor market more transparent, those same qualifications constitute barriers to easy movement within the labor market, rendering the system less permeable.

In the United States, high school students' motivation to perform well in school is hampered by an un-transparent education-career nexus. Connections between school and work are opaque in part because few jobs in the middle and lower levels of the occupational hierarchy require formal credentials. In the highly permeable American labor market, workers move rather easily among employers, and from one type of work to another. Once they are engaged in full-time employment, permeability is a great advantage to American workers. It allows upward mobility, voluntary career changes, and adaptation to economic change. Auto mechanics become chefs. Laid-off factory workers become truck drivers. Hairdressers become receptionists.

Young people in the German-speaking countries face precisely the opposite conditions—highly transparent, but not permeable. Extensive credentialing marks out a clear path from education into employment. Apprenticeship, which is the primary means of obtaining jobs in the middle levels of the occupational hierarchy, concludes with a national examination having both a written and a practical component. Only by completing the schooling and on-the-job training prescribed for a specific occupation and then passing the examination can one enter any of the 370 training occupations. (Some 20,000 additional occupations also treat this training and examination as qualifications, sometimes adding further training.) This system of very strong and highly visible connections between education and employment provides a clear answer to a young person's question, "How can I become an electronics technician, dental assistant, airplane mechanic, or office worker?" The answer is, "Do as well as

possible in school, then find the employer who offers the best apprenticeship in your chosen field and apply. If you work hard in your apprenticeship and part-time schooling and get a good grade on your qualifying examination, your training firm will probably hire you, and if they don't you will have good chances in other firms."

The trade-off is impermeability. A 3rd-year apprentice auto mechanic in Munich explained to me that he had decided to switch to auto body repair because it was a more creative occupation. He added that this would entail a second 3-year apprenticeship, including 3 additional years of part-time schooling. German adults who wish to change occupations or whose occupations have been made redundant by new technology or economic change are best advised to seek training in fields that do not have apprenticeship programs.

Ideally, young people would be able to envision a path for themselves from studenthood to satisfying employment and then, while following that path, find opportunities for changing their minds, adapting to changing economic conditions, and surpassing their original goals. However, because formal educational credentials simultaneously mark the path and place hurdles across it, transparency is purchased at the price of impermeability.

In the following analysis, I shall compare the transparency and permeability of seven countries' education-employment connections. These broad characterizations should not obscure clear and important variations within countries and across occupational fields. In all countries, my concern is with the middle levels of the occupational hierarchies: skilled jobs but not professions; requiring post-compulsory education, but less than a university degree. This caveat is very important because connections between employment and education for university graduates entering the professions are more alike than different among these countries. All are characterized by high transparency and low permeability. For example, the educational credentials required of a physician are clearly prescribed, making the path from school to career quite transparent, but those credentials are sufficiently daunting that they prevent easy movement into the profession and discourage movement out of it.

The American Model: School-Based Learning

Relative to other countries, the United States has a highly permeable but non-transparent school/work nexus in the middle levels of its occupational hierarchy. Formal qualifications for such occupations are rare and not terribly hard to acquire. Entry into a particular occupational field often requires no special training or licensing. Movement from one field to another is frequent and easy. Workers are treated as interchangeable parts. They are quickly laid off in poor economic times and just as quickly replaced when times improve.

High permeability matches the individualistic ideology prevailing in the United States. Each person is considered responsible for his or her own destiny. Demanding specific training and certification for most jobs is considered an infringement on the individual's freedom to choose an occupation and the employer's right to select freely among applicants.

High permeability, in addition to matching American economic conditions and social ideology, contributes to a relatively open society. The cost is low transparency. Because requirements for occupations and jobs are not spelled out clearly and movement appears to be highly random, a young person trying to look into the future has difficulty planning. No one can tell her or him precisely what to do in order to prepare for a certain kind of employment.

There are exceptions, to be sure. Anyone anticipating a clerical career knows that keyboard skills are essential. Occupations affecting health and safety require licensing examinations, not only for health care providers but for barbers and hairdressers and for electricians and plumbers. However, a wide range of skilled blue-collar occupations such as carpenter and auto mechanic do not require specific qualifications. The growing set of occupations with "technician" in their titles may demand advanced knowledge and skill; however, most occupations with "technician" in their titles may demand advanced knowledge and skill but allow most aspirants to achieve them in a variety of ways, including military training, community or technical colleges, proprietary (profit-making) trade schools, or informal on-the-job training.

The Japanese Model: Selective Schools

Japan has evolved an education-labor market system that exaggerates the American pattern. Its greater success in motivating young people reveals another means, in addition to formal credentials, of increasing transparency; namely, employers' use of school credentials when making hiring decisions, and the creation of strong connections between individual schools and employers.

As in the United States, the Japanese secondary education system is driven by preparation for higher education, but in even more extreme form. Elementary and junior high school are compulsory in Japan, but because high school enrollment is not compulsory, high schools have the right to select among applicants.

Selection is accomplished by means of examinations. Each high school administers its own examinations and admits the highest scoring candidates. Competition is fierce for admission to high schools with the best records of preparing their students for university entrance. At the end of high school, the same process is repeated, with universities admitting the highest scorers on their examinations and students competing for admission to the best universities. The best universities are those that are most successful at placing graduates in good jobs with the government or with prestigious firms (Rohlen, 1983).

Japanese youth who are not involved in the competition for university admission are, unlike their American counterparts, motivated to work hard in school to improve their career prospects. They enroll in less prestigious high schools, notably vocational high schools. Although such schools lack the academic rigor of more competitive schools, many vocational and academic high schools maintain long-term relationships with specific firms in which the schools recommend their best graduates and the firms hire them. The relationship is reciprocal. If the schools begin sending second-rate graduates, the firm will stop offering jobs. If the firm refuses to guarantee employment for the school's best graduates, the school will send its prize pupils elsewhere (Rosenbaum, Kariya, Settersten, & Maier, 1990). This practice enables young people to see clearly how they can move from school into desirable careers.

However, greater transparency, as compared to equivalent careers in the United States, is purchased by sacrificing permeability. Large firms offer lifetime employment. Status and pay are determined more by seniority than by performance. Any employee who remains with the firm and demonstrates proper loyalty and commitment, including long hours and short vacations, can count on a steady rise up the corporate escalator until age 50 or so, after which retirement is likely to be required.

This system of secure employment, however, does not exist in all firms. Small firms cannot always make such guarantees. Moreover, women are commonly employed even in large firms as "temporary" workers with no security or benefits regardless of how long they are actually employed.

The great strength of the Japanese system is that it motivates a remarkably high level of school achievement across a wide spectrum of the population. Japanese schools effectively impart general academic knowledge that provides a foundation for specific vocational training given by employers. From the perspective of motivation, the most striking accomplishment of the Japanese system is that the competition for desirable employment motivates school achievement even among those who have clearly lost the competition.

The German Model: Learning at Work

With respect to occupations that do not require a university degree, the German-speaking countries present the starkest contrast with the United States and Japan in terms of transparency and permeability. Germany, Austria, and Switzerland have strong apprenticeship systems that were transformed around the turn of the century to meet the demands of an industrial economy. Compulsory part-time schooling was added to on-the-job training to create what is known as the "dual system" in all three countries. Examinations were created to certify apprentices' accomplishments and qualify them for entrance into their training occupation. New occupations were added to the traditional list of crafts, including industrial, technical, and administrative occupations (e.g., machine repairer, dental lab technician, office worker).

Apprenticeship places the German-speaking countries at the opposite end of the continuum from the United States with regard to both transparency and permeability. Transparency is high. However, precisely the specificity of occupational training makes career entry and movement within the labor market more difficult—permeability is low. One cannot, as in the United States, become a carpenter simply by getting a job as a carpenter, or an auto mechanic by learning to fix one's own car. Both occupations require specific training programs, exams, and certification. As a consequence, choosing apprenticeship tends to limit young people to a particular segment of the labor market. This problem of permeability has been worsened by increasing enrollments in extended full-time schooling. Enrollment in the college preparatory *Gymnasium* and full-time vocational schools has increased in recent years and a larger proportion of the youth population has enrolled in full-time vocational schools, leaving a smaller proportion in apprenticeship.

Increasing school enrollment has two drawbacks, especially in Austria. One is a surplus (in labor market terms) of university-educated people who cannot find jobs appropriate to their educational attainment. The second, more germane to the present analysis, is that employers prefer vocational school-trained office and technical workers for middle-level positions in the same fields for which many apprentices are trained, reducing apprentices' prospects for upward mobility. Employers' preference for school graduates over apprentices holds apprentices in lower-level positions and blocks their rise through the occupational hierarchy.

Switzerland and Germany have recognized the desirability of advanced schooling for a larger proportion of their populations, and they have incorporated extended schooling with apprenticeship more rapidly than Austria. Interestingly, they have done so in two distinct ways.

In both countries, occupations that require higher levels of theoretical or abstract knowledge and skill (primarily administrative and technical occupations) require $1\frac{1}{2}$ days of school per week, while less academically challenging occupations require only 1 day. Switzerland is moving toward making $1\frac{1}{2}$ days per week standard for all occupations. Moreover, by law every apprentice who qualifies and chooses to do so may add an extra half day per week of vocational middle school, maintaining the same earnings despite spending 2 days per week off the job. Completion of this form of schooling confers the qualification required to pursue post-secondary education and training. This option establishes a direct tie between apprenticeship and higher education that is lacking in Austria.

The German answer to this same need is less planful and more individualistic. It is "double qualification" (Kaiser, Nuthmann, & Stegmann, 1985). Double qualification means that a young person completes an apprenticeship *and* the comparable course of study in a full-time vocational school. While growing enrollment in full-time secondary education in Austria has reduced enrollment in apprenticeship, in Germany growing school enrollment has been accompanied by increased enrollment in apprenticeship because the two have increasingly been combined rather than treated as mutually exclusive. As in Switzerland, the school credential opens an apprentice's path to further education. But German employers do not normally prefer applicants with school qualifications over those who qualified by means of apprenticeship.

One of the most dramatic developments in recent years in Germany has been the growing proportion of young people who graduate from the *Gymnasium*, earning the *Abitur*, which qualifies them for university study, and then enroll in an apprenticeship instead. These youth take the most prestigious apprenticeships, particularly in banking and insurance. Some then enroll in the university after completing their vocational training. Even without higher education, this combination of academic and vocational qualifications is highly valued by German employers. One consequence of the trend to combine apprenticeship with post-compulsory schooling is that the average age of apprentices has been rising.

Augmenting apprenticeship with extra schooling, whether simultaneously or sequentially, makes the education-employment nexus more permeable for those who complete both forms of education and training; they have access both to further education and to higher-level occupations. However, it can simultaneously make the system less permeable for those without the added qualifications, as in Austria.

Reducing the number of different training occupations is another approach to improving permeability. Germany has taken a dramatic step in this direction, by combining related metalworking occupations into one training program. This increases the program's flexibility because apprentices need not have made so specific an occupational choice and have a larger number of options upon completion. It also meets employers' growing need for skilled workers who are broadly trained and flexible.

Enhanced school qualifications and double qualification open access to postsecondary education and to the higher-level occupations that require such credentials, making the dual system more permeable. Combining related occupations into one comprehensive training program also increases horizontal permeability. However, neither of these adaptations appears to impair transparency, suggesting that a better balance between the two can be attained. Reducing the number of distinct paths from education to career seems to be an ideal adaptation from the perspective of optimizing both permeability and transparency.

Balancing Apprenticeship and Schooling: Scandinavia

Denmark, like the other Scandinavian countries, patterned its education and training system after Germany's in the 19th century, but over the past three decades has tried to increase that system's permeability, both horizontally, among occupations at the same status, and vertically, across social classes. Vocational schooling has been a major part of that effort, notably for the purpose of retraining adults.

Two recent adaptations of apprenticeship are of particular interest. One is a consolidation of what had become two parallel vocational training systems, one school-based, the other relying on apprenticeship. In contrast to the Austrian experience with such an arrangement, the Danes have concluded that the school-based system is inadequate. Therefore, they are phasing it out in favor of apprenticeship. What remains is an option for young people who may begin their vocational education either with full-time schooling or full-time work. However, after the first half year, the two paths converge and participants in both must alternate schooling with work experience. This means that all young people in the vocational education system must obtain an apprenticeship contract by the middle of grade 11.

The second adaptation is a consolidation of training occupations. From an array of some 350 training occupations, nearly as large as Germany's, Denmark has reduced the number of training occupations to 85. This simplifies the system in several ways. Fewer occupations means a smaller number of regulations and curriculum guides. Young people can choose broader occupational areas without, for example, making fine distinctions among different types of work with metal. Specialization is postponed until the last year or two of training. The structure of occupations resembles a tree, with a thick trunk of related occupations at the base and narrower specialties branching off above.

Because all apprentices in each of the 85 occupations receive identical training for their first 2 years, they share a common base of knowledge and skill and can change their minds about a specialty without having to begin their training again from the beginning. Similarly, if changes in the labor market require retraining, it can begin from that common base, making workers more flexible over time.

In Sweden, apprenticeship has been a common experience for non-college youth in Sweden for decades, but it was never so thoroughly integrated with schooling as in the German dual system. As of 1970, the Swedes abandoned the sharp distinction they had made between academic and vocational schooling and made all secondary schools comprehensive, more in line with American practice. At that time they determined that education should be the responsibility of the state, not of private businesses, and they relocated the majority of vocational training from the workplace to schools.

In principle, all secondary schools are now equal and all graduates are qualified to pursue higher education. Naturally, the formerly selective college preparatory schools (which had the same name used in Germany, *Gymnasium*) maintained some of their prestige, and former vocational schools are generally seen as less desirable. Furthermore, although it is possible for a secondary school graduate enrolled in a vocational course to enroll in higher education, they have access only to a limited number of less desirable programs. Enrollment in liberal arts or pre-professional courses is not possible for a vocational graduate without extensive added coursework.

Swedish vocational students are ordinarily not apprentices. They are not paid for their work. The state-run schools and not the firms are responsible for their education and training. There are exceptions, however. A few large firms maintained the apprentice schools they had before the 1970 reform. These schools are operated by private firms for the benefit of their apprentices. They teach all of the courses required by the state but add firm-specific training and experience that can be closely integrated with academic and vocational instruction.

For many Swedish youth, formal apprenticeship in the sense of being an employee as well as a student begins after secondary school graduation. In many occupations—construction is a good example—vocational training begins in secondary school, incorporates a modicum of work experience, and then continues for 2 years after graduation with a full-time apprenticeship. In these occupations, apprenticeship is continuous with vocational schooling, but there are far fewer institutional links between school and apprenticeship than in the German dual system.

The Swedish system was designed quite explicitly to enhance permeability as a matter of democratic principle. The use of modules to organize the vocational curriculum makes the Swedish vocational certification system much more flexible than the German. A module is a self-contained unit in which acceptable levels of knowledge and skill are specified. Vocational competencies may be achieved either in school or at work or both. The record of modules that a young person has completed informs an employer precisely what she or he knows and is able to do. Some graduates complete more modules than others. If an employer requires additional modules, the young person can complete them after being hired and add them to his or her credential file. The modular curriculum is ideal for adult education and retraining; indeed, the use of modules was borrowed from adult education in Denmark.

The Swedes also promote permeability with their youth centers, institutions that fulfill a distinctive obligation. Swedish schools are given responsibility for all youth until they reach age 18. Discussions are underway about raising the age to 20. That responsibility persists even when young people choose to leave school at age 16. Youth center staff are charged with maintaining contact with out-of-school youth to ensure that they have opportunities either to reenroll in school or to find employment. They do this by engaging in "door-knocking activities." That is, they are not passive, waiting for young people to get in touch; rather, they actively seek out youth, in person

and by telephone, to learn what they are doing and to offer assistance and opportunities. Their capacity to do this is enhanced by the availability of fully subsidized work placements lasting up to 6 months. In addition, youth center staff members constitute a rich professional resource. They include teachers, career counselors, nurses, and psychotherapists. Career counselors are specially trained with equal amounts of psychology, sociology, and labor market economics.

There is some loss of transparency as a result of high permeability. Lower reliance on formal credentials (and less precise credentials) than in the German-speaking countries makes entry into and movement within the labor market easier. However, Swedish youth do not have crystal clear guidelines to lead them into a specific occupation. Following high school graduation, young Swedes often try out more than one occupational field and take time off for international travel. Giving older youth a chance to try different jobs after they complete compulsory schooling is another way of increasing transparency.

Transparency Versus Permeability

Future career prospects motivate adolescents to perform well in school when adolescents can see clearly what those prospects are and how to achieve them (i.e., the education-employment nexus is transparent) and when it is possible to move readily through that system, (i.e, it is permeable). Unfortunately, these two characteristics tend to be contradictory because specific educational qualifications for employment, which increase transparency by communicating precisely what is required to enter an occupational field, simultaneously decrease permeability by establishing barriers to career entry and career change.

The United States stands at one extreme among the seven nations discussed. Lacking specific qualifications for most occupations below the professional level, it has a highly permeable system. Occupational mobility is high. The cost is that adolescents who do not intend to enroll in 4-year colleges have grave difficulty seeing the value of schooling. This is exacerbated by a peculiar impermeability in the system; namely, that employers tend to use age as a proxy for worker virtues and refuse to hire teenagers for career entry positions.

Austria stands at the opposite extreme. A traditional apprenticeship system makes career paths very clear. However, the need for very specific occupational qualifications reduces occupational mobility. And a traditional school system that is sharply divided from apprenticeship limits apprentices' option to continue their full-time schooling and to rise through the corporate ranks.

Japan has added transparency to an American-style school-based system by means of almost contractual arrangements between schools and specific firms, which motivate students to perform well even if they are not engaged in competition for university admission, so that they may gain employment recommendations from their school. Though this privilege is available to only a minority of students, school achievement is remarkably high among Japanese adolescents.

Sweden consciously increased the permeability of its system by enrolling nearly all adolescents in comprehensive high schools, thus enhancing their opportunity for further education. A current move to extend vocational studies another year and to add substantial work experience to classroom instruction represents a step in the direction of the work-based approach found in the German-speaking countries.

Denmark's recently reformed apprenticeship system maintains transparent connections between education and employment but increases permeability by combining similar occupations and delaying specialization.

Germany and Switzerland are both engaged in serious efforts to increase the permeability of their systems. Germany is doing so formally by reducing the number of separate training occupations and informally by the popular practice of double qualification. The most promising Swiss reform is the addition of more school time to apprenticeship, simultaneously deepening technical understanding, broadening general education, and qualifying apprentices for further education.

Conclusions

My principal concern has been with improving the motivation of American youth, not only because of my citizenship but because the problem is clearly greatest there. However, the other six countries could also learn from each other. Sweden is already increasing emphasis on work-based learning, borrowing from its own past, from Denmark, and from the German-speaking countries. Germany would do well to examine some of the more progressive aspects of Swiss apprenticeship, many of which are already found in some German programs but are not yet universal. Austria's system could benefit from practices in both Germany and Switzerland, but is hampered by the dominance of small businesses, whose owners too often view apprentices as cheap labor and are unwilling to make the investment required to upgrade the quality of education, even though in the long run it would make economic sense for them.

Japan is the country with which I am least familiar. Work-based learning is highly developed there, at least among large firms, but sharply separated from school-based learning. Both high school and university graduates receive rigorous training after they are hired, but I have no detailed information on the nature of that training. The results in terms of productivity indicate that it is effective. However, Japanese critics cite the sterility of school pedagogy in Japan, which demands memorization and does not reward originality. And there is a huge gap between privileged permanent employees, who are predominantly male, and "temporary" employees, predominantly females, and males of Korean and low-caste Japanese ancestry. School pedagogy and the career prospects of low-status people might be addressed using some adaptation of work-based learning combined with formal schooling in order to render education more available and more useful.

Motivating adolescents to learn in school requires attention to immediate, short-term incentives but also to the connection between school performance and career opportunities. Finding the optimal combination of transparency and permeability is the key.

The best way to test empirically the hypothesized relationship between the lack of transparency in the school/career nexus and poor school performance in the United States would be to create a more transparent system and then observe whether students' behavior changed in the predicted direction. My colleagues and I are engaged in such an effort, inspired by German-style apprenticeship. Several other groups are similarly engaged.

The utility of these educational reforms as experiments testing the motivational hypothesis will depend not only on research design and methodology, but also on whether any of the demonstration projects achieves an adequate scale. In order to achieve the predicted effect, youth apprenticeship must be available for all young people who prefer it over a long enough time period to become a dependable part of their prospects for the future. If this occurs, and if those young people who are eligible to become apprentices take their school-work more seriously and behave more responsibly in other realms, this will constitute evidence supporting the hypothesis around which this chapter has been organized.

REFERENCES

Kaiser, M., Nuthmann, R., & Stegmann, H. (Eds.). (1985). Berufliche verbleibsforschung in der diskussion (Vol. 1): Schulabgänger aus dem seundarbereich I beim Übergang in ausbildung und beruf. Nürnberg: Institut für Arbeitsmarkt-und Berufsforschung der Bundesanstalt für Arbeit.

Rohlen, T. (1983). Japan's high schools. Berkeley: University of California Press.

Rosenbaum, J. E., Kariya, T., Settersten, R., & Maier, T. (1990). Market and network theories of the transition from high school to work: Their application to industrialized societies. *Annual Review of Sociology, 16,* 263–299.

THINKING CRITICALLY

1. What is meant by "transparency"? What makes transparency a problem in the American system?

2. What is it about the Japanese system that motivates high academic achievement? What are the drawbacks of that system?

3. In what ways is the system in German-speaking countries growing more permeable? Why is it moving in this direction?

4. How are Swedish youth centers involved in the transition from school to work?

Media Use Among Moroccan Adolescents

Although media use is especially pronounced among adolescents in industrialized countries, it is now an important part of life for adolescents in most parts of the world. Of particular interest is the use of media among adolescents in developing countries, where the media they are exposed to may present ideas and images quite different from the life they know from their direct experience. In this reading, the authors describe uses of media among adolescents in Morocco, a developing country in northern Africa. Especially with regard to heterosexual relationships, what adolescents find in the media is in sharp contrast to what they see occurring among the people they know. Nevertheless, in their preferences and behavior most Moroccan adolescents continue to adhere to their local cultural traditions.

Reading 12.1

"The Mosque and the Satellite": Media and Adolescence in a Moroccan Town

S. S. Davis and D. A. Davis

Our title was suggested by Moroccan sociologist Fatima Mernissi's response to a question about how she dealt with Islam as a feminist. "As a Muslim woman I want to have two things: the mosque and the satellite, both at the same time" (Mernissi, 1993). Her explanation made it clear that the mosque stood for her Islamic cultural heritage, and the satellite for access to western technology and its products. She wants not one to replace the other, but to combine them creatively. In this she echoes the ambitions of many Moroccan youth who have similar goals, though perhaps less well articulated.

We have followed Zawiya residents' growing involvement with electronic media for 29 years, since Susan arrived in this rural town in 1965 as the first American Peace Corps volunteer and found nothing more than a few radios in the more affluent homes. When we returned from a year of fieldwork in 1982 to compare notes with the other members of the Harvard Adolescence Project, we were struck by the pervasiveness and manifest similarity of adolescents' media experience across developing countries. English-speaking Inuit (Eskimo) youth 300 miles north of the Arctic circle were sitting with their Inuktitut-speaking parents, watching the *Love Boat* or southern Canadian hockey; young men in an Aboriginal settlement in northern Australia were dressing like Afro-American teens and listening to reggae; and Moroccans were discovering Dolly Parton and arguing over who shot J. R. Ewing. These superficial similarities in media exposure suggested a universal experience mediated by Western television, films, and popular music, but it proved difficult to establish that Canadian Inuit, Australian Aboriginal, or rural Moroccan youth were in fact using these media in similar ways— taking similar lessons about lust and betrayal from J.R., or having similar fantasies to the romantic images of reggae or country music. Indeed, social scientists studying such aspects of popular culture stress the complex intermingling of different cultural productions (Abu-Lughod, 1989; Mitchell, 1989).

This paper reports our findings on the use of electronic media by a group of young Moroccans in the early 1980s, and follows some

individuals up to 1990. It offers examples of their personal reactions to the images and emotions presented by an increasing range of television, radio, recorded, and printed material, from the global entertainment industry, from the rest of the Middle East, and from Morocco itself. The rapidly expanding array of media was used by adolescents in a period of rapid social change to re-imagine many aspects of their lives, including a desire for more autonomy, for more variety in heterosexual interactions, and for more choice of a job and a mate. While male and female media consumption varied, they used media with similar goals. Much of the content of Western media images is difficult to reconcile with traditional Moroccan values rooted in Islam and a strong extended family. While the young people we interviewed and observed often seemed acutely aware of the apparent contradictions between traditional and modern ways—between the mosque and the satellite—they did not, typically, see these contradictions as irreconcilable, and most seemed eager to preserve core traditional values while hoping to reap the benefits of the affluent and exciting society promised by the media.

Zawiya: A Semirural Moroccan Town

Just across the Straits of Gibraltar from Spain, Morocco is located on the northwest corner of Africa. In climate and size Morocco resembles California, with chilly wet winters and hot dry summers. Beaches on the Mediterranean and Atlantic coasts give way to plains and mountain ranges, and finally to desert in the far south. The population is Arab and Berber, and almost completely Muslim.

Most of our data were collected in Zawiya, a semi-rural town of about 12,000 in northwestern Morocco, near the city of Meknes. Although located on the edge of a rich agricultural plain, more of the population works in commerce or trades than in agriculture. Zawiya is near Kabar, a market town of about 50,000 on a main train line, and is thus neither isolated nor urban. There are a primary and junior high school in Zawiya, and a mayor's office, post office and police station—

but there is no bank, hospital, high school, or restaurant. Government employees staff many offices and the schools, and offer a model of white-collar jobs to which many adolescents aspire. Parents, on the other hand, work mostly in blue-collar service jobs, and many grandparents were farmers. Most residents live in concrete houses on unpaved streets, and until 1988 had no running water and had to carry their supply from seven outdoor taps. Nearly all households had electricity, however, and the majority had television in 1982. While incomes vary, Zawiya lifestyles are quite similar. Yet gender roles are quite different, and the ways this affects media use are elaborated below. In general, girls spend more time in household chores and boys have more leisure, so girls stay closer to home and boys go further afield. Girls may go to a house to visit or embroider, and boys may play soccer or go to town. Walking to the high school in town and running errands in Zawiya give boys and girls a chance to meet and talk, but dating is taboo and a more serious offense for girls than boys.

Zawiya's adolescents and their families live in a rapidly changing world. Grandparents farmed the land, while their children may work in France, and Morocco is now part of the world economy. Grandparents rarely saw a car, while adolescents take trains to the capital. Rural families lived in extended family groups, but now each family lives alone, so most young wives do not have to serve an exacting mother-in-law in residence. Only a few parents attended school, while most adolescents attended primary school and many go on. Education also opens up white-collar jobs for both sexes, and in cities one sees office plaques for women doctors, dentists, and lawyers, something rare until the 1980s.

Most of the data presented here were collected in a year of fieldwork in 1982 as part of the Harvard Adolescence Project, in which postdoctoral researchers conducted parallel studies of young people in seven cultures. We gathered anthropological, sociological, and psychological data on over 100 Zawiya adolescents and their families. We lived in a house in the neighborhood we studied, and the data include partici-

pant observation of adolescents and their families. Since we had maintained regular contact with Zawiya from 1965, when Susan first arrived there, by 1982 we were seen almost as aunt and uncle to several local families.

Our research included young people from 9 to 21, and a few slightly older neighbors. While in the United States the ages 13–19 are often used to delineate adolescence, in Morocco the social changes we associate with this phase begin later and last longer. We weighed, measured, and completed sociological questionnaires and school and family histories for each of the young people. We gave psychological tests of cognitive development (D. Davis, 1987) and gender identity (S. Davis, 1983) to about 60, and conducted open-ended interviews with a group of about 20 with whom we had especially good rapport. Susan returned in 1984 and updated these interviews. Our more general statements are based on observations of and interactions with families over a period of 20 years. In 1989–1990, Susan began research on Moroccan women's relationships with their husbands and with female friends and relatives around the time of marriage, in Zawiya and also in Rabat. These data suggest current and future trends for media and gender relations.

The Moroccan Media Context

Most readers will be unfamiliar with what types of media are available in a small town on the northwest corner of Africa, so we present an overview in order to help understand the media context. We will describe the several types of media, including the increasing availability and thematic content of each and the context in which it is used, and will highlight the influences of gender and education.

Most young people in Zawiya watched some television daily by 1982. They also listened to music and news broadcasts on the radio in Arabic and/or French, and many males saw at least the occasional motion picture. Cassette players were owned by most families, and some older male adolescents spent many hours by themselves or with male friends listening to popular recordings from the Middle East, France, and the United States. The majority of both genders said they read as a leisure activity.

Gender and Education

Before presenting specific information on the various media, we want to stress that exposure to media is strongly influenced by gender and education in Zawiya. Male adolescents have greater access to family resources, including use of the family's cassette player, money to purchase tapes, and a room of their own. They have the mobility to go to the cinema, where they are often exposed to more sexually-explicit material, but female attendance is considered shameful.

Educational level determines whether one can understand the foreign languages—most often French—used in television, films, and music. Both sexes were entering elementary school in Zawiya by the 1980s, but twice as large a proportion of males (48% vs. 23%) attended secondary school, where they became adept in French (Davis & Davis, 1989, p. 62).

Television

Television is the most used of the mass media by local people, and youth are avid consumers. The first set appeared in a Zawiya cafe in 1967, and by 1982 a majority of households had one. The most prosperous families had color sets. There has always been one government channel that initially broadcast only evenings, but it now has expanded coverage. In the late 1980s a cable channel became available, and in the early 1990s satellite dishes began to appear on family rooftops in cities. By 1994 some dishes appeared in Zawiya, giving access to over 90 channels with programs from France, Italy, Germany, England, and CNN.

One might imagine that the content of television programs has changed from local to international with the wider range of channels, but it has been international from the start. Since it is much less expensive to buy than to produce programs, at first a majority came from France. News has always been broadcast by local anchorpersons in literary Arabic (not widely understood by the uneducated, who speak the colloquial form) and in French. Even if it was difficult to understand, television's visual aspect opened up new worlds to viewers: people who had never seen snow suddenly were familiar with it, and world political and entertainment figures became recognizable. Other early programming included French dramas, soccer matches, and a popular Saturday night feature that still exists: the local variety show. Each week a particular town is featured and filmed with a live audience, and one hears about local characteristics and sees typical dances and songs, often with a nationally popular singer as special guest. Television evolved to include more American programs (dubbed in French) like *Little House on the Prairie*, *The Incredible Hulk*, and *Dallas*.

An important change by the early 1980s was more Arabic programming, primarily Egyptian serials or evening soaps, often with a romantic theme. Although the Egyptian and Moroccan dialects of Arabic differ, the Egyptian is much more widely understood than French, so a larger part of the viewership could follow the plots. Another innovation is the dubbing of a Japanese produced cartoon show into literary Arabic; this popular program probably helps children learn the literary language. The cable channel and satellite access make available programs with more explicit sexual interaction than one usually sees—on the broadcast channel an extended embrace is felt to be risque, let alone bedroom scenes. In fact, the only example we saw of parents restricting media use was that some discontinued cable service because the European and American films embarrassed families watching in mixed-sex groups.

Television was the most social of the media: the family usually gathered to watch in the largest room in the house. In the past, especially in the largely French program period, few people paid close attention, and conversations went on around the set, with an occasional pause for an adolescent who understood the plot to explain it to the elders. Most Zawiya adults understand little French, since in the colonial period few rural Moroccans attended even elementary school. Adult family members often described interesting alternative plots they had elaborated while watching; sometimes there were active family debates about which character would do what, and why, based on these different understandings. As comprehension has increased, television watching has become less interactive.

Radios and Cassettes

Radios were the primary access to the mass media when we began to work in Zawiya in the mid-1960s, and not all families had one. Since then nearly every family acquired a radio, but they had been replaced by cassette players as the medium of choice for adolescent males and many females by 1982. On radio music was the main attraction, although news, soccer games, and audio advice columns were popular. Cassette players were also mainly used for music, although there were tapes of Moroccan comedians and Koranic recitation.

There was wide variety in the content of both radio and cassette music. In Arabic one heard Moroccan, Egyptian, Lebanese, and Algerian singers and musicians, in classical and popular styles. . . . A favorite radio station nationwide was Tangier-based Medi-Un, which played Arabic, European, and American music, classical and popular, with the patter between songs in the appropriate language. Requests to us by young men in Zawiya for copies of albums have over the years included Bob Dylan, Bob Marley, Kenny Rogers, and Emmylou Harris. Parents did not generally attempt to control the content of their children's listening, and in any case the French or English lyrics of imported Western music would be incomprehensible to most adults. The main adult use of radio was women listening, often with daughters while doing housework, to "Miss Laila," the Moroccan version of Dear Abby, who answered listeners' questions on relationships in Moroccan Arabic.

Since radios and cassette players are portable, the context of listening varied more than that of television watching. These media, especially cassette players, were more often used individually or in groups of peers. This was truer for boys since they had more free time and preferential access to the radio or player. Boys were also more apt to have their own room where they could listen uninterrupted, either by mother's calls for assistance or the noise of siblings playing. Teenagers and young adults borrowed these tapes from each other constantly, and we heard of several friendships strained by the non-return of a prized tape.

Films

There were three movie theaters in Kabar, two kilometers away, which showed risque films as well as spaghetti westerns, police films, and Indian romances—all imported, and dubbed in French or literary Arabic. While young women attended films in the cities, those from Zawiya rarely did since cinemas full of rowdy young men were seen as unsuitable for them.

VCRs

This new technology did not appear until after our 1982 research, but we mention it to highlight the rapid spread of media technologies. Videocassette players were still rare in Zawiya at the end of the 1980s. The local video watching we heard about was often by groups of young men and involved soft core or X-rated movies. Hannah Davis (1989) reports that multigenerational groups of women in a larger nearby town preferred videos with a romantic theme. We heard of no systematic VCR watching by groups of Zawiya women; however, even local weddings are now often taped, and girls and women occasionally enjoy watching these lengthy celebrations (see Ossman, 1994).

Print

We enter into another realm with print media, one that was nearly nonexistent in Zawiya in the mid-1960s but that has become increasingly popular as literacy rises. Young peoples' reading included newspapers, poetry, stories rented from teachers, and magazines. The most popular magazines were *photoromans*, which are like comics, but with photos and word balloons telling the often-romantic story. *L'Opinion*, one of Morocco's major French-language newspapers, had a special section, Opinions of the Young, to which youth submit poems, jokes, and personal dilemmas; by the late 1980s it appeared three times a week because of increasing interest.

Adolescent Use of Media Images

Media Exposure

In terms of the media preferences of adolescents (between 64 and 101 responded to different questions), significantly more girls than boys preferred Arabic to Western language entertainment on radio, cassettes, and television. For radio, 83% of the girls preferred Arabic programs compared to 35% of the boys; for cassettes (mostly music) 85% of girls and 56% of boys preferred Arabic. On television, 44% of girls and 12% of boys preferred Arabic programs. While boys on the average were more educated than girls (and thus more comfortable with non-Arabic languages), even among the more educated youth, girls tended to prefer Arabic media.

The two sexes in Zawiya had a very different exposure to cinema. Of girls, 80% had *never* been to a movie, while 40% of boys went occasionally and another 40% went weekly or more often. An important influence on male gender relations was the soft-core European films (and videos), portraying interpersonal behavior that is banned on television. This may lead young men to have certain physical expectations of their future spouses—or it may be so different that it will not be assimilated beyond fantasy.

We also asked about whether youth read in their leisure time: 64% of males and 61% of females said they did. This is surprising since nearly twice as many females as males were out of school at the time of the research (47% vs.

26%), and females' educational level was generally lower. We could not evaluate differences in terms of what was read because we lacked detailed enough data.

One 18-year-old boy said he enjoyed French films on TV, but not Egyptian ones, because in the former you "see some of the world," while the Egyptian films only allow you to see "inside the house." He also expressed a preference for French news broadcasts, because they are shorter and have more pictures, whereas the Arabic broadcasts are long and dull. On the other hand, his cassette listening was mostly to Moroccan bands, and his leisure reading was primarily in Arabic magazines and poetry. He said he went to the cinema 1–3 times per week (one of the highest reported rates), and preferred "boxing" and French films.

The only Zawiya girls who reported regular trips to the cinema were sisters aged 15 and 17 when interviewed. The younger said she went 3–4 times per month, and that she liked Indian and Arabic films. The older said she went about three times a year and that she liked Indian films and karate films. Both said they liked to listen to Moroccan female singers on their family's cassette player, and the older sister also mentioned liking Indian popular music.

One consequence of increased school attendance was to make more contact between the sexes possible (D. Davis, in press; Davis & Davis, 1993, in press) and the media played an important role in shaping the expected results of this contact. Marriages in Morocco were traditionally arranged by parents, based more on familial than individual compatibility, and with economic support more important than emotional attraction. After meeting potential spouses in school, young people had more idea of what they wanted in a mate. While most of the about 100 Zawiya youth we asked "Who should choose the spouse?" answered "the parents" (64% of females and 55% of males), about 25% of each sex wanted to take part in the decision. The number saying they wanted to be involved increased significantly as youth increased in age and in level of education (S. Davis, 1984). Similarly, Naamane-Guessous found that 56% of her more-educated urban

Moroccan female sample would accept arranged marriages and 25% wished to choose a spouse themselves (Naamane-Guessous, 1987, pp. 68–69).

Use of Media Images

Since dating was still taboo in Zawiya, how did one learn about interacting with the opposite sex and choosing a spouse? Young women discussed these topics intensely but their experience was limited, and an important source of such information was television programs. Many Moroccan programs originated in Egypt, the largest producer of Arabic-language media. A recurrent theme was the love match opposed by parents, who preferred a rich older man for their daughter; the love match usually triumphed. One young woman from Zawiya described how she saw the role of television:

> Girls today learn a lot from television films; they learn how to lead their lives. Those films show the problems of marriage and divorce and everything—television explains a lot. Television has made girls aware. Boys too, but mainly girls—they watch films. In Zawiya there are no cafes for them to go to, no parties, nothing—but now they see all that on TV, how girls behave with their friends. One is going to the university, her fiance asks her to go to a cafe with him. They talk, and then they marry. Some don't marry; they talk with one and then go off with another. See? They learn and don't give a damn. . . . It is the woman who is in charge, because TV shows that women have progressed like men. They have projects, they work at the post office and at stations, they do everything—there is no difference between men and women. . . . If I ask [my eight year old niece] about something, she'll know. It is TV that has caused girls to progress.

It is clear that the medium of television is playing a role in people's re-imagination of gender roles, providing examples from several cultural milieus. An urban man in his 20s, interviewed in 1989, supported this view of the expansive effect of television: "Personally, I think that today a 20 year old girl can have more experience than a 40 year old woman of the previous generation. She can have more experience than my mother, because there is television and she goes out."

In at least one case, a Zawiya youth made use of images borrowed from the media in creating a drama of his own. The young man we called "Sa'id" in our book on Moroccan adolescence (Davis & Davis, 1989) was a troubled 18-year-old when Susan interviewed him in 1984. Among the roughly 100 adolescents we questioned about leisure activity and aspirations, Sa'id stood out for the frequency of his visits to the Hindi, Arabic, and Western cinema of Kabar—one to three times a week during the summer of 1982. We were struck by the grandiosity of his career plans and by the extent to which he seemed enthralled by TV and film scenarios.

When we were back in Zawiya in 1987, we had several occasions to talk at length with Sa'id, then 21. By this time he had dropped out of school after several failures, which was not uncommon in Zawiya, and he was living at home and unemployed. His major preoccupation during this period was drama: Sa'id had joined a drama group in nearby Kabar, and had recently completed a short play of his own, titled *If the Crazy One Spoke Up* (Davis & Najmi, 1994). The setting is a mental hospital ward, where eight "crazy" inmates are interviewed by a visiting "psychological researcher" and act out the stresses that have driven them out of their minds.

The play offers a set of vivid satirical anecdotes about contemporary Moroccan life, making use of short poems, song lyrics, and dialogue in the language of the street. The script makes explicit and effective use of references to imported media as a model for, and perhaps a partial source of, the life problems faced by the characters. One of the inmates characterizes his problem as "like one of those films that they show on TV," and at the conclusion of his portrayal the interviewing psychologist agrees, saying, "All we need is the Indians, and we could make a Western film." When a jilted girl tells her boyfriend that they should struggle to overcome poverty and social barriers to their wedding, he cynically says, "Are you influenced by Egyptian movies?"

Discussion

What do these media preferences and uses mean? One might interpret girls' greater preference for Arabic programs to mean being more traditional, and espousing traditional gender roles. Yet this preference included Moroccan Arabic, Egyptian, Lebanese, and Berber songs or programs, many of which had themes of love and "modern" interactions of couples. One could argue that "Western" programs devoted a higher proportion of their time to "modern" relationships, or presented more variations and more extreme violations of traditional norms (e.g., embraces instead of flirtatious glances)—yet much of what adolescents see and listen to in the media deals with romance and couples. It is also interesting that for television viewing, about half of both boys and girls said they preferred both Arab and Western programs. Many adolescents of both sexes seem to want to see what is going on all over the world. The visual character of television makes language differences less important.

Moroccan male adolescents share the American tendency to prefer more individualis-tic and teen-focused forms of media as they get older, and spend more time with music tapes. Young women, unlike their American peers, spend more time watching television in family groups. They too enjoy music tapes, but their brothers have more access to them, and to private space in which to listen. It seems likely that popular music—and, for males, imported videotapes and commercial movies—provide a more relevant vehicle for the fantasies of later adolescence than does standard television fare. Males can select among the many tapes and films available to them, and thus develop a more individualistic taste in media. Females usually have to settle for the more limited programming on television and radio.

Both sexes in Zawiya are using media to gain new perspectives on heterosexual interactions. In a culture in which heterosexual interactions were quite limited, the media are an important source of socialization. Moroccan television portrays both Eastern and Western couples in romantic relationships, and movies and videos often contain more risque images. Popular music is listened to in several languages, and nearly all laments a lost love or celebrates a new one. While adolescents respect much of traditional culture, and some restrictions remain, a major use of media in Morocco is in the re-imagining and redefinition of the culture's rapidly changing gender roles.

REFERENCES

Abu-Lughod, L. (1989). Bedouins, cassettes, and technologies of public culture. *Middle East Report, 19,* 7–11.

Davis, D. A. (1989). Formal operational thought and the Moroccan adolescent. In J. Valsiner (Ed.), *Cultural context and child development: Towards a culture-inclusive developmental psychology.* Lewiston, NY: Hofgrefe and Hubor.

Davis, D. A. (in press). Modernizing the sexes: Changing gender relations in a Moroccan town. *Ethos.*

Davis, D. A., & Davis, S. S. (1993). Sexual values in a Moroccan town. In W. J. Lonner & R. S. Malpass (Eds.), *Psychology and culture.* Boston: Allyn and Bacon.

Davis, D. A., & Najmi, M. (1994). *If the crazy one spoke up.* Unpublished manuscript.

Davis, H. (1989). American magic in a Moroccan town. *Middle East Report, 19,* 12–17.

Davis, S. S. (1984). *Sexual politics and change in a Moroccan town.* Paper presented at the annual meeting of the Middle East Studies Association, San Francisco.

Davis, S. S. & Davis, D. A. (1989). *Adolescence in a Moroccan town: Making social sense.* New Brunswick, NJ: Rutgers University Press.

Davis, S. S., & Davis, D. A. (in press). Love conquers all? Changing gender relations in a Moroccan town. In E. J. Fernea (Ed.), *Childhood in a Muslim world.* Austin: University of Texas Press.

Mernissi, F. (1993). Interview with Terry Gross on *Fresh Air,* 12/15/93. National Public Radio, Washington, DC.

Mitchell, T. (1989). Culture across borders. *Middle East Report, 19,* 4–6.

Naamane-Guessous, S. (1987). *Au-dela de toute pudeur: La sexualite feminine au Maroc.* Casablanca: Soden.

Ossman, S. (1994). *Picturing Casablanca: Portraits of power in a modern city.* Berkeley: University of California Press.

THINKING CRITICALLY

1. Describe the differences in adolescent boys' and girls' access to media. How do these differences reflect Moroccan cultural beliefs about gender roles?

2. To what extent does Moroccan adolescents' media use reflect the influence of globalization, and to what extent is it rooted in local and national culture? Give examples.

3. Recent research and theory on media have focused on the *uses* that people make of media. What uses of media take place among the Moroccan adolescents described here?

4. For Moroccan adolescents, how is the portrayal of heterosexual relationships in the media they consume different from the heterosexual relationships they see around them? To what extent is it possible for Moroccan adolescents to have both "the mosque and the satellite" in terms of heterosexual relationships?

Media Use in Adolescents' Bedrooms

Adolescents in industrialized countries spend a lot of their time using various media, including recorded music, radio, television, magazines, computer games, and the Internet. The authors of this reading take an unusual approach to learning about adolescents' media use by having adolescents describe the contents of their bedrooms, which typically contain a variety of media representations. The result is a rich qualitative portrayal of the importance of media in adolescent's lives and of how adolescents use the materials provided in media toward constructing their own identity.

Reading 12.2

Adolescent Room Culture: Studying Media in the Context of Everyday Life

J. R. Steele and J. D. Brown

In Rachael's room the bed is covered with clothes, cassette tapes and magazines, a red phone, and a cassette player. The walls are plastered with posters of the Beatles, the B52s, and a leering rock musician with his hand stuck down in his pants. The posters cover over an Impressionist art print of a little girl with flowers. One wall is full of advertisements torn from magazines featuring muscular men and thin women modeling the latest fashions. A bulletin board is crammed with snapshots of friends and a poem illustrated with a red skull and crossbones.

This is the bedroom of a 14-year-old girl who has projected into the space of her bedroom her fears, desires, and fantasies about herself in relation to others and the larger culture. It tells a lot about who she is and what she cares about.

Sixteen-years-old and a sophomore in high school, Jack also safeguards an eclectic mix of childhood artifacts and teenage fantasies and aspirations in his bedroom. On one wall a wooden box displays a fleet of model cars, painstakingly crafted during grade school. A shelf is piled high with the audiotaped "mixes" that now occupy his time. Perched on top is a teddy bear dressed in a white sailor suit, and behind the portable TV are a hand-drawn "drugs kill" poster of a rising cobra, GI Joe cutouts, and a pen-and-pencil rendering of *Lady and the Tramp*, the flotsam of earlier years. On the wall next to his bed are more current concerns: a Ferrari Testarossa poster, a "my child is an honor student at . . ." bumper sticker, and pictures of girls clipped out of magazines. "If they look good," Jack explains, "I just put them up on the wall."

Rachael's and Jack's bedrooms underscore an important commonality between these two teenagers—one white, female, and from a city in the Southeast, the other black, male, and

J. R. Steele and J. D. Brown. "Adolescent Room Culture: Studying media in the context of everyday life" from *Journal of Youth & Adolescence*, Volume 24. Copyright © 1995. Reprinted by permission from Kluwer Academic/Plenum Publishers.

from a small Southern town. That commonality is the mass media from which they both draw as they fashion their emerging identities.

Over the past several years we have been investigating the bedrooms of adolescents like Rachael and Jack in order to learn more about the relationship between teenagers and the media. Why are the media such an essential part of so many adolescents' everyday routines? What do they take from the media, and why? Are some teens more susceptible to media influence than others? What mediates the impact of media choices and effects? These and related questions have guided our room culture project. They are stimulated by the ongoing debate among social critics and media scholars about the extent to which young people can and do resist the dominant and often potentially harmful messages presented by the mass media.

Much of the public's concern about the effects of the mass media on children and adolescents centers on unhealthy behaviors, such as early and unprotected sex and drug use. The media are seen as especially powerful for at least three reasons: (1) children and teens spend more time with the mass media than they do in school or with their parents, (2) the media are full of portrayals that glamorize risky adult behavior such as unprotected sex with multiple partners and drinking, and (3) parents and other socialization agents have shirked their responsibilities to direct youth toward less risky behavior (Gore, 1987).

Some researchers who theorize about and study the effects of the mass media have moved away from a powerful effects model and instead point to an active audience that engages in selective behavior at each step in the process of being affected by the mass media (Levy & Windahl, 1985). They suggest that adolescents will make choices about which media and genres to attend to, will pay attention to some kinds of content and not others, will identify and model some media characters, and may create new meanings and uses for what they do select. These scholars argue that the process of media effects must be seen as interactive, rather than unidirectional.

However, other scholars argue that the media do not provide the full array of life possi-

bilities and are not completely open texts, subject to an infinite number of meanings (Biocca, 1988). Rather, the media present a certain set of messages or ideas about how the world works, and although some differences in interpretation and sense making are possible, the dominant meanings will prevail. At the least, it is unlikely, given the restricted nature of most media content, that audiences will be stimulated to resist or create politically vital opposition to the existing world view (Gitlin, 1991).

In the context of this theoretical discussion, we propose a model that emphasizes a dialectical process in which the media are important cultural agents whose influence on audiences is both *amplified* and *restrained* by active individuals who interact with the media from "where they live" (Schwichtenberg, 1989, p. 293), developmentally, socially, and culturally. The model does not diminish the importance of media content, but it recognizes that individuals shape and transform media encounters in a continuous cycle of meaning making. The difference between amplified or restrained effects lies in individual and group *practices*, the everyday activities, gestures, and routines that define social relations.

The model is grounded in empirical work on adolescents' "room culture," a term used to refer to both the material artifacts contained in teens' bedrooms and the activities teenagers engage in when they are in their rooms. In the interest of seeing just how active adolescents are in sorting through and making use of the cultural "tool kit" provided by the mass media (Swidler, 1986), we have been looking closely at how teens use the mass media and related materials from popular culture in their daily lives. Daily journals, in-depth interviews conducted in teens' bedrooms, and a technique called "room touring" have allowed us to see and hear the variety of ways adolescents use the media in creating a sense of themselves.

The bedroom is an important place for most adolescents, a personal space in which they can experiment with "possible selves" (Larson, 1995; Markus & Nurius, 1986). Even adolescents who share a room typically have designated some space as their own. Csikszentmihalyi and Larson (1984) found that teens spent about 13% of their awake time in their bedrooms (second only to the 20% of time spent at school). At least some of that time is spent on identity work (McRobbie & Garber, 1975; Moffatt, 1989; Willis, 1990).

Room culture data, analyzed in the aggregate, generated the theoretical connections that ground the Adolescents' Media Practice model presented. The model posits a process of media Selection, Interaction, and Application that is constantly shaping and being shaped by Identity.

Fieldwork

Our room culture project began in spring 1987 when we worked with 19 white, middle-class girls, 11–15 years old, from North Carolina and Michigan to learn about their use of the mass media in constructing a sense of themselves as sexual human beings. In order to learn what these girls saw as "sexual," they were asked to record in personal journals whatever they saw or heard in the media about "sex and relationships." Then, after a month of journal keeping, each girl was interviewed in her bedroom. She first completed a short, self-administered questionnaire about typical patterns of media use and sexual experience, and then the journal was used as a catalyst for an open-ended interview about use of the media. Pictures of each girl's room also were taken to facilitate communication between researchers working in two different states. These photos and the bedroom culture they captured opened up an unexpectedly rich vein of information about adolescent identities and media use.

In summer 1991, another six teenagers, aged 13–15, including another white girl, one black girl, two white boys, and two black boys, were interviewed, all but one in their rooms. Four of these teens were interviewed again in spring 1992, along with two more white girls who were acquaintances of one of the authors. During this phase of research, a version of "autodriving," a technique borrowed from consumer research (Heisley & Levy, 1991; Rook, 1991), was used. Each teen, holding a tape recorder, took the interviewer on a tour of his

or her room, describing everything that held special meaning or significance.

In July, 1992, 20 rising high school seniors from across the country (11 males and 9 females, including three blacks, two Native Americans, and two students of Hispanic origin) who were attending a three-week course on the university campus were asked to interview each other about their bedrooms at home. Provided with a loosely structured interview guide, they focused on how their interview partners used mass media in their rooms, assessed how important the room was, and described how decorations and artifacts reflected personal identity.

In spring 1993, room tours were conducted with five college students (two white males, one black and two white females) in their dorm rooms. The focus this time was on the media and alcohol. During the month preceding the scheduled interviews, each student had completed a 10-day journal recording drinking behavior, attitudes toward school, and observations about alcohol messages in the university environment.

Developing a Media Practice Model

The combination of our qualitative methods, persistent focus on room culture over time, and an interdisciplinary orientation led to formulation of the Adolescents' Media Practice Model (Fig. 12.2.1). The model contributes three important dimensions to the traditional conceptualization of mass media uses and effects.

1. The model takes a practice perspective (Bentley, 1987; Bourdieu, 1977, 1990; Lave, Duguid, Fernandez, & Axel, 1992) and focuses on everyday activities and routines of media consumption. Instead of worrying about where the power lies—with a powerful media or an active audience—practice theory sees media as an integral part of the continuous process of cultural production and reproduction that characterizes everyday life. Typical adolescents interact with media all day long. They wake up to the radio, they talk with their friends about last night's episode of *90210,* and they flip through the latest issue of *Sports Illustrated* or *Seventeen* while lying around after school. It is through these everyday activities that the

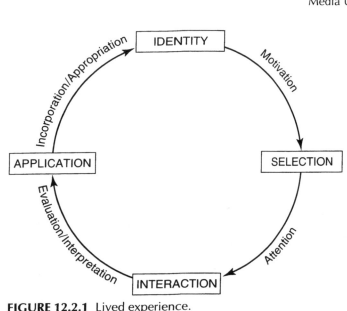

FIGURE 12.2.1 Lived experience.

media's influence is realized—not in a vacuum, but through the moment-to-moment interface between media and teenagers who come already armed with a sense of how the world is.

2. The model factors in "lived experience" (Vygotsky, 1978; Wertsch, 1991), a theoretical perspective that accounts for developmental stage, the sociocultural influences of race, class, and gender, as well as many other socializing factors, including religious background and beliefs, neighborhood influences, family life, encounters with the legal system, friendships and peer culture, success or failure in school. Not to be confused with experience in the simply historical sense (e.g., attended St. Mark's Trade School, repeated sixth grade, lettered in basketball), Vygotsky's "lived through experience," or "lived experience" as it is labeled in the model, is a complex sociogenetic construct that sees the process of development as a constant bridging—accomplished through activity and communication—between the known and the new in specific contexts (Valsiner, 1991). The term is used to position adolescent media practice in what Rogoff (1990) terms the "social sea" in which we all live.

Whether listening to music alone in the privacy of their rooms or slam-dancing at warehouse parties, adolescents carry with them their particular life histories as well as the knowledge of their peer cultures (Corsaro, 1992). It is with this embodied knowledge that they build on and transform the shared sociocultural knowledge available through the media.

3. The model incorporates identity formation, the central task of adolescent development, as a key component. Teens' sense of who they are shapes their encounters with media, and those encounters in turn shape their sense of themselves in the ongoing process of cultural production and reproduction.

In the following sections we illustrate the media components of the model with examples drawn from our room culture data.

Selection

Teens do make choices about which media and media content to attend to. This selection is sometimes quite conscious and motivated by a need to learn something or to maintain a mood. In our first study of 19 white girls and their use of sexual media content, we discovered skilled media users who attended to media that spoke to their developmental stage and sexual experience. The girls differed dramatically in their use of sexual media content (Brown, White, & Nikopoulou, 1993).

We called one group of girls "Disinterested" because they simply were less interested and tended to ignore sexual content in the media. Even with prodding, these girls preferred not talking or thinking about sex and relationships. The rooms of these girls were filled with stuffed animals and dolls and drawings by them and friends; the media were not yet in great evidence.

In contrast, the girls we labeled "Intrigued" often had surrounded themselves with sexual media content; their rooms were full of images of popular media stars and they frequently had access to a range of media, including magazines, music, and television. A third group of girls also had access to a number of media channels in their rooms, but they were most likely to have chosen images from less mainstream media. They also were the most physically mature and sexually experienced of the girls. Drawing on the work of Carol Gilligan and her colleagues who are teaching girls psychological resistance skills (Brown & Gilligan, 1992), we called these girls "Resisters" because they most consistently offered critiques of sexual media content.

"Lived Through Experience" Factored In

In subsequent studies, we again found that media selections were influenced by gender and also frequently by race. For many boys, an interest in sports guided choices. Not only did many of the boys report a preference for sports programming and magazines, they also made heavy use of sports in decorating their rooms. One summer school student wrote of her Hispanic partner, a rising high school senior: "When I chatted with Joe earlier this evening, I got the feeling that he was taking me through a tour of a *Sports Illustrated* office or a studio at the ESPN network. Joe likes sports. A lot. All of the various media in his bedroom that are important seem to be a part of his admiration for professional sports."

Arrayed on the walls of Joe's bedroom were a collage of magazine and poster cutouts of his favorite players and teams, a portrait of baseball great Don Mattingly that "reminds him of his goals in life," and a Burger King poster featuring one of the Harlem Globetrotters. Joe said he did not have a TV in his room, but that he did not really need one because the only thing he watched was sports and he could do that with his father in the living room. Joe also kept a pair of headphones hidden behind his bed so he could listen to baseball games on the radio when he was supposed to be sleeping, "something his mother doesn't approve of."

It would be inaccurate, though, to stereotype an interest in sports' media as a "boys only" phenomenon. Tanya, an African-American high school student from New York, said she watched sports on TV "most days" and displayed just three posters in her room: Spud Webb, Dominique Wilkins, and Karl Malone, all National Basketball Association stars. Still, she reported liking nonsports fare as well. The *Fresh Prince of Bel Air* was her favorite sitcom, and she watched game shows like *Family Feud* more regularly than she watched sports. Racial identification was also evident in Tanya's media choices. In addition to *Basketball Digest,* the stack of magazines on her bedstand included *Jet,* a black news magazine, and *Ebony, a* black fashion magazine. Some racial identification could be seen in her music preferences, too, which included rhythm and blues, reggae, rap, soul, and gospel.

Music Motivators

Although many of the adolescents had television sets in their rooms, most considered music systems and telephones, not TV, essential to well-being. Sixteen-year-old Emily's comment was typical for girls: "I can't be in here [her bedroom] without music. I always have music on." Boys, too, said they liked to listen to music. Willy, 17, called his stereo his "most prized possession" and like Emily, admitted to having the radio on almost all the time he was in his room (about 1½ hours daily). Jack said he listened to music "every chance I get," including during Mr. Snow's tenth grade biology class. He said he was "makin' about a 95" in that class despite the fact he would tune in his portable radio (slipped into his pocket with the wire hidden underneath his sweatshirt) whenever things started to get boring.

Motivation: Sometimes Conscious, Sometimes Not

Some teens were quite clear that they turned to specific media content to satisfy instrumental needs (Rubin, 1994). When probed about why he liked violent films like *Terminator II* and *Boyz n the Hood,* Jack said he "might want to try some moves on somebody next time you get in a fight. You learn stuff that might help you some time." Jenny, 16, said she read romance novels "all the time" because "I just like to know, to read about other people's lives and times. And forget mine." A high school junior was quite matter of fact about why he had bought a *Sports Illustrated* swimsuit calendar to hang up in his room: "To know the date and because of the girls."

At other times, media selection was habitual—e.g., "I turn on my tape player first thing in the morning to get my blood flowing correctly" or "I always watch TV after doing my homework." Our data suggest that the difference between instrumental and habitual motivators feeds directly into the quality or intensity of teens' interactions with media.

Interaction

Identifying with characters in TV shows, movies, or song lyrics; comparing, interpreting, and critiquing the physical appearance, actions, and motives of media figures; reading themselves into songs (Willis, 1990) or moving in and out of the life of a favorite romance novel heroine (Moffitt, 1993) are examples of what we categorize as media "interaction." Drawing on Hall's (1986) articulation model, Moffitt (1993) makes a convincing case that the "media experience, for some receivers, serves as an immediate reality . . . blurring the lines between the fantasy of the text and the 'reality' of lived experiences" (p. 232). Suzanne provided an apt example of this type of interaction when she described the kinds of books she liked to read: "I like to read stuff that really happens . . . that makes you feel like it's still going on."

Interpretation (Dervin, 1980) is another aspect of media interaction that is particularly important for adolescents actively engaged in "identity work" (Snow & Anderson, 1987). Teens frequently told us they liked characters or images that fit with who they were or wanted to be. For example, Danny, 15, one of the boys we interviewed twice, said he liked the TV show *Growing Pains* because there was a boy (Ben) his age in it, and "he's always into somethin'. He be doin' crazy stuff," thus suggesting both identification and motivation. Even with favorite characters, however, adolescents frequently grapple with sometimes conflicting and contradictory messages. They compare what they are seeing and hearing in the media with what they already know or thought they knew, then apply their new understandings to their lives.

Interpreting and Evaluating Media Content

Our initial study of early adolescent girls provided illustrative data on how the girls worked hard at understanding and maintaining their own standards in the face of apparently contradictory expectations. Some came to media use with clear "frames" (Graber, 1989) or "worldviews" (Kosicki & McLeod, 1990) that helped guide their interpretations of content, making them more sophisticated and consistent critics than others.

For example, many of the girls said they frequently used magazines for guidance about makeup and clothes. But some also had begun to realize that the looks projected in the magazines rarely are achieved. Maggie, 12, who, when asked if appearance is important to girls her age, replied, "Majorly!" also knew she could not look like the people in commercials: "I think most advertising is (puts on voice), 'If you use this mascara then you'll look like this, oh boy!'" Audrey, 14, similarly critiqued beauty aid commercials: "I think that they use these beautiful people to sell their products because they want fat old ladies sitting at home with curlers in their hair watching the soaps to think that if they buy Loreal's [*sic*] 10 day formula they'll end up looking that beautiful. I think that that's really stupid because for one, I know perfectly well that I don't took like Cybil Shepard and Loreal's [*sic*] 10 day formula's not going to change that."

But such critiques didn't necessarily mean that the underlying premise of such advertising was dismissed. A couple of days later the same girl reported in her journal that she had spent the afternoon at the mall buying "basically cosmetics!"

This same kind of identification, evaluation, and critiquing was evident in the room interviews and alcohol journals kept by college students. Nathan, 19, evidencing a clear sense of self, wrote that he found himself feeling "really targeted" by a Heineken beer commercial: "The scene was some people in their early thirties relaxing on their porch. Even though I'm much younger, I felt I related well in the sense that I would enjoy relaxing, conversing, and drinking on a nice, open porch. I found this ad interesting because it didn't involve girls in bikinis, big parties, or any of the other typical 'fantasy' aspects of beer advertising."

Application

Our analyses suggest that adolescents' bedrooms are important spaces where they can apply "media matter" (Rosengren & Windahl, 1989) in their everyday lives. Frequently, the adolescent is an active agent who consciously draws on the media to achieve specific purposes. We call this type of intentional, goal-oriented application *appropriation*.

Appropriation

Some typical examples of appropriation include using media to do the following:

Enhance a mood or cope with feelings: "When I need to get pumped up, like before a party, I listen to wild, loud music." (white female, 16)

Sort through cultural values and norms: "Sometimes I try to figure out what I would have done . . . (white female, 13)

Make a statement about identity: "I like it just cuz it's weird and not many people have stuff like that. I like to be different. It's just me." (white female, 16)

Emulate admired behavior: Asked why she had dyed her hair, Asta replied, "Because that's what you got to do today, Mama." (black female, 13)

Fantasize about possible selves or situations: "I would love to meet David Lee Roth one day. He would be a snob but I think it would be neat." (white female, 14).

Mood Enhancement.   Both Arnett (1995) and Larson (1995) have provided convincing evidence of teens' appropriation of media to enhance a mood or cope with the confusing emotions that teenagers must deal with. Our data, too, held numerous examples of this type of application. Suzanne, 17, told us when she had "real problems" she liked to turn on her stereo and "just wallow in it. When I feel that way I just want them [her parents] to leave me alone." Jenny said she liked "to find songs that are like the same as whatever kind of mood I'm in." Emily echoed a similar pattern: "When I'm sad I tend to listen to sad music, which doesn't exactly help in cheering me up. I listen to it much louder when I'm happy."

Cultural and Social Integration.   Movies and TV shows were often the takeoff point for reflecting on relationships and how to sort through the challenges of everyday life. Chelsea, 15, said the television show *Growing Pains* was one of her favorites because: ". . . it has a teenager in it, and there are typical problems that you would have every day. It kinda helps you look at it and say, 'Oh yeah, that's a different way to solve that problem.'" Maggie, 12, said she liked to read the "Dear Jack and Jill" letters column in *Teen* magazine: ". . . because like some of 'em are my problems and they have the answers there. Or like what kinds of clothes are gonna be in fashion this summer or stuff like that."

Several girls said they sought television shows, movies, and magazine articles that reassured them boys do have feelings and girls can refuse boys' unwanted sexual advances. Two girls said the movie *Stand by Me* was one of their favorites because "it brings out guys' feelings about how they feel about certain things. . . . Normally, they don't show guys' feelings."

Amy's room reflected the identity of a girl in developmental transition with movie posters of *Top Gun, Gone with the Wind,* and a picture of movie star Tom Cruise torn from a magazine, displayed alongside a poster of cartoon character Garfield the cat and posters of kittens, peacocks, and horses. In a number of the girls' rooms the transfer of emotional ties to males was evidenced by the juxtaposition of animal images, flowers, or pastoral scenes with pictures of idolized media males. Both Nola, 15, and Paulina, 13, who had had boyfriends and had "necked," had covered entire closet doors with pictures of male models and media stars torn from fashion and fan magazines. The rooms of younger males reflected a similar transition from childhood into the world of sexual relationships. Jack's room was filled with images of both black and white women, most in provocative poses. But the images of young women were interspersed with his own drawings of GI Joe done when he was 10 and "GI Joe crazy," and drawings of the movies *Lady and the Tramp* ("I just seen that in a magazine and I drew it"), and *Star Wars.*

Media also were frequently used as standards for comparison with the larger consumer society. Teens looked to the media for guidance on how to dress, style their hair, or select perfume and makeup. Alongside brand-name labels from clothing he had purchased, Jack had posted a picture of Arsenio Hall because "he dresses." Sometimes, media images were appropriated to make counterstatements, to resist mainstream values. Suzanne had posted a magazine photo of a young woman who had cemented her hair into a 7-inch high "mohawk" with the help of gel, hairspray, glue, spray starch, eggs, and cornstarch. Proud of the picture's shock value, she nevertheless asked, "Why would anyone want to look like that?"

Alyssa, a college sophomore, delighted in a Calvin Klein ad featuring Marky Mark in his underwear. "It's kind of fun to have a poster of a dumb boy, 'cause guys get really offended when they come in here. They're like (lowers voice to imitate), 'Aw, man, he's just good looking. He's an idiot. I don't know why you have that.'"

Media applications like these reinforce identification with the youth culture of which teenagers are members while at the same time reproducing the adult culture that makes money from their tastes and spending power, estimated at $89 billion in 1994 and growing (Zinn, 1994).

Expression of Self. Often, the bedroom was used to showcase possessions that reflected self-concept. Media and other artifacts remind teens of who they are, while at the same time telegraphing to parents and friends the selves they are constructing (Wallendorf & Arnould, 1988). Emily displayed a book of photographs, *The Family of Woman* (Mason, 1983), on her bookcase "so that everyone can see what a cultured person I am and what a neat mom I have who gives me books like that." Jenny, 16, had covered an entire door with cutouts of perfume bottles because "I think you can express yourself through, like fragrances and music."

Emulation/Modeling. A majority of the teens we interviewed had at least one image of a movie star, fashion model, musician, or famous athlete on the walls of their rooms. Occasionally, older adolescents included political figures. Still, images such as the posters of Martin Luther King and Malcolm X that were in the college dorm rooms of both an African-American girl and a white boy were relatively rare even among the older teens. Males and females typically included images of both sexes on their walls, and although both whites and blacks were more likely to include images of their own race, images of other races were displayed in a number of rooms. For example, Jack, 15, an African-American, had posters of both Joe Namath, a white football star, and Michael Jordan, a black basketball player, on his bedroom walls. Sigourney Weaver, the bald commando of *Alien III* fame, shared space with Led Zeppelin and basketball players from both the University of Tennessee and Duke University on the back of George's (17, Native American) door.

Explanations for why an image was selected frequently centered around emulation. A Native-American high school girl's room was decorated with 11 Marilyn Monroe posters because of Monroe's "beauty and accomplishments." Nathan had posted a Martin Luther King cutout because he'd "like to be a leader like that." Joe relied on a collage of sports heroes and related magazine clippings to provide "athletic inspiration." The stern looks on the athletes' faces reflected the tough, determined attitude he liked to imitate when playing baseball or basketball, he explained.

Fantasy. In our first study we found that the least sexually experienced girls tended to choose less "dangerous" male media stars who spoke more to the possibility of love than sex. Audrey, 14, wrote, "I also thought River Phoenix (Chris Chambers) was gorgeous! He was so sweet and sensitive, too, with his best friend, Gordie. Gordie reminds me of what my dad used to be like when he was a little boy."

In contrast, a more sexually experienced girl included a picture of John F. Kennedy, Jr., in her journal and wrote, "I'm in love with him. He's so sexy and good-looking." Suzanne, a high school junior when interviewed, had cut out an ad for eyeglasses featuring a bare-chested man because she "thought the guy was cute . . . maybe because I don't know him. That makes him more mysterious, and you don't need to worry about whether he's a jerk."

Incorporation

Incorporation, the other subcategory of media application, is harder to discern because it is less visible, more internal. Difficult to tease out of self-report data and not readily apparent in room decorations, incorporation is a "way of taking" meaning (Heath, 1982) from the media, often unconsciously, and making it part of the self.

Framing. Some girls brought a feminist frame to media content that led them to critique it. For Melissa, 13, and a few of the other girls, one of the main problems with sexual content in the media was that it did not allow room for female sexual desire or initiative. An advertisement for a diamond ring that featured a woman caressing a man as she sits on his lap in a rocking chair was the catalyst for this journal entry: "For once they've got the positions turned around to show how things really are. The woman can be on top, too. A woman has as many needs as a man believe it or not advertisers. It doesn't always take a diamond either to 'get in the mood.'"

Cultivation. Despite such strong feminist critiques, most of the girls we have interviewed have held an abiding faith in finding true love, a cultural model they act on in their own lives. Girls at all stages of sexual development and experience looked for and found reinforcement for a romantic myth in the media. Lang, 14, laid out the romantic fantasy script in eight pages in her journal with images cut from teen girl magazines. The series began with an ad suggesting that girls have to compete with each other for men, included ads depicting beautiful men and women in passionate embraces, and ended with the image of a happy bride and groom getting into a convertible under the headline, "We've only just begun. . . ." In keeping with cultivation theory (Gerbner, Gross, Morgan, & Signorielli, 1994), the romantic myth over time begins to seem real.

Emotional Conditioning. True to her words ("I can't be in here [her bedroom] without music"), Emily had the radio on during her room interview. At one point, she interrupted herself midsentence, exclaiming, "That's David's and my song! I can almost smell his cologne when it comes on."

Identified by Thorson (1989) as a conditioned response stored in memory, this type of media association may help to explain the cumulative effects of media exposure over a lifetime. Although space precludes a full discussion of Thorson's perspective, her insight that consumer attitudes and behavior may be affected through an "inattentive mode of processing" (p. 398) that hinges on involvement, interest, or motivation moves our thinking about adolescents' application of media messages in a useful direction. If consumers often act using memory content of which they are unaware, the implications for media effects research are important.

Conclusion

This final example returns us to the model. Like all models, the Adolescents' Media Practice Model is a "consciously simplified description in graphic form of a piece of reality" (McQuail & Windahl, 1993, p. 2). That piece of reality is what we have learned from our room culture research with adolescents. To summarize:

1. Adolescents are active in much of their use of the media. They choose which media they will attend to, and they

choose favorite characters and models to emulate and lust after (Selection). They debate and consider the meaning and significance of portrayals, images, and symbols (Interaction). And they apply those meanings in their everyday lives, sometimes actively, but at other times unconsciously (Application).

2. Basic sociocultural factors such as gender and race as well as the conditions of their own lives influence what is attended to and how media content is interpreted and applied by teens (Lived Experience).

3. Adolescents' sense of who they are and who they may someday want to become plays a central role in their use of media—affecting what media are attended to, how intensely, and to what effect—while at the same time feeding forward and changing the sense of self in the process (Identity).

Taking all of these factors into consideration, we argue that traditional categories of media activity are components of a continuous, dialectical process of cultural and social production and reproduction. The impact of this process is at once constrained and amplified by what is available in the media and by what adolescents bring to the media.

By foregrounding identity and taking a practice perspective, the model helps explain why media effects, traditionally perceived as changes in attitudes, opinions, or behavior, have been so elusive. The media's influence on adolescents' sense of themselves is complex and realized through everyday activities and routines, making effects extremely difficult to measure—not because the media are weak and the audience strong, but rather because they are intricately woven into the fabric of daily life. This view underscores the need for more longitudinal, qualitative studies that explore the relationship between adolescents' everyday media practices and identity.

Too little is known about the effects of repeated exposure to ever larger doses of media sex and violence, often unaccompanied by the types of negative outcomes that might deter emulation. What happens, for example, to children who start repeating gangsta rap lyrics from the time they are 2 or 3? What is the effect of middle school students dialing up 1–800–585-SEXX and listening to "Hi, baby, I'm wet, wild, and willing to do anything and everything to please you for only $3.99 a minute. I want to make you scream," followed by the domestic and international pay phone numbers to call?

We may not be able to design experimental studies capable of explaining the cumulative effects of such practices, but we know they exist and we know that they feed into the process of identity construction. Our data demonstrate that as teens participate more in domains of the adult world, they tend to seek and pay attention to relevant information from the media. And we have seen that even teens who come to the media with other points of view may over time be influenced by dominant media messages (Gerbner et al., 1994; McRobbie, 1982).

Our work with teens in their most intimate space has shown us the value of qualitative work. Bedrooms demonstrate that most teens draw heavily from the media, and bedrooms can say volumes about who teens are. As one teen summed it up: "I guess it's really my room in general that's just really me."

REFERENCES

Arnett, J. J. (1995). Adolescents' uses of media for self-socialization. *Journal of Youth and Adolescence, 24,* 519–533.

Bentley, G. C. (1987). Ethnicity and practice. *Comparative Studies in Society and History, 29,* 24–55.

Biocca, F. (1988). Opposing conceptions of the audience: The active and passive hemisphere of mass communication theory. In J. A. Anderson (Ed.), *Community Yearbook 11.* Beverly Hills, CA: Sage.

Bourdieu, P. (1977). *Outline of a theory of practice.* Cambridge: Cambridge University Press.

Bourdieu, P. (1990). *The logic of practice.* Stanford, CA: Stanford University Press.

Brown, J. D., White, A. B., & Nikopoulou, L. (1993). Disinterest, intrigue, and resistance: Early adolescent girls' use of sexual media content. In B. Greenberg, J. D. Brown, & N. Buerkel-Rothfuss (Eds.), *Media, sex, and the adolescent.* Cresskill, NJ: Hampton Press.

Brown, L. M., & Gilligan, C. (1992). *Meeting at the crossroads: Women's psychology and girls' development.* Cambridge, MA: Harvard University Press.

Csikszentmihalyi, M., & Larson, R. (1984). *Being adolescent: Conflict and growth in the teenage years.* New York: Basic Books.

Dervin, B. (1980). Communication gaps and inequities: Moving toward a reconceptualization. In B. Dervin & M. J. Voigt (Eds.), *Progress in communication sciences* (Vol. 2). Norwood, NJ: Ablex.

Gerbner, G., Gross, L., Morgan, M., & Signorielli, N. (1994). In J. Bryant & D. Zillmann (Eds.), *Media effects: Advances in theory and research.* Hillsdale, NJ: Lawrence Erlbaum.

Gitlin, T. (1991). The politics of communication and the communication of politics. In J. Currant & M. Gurevitch (Eds.), *Mass media and society.* New York: Edward Arnold.

Hall, S. (1986). On postmodernism and articulation: An interview with Stuart Hall. *Journal of Community Inquiry, 10,* 45–60.

Heath, S. B. (1982). What no bedtime story means: Narrative skills at home and school. *Language and Society, 11,* 49–76.

Heisley, D. D., & Levy, S. J. (1991). Autodriving: A photoelicitation technique. *Journal of Consumer Research, 18,* 257–272.

Kosicki, G. M., & McLeod, J. M. (1990). Learning from political news: Effects of media images and information-processing strategies. In S. Kraus (Ed.), *Mass communication and information processing.* Hillsdale, NJ: Lawrence Erlbaum.

Larson, R. (1995). Secrets in the bedroom: Adolescents' private use of media. *Journal of Youth and Adolescence, 24,* 535–550.

Lave, J., Duguid, P., Fernandez, N., & Axel, E. (1992). Coming of age in Birmingham: Cultural studies and conceptions of subjectivity. *Annual Review of Anthropology, 21,* 257–282.

Levy, M., & Windahl, S. (1985). *Media gratification research: Current perspectives.* Beverly Hills, CA: Sage.

Markus, H., & Nurius, P. (1986). Possible selves. *American Psychologist, 41,* 954–969.

Mason, J. (Ed.). (1983). *The family of woman.* New York: Putnam.

McQuail, D., & Windhal, S. (1993). *Communication models for the study of mass communication.* London: Longman.

McRobbie, A. (1982). "Jackie": And ideology of adolescent femininity. In B. Waites, T. Bennett & G. Martin (Eds.), *Popular culture: Past and present.* London: Croom Helm.

McRobbie, A., & Graber, J. (1975). Girls and subcultures. In S. Hall & T. Jefferson (Eds.), *Resistance through rituals: Youth subcultures in post-war Britain.* London: Hutchinson.

Moffatt, M. (1989). *Coming of age in New Jersey: College and American culture.* New Brunswick, NJ: Rutgers University Press.

Moffitt, M. A. (1993). Articulating meaning: Reconceptions of the meaning process, fantasy/reality, and identity in leisure activities. *Community Theory, 3,* 231–251.

Rogoff, B. (1990). *Apprenticeship in thinking: Cognitive development in social context.* New York: Oxford University Press.

Rook, D. W. (1991). I was observed (in absentia) and auto-driven by the consumer behavior odyssey. In R. W. Belk (Ed.), *Highways and buyways: Naturalistic research from the consumer behavior odyssey.* Provo, UT: Association for Consumer Research.

Rubin, A. M. (1994). Media uses and effects: A uses-and-gratifications perspective. In J. Bryant & D. Zillman (Eds.), *Media effects: Advances in theory and research.* Hillsdale, NJ: Lawrence Erlbaum.

Schwichtenberg, C. (1989). The "mother lode" of feminist research: Congruent paradigms in the analysis of beauty culture. In B. Dervin, L. Grossberg, B. J. O'Keefe, & Wartella, E. (Eds.), *Rethinking communication, Vol. 2, Paradigm exemplars.* Newbury Park, CA: Sage.

Snow, D. A., & Anderson, L. (1987). Identity work among the homeless: The verbal construction and avowal of personal identities. *American Journal of Sociology, 92,* 1336–1371.

Swidler, A. (1986). Culture in action: Symbols and strategies. *American Sociological Review, 51,* 273–286.

Thorson, E. (1989). Processing television commercials. In B. Dervin, L. Grossberg, B. J. O'Keefe, & E. Wartella (Eds.), *Rethinking communication: Vol. 2, Paradigm exemplars.* Newbury Park, CA: Sage.

Valsiner, J. (1991). Building theoretical bridges over a lagoon of everyday events: A review of *Apprenticeship in thinking: Cognitive development in social context* by Barbara Rogoff. *Human Development, 34,* 307–315.

Vygotsky, L. S. (1978). Mind in society: The development of higher psychological processes. In M. Cole, V. John-Steiner, S. Scribner, & E. Souberman (Eds.). Cambridge, MA: Harvard University Press.

Wallendorf, M., & Arnould, E. J. (1988). "My favorite things": A cross-cultural inquiry into object attachment, possessiveness, and social linkage. *Journal of Consumer Research, 14,* 531–547.

Wertsch, J. V. (1991). *Voices of the mind: A sociocultural approach to mediated action.* Cambridge, MA: Harvard University Press.

Willis, P. (1990). *Common culture.* Boulder, CO: Westview Press.

Zinn, L. (1994, April 11). Teens here comes the biggest wave yet. *Business Week,* p. 76 and following.

THINKING CRITICALLY

1. Explain how girls may select media content differently depending on whether they are "Disinterested," "Intrigued," or "Resisters." Do you think similar categories exist for boys?

2. In what way does putting pictures of media stars on their bedroom walls reflect adolescents' "transition from childhood into the world of sexual relationships"?

3. Think about your own use of media. Giving examples, describe the extent to which your experience fits the model described here.

4. Explain how Interpretation is similar to and different from Application. Give an example, either from the text here or from your own experience.

XIII Problems

Alcohol Use in College

Alcohol use tends to be highest in emerging adulthood and is especially high among college students. This reading examines the reasons for college students' alcohol use, focusing on the weeks following entry into college. An important feature of the study is that it includes "pro-drinking" motivations (social goals, the belief that drinking is fun) as well as "antidrinking" motivations (academic and health goals, the belief that drinking is risky). The results show that social goals and the belief that drinking is fun are especially strong predictors of college drinking.

Reading 13.1

Alcohol Use and Binge Drinking as Goal-Directed Action During the Transition to Postsecondary Education

J. L. Maggs

Alcohol use and binge drinking as goal-directed action during the transition to postsecondary education by J. L. Maggs (1999). From *Health Risks and Developmental Transitions During Adolescence*, edited by J. L. Maggs and K. Hurrelmann, pp. 345–371. Reprinted with the permission of Cambridge University Press.

When adults reminisce about their college days, a common activity is swapping tales about wild parties, experiments with bizarre and often unknown concoctions, outrageous and funny things done while drinking, and other hilariously presented, legendary exploits. Sometimes the tone of the conversation momentarily grows sober as people wonder aloud how they made it through this phase safely or remember an old friend who was not so lucky. But even in the context of such self-reflection, there is also a feeling of regret that this exciting time of life is over, a time when you shared everything with your friends, partied every weekend, and had only yourself to worry about. Of course, this mythical depiction of the carefree life of the college student does not represent the diversity of actual experiences, but as a legend it is a powerful image that evokes nostalgia in some adults, a feeling of having missed out in others, and excitement in adolescents who still have college to took forward to.

More than half of North American adolescents go on to some form of postsecondary education after completing high school (W. T. Grant Commission, 1988). In addition to greatly enhancing occupational prospects, going to college tends to slow the passage to adulthood (Sherrod, Haggerty, & Featherman, 1993). Because individuals typically leave school before commencing full-time employment or starting a family, the timing of the assumption of adult roles (e.g., worker, spouse, parent) is greatly influenced by the amount of time spent in formal education (Marini, 1984, 1985). That is, adolescents who go to college tend to start their first full-time job, marry, and have children later than those who complete their education by the end of high school. A more gradual passage toward adulthood may have many noneducational benefits (W. T. Grant Commission, 1988). For many individuals, the college years represent an opportunity to postpone the assumption of full adult responsibilities while continuing to learn, explore ideas, and pursue personal and academic interests (Pascarella & Terenzini, 1991). Likewise, individuals can experiment with various adult behaviors, values, and lifestyles. In other words, the college experience can provide a safe haven for exploration, a developmental moratorium (Sherrod et al., 1993).

This chapter focuses on the use of alcohol as a representative risk behavior during the transition to university life. The chapter argues that late adolescent and young adult alcohol use and binge drinking can be usefully conceived of as purposive action directed toward the pursuit of developmentally normative goals. The introduction discusses the characteristics of this major developmental transition, the prevalence and functions of alcohol use during adolescence and young adulthood, and the theoretical assumptions and hypotheses that guided the research. Subsequent sections describe the study, in which late adolescent university students completed questionnaires about their adjustment, goals, beliefs about alcohol, and drinking behavior on two occasions as they began their first year and were adjusting to life in a college residence.

Developmental Transitions and Risk Behaviors

Why is the transition to postsecondary education a particularly interesting time to study risk behaviors such as alcohol use? First, moving away from home to begin postsecondary education leads to dramatic changes in the physical context and in normative expectations for social and academic behavior (Aseltine & Gore, 1993; Prentice & Miller, 1993). As students begin life in this new environment, they are likely to set personal goals for the upcoming year (Cantor, Norem, Niedenthal, Langston, & Brower, 1987). Focusing on students' personal characteristics, goals, and beliefs as factors shaping their drinking behavior will advance our understanding of the functions served by risky behaviors such as binge drinking. Second, moving away from home leads to significant changes in opportunities in many domains (Cantor, 1994), not the least of which is risky behavior. University administrators and resident assistants do not and cannot care for individual adolescents and protect them from harm to the same extent as loving parents do. Thus opportunities for potentially risky activities such as eating unhealthy foods, drinking, using drugs, and having risky sex are likely to increase. Desires to experiment that were previously suppressed or limited to rare occasions may be more easily fulfilled in the new, more independent living situation. Therefore, this period of transition, during which opportunities to experiment expand greatly, provides a window into how adolescents shape their own behavior, given the opportunity.

Prevalence of Alcohol Use on Campus

High school and college students widely report using alcohol. For example, 72% of 20- to 24-year-old Canadians reported drinking alcohol regularly, and 20% of males and 4% of females reported consuming eight or more drinks on one occasion in the previous week (Siggner, 1988). The frequency and quantity of drinking increase throughout adolescence, peak in the early twenties, and then tend to decline as adult roles are initiated (Jessor, Donovan, & Costa, 1991; Kandel & Yamaguchi, 1985; Sharpe & Lowe, 1989). In addition to these age trends, alcohol use is particularly high among college students, especially those living in dormitories and fraternities/sororities (Crowley, 1991; O'Hare, 1990). The annual U.S. Monitoring the Future surveys, for example, show that among 19- to 22-year-old Americans, college students have a slightly higher annual prevalence of alcohol use than noncollege youth (87% versus 84%, respectively), a higher monthly prevalence of use (72% versus 63%), and a higher 2-week prevalence of binge drinking (40% versus 34%) (Johnston, O'Malley, & Bachman, 1994).

Functions of Alcohol Use and Binge Drinking

Alcohol consumption was selected as the focus risk behavior for this study because of the very high prevalence of alcohol use and binge drinking among late adolescent and young adult students and because of the potential for

serious negative consequences due to alcohol misuse (Siggner, 1988). The role played by drinking alcohol in adolescents' lives is paradoxical, just as it is for other so-called problem behaviors (Maggs, Almeida, & Galambos, 1995; Maggs & Hurrelmann, 1996). Despite the possibility of serious harm from binge drinking and alcohol misuse, drinking also may serve important constructive functions for adolescents, such as helping them to make friends, let off steam, indicate a transition to a more mature status, or explore personal identities (Chassin, Presson, & Sherman, 1989). Prevalence studies show that it is more normative to drink during adolescence than it is not to drink (Johnston et al., 1994; Moffitt, 1993). In fact, some scientists have argued that experimenting with risk behaviors such as drinking alcohol has become one of the developmental tasks or rites of passage of adolescence in Western societies (e.g., Baumrind, 1985; Jessor, 1987; Schulenberg, O'Malley, Bachman, Wadsworth, & Johnston, 1996; Shedler & Block, 1990). Understanding how and why adolescents use alcohol as they negotiate the transition into adulthood is essential for planning health promotion efforts aimed at minimizing the negative consequences of alcohol misuse (Leventhal & Keeshan, 1993).

Behavior as Goal-Directed Action: Theoretical Perspective and Hypotheses

The developmental action perspective provides a useful framework for understanding adolescent alcohol use. The action perspective assumes that human development is initiated and directed by the intentions and goals of developing individuals. That is, humans shape their own development through goal-directed action. The term *action* is used to denote purposive, self-directed behavior (Silbereisen & Eyferth, 1986). Applying a developmental action perspective to adolescent alcohol use, individuals are assumed to have attributes that direct their decisions about engaging in this potentially risky behavior. These attributes can be said to motivate drinking behavior (Jessor,

1987). Thus drinking can be viewed as rational, goal-directed action. In the present study, individual differences in psychosocial adjustment, personal goals, and beliefs about drinking alcohol were hypothesized to predict levels of alcohol use and binge drinking.

Summary and Hypotheses

The present study viewed students' alcohol use as a purposive behavior directed toward the attainment of instrumental, developmentally relevant goals. Participants were older adolescents moving into student residences at the start of their first year of university. The extent to which psychosocial adjustment, personal goals, and beliefs about alcohol predicted alcohol use and binge drinking was examined. The hypotheses were as follows: (1) students with more positive self-images will drink less and students who feel more accepted by their peers will drink more; (2) students with high social goals will drink more, and students with high academic goals and high health goals will drink less; and (3) beliefs about the fun and risk of alcohol will predict drinking. Finally, it was hypothesized that (4) goals and beliefs that *promote* or *encourage* drinking (social goals, the belief that drinking is fun) will be more strongly related to drinking than goals and beliefs that *hinder* or *discourage* drinking (academic goals, health goals, the belief that drinking is risky).

Method

Participants and Procedure

The participants were 344 students living in on-campus residences at a medium-sized Canadian university. The estimated response rate was 79%. The mean age was 18.7 years ($SD = 1.0$); 74% were younger than the legal drinking age of 19 years. However, participants reported experiencing relatively few obstacles to drinking. For example, when they wanted to drink, 76% reported having people to drink with, 79% were able to acquire alcohol, and 88% had a place to drink most or all of the time. Questionnaires were completed by the participants dur-

ing their first week of the fall semester as they began living in a university residence. Three weeks later, a second set of questionnaires was completed (matched $n = 169$). The collection of data concerning plans to drink and actual drinking permitted the evaluation of the extent to which psychosocial adjustment, personal goals, and beliefs about alcohol predicted planned drinking, actual drinking, and differences between planned and actual drinking. Participants were assured that all responses would be anonymous, and informed consent was obtained in writing. Although there was considerable attrition between Time 1 and Time 2, analyses revealed no significant differences between those who remained and those who dropped out with respect to demographic variables, alcohol use, or any other measured variable.

Measures

Psychosocial Adjustment. Three subscales from the Adolescent Self-Image Questionnaire (Offer, Ostrov, & Howard, 1982) assessed adolescents' feelings about themselves: Impulse Control measured adolescents' resistance to impulsive, violent, or angry behavior (9 items, e.g., "Even under pressure, I manage to remain calm"); Mastery and Coping assessed confidence in coping (10 items, e.g., "When I decide to do something, I do it"); and Emotional Tone measured positive affect (9 items, e.g., "Most of the time, I am happy"). Subjects rated items on a 6-point scale ranging from 1 = Does not describe me at all to 6 = Describes me very well, with higher scores indicating a more positive self-image. Offer et al. (1982) demonstrated the psychometric adequacy of these measures. In the present sample, alphas were .64, .67, and .80, for the three subscales, respectively. The three self-image subscales were closely interrelated. To reduce the number of predictors, the three self-image subscales were combined into one "self-image" scale.

Peer Acceptance was measured using the Offer et al. (1982) nine-item peer acceptance scale. Participants indicated how confident and positive they felt about their relationships with their peers. A sample item was "I do not have a particularly difficult time in making friends," rated on the same 6-point scale as for self-image. Mean scores were computed, with higher scores indicating that adolescents felt more accepted by their peers. Cronbach's alpha was .80.

Personal Goals. Students were asked to rate the importance of achieving certain goals during the upcoming academic year. Three categories of goals were assessed: Social Goals (six items, e.g., "make new friends"), Academic Goals (three items, e.g., "do well in all your courses"), and Health Goals (three items, e.g., "work out/participate in sports regularly"). Possible responses ranged from 1 = Not at all important to me to 5 = Very important to me. Alphas for the three scales were .80, .82, and .71, respectively.

Beliefs About Drinking Alcohol. Participants indicated how Fun and how Risky they thought it was to drink alcohol. Possible responses on these two single-item measures ranged from 1 = Not at all Fun to 4 = Very Fun and from 1 = Not at all Risky to 4 = Very Risky.

Drinking Behavior. Questions adapted from previous research were used to measure alcohol use and binge drinking (Donovan, Costa, & Jessor, 1985; Health & Welfare Canada, 1988). To measure Planned Alcohol Use, participants were asked (1) how often they planned to drink alcohol in the upcoming three weeks (possible responses ranged from 1 = Never to 6 = Every day) (frequency) and (2) how many drinks they planned to drink per average drinking occasion (possible responses ranged from 1 = none to 7 = 12 or more) (quantity). These two items were multiplied to yield a quantity-frequency estimate of alcohol use. To measure Planned Binge Drinking, participants indicated (3) how many times they planned to consume five or more drinks on one occasion in the next 3 weeks and (4) how many times they planned to get drunk in the next 3 weeks. Response formats were the same as for item (1). The mean of these two items

was taken. At Time 2, these four questions were repeated with respect to the quantity and frequency of Actual Alcohol Use and Actual Binge Drinking in the 3 weeks between Time 1 and Time 2. Coefficient alphas for the binge drinking scales were .93 for planned drinking and .92 for actual drinking.

Results

Descriptive Analyses

Levels of planned and actual drinking were similar to those found in other Canadian and American surveys (e.g., Johnston et al., 1994; Siggner, 1988). For example, 74% and 45% of students planned to use alcohol and get drunk at least once, respectively, in the upcoming 3 weeks; 72% and 49% actually did so. Plans to drink were quite closely related to actual drinking behavior, as indicated by large correlations between planned and actual alcohol use and between planned and actual binge drinking, $r =$ .69 and .67, both $p < .001$. The quantities of alcohol respondents reported actually consuming per average drinking occasion were 1 drink (9%), 2 to 3 drinks (33%), 4 to 6 drinks (34%), to 9 drinks (18%), and 10 or more drinks (7%). Two one-way MANOVAs examined gender differences in alcohol use and binge drinking. Planned and actual drinking were analyzed in separate analyses because of the different n. Both multivariate F values were significant at $p < .001$. Univariate tests showed that, relative to females, males had higher planned alcohol use, $F(1, 343) = 12.3$, $p < .001$, planned binge drinking, $F(1, 343) = 17.0$, $p < .001$, actual alcohol use, $F(1, 167) = 4.27$, $p < .05$, and actual binge drinking, $F(1, 166) = 12.2$, $p < .01$.

Prediction of Intended and Actual Drinking Behavior

The first three hypotheses stated that drinking behavior would be predicted by psychosocial adjustment, personal goals, and beliefs about alcohol. These hypotheses were evaluated using a series of multiple regression analyses. Gender was entered on a first step as a control variable because males' physical size and metabolism allow them to drink more alcohol than females. Three steps added the psychosocial adjustment variables (self-image, peer acceptance), personal goals (social, academic, and health goals), and beliefs about alcohol (fun, risk), respectively. Table 13.1.1 presents the results of these analyses, including bivariate correlations between the predictors and criterion variables, standardized regression coefficients for each predictor at the step it was added to the equation, change in R^2 for each step, and total R^2, for each of the four criterion variables.

On the first step, gender predicted 4–7% of the variance in drinking, with males drinking and binge drinking more than females, as expected. The second step examined the relationship of psychosocial adjustment with alcohol use and binge drinking. From 12% to 14% of the variance in drinking was explained by the two predictors. Inspection of the correlations shows that students who felt more accepted by their peers planned to and actually did engage in more alcohol use and binge drinking, as hypothesized. Contrary to the hypothesis, self-image was not related bivariately to alcohol use or binge drinking. Nonetheless, self-image was a consistent predictor of drinking when levels of peer acceptance were controlled. That is, peer acceptance appeared to suppress the relationship of self-image and drinking (Pedhazur, 1982). In other words, students who had a more negative self-image than their level of peer acceptance would predict tended to drink more than students whose self-image was more positive than their level of peer acceptance would predict.

The third step added the students' social, academic, and health goals to the equation, explaining an additional 6–11% of the variance in the drinking measures. The importance of social goals consistently predicted alcohol use and binge drinking, both bivariately and when entered with the other predictors. That is, students who felt it was more important that they make friends and be popular tended to drink more alcohol. The importance of academic goals and health goals was much less consistently related to drinking, and the magnitude of the bivariate correlations and regression co-

efficients was much smaller, than those for social goals. Believing academic goals were important predicted less planned binge drinking during the first 3 weeks of the semester but was not related to planned or actual alcohol use or to actual binge drinking. Believing health goals were important predicted less planned alcohol use and binge drinking but was not related to actual drinking. Only one of the eight bivariate correlations was significant.

A final step added students' beliefs about how fun and how risky they thought it was to drink alcohol. These two single-item predictors explained an additional 21–28% of the variance in planned and actual alcohol use and binge drinking. The bivariate correlations showed that the belief that drinking was fun was consistently strongly related to higher alcohol use and binge drinking ($r = .55$ to .71), and the belief that drinking was risky was consistently related to drinking less ($r = -.35$ to .41), both as hypothesized. When entered together with the other predictor variables, Fun maintained a strong positive independent prediction ($\beta = .44$ to .58) and Risk retained a minimal independent prediction ($\beta = -.05$ to $-.14$). A total of 44–57% of the variance in drinking was explained by the full set of predictors.

The Relative Salience of Motivations to Drink and Motivations to Not Drink

In order to address the hypothesis that motivations to drink would be more predictive of levels of alcohol and binge drinking than motivations to not drink or to limit drinking, a separate set of regressions was performed. The first two steps were identical to the previous analyses. On the third step, two blocks of predictors were entered simultaneously. One block contained the prodrinking characteristics and motivations to drink: social goals and the belief that drinking is fun (Block A). The other block contained the antidrinking motivations: academic goals, health goals, and the belief that drinking is risky (Block B). Because Blocks A and B were entered into the equation simultaneously, the R^2 associated with each block represents the unique contribution of the

TABLE 13.1.1 Multiple Regressions Predicting Planned and Actual Alcohol Use and Binge Drinking by Psychosocial Adjustment, Personal Goals, and Beliefs About Drinking

STEP AND PREDICTORS	PLANS TO DRINK			ACTUAL DRINKING			PLANS TO BINGE DRINK			ACTUAL BINGE DRINKING		
	r	β	ΔR^2	r	β	ΔR^2	r	β	ΔR^2	r	β	ΔR^2
Step 1: Gender	.23***	.23***	.05***	.19*	.19*	.04*	.23***	.23***	.05***	.27***	.27***	.07***
Step 2: Psychosocial adjustment												
Self-image	.06	-.26**		.02	-.29**		.01	-.31***		.01	-.29**	
Peer acceptance	.30***	.46***	.12***	.30***	.46***	.14***	.25***	.44***	.12***	.29***	.46***	.14***
Step 3: Personal goals												
Social	.43***	.36***		.29***	.23**		.40***	.33***		.33***	.23**	
Academic	-.08	-.08		-.12	-.06		-.11*	-.10*		-.15	-.06	
Health	-.05	-.13**	.11***	-.13	-.15	.06**	-.06	-.12*	.10***	-.11	-.15	.06**
Step 4: Beliefs about alcohol												
Fun	.71***	.58***		.60***	.44***		.63***	.48***		.55***	.44***	
Risk	-.35***	-.05	.28***	-.41***	-.14*	.21***	-.38***	-.12**	.22***	-.40***	-.14*	.21***
Total R^2 (adjusted R^2)			.57 (.56)***			.44 (.42)***			.49 (.47)***			.44 (.42)***

Note: $n = 340$ for Plans, $n = 164$ for Actual. r = Pearson correlation. β = standardized beta. ΔR^2 = change in R^2 for each step.

*$p < .05$. **$p < .01$. ***$p < .001$.

prodrinking and antidrinking motivations, respectively, to the prediction of alcohol use and binge drinking. The results of this analysis showed that, as hypothesized, prodrinking motivations made a substantially larger unique contribution to the prediction of alcohol use and binge drinking ($R^2 = .13$ to $.31$) than did antidrinking motivations ($R^2 = .01$ to $.03$)

Predictors of Drinking More or Less Than Intended

The previous analyses showed that the predictors of planned and actual alcohol use were very similar, and these did not vary systematically by level of drinking (i.e., alcohol use versus binge drinking). The strong relationship between planned and actual alcohol use and binge drinking indicated that plans to drink were often realized. However, these correlations between intended and actual drinking also showed that over half of the variance in actual alcohol use was not accounted for by plans to drink ($1 - .69^2 = 52\%$). A final series of analyses examined the extent to which psychosocial adjustment, personal goals, and beliefs about alcohol accounted for *differences* between intended and actual drinking. Thus these analyses examined factors that predicted drinking more or less than intended.

Table 13.1.2 presents the results of the two multiple regressions, which followed the same strategy as those reported in Table 1 with the addition in Step 1 of plans to drink and binge drink, respectively. The criterion variables were actual drinking and binge drinking at Time 2. By thus controlling for plans to drink alcohol on the first step, the remaining steps in the regression analyses examined the extent to which the set of predictors accounted for discrepancies between intentions to drink and actual drinking behavior. As before, the first step also included gender.

The results for Step 1 showed that in addition to the large and significant relationship of planned to actual drinking, gender was a significant predictor of binge drinking. Examination of the means for males and females showed that males binge drank more than

planned and females binge drank less than planned. Step 2 added self-image and peer acceptance. The pattern of results for drinking was similar to that in the previous regressions, with low self-image emerging as a predictor of drinking more than intended only when peer acceptance was included in the equation. Having high peer acceptance was related to drinking more and binge drinking more than intended. Step 3 added the three personal goals variables to the equation, with no additional significant relationships. Finally, Step 4 added beliefs about the fun and risk associated with drinking alcohol, with an additional 2% of the variance explained for drinking and 3% for binge drinking. Believing that drinking alcohol was fun predicted drinking and binge drinking more than intended during the first 3 weeks of school, and believing that drinking alcohol was risky predicted drinking less than intended.

Discussion
Psychosocial Adjustment

The relationship between the psychosocial adjustment variables and drinking behavior supported the paradox hypothesis about normative risk-taking behaviors. That is, although people who felt accepted by their peers also reported feeling good with respect to themselves in general, peer acceptance and general self-image were differentially related to alcohol use and binge drinking. Those who felt more accepted by their peers planned to and actually did drink more, and those who felt positively about their own impulse control, mastery, and emotional tone planned to drink less, consistent with previous research on younger adolescents (Maggs et al., 1995). Higher peer acceptance and more negative self-image together also predicted drinking more than planned. Subsequent analyses in the present sample supported the interpretation that the positive effect of drinking on feelings of peer acceptance suppressed the negative bivariate relationship of self-image and drinking. That is, self-image emerged as a significant predictor of

TABLE 13.1.2 Multiple Regressions Predicting Discrepancy Between Planned and Actual Alcohol Use by Self-Image, Personal Goals, and Beliefs About Drinking

STEP AND PREDICTORS	ACTUAL DRINKING			ACTUAL BINGE DRINKING		
	spr	β	ΔR^2	spr	β	ΔR^2
Step 1: Control variables						
Planned alcohol use[a]	.69***[b]	.68***		.67**[b]	.65***	
Gender	.05	.03	.47***	.21**	.16**	.48***
Step 2: Psychosocial adjustment						
Self-image	.01	−.15*		.09	−.09	
Peer acceptance	.21**	.25***	.04***	.21**	.21**	.03*
Step 3: Personal goals						
Social	−.05	−.05		.05	.02	
Academic	−.03	−.04		−.01	−.00	
Health	−.09	−.07	.01	−.04	−.03	.00
Step 4: Beliefs about alcohol						
Fun	.22**	.17*		.20**	.18*	
Risk	−.19*	−.09	.02**	−.17*	−.07	.03**
Total R^2 (adjusted R^2)			.54 (.51)***			.53 (.51)***

Note: $n = 164$. spr = semipartial correlation, controlling for Time 1 drinking measure.
β = standardized beta. ΔR^2 = change in R^2 for each step.
[a]Planned alcohol use and planned binge drinking.
[b]Correlation of Time 1 with Time 2 score.
*$p < .05$. ** $p < .01$. *** $p < .001$.

drinking only when levels of peer acceptance were controlled.

The suppression by peer acceptance of the relationship between self-image and drinking behavior may help to explain past inconsistent results with self-esteem and alcohol use (e.g., Jessor et al., 1991; Newcomb, Bentler, & Collins, 1986; Windle & Barnes, 1988). If some risk behaviors have both positive and negative antecedents and consequences for individuals, understanding the nature of these relationships may be very difficult. This finding is not surprising considering the strong contradictory messages about alcohol in North American culture (Peele, 1993). Films, television programs, beer advertisements, and popular legends about late adolescent binge drinking present a positive and alluring image of the fun and good times associated with alcohol use. In contrast, many negative images about alcohol use and abuse also abound: public service announcements against drinking and driving, minimum legal purchase ages (21 in the United States, 18 or 19 in Canada), stiff penalties for drinking and driving, alcohol-related fatality statistics, and so on. The current results are consistent with the opposing influences on adolescents (and adults) with respect to drinking alcohol. That is, drinking was associated with greater interpersonal competence and confidence in interpersonal domains but also was related to less positive psychological adjustment. Thus the paradoxical regard in which alcohol is held in North American culture was reflected at the individual level: drinking appeared to be both good and bad.

Personal Goals

Developmental role transitions such as starting university or moving away from home have important consequences for personal goal setting because they provide a basis for anticipating what is possible, acceptable, and desirable at different ages and in different contexts (Nurmi, 1993). The results for the importance of social goals supported the proposition that drinking alcohol can be a rational behavior directed toward the attainment of developmentally and situationally relevant personal goals (Cantor, 1994; Silbereisen & Eyferth, 1986). The lack of consistent inhibitory effects of academic and health goals on alcohol use or binge drinking suggests that (1) students do not view drinking during the first weeks of the semester as having a negative effect on their academic performance and health; (2) drinking is so subjectively rewarding that any negative consequences are viewed as acceptable side effects; (3) drinking behavior is guided by forces other than rational decision making; or (4) some combination of these three factors. The fact that social, academic, and health goals did not predict differences between intentions to drink and actual drinking behavior suggests that the effect of personal goals on drinking was already accounted for by intentions or plans to drink. An important caveat to these results is that all data were collected during the first month of the first year of university, before academic demands and deadlines were in full swing. It is probable that the importance of academic goals would be significantly related to variables such as the cumulative number of nights spent socializing per semester or to alcohol use data collected during midterms or final exams.

Beliefs About Fun and Risk

The magnitude of the relationship between fun and risk ratings with planned and actual drinking behavior is remarkable in light of the simplicity of the measurement of fun and risk. By themselves, the single-item measures of fun and risk accounted for 30–50% and 12–17% of the variance in drinking, respectively. These two

variables also added substantially to the prediction of planned drinking, actual drinking, and differences between planned and actual drinking above and beyond the effects of psychosocial adjustment and personal goals. This result underscores the importance of taking seriously the perspective of adolescents and the factors they consider as they make decisions about potentially risky yet immediately rewarding behaviors such as alcohol use and binge drinking (cf. Furby & Beyth-Marom, 1992). In particular, programs aiming to prevent or reduce undue risk-taking need to acknowledge the positive functions served by these behaviors.

Relative Salience of Positive Versus Negative Consequences

Prodrinking motivations (social goals, believing that drinking is fun) were much more strongly predictive of alcohol use and binge drinking than were antidrinking motivations (academic goals, health goals, believing that drinking is risky). This suggests that despite the potential dangers and disadvantages of drinking too much, the desire to partake in social activities involving alcohol is a strong force for students beginning university. Why would motivations to drink be so much more salient than motivations to not drink or to limit drinking? Positive functions of drinking, such as making friends and having fun, may be more salient because they are experienced more immediately than negative functions such as damaging one's health or failing an exam. A related possibility is that positive outcomes may seem more likely than negative ones. For example, the likelihood of meeting new people at any given party is high, whereas the likelihood of getting fat or having an accident on any given night is relatively low.

Directions for Future Research

The current results support the argument that risk behaviors play a constructive role in adolescent development (Jessor, 1987; Maggs et al., 1995; Maggs & Hurrelmann, 1996; Silbereisen & Noack, 1988). The strong relationship between prodrinking motivations and alcohol use/binge drinking underscores the importance of taking very seriously the subjective functions served by risk behaviors such as drinking for adolescents and young adults. Future research would benefit by explicitly considering adolescents and young adults as active shapers and directors of their own behavior and development within the opportunities furnished by their environments (Hurrelmann, 1989). Prevention and health promotion programs that target behavior typically assume that individuals have the power or ability to change their own behavior. We need theoretical models that test and conditions under which this assumption is true.

An important direction for future research on this topic would be to systematically incorporate normative variations in the transition to university life as an aspect of the research design, as has been done, for example, concerning the transition to junior and senior high schools (Simmons & Blyth, 1987). Inter- and intracampus variations in college housing options (e.g., dormitory versus living with parents versus off-campus housing versus fraternity/sorority house), housing policies (e.g., no alcohol versus limited use permitted), and recreational opportunities (e.g., active campus culture versus commuter community) could be examined to determine their impact on students' drinking habits, social integration, and general adjustment to campus life. Longer-term longitudinal studies are needed to assess the continuing impact of personal characteristics on social and academic behavior, as well as potential consequences of behaviors such as drinking on multiple domains of life.

REFERENCES

Aseltine, R. H., Jr., & Gore, S. (1993). Mental health and social adaptation following the transition from high school. *Journal of Research on Adolescence, 3,* 247–270.

Baumrind, D. (1985). Familial antecedents of adolescent drug use: A developmental perspective. In C. LaRue Jones & R. J. Battjes (Eds.), *Etiology of drug use: Implications for prevention. NIDA Research Monograph 56: A RAUS Report* (pp. 13–44). Rockville, MD: National Institute on Drug Use.

Cantor, N. (1994). Life task problem solving: Situational affordances and personal needs. *Personality and Social Psychology Bulletin, 20,* 235–243.

Cantor, N., Norem, J. K., Niedenthal, P. M., Langston, C. A., & Brower, A. M. (1987). Life tasks, self-concept ideals, and cognitive strategies in a life transition. *Journal of Personality and Social Psychology, 53,* 1178–1191.

Crowley, J. E. (1991). Educational status and drinking patterns: How representative are college students? *Journal of Studies on Alcohol, 52,* 10–16.

Donovan, J. E., Costa, F. M., & Jessor, R. (1985). *Health questionnaire.* Boulder, CO: University of Colorado, Institute of Behavioral Science.

Furby, L., & Beyth-Marom, R. (1992). Risk taking in adolescence: A decision-making perspective. *Developmental Review, 12,* 1–44.

Hurrelmann, K. (1989). Adolescents as productive processors of reality: Methodological perspectives. In K. Hurrelmann & U. Engel (Eds.), *The social world of adolescents: International perspectives* (pp. 107–118). Berlin: Walter de Gruyter.

Jessor, R. (1987). Problem-behavior theory, psychosocial development, and adolescent problem behavior. *British Journal of Addiction, 82,* 331–342.

Jessor, R., Donovan, J. E., & Costa, F. M. (1991). *Beyond adolescence: Problem behavior and young adult development.* New York: Cambridge University Press.

Johnston, L. D., O'Malley, P. M., & Bachman, J. G. (1994). *National survey results on drug use from the Monitoring the Future Study, 1975–1993.* Rockville, MD: National Institute on Drug Abuse.

Kandel, D. B., & Yamaguchi, K. (1985). Developmental patterns of the use of legal, illegal, and medically prescribed psychotropic drugs from adolescence to adulthood. In C. LaRue Jones (Ed.), *Etiology of drug use: Implications for prevention. NIDA Research Monograph 56: A RAUS report* (pp. 13–44). Rockville, MD: National Institute on Drug Abuse.

Leventhal, H., & Keeshan, P. (1993). Promoting healthy alternatives to substance abuse. In S. G. Millstein, A. C. Petersen, & E. O. Nightingale (Eds.), *Promoting the health of adolescents: New directions for the twenty-first century* (pp. 260–284). New York: Oxford University Press.

Maggs, J. L., Almeida, D. M., & Galambos, N. L. (1995). Risky business: The paradoxical meaning of problem drinking for young adolescents. *Journal of Early Adolescence, 15,* 339–357.

Maggs, J. L., & Hurrelmann, K. (1996). *Do substance use and delinquency have different implications for adolescents' peer relations?* Manuscript in review.

Marini, M. M. (1984). The order of events in the transition to adulthood. *Sociology of Education, 57,* 63–84.

Marini, M. M. (1985). Determinants of the timing of adult role entry. *Sociology of Education, 57,* 309–350.

Moffitt, T. E. (1993). Adolescence-limited and life-course-persistent antisocial behavior: A developmental taxonomy. *Psychological Review, 100,* 674–701.

Newcomb, M. D., Bentler, P. M., & Collins, C. (1986). Alcohol use and dissatisfaction with self and life: A longitudinal analysis. *Journal of Drug Issues, 16,* 479–494.

Nurmi, J.-E. (1993). Adolescent development in an age-graded context: The role of personal beliefs, goals, and strategies in the tackling of developmental tasks and standards. *International Journal of Behavioral Development, 16,* 169–189.

Offer, D., Ostrov, E., & Howard, K. I. (1982). *The Offer self-image questionnaire for adolescents: A manual* (3rd ed.). Chicago: Michael Reese Hospital.

O'Hare, T. M. (1990). Drinking in college: Consumption patterns, problems, sex differences, and legal drinking age. *Journal of Studies on Alcohol, 52,* 500–502.

Pascarella, E. T., & Terenzini, P. T. (1991). *How college affects students.* San Francisco: Jossey-Bass.

Pedhazur, E. J. (1982). *Multiple regression in behavioral research: Explanation and prediction* (2nd ed.). New York: Holt, Reinhart, and Wilson.

Peele, S. (1993). The conflict between public health goals and the temperance mentality. *American Journal of Public Health, 83,* 805–810.

Prentice, D. A., & Miller, D. T. (1993). Pluralistic ignorance and alcohol use on campus: Some consequences of misperceiving the social norm. *Journal of Personality and Social Psychology, 64,* 243–256.

Schulenberg, J. E., O'Malley, P. M., Bachman, J. G., Wadsworth, K. N., & Johnston, L. D. (1996). Getting drunk and growing up: Trajectories of frequent binge drinking during the transition to young adulthood. *Journal of Studies of Alcohol, 57,* 289–304.

Sharpe, D. J., & Lowe, G. (1989). Adolescents and alcohol: A review of the recent British research. *Journal of Adolescence, 12,* 295–307.

Shedler, J., & Block, J. (1990). Adolescent drug use and psychological health: A longitudinal inquiry. *American Psychologist, 45,* 612–630.

Sherrod, L. R., Haggerty, R. J., & Featherman, D. L. (1993). Introduction: Late adolescence and the transition to adulthood. *Journal of Research on Adolescence, 3,* 217–226.

Siggner, A. J. (1988). *Canada's health promotion survey: Technical report series: Special study on youth.* Ottawa: Minister of Supply and Services Canada.

Silbereisen, R. K., & Eyferth, K. (1986). Development as action in context. In R. K. Silbereisen, K. Eyferth, & G. Rudinger (Eds.), *Development as action in context: Problem behavior and normal youth development* (pp. 3–16). Berlin: Springer-Verlag.

Silbereisen, R. K., & Noack, P. (1988). On the constructive role of problem behavior in adolescence. In N. Bolger, A. Caspi, G. Downey, & M. Moorehouse (Eds.), *Persons in context: Developmental processes* (pp. 152–180). Cambridge: Cambridge University Press.

Simmons, R. G., & Blyth, D. A. (1987). *Moving into adolescence: The impact of pubertal change and school context.* New York: Aldine de Gruyter.

W. T. Grant Commission. (1988). *The forgotten half: Pathways to success for America's youth and young families.* Washington, DC: Youth and America's Future: The William T. Grant Commission on Work, Family, and Citizenship.

Windle, M., & Barnes, G. M. (1988). Similarities and differences in correlates of alcohol consumption and problem behaviors among male and female adolescents. *International Journal of the Addictions, 23,* 707–728.

THINKING CRITICALLY

1. Is all alcohol use among young people "potentially risky," as the authors assume here? If not, how would you distinguish between use and abuse?

2. What explanation do the authors give for why fun is a better predictor than risk of college students' alcohol use? What other explanation might you offer?

3. What makes drinking "fun" for many college students? How might the fun of drinking be related to the social situations—meeting many new people, looking for possible intimate relationships—in which college students typically find themselves?

4. In what ways would you predict that the results of this study would be different if it were conducted with juniors and seniors rather than first-year students?

Adolescent Problems in the East and the West

Most research on adolescent problem behavior (such as substance use, physical aggression, and school misconduct) has been conducted in the United States, and most has focused on the role of family environment and peers in such behavior. This reading takes a more cultural approach, comparing patterns of problem behavior in the United States, South Korea, and China. Family and peer variables are included, but they are placed in the broader context of differences in beliefs between cultures and the extent to which each culture has been influenced by globalization.

Reading 13.2

The Perceived Social Contexts of Adolescent Misconduct: A Comparative Study of Youths in Three Cultures

E. Greenberger, C. Chen, M. Beam, S. M. Whang, and Q. Dong

Cross-cultural research on adolescent problem behavior suggests that European and American children and adolescents are more likely to exhibit externalizing behaviors such as physical aggression, defiance, and antisocial acts than are their African and Asian peers (Achenbach, Hensley, Phares, & Grayson, 1990; Achenbach, Verhulst, Baron, & Akkerhuis, 1987; Lambert, Weisz, & Knight, 1989; Weine, Phillips, & Achenbach, 1995). These behavioral differences typically have been interpreted in terms of differences in cultural values or syndromes. Thus, cultures that are higher in "individualism" are thought to be more conducive to the overt expression of deviance than cultures that are more "collectivist"—that is, cultures in which the interdependence of selves tends to encourage suppression of behavior that is socially disapproved.

It is possible, however, that cultural differences in the level of adolescent misconduct do not emerge until middle adolescence—at least among youths of Chinese versus European ancestry. Two sets of investigators failed to find differences in rates of problem behavior of U.S. and Chinese children, early adolescents, or both (Chen, Greenberger, Lester, Dong, & Guo, 1998; Weine et al., 1995); whereas other investigators found that middle adolescents of European ancestry in Australia and the United States reported more misconduct than did their peers of Chinese ancestry in these two countries or in Hong Kong. Chen et al. (1998) suggested that differences in misconduct might emerge by middle adolescence, in response to cultural differences in the extent of parental autonomy-granting (Feldman & Rosenthal, 1990) and peers' influence on one another.

A long line of research in the United States has illuminated the family and peer correlates of misconduct (see, e.g., Jessor, 1992). In contrast, cross-cultural research on adolescent misconduct has tended to focus somewhat disproportionately on family factors (e.g., Chen et al., 1998; Feldman, Rosenthal, Monte-Reynaud, Leung, & Lau, 1991). In cultural settings that differ in their emphasis on individualistic versus collectivist values, however, the potential sources of social influence extend beyond that of family members and friends. In some cultures, the behavior and attitudes of larger social collectives (e.g., schoolmates, even though they may not be "friends," neighbors, and coworkers) also may be influential. We know of no cross-cultural studies that simultaneously assess multiple sources of social influence on adolescent misconduct.

In this study, we examined the frequency of self-reported misconduct among middle adolescents (ages 16 to 17) in the United States, China, and Korea and explored the associations between misconduct and adolescents' perceptions of the behavior and attitudes of family members, close friends, school peers, and neighborhood adults. We focused on neighborhood adults (rather than neighborhood peers) because the former may play an important role both as behavioral models and sources of social control (Reiss, 1995), and because adolescents' perceptions of neighborhood peers seem likely to overlap with their reports about their close friends and school peers.

Comparison of adolescents in the three sites from which we obtained samples is of interest because of similarities as well as differences among and between them. The three countries currently are linked by economic and political interests, and by immigration from the two Asian countries to the United States; China and Korea are linked additionally by a long political history and shared philosophical (religious) perspectives. Despite these connections,

the three countries differ considerably with respect to the social organization of, and larger societal influences on, adolescents' lives. For example, the United States, Korea, and China (and the cities in each country from which we drew our sample) differ, in declining order, in the degree to which they have experienced industrialization, had contact with the capitalist nations, and now participate in the global economy. These factors are likely to have implications for young people's emerging values and social relationships, as we suggest later.

Our hypotheses were as follows:

1. Middle adolescents' self-reported involvement in problem behaviors will differ across the three samples. Specifically, U.S. middle adolescents will engage in more misconduct than will either of their Asian counterparts, and Korean adolescents will exceed Chinese in their involvement in socially disapproved behavior. These predictions are based on a number of considerations. Globalization (Kearney, 1995) refers to the permeation of once-local communities or "cultures" by processes such as migration, tourism, commerce, and communications. The interpenetration of communities and cultures has important consequences, including a greater variety in the images of behavior, goods and products, and lifestyles to which youths are exposed. These factors, along with the existence of more diverse norms and values within a globalized community, are likely to increase the likelihood of adolescent misconduct; thus, our expectation of higher levels of problem behavior among U.S. than Korean or Chinese youths. However, Korean youths, certainly those residing in Seoul, are living in a society that has undergone and continues to experience substantial economic, political, and social change. American clothes, music, and movies are part of the world of adolescents in Korea's major city and expose youths to values, behaviors, and styles of relating to others that are discrepant from cultural traditions. In fact, appreciable intergenerational conflict, especially regarding familial obligations and expectations, has been widely reported (Whang, 1997). In contrast,

Chinese adolescents live in a society that, although changing, still adheres substantially to collectivist values and emphasizes the individual's obligation to uphold traditional ways and behave in a manner that reflects well on the family (Bond, 1996). Although Tianjin is a port city with increasing links to the Western world, it is considerably behind Seoul in the degree to which global processes have penetrated the culture. Thus, we predicted higher levels of misconduct among adolescents in Seoul than in Tianjin.

2. For analogous reasons, U.S. youths will perceive the behavior of family members, close friends, school peers, and neighborhood adults to be more deviant or potentially problematic than will Korean and Chinese youths. We expected Koreans' perceptions of the behavior and attitudes of others to fall midway between those of U.S. and Chinese youths.

3. The perceived *behavior of family members* will be significantly and positively associated with adolescents' behavior (i.e., misconduct) in all three cultural settings. We had no basis for making any predictions about possible between-group (country) differences in the extent to which family members' and adolescents' behavior would be associated. We know of no cross-cultural studies that have examined the intergenerational transmission of deviant or potentially problematic behavior or adolescents' modeling of family members' involvement in such behavior.

4. The perceived *attitudes of family members* toward adolescent misconduct will be more strongly associated with the behavior of adolescents in China and Korea than that of adolescents in the United States. This hypothesis rests on the assumption that a stronger sense of obligation to meet family expectations, and higher value-consensus among the adult generation, prevail in the two Asian countries than in the United States.

5. Perceptions of *close friends' behavior and attitudes toward misconduct* (lenient vs. disap-

proving) will be more strongly associated with the level of U.S. adolescents' misconduct than that of Chinese or Korean youths. . . . This hypothesis is based on studies that indicate that U.S. youths spend significantly more time with peers than do their Chinese and Korean counterparts (Chen et al., 1998; Fuligni & Stevenson, 1995), and on findings of Chen et al. (1998), which showed that greater time involvement with peers, typical of U.S. youths, increases friends' potential to influence each others' behavior. We made no prediction about differences in the relative effects of friends' misconduct and attitudes on the behavior of Chinese versus Korean youths.

6. Perceptions of the behavior of adolescents' *school peers* (not necessarily "friends" but nonetheless part of their daily social environment) will be more strongly associated with the level of misconduct of Chinese and Korean youths than U.S. youths. This hypothesis is based on the notion that a stronger collectivist orientation prevails in the two Asian nations than in the United States, and that for American youths, the existence of close friendship relationships, small cliques, and other groupings based on common reputation or interests may fragment or take the place of the influence of peers in general (Brown, 1990).

7. With respect to the cross-cultural relations between perceptions of neighborhood adults' behavior and adolescents' misconduct, we advanced no a priori hypotheses. On the one hand, neighborhood adults' behavior might be more strongly associated with U.S. youths' than with Asian youths' misconduct because of various factors that have weakened the authority of the American family (e.g., marital disruption, high geographic mobility) and allowed youths greater contact with nonfamilial adults (e.g., widespread youth employment; Fuligni & Stevenson, 1995; Greenberger & Steinberg, 1986). Alternatively, the Asian youths in this study might be more responsive to the norms of neighborhood adults because of concerns about how their behavior might damage the family's reputation in the community.

Method

Participants

All participants in this study were 11th graders who attended public high schools in middle- or working-class neighborhoods. Schools were selected from three coastal cities that vary in their current stage of industrial development and extent of global contacts. The 201 American youths in our study sample came from a school in the greater Los Angeles area, a metropolitan area with a high degree of industrial and postindustrial development, much foreign commerce and tourism, and a culturally diverse population. The 391 Korean youths were enrolled in five schools in Seoul, one of the most industrialized cities in Asia, comparable to Hong Kong and the major cities in Japan in regard to its linkages with other countries in the world. The 502 Chinese youths came from four schools in Tianjin, a more recently industrializing port city that, along with Beijing and Shanghai, is one of three cities under the direct jurisdiction of the Chinese national government. Of these three mainland Chinese cities, Tianjin has the lowest per capita income and the fewest college graduates (State Statistical Bureau, People's Republic of China, 1998). Among the three cities from which we sampled adolescents for this study, Tianjin clearly has the least exposure to other cultural systems, foreign visitors, and the ideas and products of the Western world.

Chinese youths were 1 year older, on average, than their American counterparts because they begin formal schooling a year later. As would be expected, substantially more Asian than U.S. adolescents were living with their still-married biological parents (58% U.S.; 88% Korea; 94% China). The three groups differed significantly with respect to level of parental education, $F(2, 1050) = 101.09$ for fathers; $F(2, 1067) = 69.33$ for mothers, both $p < .001$. As expected, in view of cultural differences in the availability of education to the parent generation, adolescents in the Chinese sample had parents with far less education than those in the Korean and U.S. samples. As well, Korean fathers in the sample had more education than

U.S. fathers. About 53% of the U.S. sample were of European background; about 16% were Latinos; approximately 11% each were of Asian or Pacific Islander origins; and 9% classified themselves as "other" or "mixed." Approximately 94% of the Chinese were of Han ancestry. Of the Korean sample, 100% were ethnic Koreans.

Procedure

All data were collected from adolescent respondents by means of anonymous, self-report questionnaires administered during a classroom period. In the United States, active consent was obtained from both adolescents and their parents through signed permission letters; of the 300 enrolled 11th graders, 83% were present on the day of testing, and 201 (83% of those present, 67% of all enrolled 11th graders) obtained the necessary consent forms and subsequently completed the survey. In China and Korea, parental permission was vested in the school, and 95% of students completed usable surveys.

Instrument development for this cross-cultural study involved several steps. The authors, whose cultural backgrounds correspond with each group examined, collaborated extensively in the operationalization of concepts and construction of measures, in some cases drawing on existing measures. Additionally, teachers, graduate students, and undergraduate college students provided input to questionnaire items. A version of the survey instrument was first written in English, with which all authors had either proficiency or substantial familiarity. The bilingual researchers involved in the study then translated the survey instrument into their native language, which was reviewed by other native language speakers who were proficient in English. Adjustments in items were made when needed.

Measures

Adolescents' Problem Behaviors were assessed by means of a 61-item scale similar to those used in research by others (Feldman et al.,

1991; Greenberger & Steinberg, 1986; Steinberg, Mounts, Lamborn, & Dornbusch, 1991). Only those items were included for which there was "opportunity" across cultures (thus, automobile-related misconduct was excluded, because Chinese youths have virtually no access to cars) and about which all authors agreed that the behavior would, or could, potentially, constitute misconduct in their respective cultural settings. The scale included 9 risk-taking items (e.g., did something or went somewhere dangerous just for the excitement); 5 items about substance use (e.g., drank hard liquor); 6 items about physical aggression toward others (e.g., got into a fist fight); 6 items pertaining to theft (stole money or property); 12 items reflecting school misconduct (e.g., cheated on test, "ditched" school for a day); and an additional 18 items covering a variety of behaviors (e.g., littered the environment, was detained or arrested by police). Respondents indicated whether they had engaged in each of the 61 behaviors "never," "once or twice," or "more often" during the past 6 months. Cronbach's alpha was .96, .92, and .91 for the U.S., Korean, and Chinese samples, respectively.

Perceived behavior of others was assessed by means of four scales. Adolescents responded to two 10-item questionnaires that assessed Perceived Behavior of Close Friends and Perceived Behavior of School Peers, and to two 7-item questionnaires that assessed Perceived Behavior of Family Members and Perceived Behavior of Neighborhood Adults. These items were drawn from several domains of the Problem Behaviors scale previously described. Adolescents indicated whether "none," "some," or "many" of their close friends, schoolmates, and adult neighbors had engaged in each of the behaviors during the past 6 months, and answered "yes" or "no" regarding family members' involvement in the listed behaviors (e.g., frequent use of alcohol or nicotine, physical aggression, theft).

Perceived attitudes of parents and close friends toward the adolescent's hypothetical involvement in misconduct were assessed by comparable 11-item scales reflecting the various domains included in our Problem Behaviors

measure. For Parental Sanctions, adolescents reported whether they thought their parents' reaction to each type of misconduct would be "would not care," "would be somewhat upset," or "would be very upset." For Close Friends' Sanctions, respondents indicated whether these friends would be likely to "approve" or "say nothing" (scored as 1) versus express disapproval (scored as 2).

The total Problem Behavior score was the dependent variable in all tests of hypotheses. Gender was included in all models, in light of consistent cross-cultural findings that boys exceed girls in their involvement in misconduct and to explore possible gender differences in the relations between the perceived behavior and attitudes of others toward misconduct and adolescents' involvement in problem behaviors.

Results

Levels of Misconduct and Sanctions Against Misconduct Across Cultural Contexts

ANOVAs and subsequent Scheffe contrasts revealed strong overall support for Hypotheses 1 and 2. Adolescents' self-reported level of involvement in misconduct differed significantly among the three groups, $F(2, 1087) = 111.14$, $p < .001$. Scheffe contrasts revealed that U.S. adolescents engaged in more misconduct than either Chinese or Korean adolescents of the same age (16 to 17 years old); and as hypothesized, Korean youths engaged in more misconduct than did Chinese youths (ps for all Scheffe contrasts reported here and later were significant at $p < .05$).

Further examination of the data revealed that four subsets of problem behavior items (see Measures) had satisfactory internal consistency and thus could be treated as subscales: risk-taking, $\alpha = .70$ to .83; physical aggression toward others, $\alpha = .70$ to .79; property violation, $\alpha = .60$ to .79; and school misconduct, $\alpha = .77$ to .85. ANOVAs of these subscales generally followed the same pattern: that is, U.S. youths > Koreans > Chinese. The exception was that U.S. and Korean adolescents did not differ significantly in level of risk taking. The largest cultural differences emerged in the domains of school misconduct, $F(2, 1089) = 98.15$, $p < .001$) and physical aggression, $F(2, 1090) = 56.38$, $p < .001$. Despite overall differences in school misconduct, we noted one striking similarity: The vast majority of adolescents in all three settings reported copying homework at least once in the past year (94% of U.S. youths, 97% of Koreans; 70% of Chinese).

Examination of items on the physical aggression subscale revealed that the proportion of U.S. youths who had committed the various acts was typically at least twice that of Koreans, Chinese youths, or both. For example, figures for the item "hit or threatened to hit someone" were 52%, 18%, and 11% in the order previously indicated. Several types of substance use were reported far more often by American adolescents; for example, marijuana use was 41% in the U.S. sample versus under 1% in each of the two Asian settings.

Perceptions of Others. Adolescents' perceptions of family members', friends', and school peers' misconduct also differed significantly, and the same pattern of subgroup differences emerged as in the case of adolescents' self-reported misconduct. Consistent with Hypothesis 2, U.S. youths perceived more problematic behavior among family members, friends, and school peers than did either of the two Asian groups, and Koreans perceived more problem behaviors in these social environments than did Chinese youths. Additionally, the three groups of adolescents differed significantly with respect to their perceptions of adult neighbors' behavior, $F(2, 1026 = 31.88$, $p < .001)$. As expected, adolescents in the United States reported more problematic behavior than did Chinese; however, Scheffe tests revealed a departure from the pattern of results for Korean and Chinese adolescents reported thus far, that is, both U.S. and Chinese participants perceived more problematic behavior among neighborhood adults than did Koreans.

ANOVAs also revealed differences among the three culture groups with respect to perceived sanctions against adolescent misconduct.

These differences were highly significant for close friends' sanctions, $F(2, 1070) = 68.06$, $p < .001$; and although significant, were more modest in the case of perceived parental sanctions, $F(2, 1078) = 5.46$, $p < .01$. In general, parents and friends were seen as less tolerant of respondents' misconduct in those cultural contexts in which adolescent misconduct was lower. Thus, as predicted (Hypothesis 2), U.S. youths perceived a lower level of negative sanctions from parents and friends than did Chinese and Koreans; and Koreans perceived friends as less disapproving of misconduct than did Chinese respondents.

Correlational Analyses

Table 13.2.1 shows the zero-order correlations between adolescents' self-reported levels of misconduct and their perceptions of others' behavior and attitudes. Because the focus of our analyses is on the subsequent multivariate analyses of association among variables, we comment only briefly on the correlational data. The data shown in Table 13.2.1 are consistent with the prediction that family members' perceived behavior and attitudes would be associated with adolescent misconduct across cultural settings (Hypotheses 3 and 4), although the correlation between family members' and adolescents' behavior was trivial in magnitude for Chinese youths. For the United States–China comparison, the correlations between family members' behavior and adolescent misconduct differed significantly ($z = 3.63$, $p < .001$).

Muitivariate Models of the Contributions of Perceived Behavior and Sanctions of Others to Adolescent Misconduct

Perceived Behavior of Others. As Table 13.2.2 indicates, sex and the perceived behavior of close friends made unique contributions to adolescent misconduct in all three cultural contexts. Boys, and adolescents who believed their friends engaged in more problematic behavior, reported engaging in more misconduct themselves. Comparisons of the unstandardized beta coefficients across samples (Table 13.2.2) tended to confirm findings from our

TABLE 13.2.1 Correlation of Perceived Behavior and Attitudes of Others With Adolescents' Self-Reported Misconduct

	UNITED STATES	KOREA	CHINA
Family members' behavior	.38***	.20***	.10*
Close friends' behavior	.70***	.52***	.50***
School peers' behavior	.05	.18***	.29***
Neighborhood adults' behavior	.33***	.20***	.25***
Parental sanctions	−.42***	−.28***	−.35***
Close friends' sanctions	−.47***	−.46***	−.39***

*p < .05. **p < .01. ***p < .001.

earlier correlational analyses (Table 13.2.1), which showed that close friends' behavior was more consequential for adolescent misconduct in the United States than in the other two countries. In the Chinese sample only, perceived behavior of school peers and family members also made independent contributions to adolescents' misconduct. Most interesting, the perceived behavior of neighborhood adults contributed uniquely to the explained variance in adolescents' misconduct in the United States but not in either of the two Asian settings.

Perceived Sanctions of Others. Perceived sanctions of parents and close friends (together with gender) accounted for roughly similar amounts of the variance in adolescent miscon-

duct across the three settings: 35% in the United States, 28% in Korea, and 26% in China. There were striking similarities across the three samples in the relations between adolescent misconduct and the perceived sanctions of parents and friends. Girls, and adolescents who believed their parents and close friends would be more disapproving of their misconduct, reported lower levels of misconduct.

Discussion

In the concluding section of this article, we highlight key findings, attempt to integrate them with results of previous research, and call attention to several limitations of the current study and to directions that future research might take.

TABLE 13.2.2 Regression of Problem Behaviors on Gender and Perceived Behavior of Others and Summary of Significant Interactions

	UNITED STATES			KOREA			CHINA		
	B	β	t	B	β	t	B	β	t
Sex	−.10	−.15	2.83**	−.08	−.23	4.37***	−.06	−.20	5.11***
Family members' behavior	.12	.08	1.19	.06	.05	.98	.08	.08	1.97*
Close friends' behavior	.39	.62	10.97***	.21	.38	6.85***	.24	.40	9.97***
School peers' behavior	−.06	−.06	1.04	−.02	−.01	0.11	.07	.14	3.40***
Neighborhood adults' behavior	.10	.13	2.15*	.05	.07	1.40	.03	.07	1.68
Sex × Neighborhood adults' behavior	Adj. R^2 = .53***			Adj. R^2 = .28***			Adj. R^2 = .32***		
	—	—	—	—	—	—	−.01	−.08	2.23*

*p < .05. **p < .01. ***p < .001.

Levels of Misconduct and Related Behaviors and Sanctions of Others

As predicted, a sample of middle adolescents living in the greater Los Angeles area reported significantly more misconduct than their 16- to 17-year-old peers in Seoul and Tianjin; as well, the Korean adolescents significantly exceeded Chinese youths in misconduct. The same pattern of findings emerged in relation to adolescents' perceptions of the behavior of family members, close friends, school peers, and neighborhood adults. Relatedly, U.S. 16- to 17-year-olds viewed their parents and friends as more tolerant (i.e., less disapproving) of their misconduct than did either Chinese or Koreans; and Koreans viewed their friends as more tolerant of misconduct than did their Chinese peers. In summary, adolescents reported consistent levels of problem behaviors and attitudes toward such behavior across the various social contexts they traverse within their different cultural settings.

One possible interpretation of the findings previously summarized is that societies that have more extensive global contacts and are exposed to more individualistic values present adolescents with a wider choice of behavioral options. These options include ones that depart from traditional norms and that may not be sanctioned by adults. In point of fact, the multiplicity of values and ensuing loss of value consensus in the community (Baumeister & Tice, 1986) also may affect the behavior and attitudes of adults. The significant mean differences on most measures of behavior and attitudes between youths in Seoul and in a Chinese city that more recently has been launched into the world system tend to support the view that social and economic change alters the normative context of adolescent development. Differences among the three samples in the amount of variance that was detected on most measures included in this study also support the view that adolescents in more globally connected and culturally diverse settings are growing up in environments characterized by more heterogeneous norms. Indeed, because stage of industrialization, degree of globalization, and the extent of diversity of local populations are likely to covary, it will be difficult to pinpoint the effects of each.

The findings of this study are consistent with the findings of Feldman et al. (1991) regarding cross-cultural differences in middle adolescents' level of misconduct. The current findings are also consistent with the argument of Chen et al. (1998) that rates of misconduct for Chinese and U.S. youths—similar in early adolescence—would be likely to diverge as youths entered middle adolescence. These authors' prediction was based in part on the stronger associations that had emerged between misconduct and the perceived peer behavior and attitudes of peers among U.S. than among Korean (Seoul) and Chinese (Beijing) adolescents. The convergence of findings from the Chen et al. (1998) study and this study, showing that youths from the more industrialized Asian locations (Taiwan and Seoul) tended to report more problem behavior and lax attitudes toward such behavior than youths in the more traditional Chinese environments (Beijing and Tianjin), further strengthens our conjecture that macrosocial factors and adolescent misconduct are linked.

Cross-Cultural Similarities

Several findings were replicated cross-culturally in this study: (a) A higher average level of involvement in problematic behaviors was reported by boys than girls; (b) adolescents who perceived their friends as engaging in more misbehavior engaged in more misbehavior themselves; and (c) youths who believed their parents and close friends would respond less negatively to their misconduct engaged in more misconduct. As well, the strong association in three different cultural settings between close friends' perceived behavior and attitudes toward misconduct and adolescents' own involvement in misconduct underscores the importance of peers in adolescent development. Despite the strong influence of close friends' perceived behavior across settings, perceived parental and friends' sanctions contributed uniquely to lower levels of misconduct among the groups. Most interesting, the relative effect of friends' sanctions vis-à-vis parents' sanctions was greatest among Koreans, the group in which the adolescent generation is shifting away from traditional values (Whang, 1997). The greater importance of friends' than parents' sanctions in this setting is consistent with Mead's (1928/1978) suggestion that peer influences may be especially strong in rapidly changing societies, where "old ways" are no longer sufficient for successful adaptation in the future.

School Peers', Neighborhood Adults', and Adolescents' Misconduct

The fact that perceived behavior of school peers was not related to U.S. adolescents' own level of problem behavior seems to indicate that students in U.S. high schools form mutually indifferent peer groups (i.e., "If you are not a close friend, what I believe *you* do and think is of no importance to my views and behavior"). In contrast, the finding that both close friends' and school peers' misconduct were related to Chinese adolescents' behavior suggests a social environment in which close peers' and school peers' levels of misconduct each adds to the explanation of adolescents' involvement in such behavior.

The association between perceived behavior of neighborhood adults and adolescent misconduct was stronger for U.S. than Chinese or Korean youths: That is, the neighborhood adults "effect" emerged, when other variables were controlled, in the U.S. sample but not in either of the other samples. Adolescents in the two Asian settings, compared to U.S. youths, seem to live in or perceive that they live in neighborhoods where the adults' behavior is more similar to that of their family members. It makes intuitive sense that Korean and Chinese youths live in more homogenous cross-context settings. In contrast, youths in the United States are more likely to live in culturally diverse

and value-heterogeneous neighborhoods, due largely to economic factors that allow or oblige families with different values to live in close proximity. . . .

Limitations and Future Research Directions

The models tested in this study may not have included measures of other social contexts that are important to Asian youths, for example, the behavior and attitudes of teachers (Chen & Dong, 1999). Differences in school dropout and survey participation rates of the populations that were sampled also merit brief commentary. The higher dropout and lower participation rates of U.S. youths strongly suggest that the results of this study underestimate the already significant U.S. versus Korean and Chinese means on various measures of problematic behavior, troubled relationships, and antisocial attitudes (e.g., U.S. vs. Asian youths' mean levels of misconduct). This is all the more so when readers recall that automobile-related misconduct was eliminated from the problem behavior scale because it was not cross-culturally relevant.

Researchers' agendas should include further exploration of how adolescent behavior responds to macrolevel changes in various societies, especially to global influences that may undermine core cultural values. Cross-sectional studies, and those that focus exclusively on adolescents (both characteristics of this study), leave important questions unanswered, such as the order in which behavioral and attitudinal change occurs in adolescents and the adult generation and who most influences whom. Longitudinal studies that also include explicit measures of degree of industrialization, global linkages, and local population diversity would be especially valuable in clarifying whether these societal parameters, either as a group or individually, lead to alterations in adolescents' behavior and attitudes and their perceptions of the behavior and attitudes of people in the various social contexts of consequence to them.

REFERENCES

Achenbach, T. M., Hensley, V. R., Phares, V., & Grayson, D. (1990). Problems and competencies reported by parents of Australian and American children. *Journal of Child Psychology and Psychiatry, 31,* 265–286.

Achenbach, T. M., Verhulst, F. C., Baron, G. D., & Akkerhuis, G. W. (1987). Epidemiological comparisons of American and Dutch children: I. Behavioral/emotional problems and competencies reported by parents for ages 4 to 16. *Journal of American Academy of Child and Adolescent Psychiatry, 26,* 317–325.

Baumeister, R., & Tice, D. (1986). How adolescence became the struggle for the self: A historical transformation of psychological development. In J. Suls & A. Greenwald (Eds.), *Psychological perspectives on the self* (Vol. 3, pp. 183–201). Hillsdale, NJ: Erlbaum.

Brown, B. B. (1990). Peer groups and peer cultures. In S. S. Feldman & G. R. Elliot (Eds.), *At the threshold: The developing adolescent* (pp. 171–196). Cambridge, MA: Harvard University Press.

Chen, C., & Dong, Q. (1999). *The role of relationships with teachers in adolescent development among a national sample of Chinese urban youth.* Manuscript submitted for publication.

Chen, C., Greenberger, E., Lester, J., Dong, Q., & Guo, M.-S. (1998). A cross-cultural study of family and peer correlates of adolescent misconduct. *Developmental Psychology, 34,* 770–781.

Feldman, S. S., & Rosenthal, D. (1990). The acculturation of autonomy expectations in Chinese high schoolers residing in two western nations. *International Journal of Psychology, 25,* 259–281.

Feldman, S. S., Rosenthal, D. A., Monte-Reynaud, R., Leung, K., & Lau, S. (1991). Ain't misbehaving: Adolescent values and family environments as correlates of misconduct in Australia, Hong Kong, and the United States. *Journal of Research on Adolescence, 1,* 109–134.

Fuligni, A. J., & Stevenson, H. W. (1995). Time use and mathematics achievement among American, Chinese, and Japanese high schoolers. *Child Development, 66,* 830–842.

Greenberger, E., & Steinberg, L. (1986). *When teenagers work: The psychosocial costs of adolescent employment.* New York: Basic Books.

Jessor, R. (1992). Risk behavior in adolescence: A psychosocial framework for understanding and action. *Developmental Review, 12,* 374–390.

Lambert, M. C., Weisz, J. R., & Knight, F. (1989). Over- and undercontrolled clinic referral problems of Jamaican and American children and adolescents: The culture-general and the culture-specific. *Journal of Counseling and Clinical Psychology, 57,* 467–472.

Mead, M. (1928/1978). *Culture and commitment.* New York: Anchor.

Reiss, A. J., Jr. (1995). Community influence on adolescent behavior. In M. Rutter (Ed.), *Psychosocial disturbances in young people: Challenges for prevention* (pp. 305–332). New York: Cambridge University Press.

State Statistical Bureau of China, People's Republic of China. (1998). *China statistical yearbook.* Beijing: China Statistical Publishing House.

Steinberg, L. (1998). *Adolescence* (5th ed.). New York: McGraw-Hill.

Steinberg, L., Mounts, N. S., Lamborn, S. D., & Dornbusch, S. M. (1991). Authoritative parenting and adolescent adjustment across varied ecological niches. *Journal of Research on Adolescence, 1,* 19–36.

Weine, A. M., Phillips, J. S., & Achenbach, T. M. (1995). Behavioral and emotional problems among Chinese and American children: Parent and teacher reports for ages 6 to 13. *Journal of Abnormal Child Psychology, 23,* 619–639.

Whang, S.-M. (1997). The sociocognitive analysis of the phenomenon of the generation gap between parents and their adolescent child: The differential construction of representational categories of their relationships and problem behaviors in daily life. *Korean Journal of Developmental Psychology, 10,* 152–166.

THINKING CRITICALLY

1. On what basis do the authors argue that globalization leads to greater adolescent misconduct? Do you agree with their argument?

2. Do the findings of a correlation between adolescents' misconduct and their perceptions of their friends' misconduct show that adolescent friends cause or pressure each other into misconduct? Why or why not?

3. Why do the authors include perceptions of neighborhood adults' behavior in the study? What is the meaning of the finding that this variable is related to adolescents' misconduct only in the U.S. sample?

4. How can the results of this reading be explained in terms of the individualism of American society and the collectivism of Asian societies? Include an explanation of why Korean adolescents fall in between American and Chinese adolescents on measures of misconduct.

Index